CSR, Sustainability, Ethics & Governance

In recent years the discussion concerning the relation between business and society has made immense strides. This has in turn led to a broad academic and practical discussion on innovative management concepts, such as Corporate Social Responsibility, Corporate Governance and Sustainability Management. This series offers a comprehensive overview of the latest theoretical and empirical research and provides sound concepts for sustainable business strategies. In order to do so, it combines the insights of leading researchers and thinkers in the fields of management theory and the social sciences – and from all over the world, thus contributing to the interdisciplinary and intercultural discussion on the role of business in society. The underlying intention of this series is to help solve the world's most challenging problems by developing new management concepts that create value for business and society alike. In order to support those managers, researchers and students who are pursuing sustainable business approaches for our common future, the series offers them access to cutting-edge management approaches.

CSR, Sustainability, Ethics & Governance is accepted by the Norwegian Register for Scientific Journals, Series and Publishers, maintained and operated by the Norwegian Social Science Data Services (NSD)

Anna Maria Fellegara • Riccardo Torelli •
Andrea Caccialanza
Editors

Sustainable Transition of Meat and Cured Meat Supply Chain

A Transdisciplinary Approach

Springer

Editors
Anna Maria Fellegara
Department of Economic and Social Sciences
Università Cattolica del Sacro Cuore
Piacenza, Italy

Riccardo Torelli
Department of Economic and Social Sciences
Università Cattolica del Sacro Cuore
Piacenza, Italy

Andrea Caccialanza
Department of Economic and Social Sciences
Università Cattolica del Sacro Cuore
Piacenza, Italy

ISSN 2196-7075 ISSN 2196-7083 (electronic)
CSR, Sustainability, Ethics & Governance
ISBN 978-3-031-34976-8 ISBN 978-3-031-34977-5 (eBook)
https://doi.org/10.1007/978-3-031-34977-5

Università Cattolica del Sacro Cuore contributed to the funding of this research project and its publication (D.3.2. 2020—R2104500099—VIS—Valore Impresa Sostenibile).

This Springer imprint is published by the registered company Springer Nature Switzerland AG
The registered company address is: Gewerbestrasse 11, 6330 Cham, Switzerland

Foreword

Livestock farming and animal production chains have been under pressure in recent years. In countries with advanced economies, the attention and sensitivity of civil society toward farming ethical issues and sustainability have grown exponentially.

Such a trend influences the markets—reacting with more targeted product offers (e.g., free-range eggs)—and the communication channels—fostering news and articles on the topics released regularly.

Based on claims and simplified notions, the marketing language style characterizes a large portion of the media (beyond social media), contributing to a biased representation of livestock farming and breeding and generating an inaccurate and sometimes incorrect public opinion about animal production.

In point of fact, animal farming, which played a crucial role in the development of humankind, is particularly complex because of the multiple interactions with the environment and ecosystems, both positive and negative.

Indeed, a robust analysis of the meat supply chain, also related to sustainability, requires a multilevel analytical rigorous approach.

This book explores the supply chain through the magnifying glass of sixteen research focuses, described one by one in dedicated chapter and addressing various topics and issues, resulting in a composite analysis of sustainability in the broadest sense.

This multidisciplinary and interdisciplinary approach provides the reader with a comprehensive overview of the many aspects that constitute the sustainability of the cured meat supply chain.

Which attitudes and expectations have the younger generation towards cured meat consumption? Which are the leverages available for the farmer to improve the production process? How to overcome the critical points of the transformation phase? How to share the social responsibility of the players operating within a supply chain? How to combine social, environmental, and economic sustainability? How to adapt farming to climate change?

These are just a few examples of the big questions addressed by the authors, sometimes resulting in detailed explanations and sometimes in just an admission of lack of enough knowledge and information and the need for further investigation.

Fortunately, the increasing demand for more sustainable and sensitive animal production fostered the scientific research that produced significant knowledge progress.

The hope is that the new acquisitions, with theoretical and practical implications, will be exploited by decision-makers because the future of animal production requires strategic short- and medium-term decisions based on scientific and technical robust information.

General manager AIA (Italian Breeders Association), Rome, Italy
March 29th 2023

Mauro Donda

Disclaimer

All contributions included in this volume underwent a blind peer review process. The volume editors managed, monitored, and verified the entire process.

Contents

About the Editors

Anna Maria Fellegara is a Full Professor of Business Economics and Dean of the Faculty of Economics and Law of the Università Cattolica del Sacro Cuore (Piacenza, Italy). She is the Vice President of SIDREA—Italian Society of Accounting and Business Economics and a member of AIDEA—Italian Academy of Business Economics. She is currently a professor of Accounting and Financial Statements, Integrated Reporting, Financial Statement Analysis, and Corporate Control Systems. Coordinator of national inter-university research on financial statements and consolidated financial statements; on the application of national and international accounting standards. Member of the scientific committee of the Emilia Romagna Higher Education School of the Order of Chartered Accountants and Accounting Experts. Member of the Management Committee of the Cariparma-Crédit Agricole Campus for the training of the group's human resources. The scientific production of recent years has concerned the topics of information on ownership structures and governance structures, disclosure on corporate governance in groups as a tool for protecting widespread interests and assessing creditworthiness. The topics of sustainability were developed with reference to the levels of economic-financial disclosure and the choices of integrated reporting in companies and national groups. She is the Director of the Research Centre for Responsibility, Ethics and Sustainability in Management—RES.m HUB.

Riccardo Torelli is an Assistant Professor in Corporate Sustainability, Responsibility and Ethics at the Faculty of Economics and Law (Department of Economic and Social Sciences) of Università Cattolica del Sacro Cuore (Piacenza, Italy). He is also a Lecturer of Corporate Social Responsibility and Sustainable Business Strategy. His research focuses on corporate sustainability and SDGs, CSR and business ethics, non-financial reporting, and greenwashing. He is a member of Centre for Social and Environmental Accounting Research (CSEAR), European Business Ethics Network (EBEN), and Associate Editor of Corporate Social Responsibility and Environmental Management journal and of Journal of Public Affairs. He has published several international contributions, in particular in Journal of Business Ethics, Business Strategy and the Environment, Corporate Social Responsibility and Environmental Management, Journal of Cleaner Production, Sustainability Accounting Management and Policy Journal, Social Responsibility Journal, and in some Springer edited books. He is a member of several interdisciplinary projects on business sustainability. He is also the co-founder and secretary of the Research Centre for Responsibility, Ethics and Sustainability in Management—RES.m HUB.

Andrea Caccialanza is a Ph.D. Candidate in Università Cattolica del Sacro Cuore, Piacenza (Italy). His research covers topics such as sustainability reporting determinants in agri-food systems, food production systems and supply chains, SDGs and gender equality, sustainability and social impact in megaprojects. He is a member of the Center for Social and Environmental Accounting Research (CSEAR), the Italian Association for Management and Marketing studies (SIMA-SIM), the Italian society of accounting and business administration teachers (SIDREA), and the European Business Ethics Network (EBEN). He is also a member of the Research Centre for Responsibility, Ethics and Sustainability in Management—RES.m HUB.

Introduction

Anna Maria Fellegara, Riccardo Torelli, and Andrea Caccialanza

Sustainability and sustainable development are now benchmark concepts in business administration and management. Despite the increasingly widespread familiarity with these concepts, for many companies, especially small and medium-sized ones, it is still unclear the benefit that adopting a sustainable strategy could bring and above all the real extent of the investment required, in financial, organisational, human and relational terms. Moreover, the legal instruments through which such a strategy could be implemented and the tax benefits that could derive from it are sometimes not very well understood, especially in light of the forthcoming regulatory interventions aimed at facilitating such paths, also in connection with the use of EU funds. Taking as its reference, the articulation of research topics of interest for Università Cattolica del Sacro Cuore, and in particular the topic about the redefinition of development models oriented towards a sustainable and inclusive economic and financial system, the VIS—Valore Impresa Sostenibile (Sustainable Company Value) project set out to develop and implement a self-assessment model for sustainable innovation and change in companies in the cured meat supply chain. This push to turn towards practices of responsibility, sustainability (social, environmental and economic) and respect for ethical-moral values is tangibly present in the founding principles of the Università Cattolica del Sacro Cuore. The principles of integral humanism (Maritain, 1936) to which the Social Doctrine of the Church tends (Pontifical Council of Justice and Peace, 2004), have represented, and continue to do so, key values of the pedagogical and scientific research action of this University. These core values, strengthened and further actualised by the work of Pope Francis, Laudato si' (2015), offer spiritual nourishment and encouragement, as well as

A. M. Fellegara · R. Torelli (✉) · A. Caccialanza
Department of Economic and Social Sciences, Università Cattolica del Sacro Cuore, Piacenza, Italy
e-mail: annamaria.fellegara@unicatt.it; riccardo.torelli2@unicatt.it; andrea.caccialanza@unicatt.it

A. M. Fellegara et al. (eds.), *Sustainable Transition of Meat and Cured Meat Supply Chain*, CSR, Sustainability, Ethics & Governance,
https://doi.org/10.1007/978-3-031-34977-5_1

scientific inspiration, in concentrating one's energies and skills towards the search for interventions, models, practices, strategies and actions for a humanity able to feel empathy and to grant the other respect, acceptance and care.

The deepening of knowledge on how to effectively implement a sustainability orientation and innovate corporate business models, as well as assessing the sustainability of a company, is particularly relevant with reference to the agri-food chain as confirmed by the relevant literature.

The main scientific contributions declining the theme of sustainability in this supply chain dwell on the dynamics of implementing sustainability within organisations (Singh & Abhilash, 2018; Schmitt et al., 2017; Menozzi et al., 2015; Epstein et al., 2010), on the concept of sustainable innovation (Langendahl et al., 2016; Boons et al., 2013; Larson, 2000) on the role of the supply chain in fostering the adoption of a sustainability orientation (León-Bravo et al., 2017; Cagliano et al., 2016; Canfora, 2016), on the role of the consumer and its expectations (Grunert, 2011), on the link between sustainability practices and forms of typical product protection (Arfini et al., 2019; Chkanikova & Lehner, 2015).

The VIS project builds on this debate by adopting a trans-disciplinary perspective implemented by an intra-university, inter-faculty and inter-disciplinary working group, coordinated by Prof. Daniele Cerrato, Full Professor of Business Economics, from the Faculty of Economics and Law of Piacenza and including researchers from the Faculty of Agricultural, Food and Environmental Sciences and the Faculty of Education.

Starting from the need to support the measurement and evaluation of the impacts that sustainability can produce at the level of the individual company and, above all, along the supply chain, the VIS project aimed to develop, by comparing with the existing literature and proceeding with an in-depth analysis in the field, an analysis and design model for innovation and change designed to accompany and facilitate innovation and sustainable development in the cured meat supply chain.

The choice of the cured meat supply chain originates from the importance that companies in this sector have in the Italian gastronomic tradition as well as from the opportunity to investigate the potential positive effects that sustainability can generate with respect to this type of production. The presence in the Po Valley territories of some of the most important cured meat factories and sector associations that promote and enhance, among other things, some of the best-known legal protection brands, is a useful condition for the development of specific collaborations aimed at ensuring as far as possible an integration between research and the production of positive spin-offs for the production fabric. Lombardy and Emilia-Romagna, the reference territories for the Po Valley offices of the University, are, moreover, the two territories with the highest number of PGI and PDO specialities in the cured meat sector.

VIS is a research-intervention project, which aimed to involve and accompany companies and organisations in the supply chain in a process of in-depth analysis and development of knowledge and strategies for sustainability. The project also aimed to effectively disseminate the knowledge developed both to those directly involved, companies and trade associations, and more generally to the communities affected by the supply chain's activities (customers, citizens, institutions, third sector).

The project, which covered a 24-month period (from April first, 2021), involved intense research and scientific coordination between the three research units involved: the unit of the Faculty of Economics and Law led by Prof. Davide Galli, Associate Professor in Business Economics, and subsequently by Prof. Anna Maria Fellegara, Full Professor of Business Economics; the unit of the Faculty of Agricultural, Food and Environmental Sciences led by Prof. Paolo Ajmone Marsan, Full Professor of General Zootechnics and Genetic Improvement; the unit of the Faculty of Education led by Prof. Cristina Birbes, Associate Professor of General and Social Pedagogy.

During the 2-year period of activity, the research project team has organised several internal meetings and with different professional actors in the production chain at both company and association levels, created a multi-stakeholder network, presented research at various national and international conferences and produced scientific and divulgative outputs of different typology, one of which is this book. This is intended to collect and organise the evidence that emerged within the research groups belonging to the different Faculties, proposing complementary perspectives on the main challenges that the cured meat supply chain is called to face today and in the immediate future.

What makes the approach adopted by this volume innovative is the transdisciplinary perspective that this project sought to promote. In a perspective of increasing collegiality, preliminary thematic meetings were organised within groups of researchers from the same Faculties, later followed by collective moments of discussion on the several topics and challenges under analysis. This inductive approach led to the emergence of an increasing number of research questions, linking complementary perspectives and theoretical backgrounds. Therefore, in a perspective of progressive granularity, contributions were systematised on the basis of increasingly circumscribed categories of analysis.

The debate started from the analysis of the need to consume meat-based products, thus raising the issue of education for consumption and the understanding of the challenges for a sustainable consumption education of cured meats. A further focus was placed on the context of consumption by Generation Z, thus emphasising the commitment on the part of families, schools and the business and civil community (chapter "Generation Z and sustainable cured meat consumption: Educational challenges and pedagogical perspectives").

From the focus on the need for food (and meat) consumption, the debate then shifted to the analysis of the product itself and the production conditions to be met in order to consider that impact on the environment and community legitimate. The book, therefore, addresses the environmental impact of pig production, as well as measures to minimise the impact at the breeding supply chain level. A further focus on this theme is therefore on innovative techniques developed in the breeding phase (chapter "Sustainability of Swine Breeding: Future Challenges and Opportunities"). The dynamics strictly related to livestock farming are complemented by an excursus of what are the implications in terms of sustainability from the workers' human rights point of view. In particular, this focus takes inspiration from both the experience of certain foreign legal systems and recent European Union acts related to this field (chapter "Sustainable Development of Meat Supply Chain and Human Rights"). The challenges for a greater awareness of the role of sustainability a production system can be understood as a growing attention to the challenges that a farm must face in view of the intensification of the effects of climate change. Therefore, genetics can also play a role in a long-term perspective in this context. An additional focus is proposed to the better understanding of the genetic control of the main sustainability-related traits and on how the genetic information can be applied to the supply chain (chapter "Genomics for Sustainable Cured Pork Supply Chain"). To the study of specific genetics' markers is also followed by a deepening of the factors that determine the quality of production, as well as the influence of animal nutrition on the quality of the meat produced. In addition, a further aspect of contextualisation is offered with respect to the production system of protected designations of origin, as well as for the enhancement of the valorisation of co-products (chapter "The Quality of Heavy Pork Meat: The Role of PDO Production Specifications"). The debate on animal husbandry practices also implies the inclusion of an ethical dynamic in providing dignified living conditions for animals reared. A further study emphasises methodologies for the assessment of animal welfare, as well as the improvement of the reference standards also from a regulatory point of view (chapter "Animal Welfare in Swine Production").

The debate on institutional factors that could influence the levels of sustainability agri-food production systems cannot exclude the impact of taxation. This contribution analyses precisely how taxation can leverage steer production chains towards more sustainable behaviours (chapter "Taxation and Ecological Transition in Production Chains"). In addition, the production systems linked to protected geographical designations do not only affect primary production, but also have a well-defined regulatory dimension. A contribution therefore analyses the interactions linking EU geographical indications with farmers and the land, highlighting which role does the geographical indications regulatory framework plays with regard to the protection of farm animal biodiversity (chapter "Protecting Farm Animal Biodiversity Through Geographical Indications: A Legal Analysis").

From the areas related to the analysis of the product and regulatory systems, it has been also focused on a section of contributions dedicated to the specific production systems and the different perspectives of analysis. In this context, an in-depth analysis was dedicated to the analysis of the overall performance of the sector, as well as the strategies implemented in the Italian meat industry. More specifically, the focus was on the financial performance operating in the sector, in addition to the directions of corporate expansion implemented by companies (chapter "Firm Financial Performance and Growth in the Italian Meat Industry: A Longitudinal Analysis"). Climate change has already been mentioned as one of the risks associated with maintaining production capacity and as one of the challenges of this production system. Therefore, starting from the identification of evidence from the literature on the climate change in the agrifood system, a contribute analyses strategic, operational and governance tools used to manage risks in cured meat supply chain (chapter "Climate Change Risk Management and Firms' Adaptive Responses: Evidence from the Livestock Industry"). On the other hand, a further contribute proposes the identification of the specific risks at supply chain level during the ecological transition process that can generate significant repercussions on company' financial stability (chapter "A Specific Risk Approach to the Meat and Cured Meat Supply Chain"). Another delicate phase in the life of a company, also in the meat supply chain context, is the generational transition. Consequently, one chapter is aimed to highlight the peculiarities of the succession in family-owned businesses and to discuss the main difficulties encountered by second and third-generation entrepreneurs during the succession process (chapter "Managing Generational Handover in Family Business: Some Case Studies in the Charcuterie Factories").

The volume, therefore, at first traces the analysis of needs, then describes the conditions for these productions to fall within the conditions of sustainability of the product and the production systems themselves. The last two steps of the reasoning are overall aimed at understanding the role of communication and reporting the results achieved by the industry as a whole. This excursus takes its start from the impact that digital communication has on young people, proposing the results of a quantitative study proposed to the segment of Generation Z, defined as 'digital native' (chapter "Generation Z, Consumption of Cured Meats, Lifestyles").

From the analysis of the recipients of the communication, it has then been analysed the company itself as promoter of a communication on sustainability issues with three additional contributions. The first proposes a sampling analysis of the extent and the diffusion of sustainability reporting at the tier of the whole Italian food manufacturing, including different food categories. This focus is the preliminary attempt to systematise the effects of the implementation of the recently approved of the Corporate Sustainability Reporting Directive (chapter "The Sustainability of Meat and Cured Meat Supply Chain: Where Are We Now?"). Secondly, another chapter discusses the diffusion of sustainability practices and accountability principles at the transformation' tier of meat and cured Italian meat supply chain. For each of the communication area involved, it has been mapped and discussed several themes, indicators and the implementation of international standards and diffused best practices (chapter "The Spread of Sustainability Reporting in the Italian Food Manufacturing Context"). Finally, the last chapter introduces the reader to the proposed VIS self-assessment tool for the meat and cured Italian meat supply chain. Starting from the FAO' SAFA framework, the model represents a 'ready to use' tool for all the small and medium enterprises both at farm and transformation level. Moreover, this model allows the operator also to establish a time-series analysis of its sustainability performance and a useful scheme for the whole meat and cured meat supply chain (chapter "The VIS Assessment Tool for the Cured Meat Italian Supply Chain: Fostering Accountability for Sustainability Through a FAO SAFA-Based Framework").

In conclusion, without claiming to offer a completely comprehensive picture of the challenges this fair faces in the present and near future, this volume aims to raise awareness of the issue of the transition to more sustainable production models. The transdisciplinary approach adopted has proved to be effective in restoring the complexity of the challenges to be faced to the research group and to industry operators, as well as a valid starting point for further analysis in this and other agri-food supply chains.

References

Arfini, F., Antonioli, F., Cozzi, E., Donati, M., Guareschi, M., Mancini, M. C., & Veneziani, M. (2019). Sustainability, innovation and rural development: The case of Parmigiano-Reggiano PDO. *Sustainability, 11*(18), 4978.

Boons, F., Montalvo, C., Quist, J., & Wagner, M. (2013). Sustainable innovation, business models and economic performance: An overview. *Journal of Cleaner Production, 45*, 1–8.

Cagliano, R., Worley, C. G., & Caniato, F. F. (2016). The challenge of sustainable innovation in agri-food supply chains. *Organizing for Sustainable Effectiveness, 5*, 1–30.

Canfora, I. (2016). Is the short food supply chain an efficient solution for sustainability in food market. *Agriculture and Agricultural Science Procedia, 8*(1), 402–407.

Chkanikova, O., & Lehner, M. (2015). Private eco-brands and green market development: Towards new forms of sustainability governance in the food retailing. *Journal of Cleaner Production, 107*, 74–84.

Epstein, M. J., Buhovac, A. R., & Yuthas, K. (2010). Implementing sustainability: The role of leadership and organizational culture. *Strategic Finance, 91*(10), 41.

Grunert, K. G. (2011). Sustainability in the food sector: A consumer behaviour perspective. *International Journal on Food System Dynamics, 2*(3), 207–218.

Langendahl, P. A., Cook, M., & Potter, S. (2016). Sustainable innovation journeys: Exploring the dynamics of firm practices as part of transitions to more sustainable food and farming. *Local Environment, 21*(1), 105–123.

Larson, A. L. (2000). Sustainable innovation through an entrepreneurship lens. *Business Strategy and the Environment, 9*(5), 304–317.

León-Bravo, V., Caniato, F., Caridi, M., & Johnsen, T. (2017). Collaboration for sustainability in the food supply chain: A multi-stage study in Italy. *Sustainability, 9*(7), 1253.

Maritain, J. (1936). *Humanisme intégral. Problèmes temporels et spirituels d'une nouvelle chrétienté*, Aubier, Paris.

Menozzi, D., Fioravanzi, M., & Donati, M. (2015). Farmer's motivation to adopt sustainable agricultural practices. *Bio-based and Applied Economics, 4*(2), 125–147.

Pontifical Council of Justice and Peace. (2004). *Compendium of the Social Doctrine of the Church.*

Pope Francis. (2015). *Encyclical letter Laudato si' of the Holy Father Francis.*

Schmitt, E., Galli, F., Menozzi, D., Maye, D., Touzard, J. M., Marescotti, A., Six, J., & Brunori, G. (2017). Comparing the sustainability of local and global food products in Europe. *Journal of Cleaner Production, 165*, 346–359.

Singh, A., & Abhilash, P. C. (2018). Agricultural biodiversity for sustainable food production. *Journal of Cleaner Production, 172*, 1368–1369.

Generation Z and Sustainable Cured Meat Consumption: Educational Challenges and Pedagogical Perspectives

Cristina Birbes and Sara Bornatici

1 Introduction

The (theme of the) relationship between food, consumption and sustainability is, today, a field being widely investigated and explored from a multidisciplinary perspective (IPCC, 2022; Baldock & Hart, 2021; Berners-Lee et al., 2018; Bornatici, 2017; Birbes, 2012). Food is configured as a complex and multifaceted object that touches different dimensions of people's lives. If it is essential to monitor its quality and its usability in concrete terms, equally important is the investigation of the impacts that this object has on the socioeducational dimension. The experience of eating is often linked to the internalization of the educational models to which one has been exposed during one's history and to the particular emotional component that this dimension evokes. Food gives meaning to our sociality and our feelings and receives meaning from them. It cannot be experienced only as a product within a market but must be sought in terms of its profound meaning for humanity (Birbes, 2012).

The promotion of well-being through attention to the quality of the food consumed is, therefore, also reflected in the area of the nourishment practices to which a person is subjected, which are rooted in a culture that is the result of historical and symbolic processes connected to the development of different societies over time.

C. Birbes
Alta Scuola per l'Ambiente, Università Cattolica del Sacro Cuore, Brescia, Italy

S. Bornatici (✉)
Facoltà di Medicina e Chirurgia, Dipartimento di Scienze Cliniche e Sperimentali, Università degli Studi di Brescia, Brescia, Italy
e-mail: sara.bornatici@unibs.it

A. M. Fellegara et al. (eds.), *Sustainable Transition of Meat and Cured Meat Supply Chain*, CSR, Sustainability, Ethics & Governance,
https://doi.org/10.1007/978-3-031-34977-5_2

When we refer to food, we are often led to categorize it as a material object designed to satisfy a primary need of humanity and all living beings. The act of eating is extremely necessary to ensure the survival of every living being.

Hence, food cannot be limited to its utilitarian function, capable of merely satisfying a primary human need. It assumes a symbolic function and value that makes it something more. It may seem strange that food could have configured such an important ingredient in human affairs, marking everything that humans have done throughout history. As Morin (2015) states, however, eating is an anthropological act. Food and food practices have always regulated humans' relationship with the world around them and their inner dimension. Food can be defined as a descriptor of the lifestyle of the human being and a means of expression of the sociality through which encounter and exchange between peoples and generations are generated. It becomes the mirror of the history and traditions of a territory because it is able to express identities, symbols and values that go beyond nutritional aspects.

Food and nutrition are, then, constituted as complex themes of investigation, as they relate, in an integrated way, to different dimensions of the lives of people and societies. Food practices can be defined as real food cultures, where food is constituted as a fundamental cultural index because it affirms itself as an instrument of identity construction. Food, as stated by Montanari (2004), is the first medium for contacting different cultures because eating the food of others is easier than decoding their language. Food, today more than ever, in a globalized world in which different cultures converge and coexist, can be a tool to initially "taste" the culture of other peoples and to "taste" one's own culture, from the perspective of reciprocity (Montanari, 2004).

The consumption of the food and food cultures of a community also suggest to us what relationship food has with the constructs of time and space. If we take Western culture as an example, it is evident that there is a link between food and temporality, a link that reflects the historical and social phenomena to which it is subject. A fast logic, characterized by praise and the triumph of speed (Tomlinson, 2007), has also imposed itself on the consumption of food; during the lockdown period following the COVID-19 pandemic, this trend was accelerated.

As reported in "The impact of the COVID-19 emergency on the eating habits of Italians during the quarantine period" (Grant et al., 2021), published by the Observatory on Food Surpluses, Recoveries and Waste (OERSA), this confinement period had, and is still having, important social repercussions from not only a socioeconomic point of view but also a psychological-behavioural perspective, having manifested itself in consumption practices and in the reshaping of lifestyles. This reflection shows how food practices are closely interconnected to the social and historical context in which one is immersed. Food, therefore, has done more than nourish over the centuries: it has been a catalyst for social transformation and organization and economic expansion (Standage, 2010). Eating is thus a behaviour that develops beyond its specific purpose; it is a situational element, and the circumstances of consumption determine its semantic meaning. Eating food generates identification with certain values and ideals, communicates our thinking and materializes the structures that orient us.

Food and the processes of its preparation convey, then, fundamental cultural meanings through which subjects constitute their sense of home and belonging to a social group, assimilating the habits, tastes, prescriptions and hierarchies that allow them to reconnect the here and now to history and family memory. Food is not only a glue between generations, a medium that expresses the prolongation of maternal dependence; it is also confirmed, in Euro-American contexts, as a fundamental component of parental thinking that maintains a close bond with a person and the creation of bonds between people (Grilli, 2014).

From a pedagogical perspective, it may be interesting, in the context of the ongoing ecological transition, to understand people's levels of concern and perceptions in relation to food, nutrition and sustainability to better orient current generations towards acting in a certain direction. The transition to sustainability requires more environmentally aware, social and economic food choices. Any substantial transition to a just and sustainable world calls into question the choices of the global consumer who, increasingly and particularly in high-income countries, assumes food consumption lifestyles based on products with a deep environmental footprint (Bogueva & Marinova, 2022).

Talking about sustainability also means talking about food sustainability. Growing sensitivity towards the sustainability of food leads to increasing attention on the elements that define its main characteristics: healthiness, safety, environmentally friendly production and economic profitability for companies and consumers. The debate on sustainable diets is open and dynamic, and the components to be considered are diverse and evolving.

2 Research Focus: Human Development Work Unit

A particular area of interest in reference to food sustainability is linked to the production of meat and cured meats—for several centuries, these have been part of the Mediterranean diet and Italian food culture—which at the same time have been increasingly subject to attention and criticism based on nutritional, ethical and environmental reasons (Bernardi et al., 2019).

A special report from the *Intergovernmental Panel on Climate Change* (IPCC, 2019) documents how between 10.8 and 19.1 billion tonnes of CO_2 equivalent emissions per year come from food and have a considerable impact on the four pillars of food security—availability, access, use and stability. Food is big business: the 100 largest food and beverage companies worldwide include 10 major meat producers and processors.

In particular, global meat companies play an important role in determining how meat and feed products are produced, transported and traded. In this context, the attitudes and values of adolescents and young people often anticipate the future and can configure important agents of environmental, social and economic change (Loader et al., 2014). Nevertheless, the future of food will be increasingly sustainable due to the decisive push in this area among younger generations, who are at the centre of the ecological transition as agents of change.

In this context, Goal 12 of the *2030 Agenda*, “Ensure sustainable patterns of production and consumption” (United Nations, 2015), deserves particular attention, as it aims at a radical change in the ways in which goods and services are currently produced and consumed. Production and consumption are, therefore, united in the same objective, as inseparable dimensions of the market on which it is necessary to act following a unitary strategy that involves, at the same time, economic operators and citizens-consumers.

The Human Development work unit within the VIS (Valore Impresa Sostenibile) project is intended to address the “consumption of cured meats, Generation Z and sustainability” triad, an educational challenge that identifies training opportunities in the family, at school and in the local community. The focal perspective is that of the Gen Z consumer, adopted to explore not only the salient motivations for the consumption of cured meats and highlight the factors that can guide consumption choices towards greater sustainability but also the obstacles that can condition the relevant decision-making process. Accordingly, the aim of this study is to probe the consumption habits of cured meats among young people in the age group from 15 to 25 years by investigating consumption methods, purchasing influences (see contribution by Zane/Molinari), selection criteria and sustainability evaluations as a parameter of product choice. In particular, we seek to highlight some aspects related to the cultural dimension connected to the consumption of cured meats by Generation Z: what is changing in the set of knowledge, opinions, attitudes, perceptions, practices that we indicate with the term youth food culture. The culture of consumption contributes decisively to the renewed critical capacity of the consumer, understood not necessarily as a way of rejecting or denying consumerism but as the ability and possibility to redefine the symbolic meanings of consumer goods. Moreover, to think sustainably about cured meats, all edible material and packaging as well as the complete purchase process must be considered to mirror the importance of reflecting on the entire experience underlying the consumption of a food, i.e., the entire consumption process.

The Treccani Encyclopedia defines Generation Z as those born between 1997 and 2012, the generation of the near future, also called *Gen Z, zoomers,* the *iGeneration, postmillennials or Homelanders*. It is also necessary to frame the context in which Generation Z were raised. The contemporary era is that of sustainable transition, of collective and global duty and responsibility, which includes a particularly profound change in the paradigms of society and economy, the transition from one way of being or living to another. The Next Generation EU and the Green New Deal are the most recent regulatory interventions of the European Union focused on supporting the sustainable transition in a context where consumers and financial institutions are giving increasing attention to sustainability issues. Consumers’ interest is also growing in the final product, from its organoleptic characteristics to its nutritional values and packaging, across the entire production chain. Hence, there is a strong tendency to seek more information on cultivation and breeding methods, the use of pesticides and the origin of raw materials. Organic, GMO-free, biodiversity, Slow

Food, locally grown produce, fair trade, veg and cruelty-free are examples of forms of resistance in the culture of conservation that are shaping the demand for consumption.

Over the last century, the increased presence and rapid transformation of media in the daily life of adolescents and young people and the availability of touchscreen devices and intelligent features during the first years of life have transformed their relationship with consumption. Their constant connections with their peer group and a multitude of sources of information have given this demographic an extraordinary range of options when making choices.

Young people under 25 have suffered greatly from the limitations imposed by the COVID-19 pandemic, specifically, from the loss, for months, of the possibility of interacting in person with their peers, attending school in person, being able to socialize in the best ways or even shopping directly in a store.

Generation Z is the next generation of consumers who, at 32% of the world's population, will make up the majority of the workforce by 2030. The next great change in buying habits will be driven by Generation Z, considered the most critical group, with a very different perspective on buying and consumption than previous generations. They are the ones who will have great purchasing power in the coming decades, which means that the market, including the food and feed industries, will have to earn their trust.

Without an adequate understanding of this generation, the world of production and commerce will find it difficult to interact with and retain this consumer target.

Furthermore, the future of food is becoming increasingly sustainable due the decisive push from young people in this area. This is highlighted in research conducted by AstraRicerche for McDonald's (2021), which explores the expectations and behaviours of Generation Z regarding the ecological transition in the agri-food chain. This report shows that the younger generations are clearly aware of the concept of ecological transition in the food supply chain and are very curious about it, whereby, e.g., they state that they want to know more. For members of Generation Z, the relevance of nutrition has also increased substantially in the last 5 years, and this interest in food is leading young people to visit festivals, events and themed fairs, both within and outside their own region.

The new generations have to deal, every day, with factors of social transformation that strongly and, unfortunately, negatively affect eating behaviours and choices made at the table. These phenomena include the following examples:

The destructuring of meal preparation, which manifests itself in the research on and consumption of ready-to-cook and ready-to-eat foods. From this perspective, food choice favours products that have good service content and are suitable to be consumed instantly compared to fresh food;

The destructuring of the food day, which manifests itself by shattering the traditional consumption rhythm (breakfast, snack, lunch, snack, dinner) and multiplying the opportunities for instant and unregulated consumption of foods available at any time of day, in every season and in every situation—often of inadequate nutritional quality and with a strong environmental impact;

The spread of meals outside the home, which delegates to public and private management companies the task of choosing the qualities, combinations and portions of everyday foods, accentuating in users an inevitable passivity with respect to consumption patterns and eating styles.

Clearly, outlining the evolutionary perspectives on the consumption of meat and cured meats is a difficult challenge. Many economic, demographic, environmental, social, climatic and technological variables intervene to change the course of events.

3 Cured Meat Culture and Generation Z

The issue of the consumption of cured meats among Generation Z is particularly complex and remains little investigated in the national and international pedagogical literature. This has required prudence in defining this study's methodological framework, the elaboration of its tools, the analysis of the data and the interpretation of the results.

The survey "sustainability and cured meats in Generation Z", following what emerged from the questionnaire (see contribution by Zane/Molinari), has been further developed in the management of two focus groups, representing this consolidated qualitative method in educational research (Baldacci & Frabboni, 2013; De Ketele & Roegiers, 1996; Trinchero, 2002; Viganò, 2003). Thus, it has enabled us to examine the extant quantitative data and to raise further questions. It was decided to propose a focus group to give the floor directly to the focal students without proposing any standardized categories within which to place their possible responses to prompts. Small group discussion, characteristic of this survey tool, in our opinion, proved to be effective in allowing participants to express themselves through a usual form of communication, namely peer discussion.

The meetings took place online and were recorded. The first focus group was attended by 10 students (4 males and 6 females) and the second by 8 (3 males and 5 females); all participants came from the Università Cattolica del Sacro Cuore and were enrolled in degree courses in which the theme of sustainability is addressed during specific courses.

Attendance to the focus group was garnered through a response to an invitation email sent to those who had already participated in the questionnaire that had comprised the subject of the first phase of the research conducted by the Human Development work unit.

The two groups were homogeneous in terms of age and heterogeneous in geographical and academic origin.

The most represented gender was the female gender; 98% of the focal sample declared that they consumed cured meats.

From the analysis, a rich and highly articulated youth food culture emerged. The focus group began with the question: "*Why do you consume or not consume cold cuts*"?

Among the emergent reasons, the majority identify the consumption of cured meats with pleasure and gluttony. Importance is also attached to wealth and respect for family and local traditions. Those who do not eat cured meats do so for ethical or environmental reasons, and some consume them in moderation for reasons of diet or food intolerance.

A theme that emerges is connected to the possibility of quickly preparing meals with cold cuts: "*eating a good salami allows you to quickly prepare a good dish and to comfortably carry a good food*"; "*I eat them because I can easily bring a sandwich to school*"; "*they are convenient to prepare when I have to eat a fast, packed lunch*". A further aspect concerns conviviality, an identification with feeling good among company in the context of aperitifs, parties or moments of sociability. The participants declare that they know little about the place of origin of cured meats, but in their intentions, there is the desire to read more about the origin of these products. If in general the attention towards pollution and the fight against waste have increased, it is not possible to grasp the close link between sustainability and cured meats, also understood as production, distribution and consumption.

Hermeneutic analysis of the focus groups has made it possible to reveal individual meanings and perspectives with respect to the focal issues, to go beyond the responses, highlighting some implicit elements in relation to the link between consumption, cured meats and sustainability.

Analysis of the contents of students' contributions thus shows that the salient factors in and/or processes for their involvement in sustainable actions are attributable to different levels.

The categories at the individual level mentioned by the students are skills and information, motivation, personal values and sense of responsibility and attitude towards the future: "*I buy it (food product) because there is quality*"; "*I buy it because it suits me*"; "*I buy it because one is worth the other*"; "*...but, you don't go to the supermarket with the idea of buying a product that will have the least impact on the environment [...] because you don't know how to evaluate it, you don't have the information*".

The expressed reasons also refer to external factors that can affect purchasing and consumption choices: "*I do not believe that sustainable actions in the purchase of cured meats will save the world, because I do not believe that everyone does [this]; there will always be someone who will not*".

On the other hand, there is a sense of disempowerment regarding the role of young people in society, since, according to some participants, the possibility of implementing real change depends, above all, on the decisions of institutions: "*I think we are still too young for these things;, we need to focus on who has the power. They are the ones who ultimately decide for all generations*".

In particular, the perception of trust is a category that transversally influences different aspects, i.e., the relationship with institutions, the economic market and the system in general:.

"*[...] Journalists and mass media then exaggerate [things]... And, all this makes us even more confused and ignorant*"; "*At the supermarket, organic things do not even have shelves. They are hidden in the corners. You walk by and you don't even see them unless you're really interested".*

A further element pointed out by the focus group participants is the risk, on the part of some companies producing cured meats, of using greenwashing in their communications with consumers, a strategy aimed at minimizing the true social, environmental and economic impact of their products. As a participant in the focus group stated, *"there is so much greenwashing, many words but few concrete certifications, that it becomes difficult for the consumer to be responsible, especially if you do not know the terms used to define sustainability in the supply chain"*. The use of vague and misleading language for consumers and the use of declarations of organic or green certifications whose existence is difficult to verify are thus some of the techniques more widespread than *greenwashing*. In the meat trade, terms such as "regenerative pasture" or "low-carbon chicken" are just a few expressions frequently used in marketing but for which there are no standards or scientific definitions, leaving these ideas vulnerable to being used in a plot for greenwashing.

Hence, companies wishing to emphasize the environmental characteristics of their products, thereby gaining the confidence of consumers, must provide consumers with complete and truthful information.

Pedagogical reflection can help prevent episodes of greenwashing from a dual perspective. On the one hand, it is a matter of compelling companies, in identifying relevant consumer-oriented measures, to integrate a green transition into their corporate identity and organizational design, making sustainability a lever for development and, on the other hand, of training consumers in deciphering *marketing* messages, in distinguishing the serious and sustainable commitment of virtuous companies from greenwashing.

The debate on consumption and sustainable production questions companies regarding their sustainability in terms of how their products and services reflect the lifestyles of customers, in terms of the belief that "façade" interventions are not enough. In fact, it is necessary to redefine a business model in depth, to propose socioenvironmental performance improvement and to not hesitate to intervene to influence consumer habits in a more responsible sense. It is up to companies to intensify the demand for precise information on the nutritional characteristics of products, reiterating the importance of an effective guarantee regarding the requirements of health, safety, environmental impact and production processes.

The points of sale and purchase of cured meats, whether supermarkets or small family-run shops, are interposed between producers and consumers and, if pedagogically oriented, can become educational laboratories, informal places for food education that present themselves as important allies of formal education.

Although the on-the-shelf presence of products that are not only ecological and organic but also fair trade and have reduced packaging, as well as the adoption of environmental management measures, is no longer a sporadic exception within the points of sale in large-scale distribution, the relationship between environmental awareness and purchasing choice needs to be further deepened according to the participants: two state that they do *not buy products linked to a sustainable supply chain,* despite being aware of environmental problems, and only one out of *18 students reported paying attention when choosing the point of sale.*

Another interesting element is the identification of the sustainability of products with sustainable packaging. "*I look more at sustainability by linking it to other aspects, for example, packaging*", stated one participant, whose statement was then reiterated and confirmed by others. Without wishing to deny the importance of the sustainability of packaging and the numerous initiatives to reduce plastic, the excessive attention given to the way in which a product is presented can deceive a consumer if he or she is not trained in the first years of life in making a critical product choice. The risk that can be glimpsed, then, is that we could lose sight of the need and the real characteristics of a product itself, beyond the packaging or advertising message that accompanies it.

Numerous studies on the symbolic value of food attest that product choice is strongly influenced by the meaning attributed to a food choice and by the private and public value that this type of consumption possesses (Russo, 2011).

Generation Z is more likely to declare, in principle, that they care about the environment more than other generations; however, established beliefs do not necessarily translate into concrete actions. In this study, although concerns were expressed about the environmental footprint of food of animal origin and the consumption of soil and water linked to the production of cured meats, only three participants stated that they personally address these when buying and choosing the cured meats they consume and expressed a desire to become more informed. These young participants are increasingly aware of the climatic costs of their actions and choices, but, generally, they are not willing to radically change their diet: one participant declares to have reduced her consumption of cold cuts but does not feel ready to cease this because this food is part of her roots and family traditions. It is an opportunity for socializing and sharing. These young Gen Zers also state that they are willing to change their consumption habits of cured meats, in terms of sustainability, if prompted by adequate scientific evidence that justifies the change: *"I am willing to change my habits if I receive scientific data of a certain type, data on actual water waste, for example; scientifically made information with evidence"*.

While no particular comments emerge in relation to the price of a product, a recurring theme is the concern for animal welfare, i.e., that the meat used to make cured meats comes from farms they define as "ethical".

In both focus groups, the Zers declare that they do not usually read labels and do not know the sustainability criteria for cured meats. Students who come from faculties oriented to the theme of sustainability, however, report that addressing some thematic aspects in the classroom during lectures has helped them reflect on the theme and raise awareness in terms of changing, albeit limitedly, some consumption habits.

The family turns out to be the context that most influences and accompanies the choices of young people. In particular, it functions as the backbone of social coexistence in its relational dimension and in that linked to consumption. Family lifestyles thus play a critical role in determining the creation of sustainable forms of habitus, from both a social and environmental point of view.

When asked, "What would you recommend to cured meat producers in order to communicate their sustainability practices to consumers?", the focus group participants suggested making all certifications more visible, investing in them to position them on the market in an irrefutable way and to define strategies for companies to be closer to their consumers and communicate their efforts in a transparent way.

A noteworthy aspect for these students is the importance of making evident the origin of a product and the guarantee of the use of *Italian meat* in the production of cured meats. Today, the competitiveness of products is increasingly based on the possibility of communicating and assuring the customer that they come from contexts known and recognized as excellent. In this light, giving new impetus and innovating production according to the criterion of particularity imply new logics and significant training actions oriented towards research and the construction of meaning to help producers and consumers reinterpret and give a new identity to this important market sector.

4 Challenges and Educational Perspectives for Sustainable Cured Meat Consumption

Only a food culture more attentive to the values of quality, particularity and sustainability in all its forms can successfully address the food issues of our century, from those related to the access to food to the prevention of a wide range of diseases and to respect for the environment. Proper, good nutrition, not understood in terms of restrictions and therapy but in educational terms, should become the subject of teaching, which also favours the recovery and consolidation of local traditions, to ensure a lifestyle based on respect for oneself and one's territory.

The particularity of a dish is linked to its territoriality. This term, from the French terroir, recalls the environment in a cultural, economic, morphological sense, focusing on biodiversity and the local and includes the human in his or her social and historical interactions. Territory from this perspective specifies the quality of a product, whether it is good and if possible, fair, that is, produced while respecting both the natural and social environments. The particularity of a food thus expresses its ability to convey the customs and traditions of a place, helping build its identity.

Today's food, as M. Franchi recalls, is flexible: "it adapts to the situations in which it is consumed, intertwines with them, gives rise to varied phenomena of hybridization, breaks down into ever smaller and more transportable portions, dresses in different forms, is continuously transformed into 'other': spectacle, symbol, care, sociability, communication" (Franchi, 2009, p. 11). Today, we discuss the sustainable quality of nutrition, which takes into account health in relation to humans (emotionally, psychologically, in terms of taste), the environment (ecological value) and society (cultural, economic, political value). Deciding what is good to eat generates a certain apprehension and difficulty of choice: humans are stunned today more than in the past by the excess of supply and information; they do not know, in depth, the industrial processes, composition of food or consequences for health of what they eat.

Choosing what to eat has the power to change the world. We also build a certain food culture through the choices we make. Learning to choose is therefore a primary goal of nutrition education.

Educating for sustainable consumption requires processes of shared responsibility geared towards global well-being and from the perspective of a culture of sustainability. First, there is the need to put in place training courses at different levels of the supply chain to spread among workers an analytical knowledge of their products and the ability to communicate this to consumers and stakeholders and grasp the information needs of the latter. For example, it would be interesting to help companies promote, through the organization of events open to citizens or workshops dedicated to families, correct and healthy lifestyles, starting from the knowledge of the focal company's products itself. To transfer these issues in a comprehensible and immediate way, thereby integrating product/service communication with the dimensions of sustainability, sustainable educational communication is more necessary than ever; it must be based on a new paradigm that takes into account complexity and offers an unprecedented look at the environment and processes. Second, without any advocation of a particular temporal order, as it is necessary that these two paths develop jointly, the activation of educational paths in the school, family and social spheres can no longer be postponed to ensure consumers know how to choose and open themselves to change in terms of assuming responsibility for a sustainable way of life. Strengthening the alliance between person, local identity and local brand is a useful strategy to prevent the ignorance of the citizen/consumer and the simultaneous indecision of producers, affecting the image of a company and, at the same time, the attractiveness of its products.

An interesting element for overcoming uncritical habits and routines by virtue of the close link between individual behaviour and context is the importance of promoting more sustainable behaviours, moments of social learning, participatory problem-solving, comparison and shared discussion.

The discourse around food is characterized as an opportunity to interpret, between the local and global, new lifestyles and daily experiences of consumers. That is, it is an opportunity to spread a new culture of the planet that alludes to responsibility and participation.

The challenges of healthy eating are issues that challenge everyone. Pedagogical reflection, answering calls to explore new frontiers of research and action for sustainable well-being, confirms the relevance of training in the discourse on nutrition, recalling, among others, the themes of nutrition, human health and inclusion. Food is a material and symbolic "place", generative of experience and knowledge, of culture and science, of dialogue and comparison. It is necessary to create real *food education* oriented towards greater ethical responsibility from a perspective that is not an obstacle to the fulfillment of each person.

Identifying some levers that stimulate consumer behaviour, i.e., affect purchasing styles and stimulate the demand for products attentive to sustainability, is a useful means for improving direct business strategies aimed at encouraging sustainable cured meat consumption. This is certainly a complex and multifaceted challenge that must be accepted by policy-makers with the support of the various parties involved: producers, processors, distributors, technicians, researchers, trade representatives and consumers.

It is important that the changes leading to the sustainability of the food system start from the bottom, that the ecological transition is conducted not only by the state or the market but also the values of individual protagonists and that the responsibility of civil society and the younger generations is recognized.

Consumer information is, therefore, a key element in sustainable development strategies, not only at the European level but also at the national level. The use of consumer information tools in relation to sustainability objectives poses numerous challenges of which we must be aware.

It is necessary to address the fact that citizens-consumers alone, via their purchasing choices, cannot change the entire production system because these choices move, in any case, within a system that is designed with the choices and actions of multiple actors, starting with economic operators and institutions. This reiterates the importance of informed and conscious participation that includes more points of view and more space and time for reflection on any action. It is thus necessary to consider the urgency of training courses aimed at parents, teachers, canteen staff and food companies that go beyond a notional-nutritional and taxation-precept approach. The complexity of food touches the past and the present, time and space, nature and culture, near and far, body and mind, thoughts and feelings: it touches humanity in its entirety.

"I do not consider myself sustainable regarding the consumption of cured meats, but even in this consumption I can improve myself": this statement leads us to reflect on how if, on the one hand, the interest of Generation Z consumers in food issues has increased. On the other hand, the attention to "eating well" or at least "eating better" is not sufficiently widespread and therefore should be addressed through adequate food education. Producers, suppliers and consumers must be able to travel together on a stretch of road towards greater food awareness, building a concrete training alliance across the entire supply chain in terms of sustainability. A diet oriented to sustainability and attention to different and better nourishment can contribute, more than many other economic and social factor, to significantly changing our way of living and being together, with a consequent increase in the confidence in a future of greater individual, family and community well-being.

The focal object in this research, if in some ways it seems very distant from the educational dimension, in reality can only feed on it. For sustainable cured meat consumption, we need more education and investment in the new generations, engines of change. Nutrition and consumption are "formative" acts, an integral part of our life experience, through which pedagogy can contribute to deciphering the educational sense of sustainable choices, on which human survival depends. Committing to a more adequate management of the Earth's goods means confronting a change that has important ethical, ecological and economic repercussions; it alludes to educating people who draw on resources in a fair and responsible way, thus generating new lifestyles.

It has thus emerged that the adoption of green behaviours requires systematic action to raise awareness on the issue, understood as the training and involvement of businesses and citizens, educating even the youngest to act responsibly in their daily choices.

On the one hand, if the consumer has the opportunity to manage his or her relationship with food in an active and creative way, contributing to the formation of his or her identity, on the other hand, we cannot but consider the risk that basing his or her identity on consumption leads to a commodification of life. Pedagogical reflection, in contrast, can enrich the paradigm of food with meaning, enhancing it in the context of an economy in which innovation is not played out exclusively before the introduction of new distribution formulas or new levers of communication and marketing. No preventive action can be separated from a rigorous education programme that can take place in different contexts: families, schools, universities, businesses, supermarkets and territories.

The crucial role of citizens-consumers and, therefore, of the information addressed to them in sustainable development strategies must be promoted with the awareness that the active participation of citizens cannot be reduced to the dimension of consumption alone. Strategies that truly want to make citizens an active part of the transition towards a fully sustainable world cannot relegate them to the sole role of individual-consumer but must provide solutions that guarantee the full, effective and active participation of citizens in achieving the Sustainable Development Goals in multiple forms and at every level. That is, they must include the full participation of each person in public life and decision-making processes, favouring forms of active citizenship that are independent of the individual's purchasing power. The ecological transition in the cured meat supply chain thus requires a "virtuous circle of responsibility": the involvement of all institutional, social, economic and individual actors in a common commitment aimed at promoting the civic engagement necessary for change leading to a more sustainable future.

References

Baldacci, M., & Frabboni, F. (2013). *Manuale di metodologia della ricerca educativa*. UTET.

Baldock, D., & Hart, K. (2021). *Pathways towards a legislative framework for sustainable food systems in the EU*. Institute for European Environmental Policy.

Bernardi, E., Capri, E., & Pulina, G. (2019). *The sustainability of meat and cured meats in Italy. Nutritionaspect, food safety, environmental impact, animalwelfare, circular economy, no waste*. Franco Angeli.

Berners-Lee, M., Kennelly, C., Watson, R., & Hewitt, C. N. (2018). Current global food production is sufficient to meet human nutritional needs in 2050 provided there is radical societal adaptation. *Elementa: Science of the Anthropocene, 6*(52), 1–14.

Birbes, C. (2012). *Nutrirsi di relazione. Una riflessione pedagogica tra cibo e educazione*. Pensa Multimedia.

Bogueva, D., & Marinova, D. (2022). Australian Generation Z and the nexus between climate change and alternative proteins. *Animals, 12*(19), 2512.

Bornatici, S. (2017). *Dal banco alla tavola. Percorsi educativi, spreco alimentare, didattica sociale*. Pensa Multimedia.
De Ketele, J. M., & Roegiers, X. (1996). *Méthodologie du recueil d'informations: Fondements des méthodes d'observations, de questionnaires, d'interviews et d'études de documents*. De Boeck.
Franchi, M. (2009). *Il cibo flessibile. Nuovi comportamenti di consumo*. Carocci.
Grant, F., Scalvedi, M. L., Scognamiglio, U., Turrini, A., & Rossi, L. (2021). Eating habits during the COVID-19 lockdown in Italy: The nutritional and lifestyle side effects of the pandemic. *Nutrients, 13*(7), 2279.
Grilli, S. (2014). Case, cibo e famiglia. Pratiche dell'abitare e della relazionalità parentale. *Lares, 80*(3), 469–490.
Intergovernmental Panel on Climate Change (IPCC). (2019). *Climate change and land: An IPCC special report on climate change, desertification, land degradation, sustainable land management, food security, and greenhouse gas fluxes in terrestrial ecosystems*. Accessed February 20, 2023, from https://www.ipcc.ch/srccl/
Intergovernmental Panel on Climate Change IPCC. (2022). *Sixth assessment report – Chapter 7: Agriculture, Forestry and other Land Uses (AFOLU)*. Accessed February 20, 2023, from https://www.ipcc.ch/report/ar6/wg3/
Loader, B. et al. (2014). 'The networked young citizen: Social media, political participation and civic engagement'. *Information, Communication & Society* (pp. 143–150).
Montanari, M. (2004). *Il cibo come cultura*. Laterza.
Morin, E. (2015). *Insegnare a vivere. Manifesto per cambiare l'educazione*. Raffaello Cortina.
Russo, V. (2011). Le 'nuove' sensibilità dei consumatori e il cambiamento nei processi di comunicazione. In V. Russo, S. Marelli, & A. Angelini (Eds.), *Consumo critico, alimentazione e comunicazione. Valori e comportamenti per un consumo sostenibile* (pp. 24–72). FrancoAngeli.
Standage, T. (2010). *Una storia commestibile dell'umanità*. Torino: Codice, Torino.
Tomlinson, J. (2007). The Culture of Speed. The Coming of Immediacy.Sage Publications.
Trinchero, R. (2002). *Manuale di ricerca educativa*. Franco Angeli.
United Nations (2015). *Transforming our world: The 2030 Agenda for sustainable development.*
Viganò, R. (2003). *Professionalità pedagogica e ricerca*. Vita e Pensiero.

Sustainability of Swine Breeding: Future Challenges and Opportunities

Federico Froldi, Giulia Ferronato, and Aldo Prandini

1 Introduction: From Global Trends to the Environmental Impact of the Pig Sector

The agricultural sector, livestock farming and the global food system have important objectives to maintain, i.e., ensuring continuous food production and food security, while guaranteeing the protection of the planet in terms of environmental, social and economic sustainability (UN/DESA, 2021). The world's demand for animal proteins (meat, milk and eggs) has increased in recent decades. This means an improved quality of life both socially and economically, with a trend primarily driven by growing populations and incomes (FAOSTAT, 2016). Meat production has increased considerably worldwide since the sixties. Global average meat supply has grown from 20 kg/year in 1961 to 43 kg in the last decade and specifically, the average person consumed around 16 kg of pork, 15 of poultry, 9 of beef/buffalo meat and 2 kg of mutton and goat (Ritchie & Roser, 2019). At a global level, the dominant livestock are poultry, cattle (including animals for beef and buffalo meat), pig, and sheep and goat to a lesser extent (Ritchie & Roser, 2019).

Pursuing sustainability means creating and maintaining conditions in which man and nature can be in productive harmony to sustain present and future generations (National Research Council, 2011). Thus, farming activities and management play an essential role in achieving sustainability of the entire supply chain (Steinfeld

Since 13/01/2022, the author is affiliated with the Department of Civil Engineering, Architecture, Environment, Land Planning, and Mathematics (DICATAM), Università degli Studi di Brescia, Brescia, Italy; email: giulia.ferronato@unibs.it

F. Froldi (✉) · G. Ferronato · A. Prandini
Department of Animal Science, Food and Nutrition (DiANA), Università Cattolica del Sacro Cuore, Piacenza, Italy
e-mail: federico.froldi@unicatt.it

A. M. Fellegara et al. (eds.), *Sustainable Transition of Meat and Cured Meat Supply Chain*, CSR, Sustainability, Ethics & Governance,
https://doi.org/10.1007/978-3-031-34977-5_3

et al., 2006; Gerber et al., 2013). Although livestock farming is very important for producing food of high nutritional value, it is also responsible for environmental impacts in terms of greenhouse gas (GHG) emissions, volatile substances, land use, freshwater and marine eutrophication and acidification (FAO, 2018).

The general trend in livestock supply chains is improving, even though, in absolute terms, meat production has a more significant environmental impact than vegetable production due to the breeding phase that is not foreseen in vegetable supply chains. Although it is a very complex phase, animal breeding shows variable impacts depending on the farming practices and the species raised. Globally, the livestock sector is responsible for 14.5% of the anthropogenic GHG emission, 7.1 gigatonnes CO_2-eq per annum, and represents a significant source of GHG emissions worldwide, generating carbon dioxide (CO_2), methane (CH_4) and nitrous oxide (N_2O) throughout the production process (Gerber et al., 2013; Hristov et al., 2013). Globally, 62% of GHG emissions from the livestock sector are attributable to cattle, followed by pigs, poultry and buffaloes for about 10% each, small ruminants for 7% and other poultry for 1% (FAO-GLEAM, 2017).

In Europe and Italy, the agricultural sector is responsible for about 93% of ammonia (NH_3) emissions, mainly from livestock farming (EEA, 2019), largely generated by manure management and synthetic fertilisers (McIlroy et al., 2019). In this context, although more efficient than beef production, pig farming is responsible for significant emissions of NH_3, secondary atmospheric particulate matter (PM_{10} and $PM_{2.5}$) and odours (Volatile Organic Compounds, VOCs) (Philippe et al., 2011). Italian livestock farming, including pig farming, has taken up the challenge to reduce NH_3 and PM emissions by 16% and 40%, respectively, by 2030 (ISPRA, 2022). Initiatives include optimising animal nutrition, reducing protein intake (precision feeding application), genetic improvement of production efficiency in heavy pigs and better management of animal housing and livestock manure. The national tradition of pig farming and high production efficiency demonstrate the sector's ability to engage in actual mitigation actions to improve its environmental performance and to remain competitive in the market.

2 Sustainable National Pig Production

Italian production is mainly directed towards breeding heavy pigs destined for producing high-quality cured meats and dry-cured ham, mainly incorporated in chains certified with the Protected Designation of Origin (PDO) label. In Italy, slaughtering takes place at the live weight of the pig, born and bred in the national territory, which is around 160–180 kg and at the age of 9 months, in compliance with the specifications of the Parma Ham and San Daniele Ham PDOs. In Europe, on the other hand, production is aimed at light pigs, slaughtered at a lower weight (around 110–120 kg) and aimed at the sale of fresh meat where lean cuts are more appreciated. In the European context, the largest pig producers in Europe are Germany, Spain and France. Italy ranks seventh in terms of the volume of meat produced, with

22 PDOs and 16 PGIs (Protected Geographical Indication) recognised (ANAS, 2022).

Given the significant tradition of pig breeding and the processing of the resulting products reflected in their excellence and context, a consolidated responsibility of the pig supply chain comes into play, which concerns not only the production phase, i.e., breeding, but also the entire supply chain as a whole. The challenge of sustainable development of the pork supply chain must and will have to intervene not only in implementing farming practices that respect animal welfare and the environment but also in fostering greater awareness and information to the end users of pork, the consumers. The national production system is a certified system of excellence; targeted and real communication of proximity to consumers could help to stimulate and consolidate pork consumption in the country and abroad. In this context, the new Common Agricultural Policy (CAP) has focused on sustainability and transitioning to a new production model.

A recent national survey by Ismea-Rete Rurale (2021) shows the sensitivity of producers to monitor their environmental performance to identify the main critical issues, such as managing livestock manure, from its storage to its distribution to the field. The new generations, therefore, have the necessary tools for the sector's sustainable, technological and digital development, with the objectives of environmental protection, social inclusion and market maintenance. The latter is explained by the rebalancing of the value chain, i.e., the improvement of the position of farmers and the structure of the chain itself, to reduce the gap between the distribution of value between farmers and retailers. On the other hand, social inclusion could be accentuated through actions and opportunities for revitalising pig farming, which also has environmental and economic spin-offs. These opportunities could be realised in protecting biodiversity and valorising autochthonous breeds as levers to relaunch the pig farming sector in fragmented and sometimes disadvantaged territorial areas. Investing in the sustainability of heavy pig farming through genetic improvement both of the behaviour (docility) of pigs and, therefore, of their state of well-being and resistance to respiratory and enteric diseases is part of a path of sustainability of production in all fields that involves intensive national pig farming (ANAS, 2022).

In recent years, some terminologies such as "precision agriculture," "intelligent agriculture" and "digital agriculture" have become common in politics and popular language, with public funds and media attention dedicated to carrying out the so-called "fourth agricultural revolution" (Barrett & Rose, 2020). Today, thanks to various forms of funding, including the European National Recovery and Resilience Plan, a path is being taken towards the continuous and constant improvement of the pig sector based on investments in quality and the environment. In this regard, the European Commission, in the CAP for the period 2021–2027, has proposed setting ambitious targets for environmental and climate action (Council of the European Union, 2020).

On the global level, however, population growth and the increase in the consumption of food of animal origin necessarily lead to the failure to achieve the

Sustainable Development Goals if concrete actions are not implemented in the short term (Isermeyer, 2020).

3 Life Cycle Assessment Analysis

The most conventional method and tool used to assess the environmental impact of a complex food system is Life Cycle Assessment (LCA) (McAuliffe et al., 2016). LCA analyses the entire life cycle (or part of it) of a system or product, covering a wide range of environmental impacts, for which quantitative estimation is carried out (Hauschild et al., 2018). Therefore, LCA is a system of analysis that studies environmental aspects from raw material supply to production, use, end-of-life, recycling and final disposal from the cradle to the grave (ISO, 2006a). LCA is regulated by the International Organization for Standardization (ISO) 14,040 and 14,044 (ISO, 2006a, b).

A typical LCA study consists of four well-defined phases:

- Goal and scope definition;
- Inventory analysis;
- Impacts assessment;
- Interpretation of the results obtained.

3.1 Goal and Scope Definition

Defining the objective and scope is the first phase of any LCA study. The objective establishes the context of the LCA study and forms the basis for delineating the scope (ISO, 2006a). The definition of the objective must consider some essential aspects: the application of the results, the audience to whom the results are addressed, the limitations resulting from the methodological choices applied and the reasons for conducting the study.

The scope of reference includes the production system, the functional unit (FU), system boundaries, parameters to be used in the assessment, allocation procedures and other relevant factors reported in ISO (2006a).

3.2 Inventory Analysis

The second part of LCA is the creation of the life cycle inventory (LCI) and its analysis. This consists of collecting data on the processes involved in the system under study (i.e., the product) and the system boundaries under consideration (i.e., the life cycle stages). The LCI is thus represented by collecting and quantifying inputs and outputs for a given product throughout the life cycle (ISO, 2006a). The LCI analysis results in a list of quantified physical elements for the product system that is associated with the service or function described by the FU (Hauschild et al., 2018).

3.3 *Impacts Assessment*

Life cycle environmental impact assessment (LCIA) aims to provide additional information to the LCI assessment to understand the results and better interpret their environmental significance. The LCIA is a relative FU-based approach and groups indicator results for different impact categories, representing the LCIA profile for the product system (ISO, 2006b). Mandatory and optional elements characterise the LCIA phase; mandatory elements are environmental mechanisms that involve processing LCI data by classifying impact categories to the data and then applying characterisation factors to them to calculate a category indicator value.

3.4 *Interpretation of the Obtained Results*

Interpretation of the results is the most critical phase of the LCA study. This phase consists of identifying relevant issues based on the LCI and LCIA, highlighting their critical issues and evaluating the sensitivity of the data, limitations and possible recommendations derived from the LCA (ISO, 2006b).

Interpretation of the results must ensure compliance with the quality requirements of the LCA study, identifying concrete actions to improve product environmental performance. The scientific literature reports that different choices in LCA can significantly impact the overall results and classification of the products being evaluated (Sala et al., 2020).

4 Application of LCA to Pig Production

Pig farming, and animal husbandry in general, is a complex system involving multiple inputs. Numerous LCA studies in the scientific literature have addressed the environmental problem that pig farming can generate (Dourmad et al., 2014; Mackenzie et al., 2015). Most studies focus on estimating the environmental impact in the production phase of pigs at 90–120 kg live weight destined for fresh meat consumption outside Italy, limiting the system's boundaries to the farm gate. Other studies also include the slaughter phase, expressing the functional unit per kg of carcass or kg of meat product. Regarding a supply chain approach, Italian pig production shows environmental performance potentials that tend to be higher than those reported in other countries (Bava et al., 2017; Cesari et al., 2017). These impacts depend on the typicalities that characterise the national production system, i.e., the production of carcasses with a higher weight than other markets. In fact, most Italian pig production is aimed at raising heavy pigs of 160–180 kg live weight in compliance with the production specifications of "Prosciutto di Parma PDO" and "Prosciutto di San Daniele PDO". Therefore, the impact per kg of product is penalised by a prolonged fattening phase of at least 9 months and a worsening conversion index (3.6–3.7 kg/kg).

Another functional unit applicable to meat production, instead of mass, is the integration of primary nutritional values (McLaren et al., 2021). For example, given the high protein intake of animal products, the kg of protein best represents the functional unit in livestock production. A study by Zucali et al. (2017) regarding meat and milk production in the Po Valley showed that pork production, followed by poultry meat and bovine milk, was characterised by the lowest global warming potential. In its national context, Italian pig breeding is an efficient system as there is optimisation in the use of resources and careful management from crop production to breeding practices and manure management.

According to Vonderohe et al. (2022) and Bava et al. (2017), environmental sustainability investigated through LCA, applied to pork production, allows the identification of the main hotspots, represented by: (i) feed production and purchase (nutrient balance); (ii) energy use; (iii) water use; (iv) manure management. In this regard, Bava et al. (2017) stated that the feed chain is the first source of GHG, contributing about 70% of the total impact, mainly due to purchased feed and with negative effects on key impact indicators, i.e., climate change. This is followed by animal manure management (about 20% of the total impact) with effects on climate change and indicators such as eutrophication and acidification for NH_3 emissions. The latter is also influenced by energy use, and negative effects are also found for climate change, as well as water use, mainly for crop irrigation.

4.1 *Effects of Feed on Environmental Impact and Sustainable Approaches*

Pig farming is characterised by its ability to convert feed such as grains and their derivatives into meat, i.e., protein and fat. The added value of this production direction is the possibility of including feed such as co-products, by-products and former foodstuffs in the animals' diet.

The production of feed and the formulation of diets for the different stages of animal husbandry have the most significant environmental impact within the product life cycle of the pig industry. The sourcing of raw materials and co-products within globalised markets means that feed has a special position in these LCA studies. The sourcing of feed and their derivatives from geographic areas other than national represents and explains the most significant impact attributed to the product unit under study. In pig farming and monogastric in general, protein sources derived from soybean are commonly used, which has a significant environmental impact when produced in areas of the world subject to land use change (LUC). Europe, and consequently Italy, uses a large part of the soybean and soybean meal for livestock from South America.

Andretta et al. (2022) also defined the distance between the place of production of feedstuffs and their use and transport as relevant. However, changes in the product specifications of Italian PDOs are planned, i.e., 50% of the feed supply will have to come from within the PDO regions' borders, which will positively impact the environmental impact of food purchasing and production. Nevertheless, there could be two ways to reduce the impact of food and feed in the product LCA study: (i) locally produced high-protein dietary components, replacing those imported from other countries; (ii) improving feed efficiency to simultaneously improve the sustainability of pig production in terms of economics and environmental impact. Some considerations in this regard are, however, necessary. The PDO regulations provide a list of feeds that can be used to feed pigs based on the nutritional and organoleptic characteristics they transfer to the meat. Therefore, protein or energy sources that perform better from an environmental sustainability point of view may not be considered.

Furthermore, replacing soya with other protein feeds must not compromise feed conversion efficiency, i.e., more feed must not be used to achieve the expected weight gains. In fact, it would be desirable to optimise the available feed resources to reduce the amounts of feed needed by the animals to complete the production cycle by means of diets that follow the concept of "precision feeding". Precision feeding involves using automatic feeding stations that allow pigs to be fed individually with dynamic *ad hoc* diets throughout the production cycle. Andretta et al. (2016) showed a 40% reduction in the use of nitrogen components in rations fed through precision feeding techniques while reducing the potential environmental pollution.

Another interesting aspect is the supplementation of synthetic amino acids, i.e., essential amino acids, enzymes and other micronutrients in diets to meet the needs of animals. Such supplementation is particularly recommended in diets that are very rich in cereals where there is a risk of excess total protein intake leading to inefficiency in feed-to-meat conversion. In Europe, synthetic Lysine, Methionine, Threonine and Tryptophan make it possible to cope with deficiencies of essential amino acids in pig diets where there is a shortage of protein intake from soybean meal and helps prevent gastrointestinal disorders. These dietary arrangements have significant environmental benefits, as reported by Kebreab et al. (2016), i.e., they can reduce GHG emissions by more than 50% due to reduced land use for soybean cultivation and less LUC.

Phosphorus assimilation is another critical dietary aspect. In pig diets, phosphorous is present in feedstuffs (cereals and oilseeds). Still, it is not readily bioavailable from the animal organism with possible physiological and environmental consequences (manure excretion). In pigs, unlike ruminants, there is no production of the enzyme phytase capable of hydrolysing phosphorus bound in organic form. Therefore, the use of the enzyme phytase, industrially produced and added to feed, has long been widespread. This can limit the intake of phosphoric salts in the diet and reduce phosphorous excretion. Phosphorous assimilation is very important as deficiencies lead to reduced production performance in sows and fattening pigs, with reduced assimilation of calcium, iron, copper and amino acids. On the other hand, an excess of phosphorous leads to a consequent calcium deficiency and losses of the phosphorous itself in manure, mainly in feces. The phosphorous contained in feces, together with nitrogen and potassium, is responsible for the eutrophication of water due to the proliferation of aquatic vegetation, representing a real environmental problem. Since the 1980s, phosphorus excretion in growing and fattening pigs has been more than halved (Crovetto et al., 2018).

Feeding practices adopted at various levels, from the sourcing of raw materials to the feeding technology adopted, must ensure the productivity and efficiency of pig farming and contain environmental emissions to promote sustainable development of the supply chain.

5 Genetic Improvement and Environmental Impact

Genetic improvement has had a significant impact on improving sow productivity in recent decades. Breeding efficiency lies in various aspects, including an improved conversion index, a 55% increase in the number of piglets bred per sow (up to more than 30 weaned piglets/year per sow), an increase in the expected number of piglets born alive per sow and a 22% increase in the meat production index (Ramaekers, 2022). Genetic improvement plays an important role in the sustainability of the national pig sector. The selection of more efficient genetic lines has positive effects on the environmental impact of pigs, thanks to the fulfillment of dietary and nutritional requirements and the optimisation of diet formulations in the context of environmental adaptation. Production performance today is optimal but requires high inputs to avoid non-expression of the phenotypic potential of reared animals. In this respect, the animal's environment must be monitored to make the rearing conditions optimal, avoid high temperatures and provide quality food and general well-being. A lack of these measures would penalise the production performance of the selected genetic lines and thus increase their environmental impact. An improvement in the conversion index translates, in breeding, into a decrease in the excreta produced, which for fattening pigs, for example, would be 2.7% for a reduction in the conversion index of 0.1 unit (i.e., from 3.7 to 3.6). With the same digestibility of the nitrogen component, this corresponds to a decrease in excreted nitrogen of about 230 g/head at a nitrogen retention efficiency of 28% and about 8.8 kg of excreted N/head.

According to Bava et al. (2017), the most efficient type of farming, in terms of live weight per sow, has a much lower potential impact per kg live weight than less efficient farms and is similar to those reported on pigs slaughtered at lower weights. On the other hand, it is required to consider, as is also the case in cattle breeding, the periods of non-productivity of the animals. Such periods when animals are neither gestating nor lactating represent an environmental cost in terms of the use of inputs such as feed, energy and resources in general that serve to maintain the animal and that at the same time are related to GHG emissions (Pietramale et al., 2021).

6 The Use of Energy and Its Optimisation

Energy is used for various activities inside and outside the farm. Inside the barns, energy use relates to the preparation and distribution of the daily feed, the handling of animal manure and the use of operating machinery, lighting, heating and ventilation, while outside, it relates to transport, the production of feed from the cultivation of the fields to the harvesting of the products (De Corato & Cancellara, 2014). Energy sources (i.e., electricity and heat) are mainly derived from fossil fuels and diesel for operating machinery and food production (Tallaksen et al., 2020).

Reducing energy consumption in livestock farming represents an excellent opportunity for livestock farmers, who can now take various measures to cope with increased energy costs and combat extreme weather conditions. Some managerial interventions include: (i) the use of inverters that consist of lower energy consumption in ventilation and manure handling systems; (ii) thermal insulation of the barns; (iii) using the effect of natural lighting or light-emitting diode lights to reduce consumption considerably; (iv) installing solar panels for energy self-production or building an anaerobic digester, the latter an opportunity that is economically burdensome and feasible for large livestock farms, but which also allows for an income supplement in the current national energy demand.

7 Water Use in Swine Production

FAO (2016) estimates that approximately 69% of all water withdrawn from renewable freshwater resources is used for irrigation, livestock and aquaculture (IDF, 2017). Increasing water is needed to meet growing water requirements in livestock production, from feed production to product supply (Steinfeld et al., 2006). An animal system's water footprint (WF) consists of different elements: the indirect water footprint of the feed and the direct water footprint associated to the potable water and service water consumed (Chapagain & Hoekstra, 2004). In the pig farming system, water is used for drinking the animals, preparing the animals' feeding, cleaning the animals and washing barns, buildings and equipment and irrigating crops. Even though the cleaning of equipment is critical to maintaining animal health, it generates wastewater that has a negative effect on the environment due to the use of detergents with nitrate (NO_3–N) and phosphate (PO_4^-) contents (Al-Bahouh et al., 2020).

WF is a measure of the amount of water used over a product's life cycle. The WF is a multi-dimensional indicator that explains the time and location of water use and the amount of water required to assimilate chemicals in water bodies (Hoekstra et al., 2011). The WF can help reverse the trend in water depletion, as it provides information on the relationship between the effect of production on water quantity and quality (Hoekstra & Chapagain, 2008). WF reflects the total water use by its elements, which include the green WF (consumption of rainwater), blue WF (surface and groundwater depletion) and the grey WF (the water required to dilute polluted water) (Al-Bahouh et al., 2020).

In the pig farming industry, 80% of the water component is green water, i.e., rainwater that has been retained by the soil and becomes available to satisfy crop needs (Mekonnen & Hoekstra, 2010). Therefore, direct water consumption on the farm is due to washing (grey water) and drinking water (blue water). Biosecurity and farm prevention protocols make it possible to reduce water inputs for cleaning while ensuring appropriate hygiene standards. Adopting technological watering systems can limit consumption, minimising waste without affecting animal welfare.

8 Emission Reduction Measures, from the Regulatory Framework to Its Applicability

The need to reduce pollutant emissions from the livestock sector is a well-known practice, and Italy has made commitments under international protocols and European directives in this regard. However, in recent years, emissions have remained stable or increased in some areas of the country, so more reduction efforts are needed, particularly in the pig sector. In the national area, 77% of pig farms are located in the North (ANAS, 2022), in an unfavourable climatic context accentuated by the presence of the Alps. This mountain range hinders air exchange in the Po Valley, causing stagnation of atmospheric pollutants that can threaten humans and animals.

To prevent or drastically reduce emissions of GHG, NH_3, as well as odour and dust, specific techniques are adopted, which affect the management of manure in the barn during storage and distribution to the field. The objectives to be pursued, first of all, must improve the health status of farmed animals, helping to reduce emissions of these substances and prevent nutrient loss during storage and subsequent utilisation of the manure itself.

The regulation of emissions lies in the EU directive 2016/2284, known as the NEC (National emission ceiling) directive. This directive limits member states' emissions of pollutants, including NH_3. The target set by the directive is a 5% reduction in NH_3 emissions for each year from 2020 to 2029 (as stipulated by the 2012 update of the Gothenburg Protocol) and 16% from 2030, compared to 2005 emissions (ISPRA, 2022). For intensive pig farms and also poultry farms, there is a specific directive, Directive 2010/75/EU IED (Industrial Emission Directive), implemented by the national Legislative Decree 46/2014, which aims to expand the scope of the previous legislation (IPPC—Integrated Pollution and Prevention

Control) and at the same time restrict the discretion of Member States regarding the conditions for issuing the Integrated Environmental Authorisation (AIA). This authorisation concerns intensive pig farms with more than 2000 production pig places (over 30 kg) or more than 750 breeding sows. It is inherent to an administrative procedure governing pollution control to safeguard and protect the environment, preserving air, water and soil quality in compliance with the IED Directive.

The IED Directive, in turn, sanctions the use of the Best Available Techniques (BAT) related to pig farming (including poultry farming) for the operation of the business. These techniques cover the processes and activities that take place on farms: (i) feed management of animals; (ii) feed preparation (from milling and mixing to the storage of feed and raw materials); (iii) husbandry (housing and buildings); (iv) collection and storage of livestock manure; (v) treatment of livestock manure; (vi) spreading and agronomic valorisation of livestock manure. BATs are associated with limit values for emissions (i.e., NH_3, odours and dust) and operating conditions (i.e., energy consumption, no repercussions on animal welfare) that are useful for correctly constructing barns by the planned techniques and good agricultural practices. In this regard, the NEC directive requires member states to establish "an indicative national code of good agricultural practice for the control of ammonia emissions" that is in line with the "Framework code of good agricultural practice for the reduction of ammonia emissions" (UNECE, 2015).

9 The Best Available Techniques: The Barns

Depending on the production management of the herd (weaning, fattening, reproduction), the buildings are specialised and correctly dimensioned, i.e., there are specific subdivisions into rooms for definite breeding activities. Thus, it is possible to move from the simplicity of fattening farms with more standardised structures (Chiumenti, 2004) to more complex structures, as in the case of reproduction. From an environmental point of view, the manure removal systems and how barns are cleaned represent and influence their construction techniques. In livestock farms, as is well known, it is necessary to reduce NH_3, odour and dust emissions through measures that include: (i) reducing the contact surfaces between manure and the atmosphere; (ii) increasing the frequency of manure removal from barns and areas where animals live; (iii) separating manure into two fractions, solid and liquid; (iv) maintaining clean and dry litter by periodically removing it and renewing it.

However, it is important to know the barn types that can be distinguished into Non-BAT and BAT. These technologies mainly affect NH_3 emissions at the barn ranging from 0.70 kg NH_3/animal place/year for weaned piglets for BAT associates high emission values between 5.65 kg NH_3/animal place/year for fattening pigs.

Older barns with long-term manure storage in deep pits inside the enclosure are still allowed (Non-BAT). Still, new barns cannot adopt these techniques unless structural and managerial measures are taken to reduce NH_3 emissions. Under such conditions, NH_3 emissions are between 0.7 and 7.5 kg NH_3/animal place/

year, representing emission limit values (Santonja et al., 2017). A justification for these facilities could be air filtration that would reduce 0.03–0.40 kg NH_3/animal place/year, making animal husbandry sustainable.

Innovative techniques implemented on most pig farms involve the removal of manure frequently (once or twice a week). The most common technique is the vacuum removal system, whereby a valve is opened at the end of a main conducting pipe, allowing the manure to be conveyed outside the barns using a vacuum. Depending on the category of animals reared, emission levels of between 0.53–5.6 kg of NH_3/animal place/year are obtained. The technique of recirculating the liquid fraction of slurry is difficult to apply to existing barns once or twice a day, which allows the storage pits or gutters to be kept clean at all times but may cause peaks of unpleasant odours during recirculation. This technique has advantages when combined with an anaerobic digestion plant, but this will be discussed in the next section.

Other company precautions lie in the separation of manure and sewage through suitable flooring (partly solid and partly slotted), the design of which allows for the rapid collection of liquid fractions (wash water and sewage) that flow into a main connection. In this way, emission surfaces are significantly reduced, making such building technologies optimal in delivery and gestation rooms.

Not all rearing systems create favourable conditions for reducing volatile emissions in the barn. Optimal solutions from a welfare point of view may not be the best in terms of controlling emissions in the barn. The use of organic litter (i.e., straw), which due to its high C:N ratio, could undergo composting of organic matter, increasing NH_3 emissions as a result of increased litter temperature (Mrad & Salvò, 2017). In addition, CH_4, N_2O and unpleasant odours could be emitted.

10 Good Agricultural Practices: The Manure Storage

Proper manure management on pig farms involves storage and management that must follow the constraints imposed by European Directive 91/676/EEC, the Nitrates Directive, which concerns the protection of water against pollution caused by nitrates from agricultural sources. Nowadays, there are great opportunities for the valorisation of livestock manure financed by regional Rural Development Plans (RDPs) to maintain the fertilising capacity of manure in storage until the field.

Environmental sustainability in reducing emissions of volatile substances and potential sources of diffuse pollution of surface and groundwater bodies is the priority for newly built storage facilities and adaptations of older barns, as seen for housing types. Farmers have various alternatives depending on the farm's size and type of storage. The types of storage for non-palpable liquid manure are represented by vertical tanks made of reinforced concrete, steel or underground ponds; for palatable manure, on the other hand, slabs or silos. To avoid, as far as possible, the volatilisation of NH_3 by exposure of the liquid manure to atmospheric air, reducing the surface-to-volume ratio of the storage facilities is necessary. These interventions, in addition to their environmental benefit, prevent denitrification due to the action of the wind on the storage surface and thus, the emission of unpleasant odours. Many measures can be taken, depending on the size and volume of storage, and depending on these, greater or lesser NH_3 reductions can be achieved. Among the most common systems for covering storage tanks are rigid lid or roof, flexible cover and floating plastic bodies, which achieve NH_3 reductions of between 80–60%, respectively. These create a barrier between manure surface and air, reducing emissions (Santonja et al., 2017).

Small farms in disadvantaged areas or those unable to build permanent storage facilities can store manure in fully sealed storage bags that allow 100% NH_3 reductions. In the case of solid manure, there is no alternative to dedicated heaps other than coverings that reduce the action of wind, rainwater and solar radiation, thus ensuring the proper development of aerobic fermentations of the stored material (UNECE, 2015). Although advantageous, these measures require considerable economic investments and could require financial support.

Among the possibilities to make pig farming and the supply chain increasingly green is the anaerobic digestion of manure, whether liquid or solid. Anaerobic digestion provides a promising practice to mitigate GHG emissions from harvested livestock manure by stabilising organic carbon through the reduction of readily degradable carbon meanwhile increasing nitrogen plant availability when the digestate is distributed as a soil fertiliser. Nowadays, anaerobic digestion is a technology widely adopted by farmers due to its environmental benefits and economic return thanks to electricity production (self-used or sold) and thermal energy. Given the considerable production costs, the future could be represented by consortium anaerobic digestion plants, for which a protection consortium or stakeholder builds a plant in strategic areas where manure from several farms flows, creating a territorial economy in the value chain.

11 Good Agricultural Practices: The Application of Manure to the Field

Pig manure has a high fertilising power when used in an agronomically efficient way due to its high ammoniacal nitrogen content (Sommer et al., 2013). Such manure lends itself to innovative and sustainable distribution techniques that reduce air exposure by improving the infiltration of manure into the soil, following the current BAT. Therefore, these techniques are necessary to achieve NH_3 and GHG emission reduction targets, especially N_2O (ISPRA, 2022). Low-emission manure application techniques include machinery such as an injector or band spreader, which represent the most effective means to improve the infiltration of slurries; the techniques are as follows: (i) band spreading slurry (trailing hose, with a 30–35% in NH_3 reduction; (ii) band spreading (trailing shoe, with a 30–60% in NH_3 reduction); (iii) injection slurry (open slot, with 70% in NH_3 reduction); injection slurry (closed slot, with

80–90% in NH_3 reduction); (iv) incorporation of surface-applied slurry (with 30–90% in NH_3 reduction) (UNECE, 2015).

Significant NH_3 reductions (around 30%) also occur through fertigation in pivot or hose irrigation systems. Most farms, given the considerable costs of synthetic chemical fertilisers (i.e., urea and ammonium nitrate), make the most of organic fertilisers. Greater efficiency in using slurry equals less dependence on chemical fertilisers and can lead to higher crop yields, which translates into lower feed purchases. Therefore, the impact of pig farming can be reduced and is being reduced over the years, considerably, thanks to targeted and specific measures, which lead to a lower use of inputs and their optimisation, also considering the economic feasibility of the measures and techniques adopted and their applicability.

12 Conclusions

The Italian pig supply chain plays a key role in the national and international markets and bears significant environmental responsibility. The approach to climate change and the environmental impacts of livestock breeding shows that breeders are attentive to adopting mitigation actions to improve their product's environmental performance. Therefore, the livestock breeding of the future is ready to face critical issues, overcome challenges and seize opportunities at various levels in accordance with European policies for the sustainable development of the whole chain.

References

Al-Bahouh, M., Osborne, V., Wright, T., Dixon, M., & Gordon, R. (2020). Blue and grey water footprints of dairy farms in Kuwait. *JWARP, 12*, 618–635. https://doi.org/10.4236/jwarp.2020.127038

ANAS. (2022). http://www.anas.it/files/documenti/Relazioneassembleadeisoci2022.pdf

Andretta, I., Hauschild, L., Kipper, M., Remus, A., & Garcia-Launay, F. (Eds.). (2022). *Strategies for mitigating the environmental impacts of pig and poultry production*. Frontiers Media SA. https://doi.org/10.3389/978-2-83250-100-9

Andretta, I., Pomar, C., Rivest, J., Pomar, J., & Radunz, J. (2016). Precision feeding can significantly reduce lysine intake and nitrogen excretion without compromising the performance of growing pigs. *Animal, 10*, 113747. https://doi.org/10.1017/S1751731115003067

Barrett, H., & Rose, D. C. (2020). Perceptions of the fourth agricultural revolution: What's in, what's out, and what consequences are anticipated? *Sociologia Ruralis* soru.12324. https://doi.org/10.1111/soru.12324.

Bava, L., Zucali, M., Sandrucci, A., & Tamburini, A. (2017). Environmental impact of the typical heavy pig production in Italy. *Journal of Cleaner Production, 140*, 685–691.

Cesari, V., Zucali, M., Sandrucci, A., Tamburini, A., Bava, L., & Toschi, I. (2017). Environmental impact assessment of an Italian vertically integrated broiler system through a Life Cycle approach. *Journal of Cleaner Production, 143*, 904–911.

Chapagain, A. K., & Hoekstra, A. Y. (2004). *Water footprints of nations*, Value of Water Research Report Series No. 16, UNESCO-IHE, Delft, the Netherlands.

Chiumenti, R. (2004). *Costruzioni rurali*. Rcs Libri-Edagricole Scolastico.

Council of the European Union. (2020). Proposal for a Regulation of the European Parliament and of The Council establishing rules on support for strategic plans to be drawn up by Member States under the Common agricultural policy (CAP Strategic Plans) and financed by the European Agricultural Guarantee Fund (EAGF) and by the European Agricultural Fund for Rural Development (EAFRD) and repealing Regulation (EU) No 1305/2013 of the European Parliament and of the Council and Regulation (EU) No 1307/2013 of the European Parliament and of the Council – General Approach (Annexes I–XIII).

Crovetto, G. M., Cesari, V., Colombini, S., Galassi, G., Prandini, A., Rapetti, L., Schiavon, S., Sigolo, S., & Toschi, V. (2018). *Rilascio di macro e micro nutrienti nelle filiere produttive*. Capitolo in: Allevamento animale e sostenibilità ambientale. Le tecnologie. A cura di Bruno Stefanon, Marcello Mele, Giuseppe Pulina Franco Angeli Editore, 2018 codice ISBN: 9788891771469.

De Corato, U., & Cancellara, F. (2014). *L'efficienza energetica nel comparto zootecnico (RT/2014/16/ENEA)*. https://doi.org/10.13140/2.1.1510.3043.

Decreto legislativo 46 del 4 marzo. (2014). *Attuazione della direttiva 2010/75/UE relativa alle emissioni industriali (prevenzione e riduzione integrate dell'inquinamento)*. (14G00058) (GU Serie Generale n.72 del 27-03-2014 – Suppl. Ordinario n. 27).

Direttiva (UE) 2016/2284 del Parlamento Europeo e del Consiglio del 14 dicembre 2016 concernente la riduzione delle emissioni nazionali di determinati inquinanti atmosferici.

Direttiva 2010/75/UE del Parlamento Europeo e del Consiglio, 24 novembre 2010. Emissioni industriali (prevenzione e riduzione integrate dell'inquinamento).

Dourmad, J. Y., Ryschawy, J., Trousson, T., Bonneau, M., Gonzàlez, J., Houwers, H. W. J., Hviid, M., Zimmer, C., Nguyen, T. L. T., & Morgensen, L. (2014). Evaluating environmental impacts of contrasting pig farming systems with life cycle assessment. *Animal, 8*, 2027–2037. https://doi.org/10.1017/S1751731114002134

EEA. (2019). *EMEP/EEA air pollutant emission inventory* Guidebook 2019.

FAO. (2016). *The global dairy sector: Facts*. Available from https://www.fil-idf.org/wpcontent/uploads/2016/12/FAO-Global-Facts-1.pdf

FAO. (2017). *Global Livestock Environmental Assessment Model (GLEAM) [versione online]*. Roma. Consultabile nella sezione "Results" del sito web: www.fao.org/gleam/en/

FAO. (2018). *Building climate resilience for food security and nutrition*. The State of Food Security and Nutrition in the World. FAO, Rome.

FAOSTAT. (2016). *FAOSTAT*. Food and Agriculture Organization of the United Nations, Rome, Italy.

Gerber, P. J., Steinfeld, H., Henderson, B., Mottet, A., Opio, C., Dijkman, J., Falcucci, A., & Tempio, G. (2013). *Tackling climate change through livestock – A global assessment of emissions and mitigation opportunities*. Food and Agriculture Organization of the United Nations (FAO), Rome.

Hauschild, M. Z., Rosenbaum, R. K., & Olsen, S. I. (Eds.). (2018). *Life cycle assessment*. Springer. https://doi.org/10.1007/978-3-319-56475-3

Hoekstra, A. K., & Chapagain, A. Y. (2008). *Globalization of Water: Sharing the planet's freshwater resources*. https://doi.org/10.1002/9780470696224

Hoekstra, A. Y., Chapagain, A. K., Aldaya, M. M., & Mekonnen, M. M. (2011). *The water footprint assessment manual: Setting the global standard*. Earthscan. https://waterfootprint.org/media/downloads/TheWaterFootprintAssessmentManual_2.pd

Hristov, A. N., Oh, J., Lee, C., Meinen, R., Montes, F., Ott, T., Firkins, J., Rotz, A., Dell, C., Adesogan, A., Yang, W., Tricarico, J., Kebreab, E., Waghorn, G., Dijkstra, J., & Oosting, S. (2013). Mitigation of greenhouse gas emissions in livestock production – A review of technical options for non-CO_2 emissions. In P. J. Gerber, B. Henderson, & H. P. S. Makkar (Eds.), *FAO Animal Production and Health Paper No. 177*. FAO. https://doi.org/10.18356/3e9d869f-en

IDF. (2017). *The IDF guide to water footprint methodology for dairy sector.* Bulletin of the International Dairy Federation 486/2017. International Dairy Federation.

Isermeyer, F. (2020). Paradigm shift in livestock farming. *Landbauforschung: Journal of Sustainable and Organic Agricultural Systems*, 23–26. https://doi.org/10.3220/LBF1592238146000

Ismea-Rete Rurale (2021) La filiera suinicola nazionale. Criticità ed opportunità di rilancio, pdf presentation at link: https://www.reterurale.it/flex/cm/pages/ServeBLOB.php/L/IT/IDPagina/1377

ISO. (2006a). *ISO 14040: Environmental management – Life cycle assessment – Principles and framework.* Int. Organ. Stand.

ISO. (2006b). *ISO 14044: Environmental management – Life cycle assessment – Requirements and guidelines*, ISO 14044, International Organization for Standardization.

Italian National Institute for environmental protection and research- Istituto Superiore per la Protezione e la Ricerca Ambientale [ISPRA]. (2022). Accessed November, 2022, from http://emissioni.sina.isprambiente.it/serie-storiche-emissioni/

Kebreab, E., Liedke, A., Caro, D., Diemling, S., Binder, M., & Finkbeiner, M. (2016). Environmental impact of using specialty feed ingredients in swine and poultry production: a life cycle assessment. *J. Animal Sci., 94*, 2664e2681.

Mackenzie, S. G., Leinonen, I., Ferguson, N., & Kyriazakis, I. (2015). Accounting for uncertainty in the quantification of the environmental impacts of Canadian pig farming systems. *Journal of Animal Science, 93*(6), 3130–3143.

McAuliffe, G. A., Chapman, D. V., & Sage, C. L. (2016). A thematic review of life cycle assessment (LCA) applied to pig production. *Environmental Impact Assessment Review, 56*, 12–22.

McIlroy, J. P., McGeough, K. L., Laughlin, R. J., & Carolan, R. (2019). Abatement of ammonia emissions from dairy cow house concrete floor surfaces through additive application. *Biosystems Engineering, 188*, 320–330. https://doi.org/10.1016/j.biosystemseng.2019.10.016

McLaren, S., Berardy, A., Henderson, A., Holden, N., Huppertz, T., Jolliet, O., De Camillis, C., Renouf, M., Rugani, B., & Saarinen, M., et al. (2021). *Integration of environment and nutrition in life cycle assessment of food items: Opportunities and challenges.* Food and Agriculture Organization of the United Nations FAO: Rome, Italy.

Mekonnen, M. M., & Hoekstra, A. Y. (2010). A global and high-resolution assessment of the green, blue and grey water footprint of wheat. *Hydrology and Earth System Sciences, 14*, 1259–1276. https://doi.org/10.5194/hess-14-1259-2010

Mrad, M., & Salvò, R. (2017). *Migliori tecniche disponibili per gli allevamenti suinicoli e avicoli.* Guida tecnica per una zootecnia sostenibile, Regione Veneto, Direzione Agroambiente, caccia e pesca, Unità operativa agroambiente. http://piave.veneto.it/resource/resolver?resourceId=26070bcc-f4e0-40e4-b9c5-7f3850ddb98a/Guida_tecnica_zootecnia_sostenibile_2017.pdf

National Research Council. (2011). *Sustainability and the U.S. EPA.* Washington, DC: The National Academies Press. https://doi.org/10.17226/13152.

Philippe, F. X., Cabaraux, J. F., & Nicks, B. (2011). Ammonia emissions from pig houses: Influencing factors and mitigation techniques. *Agriculture, Ecosystems and Environment, 141*, 245–260.

Pietramale, R. T. R., Caldara, F. R., Barbosa, D. K., Da Rosa, C. O., Vanzela, M., Pàdua, A. B., & Ruviaro, C. F. (2021). How much the reproductive losses of sows can be impacting the carbon footprint in swine production? *Livestock Science, 250*, 104594.

Ramaekers, P. (2022). *How to improve reproductive efficiency along the career with good management of live weight and back fat thickness in gilts.* https://www.3tre3.it/articoli/come-migliorare-lefficienza-riproduttiva-lungo-la-carriera_247/

Ritchie, H., & Roser, M. (2019). *Meat and dairy production.* https://ourworldindata.org/meatproduction

Sala, S., Laurent, A., Vieira, M., & Van Hoof, G. (2020). Implications of LCA and LCIA choices on interpretation of results and on decision support. *International Journal of Life Cycle Assessment, 25*, 2311–2314. https://doi.org/10.1007/s11367-020-01845-2

Santonja, G. G., Georgitzikis, K., Scalet, B. M., Montobbio, P., Roudier, S., & Sancho, L. D. (2017). *Best Available Techniques (BAT) reference document for the intensive rearing of poultry or pigs EUR 28674 EN*. https://doi.org/10.2760/020485 858p

Sommer, S. G., Christensen, M. L., Schmidt, T., & Jensen, L. S. (2013). *Animal manure recycling: Treatment and Management*. Wiley.

Steinfeld, H., Gerber, P., Wassenaar, T., Castel, V., Rosales, M., & de Haan, C. (2006). *Livestock's long shadow: Environmental issues and options*. FAO.

Tallaksen, J., Johnston, L., Sharpe, K., Reese, M., & Buchanan, E. (2020). Reducing life cycle fossil energy and greenhouse gas emissions for Midwest swine production systems. *Journal of Cleaner Production, 246*, 118998. https://doi.org/10.1016/j.jclepro.2019.118998

UN/DESA. (2021). *Policy Brief #105: Circular agriculture for sustainable rural development*. United Nations: Department of Economic and Social Affairs, Economic Analysis.. https://www.un.org/development/desa/dpad/publication/un-desa-policy-brief-105-circular-agriculture-for-sustainable-rural-development/

Unece. (2015). *Framework code for good agricultural practice for reducing ammonia emissions*. http://www.unece.org/environmental-policy/conventions/envlrtapwelcome/publications.html

Vonderohe CE, Brizgys LA, Richert JA, J.S. Radcliffe JS. (2022). How sustainable is sustainability? Anim. Front. 12:7–17. https://doi.org/10.1093/af/vfac085.

Zucali, M., Tamburini, A., Sandrucci, A., & Bava, L. (2017). Global warming and mitigation potential of milk and meat production in Lombardy (Italy). *Journal of Cleaner Production, 153*, 474–482. https://doi.org/10.1016/j.jclepro.2016.11.037

Sustainable Development of Meat Supply Chain and Human Rights

Francesco Zecchin

1 Social Sustainability, Private Law and Human Rights

For a long time, the most widespread model of economic development had been the linear and limitless one. But since the 1970s, the idea that industrial productivity had to deal with the environmental problems began to broadcast (Meadows et al., 1972). As a result, it started a process which has been gradually led to a new concept of economic development, that is, the sustainable one. However, its purpose is no longer restricted to ecology but embraces economic efficiency and the quality of people's life, as well. These dimensions are so closely linked that it is common to hear talk of a sustainability triangle (Davico, 2004). But, while with reference to ecology and economics, the debate is well nourished, and it is reflected in several statutory interventions, this is not the case for social sustainability. Even where the idea of sustainable development has perhaps been strongest recognised, i.e. in the European Union, it is conceived and implemented exclusively in the economic and environmental meaning (Art. 3, para. 3, Treaty on European Union). Of course, there have been initiatives by European bodies to emphasise sustainability in social terms (Sciaudone, 2003), and the most recent is the Proposal for a Directive of the European Parliament and of the Council on Corporate Sustainability Due Diligence and amending Directive (EU) 2019/1937, which aims to amend Directive (EU) 2019/193 of 23 February 2022 (Carella, 2022). But so far, the step of transforming these intentions into rules has not yet been taken.

In any case, a broadening of sustainability's concept is to be welcomed. It would be contradictory to talk about sustainability only in the key to a balanced ecosystem and an efficient economy, without considering living conditions of human beings

F. Zecchin (✉)
Department of Law – Università Cattolica del Sacro Cuore, Piacenza, Italy
e-mail: francesco.zecchin@unicatt.it

A. M. Fellegara et al. (eds.), *Sustainable Transition of Meat and Cured Meat Supply Chain*, CSR, Sustainability, Ethics & Governance,
https://doi.org/10.1007/978-3-031-34977-5_4

who populate the former, and who are the actors of the latter (Sciaudone, 2003), indeed. This is suggested, after all, by the Latin etymology of the word *sustĭnēre*, i.e. to keep up, which was often used in an extensive sense to express the idea of guarding and protecting someone from possible assaulters (*venientes sustĭnēre* and *sustĭnēre vim hostium*).

It is precisely in this direction, perhaps more so than the environmental and economic ones, that private law can help to a more sustainable development. Above all, because it is in the case of social sustainability that people are involved not through the medium of market or climatic conditions, but directly. Moreover, private law has now taken on as its task not only to react to an aggression against human beings in one of the interests that mark their essential nature, that is, human rights (Castronovo, 2018; Navarretta, 1996), as in the case of non-pecuniary losses (Zecchin, 2020), but also to find tools that preventively make their injury less likely (Mazzamuto & Plaia, 2007), as it is demonstrated in the privacy field (Piraino, 2006).

Well, one sector in which attempts are being made in sustainability perspective is the corporate one. Indeed, it is well known that enterprises' behaviour strongly affects environmental balance and economic efficiency, so much so that over time they have been charged with several duties, whose aim is to achieve this goals (Strampelli, 2021). But a company also strongly influences the life's quality of the people who work for it, with effects that often concern human rights (Martin & Bravo, 2015; v Falkenhausen, 2020).

Within the framework of a supply chain, moreover, the opportunity to impact on the quality of development exceeds the individual firm sphere, at least for those in a dominant position. Whoever is at the top of a supply chain, indeed, influences the behaviour of other companies involved in the production cycle, not only from the social and economic sustainability's point of view, but also from the social one. When the dominant company imposes, even if lawfully, specific production procedures on other players of the supply chain, it necessarily affects the quality of working life not only of its own employees but also of those of other companies (Strampelli, 2021). It was not by a chance that since the beginning of the 2000s, debates have begun both on how to better protect workers' rights in supply chains, and on what the role of the dominant player, national or international, might be (v Falkenhausen, 2020).

After all, it is precisely in the context of labour juridical relations within enterprises that the issue of preserving personal dimension of debtor-worker has historically arisen. In Italy, this is clearly demonstrated by the Art. 2087 of the Civil Code, which obliges entrepreneur—i.e. at least literally not all employers—to "protect the physical integrity and moral personality of employees". This trend of law policy was then grown stronger in our Constitution. As far as employers are concerned, on one hand, in the Art. 41, par. 2, according to which private economic initiative, especially if exercised by an enterprise (Buonocore, 2007), "cannot be carried out against social utility or in such a way as to damage health, environment, security, freedom, and human dignity". It could be said, in the light of the recent constitutional reform and summing up, in respect of the environment and human rights. With reference to workers, on the other hand, in the Artt. 35, 36, 37 and 38, which draw a protective structure of workers that can also be read as a buffer against the unavoidable negative effects of economic development on human rights, like wage guarantee fund or mobility treatment (Mengoni, 2011).

In addition, the role of dominant undertakings regarding the human rights of the employees who work for other supply chain companies is internationally recognised. In other words, the issue of corporate social responsibility nowadays has an international profile, as there is an increasing awareness of the need for a minimum protection's level of the human rights not only of one's own employees but also of those who work within a supply chain by the company at the top (Brino & Gragnoli, 2018). For instance, the United Nations Human Rights Council adopted the *Guiding Principles on Business and Human Rights*, whose Art. 13 provides that "The responsibility to respect human rights requires that business enterprises: (a) Avoid causing or contributing to adverse human rights impacts through their own activities, and address such impacts when they occur; (b) Seek to prevent or mitigate adverse human rights impacts that are directly linked to their operations, products or services by their business relationships, even if they have not contributed to those impacts". The Organization for Economic Cooperation and Development has also updated its guidelines, by adding a section dedicated to the human rights which provides that "Enterprises should seek ways to prevent or mitigate adverse human rights impacts that are directly linked to their business operations, products or services by a business relationship, even if they do not contribute to those impacts".

And this is a huge step, because it has to be mentioned that sustainable development has an international nature, hence if domestic or single answers did not find support in other legal systems, they would be greatly weakened, if not even unrealistic. In other words, sustainability issues go beyond local areas, they are quite independent of them and must therefore be managed from a global perspective. This is true not just for environmental balance or economic efficiency, but also for the quality of life, even more so since in a global context the risk that a human rights violation be "de-personalised" is greatest (Teubner, 2006). The complexity of international markets, indeed, leads to a high degree of fragmentation of the production process (Brino & Gragnoli, 2018), which often works to hide the responsibilities of the dominant company behind the so-called corporate veil of the several international other companies involved in the chain (Sanger, 2012).

To summarise, the idea that is taking hold is the whole production chain shall be socially sustainable, at least in terms of protecting the human rights of its workers. And both the individual companies with respect to their own employees and the companies that directly or indirectly control the chain with respect to the employees of others are entrusted with this task.

2 Human Rights' Duties of Protection as an Individual Company of a Meat Supply Chain

About the supply chain's social sustainability from the perspective of human rights protection by the company of which one is an employee, the issue must be approached in the key to the so-called duties of protection (Nogler, 2002). The Italian legal system—like many other European ones, for instance, German and French—has long adopted the idea that existence of a special legal relationship, such as a contract, triggers on parties not only duty to perform and the ones that are instrumental to this aim, so-called supplementary instrumental obligations (Betti, 1954), but also other duties which are independent of the performance one, and whose purpose is to avoid that parties involved in an obligation due to it suffer damage to their property or their person (Castronovo, 1990; Nicolussi, 2015).

This is especially important in labour contracts, because contrary to what happens in other types of legal relationships, like sales or leasing, worker as person is directly involved in the performance (Castronovo, 2006). Moreover, following our legal system job is one of the favoured opportunities for human personality development (Article 3 of the Constitution).

Labour contracts, in other words, no longer end with the employees' performance and the wage by the employers. The relationship is far more complex, and not just from the perspective of company benefits, like the welfare one, which are discretionary choices, but also regarding the employers' duties. In addition to paying salary, all actions necessary to prevent the employees from suffering personal injury in fulfilling the performance have to be carried out, indeed (Castronovo, 2006). Since this is a duty, if employer does not perform, compensation for damages will be regulated not by the rules of tort law, as was in the past under the so-called cumulative liability rule (Del Punta, 2006; Albi, 2008a, b), but under the contract law ones.

On the one hand, this brings legal form to match with reality, because employer and employees are note like two drivers who make a car accident (Castronovo, 2006). The labour contract shows that there is a legal relationship before the injury of human rights (Nogler, 2002): the latter occurs because there is the former, indeed. On the other hand, the application of contractual liability rules leads to several advantages for the employee. Above all, in terms of specific performance before damage, which would not be conceivable if the law was the tort one (Albanese, 2021; Nicolussi, 2022); of the burden of proof, which is not the same as in case of breach of contract, but much lighter than in case of tort (Nicolussi, 2015); and finally of limitation time to claim compensation, which is not 5 but 10 years.

One question that might arise is: what does it mean that worker has not to be harmed in his or her person? Well, an answer can come looking to the Article 2 of the Italian Constitution, according to which "The Republic recognises and guarantees the inviolable rights of person, both as an individual and in social groups where human personality is expressed. The Republic expects that the fundamental duties of political, economic, and social solidarity be fulfilled". In other words, it is with reference to the human rights recognised by the Constitution that the "person of the other contracting party", as objects of protection's duties, has a clearer meaning (Nicolussi, 2015).

However, there is no list of human rights; hence, they must be identified by looking at the whole legal system. This is a very difficult task, especially since we live in a society that is no longer homogeneous (Mengoni, 1985; Femia, 1996), and if the plurality of views that distinguish the list of human rights and their content were to be uncritically accepted in the legal framework, we would end up with an employer's liability too vague (Zecchin, 2020). As a result, it would no longer be possible whether a behaviour is a breach of a duty of protection (Femia, 1996; Nogler, 2006).

From a general private law point of view, the concept of good faith can be helpful. The protection of the employees' human rights is carried out within the framework of a duty which law places on fairness (art. 1175 Italian Civil Code), it thus requires that the protection's content be intersubjectively identifiable. The objectivity's share that the reference to Article 2 of the Constitution fails to provide in today's cultural climate is, in other words, compensated through the medium of good faith. It ontologically refers to an objective order of values and imposes the neglect of what is related exclusively to the subjectivity of obligations' parties (Barcellona, 2008).

Furthermore, there is a rule in the Italian civil code that both confirms the presence of these protection's duties on the part of employers (Mengoni, 2011) and points out perhaps the two most important personal subjective legal situations that must be safeguarded in workplace (Castronovo, 2006). This is the already mentioned Art. 2087, which is a development of a late nineteenth century norm dedicated to work accidents (Art. 3 law no. 80 of 17 March 1898). The norm is entitled "Protection of working conditions" and rules that "The entrepreneur is obliged to implement the provisions which are necessary to protect the physical integrity and moral personality of the employees, according to the particular nature of the work, experience and technique". The historical-systematic worth of this disposition is precisely in allowing the protection of worker's person in patrimonial structures of employment contracts (Castronovo, 2006). And not only by providing protection for employee's health, but also by attaching importance to another aspect of employee's life needs (Mengoni, 2011).

The main problem lies in identifying the meaning of "physical integrity "and "moral personality" in our pluralistic society. If a generic discomfort caused by the working environment or an injury to one's own *Weltanschauung* was enough to complete the violation of the protection's duty established by this rule, the range of the employer's duty of protection would become so broad that it would be independent of the link with the injury to physical integrity or to moral personality stated by the law, in fact (Nogler, 2010). In other words, it is necessary a typification that prevents the risk of employer being held liable for any personal upset complained by employee.

To be more precise, if by physical integrity is meant a "state of complete physical, mental and social well-being and not simply the absence of disease or infirmity"

(Preamble to the Constitution of the World Health Organization adopted by the International Health Conference, New York, 19–22 June 1946 and entered into force on 7 April 1948), as some authors have suggested (Durante, 2001; Riccio, 2009), the employer's duty of protection would be limitless. Virtually all employer misconduct can be said to affect, at least to some extent, the moral balance of the injured person, indeed. But the fact is that the law has chosen to make liability only in the case of an injury to health. Therefore, only an objective concept of health, i.e. as the absence of illness, can make employers aware of what they have to do (Albi, 2008a, b). Not surprisingly, in private law this is the meaning of the word "health". This is well demonstrated both by Articles 138 and 139 of Legislative Decree no. 209 of 7 September 2005, which explicitly tie biologic damage to a "temporary or permanent injury to the person's psycho-physical integrity which can be medically assessed", and by Article 1580 of the Italian Civil Code, which allows termination of a rental when "defects of the good or of a substantial part of it endanger health of tenant or their family members or employees". In other words, employer has to prevent employees from being at risk of suffering illnesses because of the tasks they perform. And after all, for job absence justified by illness, labour law refers to a strict sense concept of health, so much to require medical certification (Piccinini, 2010).

With particular focus on meat supply chain, the principal legal reference for identifying the employer's behaviour to avoid health damage of employees is the Legislative Decree no. 81 of 9 April 2001, which applies to all enterprises, to agri-food ones, as well. Its aims to improve the workplaces' healthiness and safety, above all by imposing an obligation on all employers to introduce an organisational model intended to identify and remove or mitigate risk factors in their company (Scarcella, 2013). In meat production, especially, risks of injury are linked to building structures and use of equipment, machinery and chemicals in the various production stages (first and second). The employer is therefore obliged to comply with a few protocols to prevent injuries to the health of its workers, including non-employees.

Moving on the concept of "moral personality", the issue is more complicated, because it is itself an uncertain borders concept (Del Punta, 2006). But proceeding from the identification of a "sufficiently socially significant" loss (Nogler, 2010), and drawing inspiration from other rules (Del Punta, 2006), it was avoided that employers would be held liable for any upset that the worker traced back to the work environment. The two most significant cases are demotion and mobbing (Nogler, 2002). The former refers to the situation of assignment to tasks lower than those for which one had been employed—which the new Art. 2103 of the Italian Civil Code, however, allowed if there are specific circumstances (Garilli, 2016)—or forced inactivity to work (Albi, 2008a, b). The latter has been connected by the courts to a behaviour with distinctive features (Mazzamuto, 2003; Ghirardi, 2015), both from a subjective point of view, i.e. the malice of the person who carries out the harmful conduct, and from the continuity of the hostile behaviour or offensive one in terms of sexual or discriminatory, i.e. the so-called persecutory design (Albi, 2008a, b).

Beyond the Art. 2087, another important subjective legal situation that, perhaps even in special terms in the meat industry, must be considered is the right to rest.

Even more so since its legal reference is the Art. 36 of the Italian Constitution (Nogler, 2002). In this case, employers have to comply with working hours, holiday and rest rules, which are not only intended in the key to restoring employees' psychophysical energies, but also of the already mentioned right to the growth of one's personality (Albi, 2008a, b).

3 Human Rights' Duties of Protection as Dominant Undertaking of a Meat Supply Chain

Once the boundaries of companies' social responsibility towards their employees' human rights have been clarified, particularly in case of one which is involved in a meat supply chain, it is possible to deal with the issue of liability that the dominant undertaking might have about human rights of partner companis' employees. *De iure conditio* there are no such obligations, not even in the recent Legislative Decree no. 198 of 8 November 2021, dedicated to unfair trading practices in business-to-business relationships in the agricultural and food supply chain.

However, it is possible to check whether there is a glimmer of hope to support the supply chain sustainability from this point of view, as well. The question would deserve a vaster and deeper treatment than this writing; therefore, here it is possible to outline some of the directions in which it could be approached, highlighting its problematic issues.

A first option would be to rely on the Art. 9 of Law no. 192 of 18 June 1998, which forbids the abuse of a client's or supplier's state of economic dependence. Now, firstly, this rule is laid down in a legislation concerning subcontracting, and this type of agreement is widely used in supply chains, including that of meat. In any case, it is an almost accepted fact that it is applicable to all contracts which have a business party that finds itself in a position to bring about excessive imbalances in the rights and obligations pertaining to its commercial relations with another one (Albanese, 1999). And this is a very frequent situation in the meat supply chains, regardless of the type of contract concluded.

But there are some critical issues, too. The first one is that the law aims to protect freedom of negotiation of weak enterprises (Albanese, 2008). As a result, the cases in point that might be considered in our discussion would be only whose contractual conditions set between dominant undertaking and other companies are first of all unbalanced in economic terms and only secondarily culminate in a risk for the workers' human rights of the weak enterprises. For instance, consider a price that is so low as to be inconsistent with the costs necessary to comply with the minimum safety standards of healthiness and safety workplace or to respect the right to rest. On the contrary, if the injury did not result from an economically unbalanced clause—as in the case where the bad workplaces hygiene does not depend on the abuse of dominant position—the Art. 9 of Law 192/98 could not be applied.

The second one is the fact that normally the relationship between dominant undertaking and companies whose workers suffer violations of human rights is indirect, because there are several links in the production chain that divide these two legal entities (Brino & Gragnoli, 2018). As a result, indirect—so to speak—abuse of a dominant position should also be included in the cases covered by the Art. 9 of Law 192/98, and this is not to be taken for granted (Maugeri, 2009; Barba, 2015).

The third problem is the need to take advantage of the economic dependence of the other company, which is required by the law. This is not always the case in supply chains, whose contractual conditions are often particularly favourable to the dominant undertaking because not so much to its behaviour, but rather to the economic system (Brino & Gragnoli, 2018).

The last one arises from the fact that the Art. 9 of Law 192/98 lays down a prohibition, so that in case of violation, the consequence is contract nullity on the ground of contrariety to a mandatory provision (Albanese, 2008), as the third paragraph of the rule makes clear. In other words, an employee who has suffered an injury to his human right cannot bring an action for damages directly against the company that has abused its dominant position. First, the worker would have to succeed in claiming nullity of the contract between the two companies. And this could jeopardies their employment, since the company for which their works would probably lose not the only order, maybe, but certainly the most economically significant one. Only then the employee could claim damages.

Perhaps a better alternative would be to apply the duties of protection once again. The mentioned subcontracting law could however be used to check whether there is a supply chain (Art. 1 and Art. 4) and whether there is a dominant undertaking (Art. 9 para. 1 and para. 2) (Albanese, 2008). It would then have to be seen if the duty of protection that dominant company has regarding the human rights of its workers could be extended to those of the other enterprises that are part of its supply chain. After all, in the wake of the new Articles 2497 et seq. of the Italian Civil Code in defense of shareholders and creditors against the event of improper direction and coordination activities, a legal scholar has already proposed the liability of "a parent company that imposes on its industrial subsidiaries production procedures that do not properly protect the physical integrity or moral personality of employees, exposing them to liability under the Art. 2087 and the consequent financial losses, to the detriment of their shareholders and creditors" (Galgano, 2014). It is, therefore, allowed to cross the border of the subjective sphere of a company because of a power's exercise that does not only give rise to rights but also to duties (Teubner, 2006), as it happens in the procurement field about salary, social security and insurance contributions, at least to some extent (Villa, 2017; Gualandi, 2021).

As the already mentioned Art. 13 of the United Nation Guiding Principles on Business and Human Rights and the new guidelines of the Organization for Economic Cooperation and Development recognises, dominating a supply chain means being able to strongly influence not only one's own contracts, but also the ones that will be agreed to comply with it, and without necessarily abusing (v Falkenhausen, 2020). Regarding the latters, workers of companies that do not dominate the supply chain are involved in the performance. As a result, these employees suffer a specific risk of injury to their human rights that is in part conditioned by the company that controls the supply chain (Castronovo, 1978). In other words, the connection between the contract of the dominant undertaking and those that are then concluded to comply with it gives rise to a duty of protection on the part of this player. It will be liable for any violations of human rights of workers involved that its position of power would have prevented.

Of course, the content of this duty of protection—as much as towards one's own workers—could be positive or negative depending on the real situation (Mengoni, 2011). In our case it would consist of the inclusion or non-inclusion of clauses. But in anyway, it would have to be discounted by the fact that the dominant company, despite its position, would not be able to directly affect the internal management of the other supply chain's companies. The liability of dominant enterprise will therefore be limited to what it would have been able to avoid, of course.

This is, moreover, the path followed both by France law, with the *loi 2017–399 relative au devoir de vigilance des sociétés mères et des entreprises donneuses d'ordre*, and the Germany one, with the *Gesetz über die unternehmerischen Sorgfaltspflichten zur Vermeidung von Menschenrechtsverletzungen in Lieferketten* of 16 June 2021, though with reference to supply chains that are not national, but international. However, the aim is precisely to protect the human rights of workers in the lowest links of an international supply chains by laying a duty of protection on the dominant undertaking (Zecchin, 2023). And the European Union is also moving in this direction, with the already mentioned Proposal for a Directive of the European Parliament and of the Council on Corporate Sustainability Due Diligence and amending Directive (EU) 2019/1937, which aims to amend Directive (EU) 2019/193 of 23 February 2022 (Carella, 2022).

But, perhaps paradoxically, there is not such a law for national supply chain, neither in France and Germany, nor Italy; hence, our hypothesis has to deal with a great legal obstacle, which is the so-called privity of contract. It lays down that a contract does not just confer duties, but also rights on someone who is not a party to a contract (Atiyah, 1995).

To overcome this difficulty, the approach followed by another legal scholar regarding the issue of product liability before the answer of European Union Law (Castronovo, 1979) could perhaps useful. The problems are in many respects similar, indeed, and not only because there is not a regulation, as it was in relation to defective products. The idea, that is, would be revise the private autonomy concept in the Constitution's view.

In more detail, whether in the past the solidarity's principle was such as to make manufacturer liable under Article 1492(2) of the Italian Civil Code for the damage suffered by consumer, despite the fact that the relationship between the former and the latter was through a chain of sales (Castronovo, 1979), today it could be the basis for protecting human rights of workers that are violated because of contractual conditions indirectly imposed on all the supply chain companies by the dominant one.

After all, in the eyes of Italian constitutional system, economic efficiency cannot be the only sustainability goal of the market, which must also include ecology and the quality of people living it, that is, environmental and social sustainability (Mengoni, 2011). From this point of view, the solidarity principle is the legal tool that gives formal relevance to interests—above all human rights—of persons who are not party to the contract, but who are affected by its effects (Castronovo, 1979). It is by means of solidarity, in other words, that the profit making of supply chains—including the meat one—could be overcome in defense of a vision that goes beyond individual interest to achieve the general aims of Italian legal system, such as protection of human rights.

The distribution of protection's duties to the dominant player in the supply chain must, however, be clarified. The rule cannot be rigidly applied and token out of the context. Performing and protecting are not the same thing, and only the duty to perform traditionally implies specific performance, that is, an action to fulfil although the breach of contract and not to claim compensation of damages (Nicolussi, 2021). This would means that the employee could not act against the dominant company to remove the risk situation to their human rights, but would have to wait for the injury, and then claim damages. That is, the worker would be obliged to perform their service in situations of danger to their person, and later be compensated: an unacceptable paradox. In individual cases, at least it is allowed that reaction to the violation of protection's duties is not only compensatory, indeed (Albanese, 2021; Nicolussi, 2021). At least when it comes to juridical duration relationships, which in addition impact on primary personal assets, the option of preventive action is recognised. Even more so since in cases such as ours, duties of protection already have a fixed content, and they could perhaps be formulated linguistically better as duties "with a protective purpose". Not surprisingly, both the French and the German law—mentioned above regarding the protection of workers human rights within the international supply chains—provided for preventive proception tools, like right of complaint in front of the dominant undertaking, whose aim is to avoid personal damage rather than compensate it (Zecchin, 2023).

References

Albanese, A. (1999). *Abuso di dipendenza economica: Nullità del contratto e riequilibrio del rapporto*, in Eur. e dir. priv. pp. 1179–1220.

Albanese, A. (2008). *Contratto mercato responsabilità*. Giuffrè.

Albanese, A. (2021). *Buonafede contratto legge*, in Eur. e dir. priv. pp. 31–89.

Albi, P. (2008a). *Adempimento dell'obbligo di sicurezza e tutela della persona*. Giuffrè.

Albi, P. (2008b). *Il danno non patrimoniale e il rapporto di lavoro*. In E. Navarretta (Eds), *Il danno non patrimoniale. Principi, regole e tabelle per la liquidazione*, Giuffrè, Milano, pp. 561–592.

Atiyah, P. S. (1995). *An introduction to the law of contract*. Clarendon Press.

Barba, A. (2015). *Reti di impresa e abuso di dipendenza economica*, in Contr. impr. pp. 1264–1351.

Barcellona, M. (2008). *Il danno non patrimoniale*. Giuffrè.

Betti, E. (1954). *Teoria generale delle obbligazioni. I. Prolegomeni: funzione economico-sociale dei rapporti d'obbligazione*, Giuffrè.

Brino, V., & Gragnoli, E. (2018). *Le imprese multinazionali e il rapporto di lavoro*, in Riv. giur. lav. pp. 209–219.
Buonocore, V. (2007). *Impresa*, in Enc. dir. – Ann. I, pp. 760-854.
Carella, G. (2022). *La responsabilità civile dell'impresa transnazionale per violazioni ambientali e dei diritti umani: il contributo della proposta di direttiva sulla "due diligence" societaria a fini di sostenibilità*, in Freedom, Security & Justice: European Legal Studies, fasc. 2, pp. 10–41.
Castronovo, C. (1978). *Obblighi di protezione e tutela del terzo*, in *Jus* pp. 123–179.
Castronovo, C. (1979). *Problema e sistema nel danno da prodotti*. Giuffrè.
Castronovo, C. (1990). *Obblighi di protezione*, in Enc. giur. Treccani, pp. 1–9.
Castronovo, C. (2006). *Danno alla persona nel rapporto di lavoro*, in Eur. e dir. priv. pp. 1341–1352.
Castronovo, C. (2018). *Responsabilità civile*. Giuffrè.
Davico, L. (2004). *Sviluppo sostenibile. Le dimensioni sociali*. Carocci.
Del Punta, R. (2006). *Diritti della persona e contratto di lavoro*, in Dir. lav. e rel. ind. pp. 195–268.
Durante, V. (2001). *Dimensioni della salute: Dalla definizione dell'OMS al diritto attuale*, in Nuova giur. civ. comm., II, pp. 132–148.
Femia, P. (1996). *Interessi e conflitti culturali nell'autonomia privata e nella responsabilità civile*. ESI.
Galgano, F. (2014). *Tratt. dir. civ.*, 4, 3° ed. edited by di Zorzi Galgano N., Cedam, Padova.
Garilli, A. (2016). *La nuova disciplina delle mansioni tra flessibilità organizzativa e tutela del prestatore di lavoro*, in Giorn. dir. lav. rel. ind. pp. 129–147.
Ghirardi, N. (2015). *Alla ricerca della fattispecie «mobbing»*, in Riv. giur. lav. prev. soc. pp. 361–387.
Gualandi, S. (2021). *Human Rights Due Diligence: Tendenze globali e insidie per l'ordinamento giuslavoristico italiano*, in Studium iuris pp. 565–574.
Martin, J., & Bravo, K. E. (2015). *The business and human rights landscape: Moving forward, Looking Back*. Cambridge University Press.
Maugeri, M. R. (2009). *Reti di imprese, contratto di rete e reti contrattuali*, in Obb. e contr. pp. 951–962.
Mazzamuto, S. (2003). *Una rilettura del mobbing: obbligo di protezione e condotte plurime di inadempimento*, in Eur. dir. priv. pp. 627–695.
Mazzamuto, S., & Plaia, A. (2007). *I rimedi*. In C. Castronovo & S. Mazzamuto (Eds.), *Manuale di diritto privato europeo*. II, Giuffrè.
Meadows, D. L., Meadows, D. H., Randers, J., & Behrens, W. W. (1972). *The limits to growth*. Universe Books.
Mengoni, L. (1985). *Diritto e valori*. Il Mulino.
Mengoni, L., (2011). *Scritti I. Metodo e teoria giuridica*, C. Castronovo, A. Albanese, A. Nicolussi (Eds.), Giuffrè.
Navarretta, E. (1996). *Diritti inviolabili e risarcimento del danno*. Giappichelli.
Nicolussi, A. (2015). *Obblighi di protezione*, in Enc. dir. – Ann. VIII, pp. 659–664.
Nicolussi, A. (2021). *Le obbligazioni*. Wolters Kluwer - Cedam.
Nicolussi, A. (2022). *L'obbligazione oltre il principio del contratto. Comportamenti socialmente tipici e relazioni di affidamento*, in *Per i cento anni dalla nascita di Renato Scognamiglio*, I, Jovene, Napoli, pp. 683–699.
Nogler, L. (2002). *Danni personali e rapporto di lavoro*, in Riv. it. dir. lav. pp. 287–310.
Nogler, L. (2006). *La "deriva" risarcitoria della tutela dei diritti inviolabili del lavoratore dipendente*, in Quad. dir. lav. pp. 63–89.
Nogler, L. (2010). *Danno non patrimoniale e rapporto di lavoro,* in S. Patti (Eds), *Responsabilità civile. Danno non patrimoniale*, Torino, Giappichelli, pp. 581–612.
Piccinini, I. (2010). *Malattia*, in P. Lambertucci (Eds.), *Diritto del lavoro*, Giuffrè, Milano, pp. 471–481.
Piraino, F. (2006). *La liceità e la correttezza*. In R. Panetta (Eds.), *Libera circolazione e protezione dei dati personali*, Milano, Giuffrè, pp. 745–916.

Riccio, A. (2009). *Verso l'atipicità del danno non patrimoniale: il mancato rispetto dei vincoli derivanti dalla Convenzione Europea dei diritti dell'uomo solleva una nuova questione di costituzionalità dell'art. 2059 c.c.?*, in Contr. e impr. pp. 277–284.
Sanger, A. (2012). *Crossing the Corporate Veil: The Duty of Care Owed by a Parent Company to the Employees of its Subsidiary*, in Cambridge Law Journal pp. 478–481.
Scarcella, A. (2013). *Sicurezza semplificata per le imprese agricole*, in Igiene e sic. sul lavoro pp. 297–307.
Sciaudone, F. (2003). *Iniziative comunitarie in tema di responsabilità sociale delle imprese: prime riflession,i* in Dir. pubb. comp. ed eur., 2003, pp. 1419–1429.
Strampelli, G. (2021). *La strategia dell'Unione europea per il capitalismo sostenibile: l'oscillazione del pendolo tra amministratori, soci e stakeholders*, in Riv. delle soc. pp. 365–374.
Teubner, E. (2006). La matrice anonima. *Quando "privati" attori transnazionali violano i diritti dell'uomo*, in Riv. crit. dir. priv. pp. 9–37.
v Falkenhausen, M. (2020). *Menschenrechtsschutz durch Deliktsrecht Unternehmerische. Pflichten in internationalen Lieferketten*. Mohr Siebeck.
Villa, E. (2017). *La responsabilità solidale come tecnica di tutela del lavoratore*. Bologna University Press.
Zecchin, F. (2020). *Il danno non patrimoniale dal torto al contratto*. Giuffrè-Francis Lefebvre.
Zecchin, F. (2023). *Sviluppo sostenibile delle catene di fornitura internazionali e diritti umani*, in *Jus* pp. 397–429.

Genomics for Sustainable Cured Pork Supply Chain

Matilde Maria Passamonti, Riccardo Negrini, and Paolo Ajmone-Marsan

1 Introduction: Why Genetics?

Animal welfare, production efficiency, food safety and food quality contribute together to improve the sustainability of pig production systems (Gamborg & Sandøe, 2005). Economic and functional traits, such as product quality, disease tolerance and fertility, are controlled by the combined effect of many genes and the environment. When genetics explains a large proportion of the phenotypic variation in a trait, breeding programmes can improve the trait, using information on the genes and genomic regions controlling it. This information is referred to as "molecular genetics".

An example of a molecular genetic contribution to improved animal welfare and food quality in pig farming is related to *porcine stress syndrome (PSS). PSS* is a heritable neuromuscular disorder causing muscle rigidity, hyperthermia, cardiac arrhythmia and sudden death. It is also associated with *pale, soft and exudative* meat (*PSE*), triggered by stress conditions that cause a high meat acidification rate in the first hours after slaughter. As PSE compromises both fresh and cured pork meat quality, it results in economic losses, estimated around 20 million dollars/year for the Australian and UK livestock industry and 32 million dollars/year for the USA in the 1990s (Meade & Miller, 1990; Owen et al., 2000; Trevisan & Brum, 2020). A test for PSE risk was based on the halothane test. Piglets that are homozygote for the PSS-causing gene suffer from a spastic contraction of the rear part of the body and fever when inhaling halothane anaesthetic gas. As the trait is recessive, the test was unable to identify carrier animals heterozygous for the causal mutation. Therefore, it

M. M. Passamonti · R. Negrini · P. Ajmone-Marsan (✉)
Department of Animal Science, Food and Nutrition (DiANA) and Nutrigenomic and Proteomic Research Center (PRONUTRIGEN), Università Cattolica del Sacro Cuore, Piacenza, Italy
e-mail: paolo.ajmone@unicatt.it

A. M. Fellegara et al. (eds.), *Sustainable Transition of Meat and Cured Meat Supply Chain*, CSR, Sustainability, Ethics & Governance,
https://doi.org/10.1007/978-3-031-34977-5_5

was not possible to eliminate the defective gene from carrier pig breeds. Molecular genetic studies found that PSS was caused by a genetic mutation in the *ryanodine receptor 1 gene (RYR1),* commonly known as the halothane gene (Fujii et al., 1991). Identification of the mutation allowed the molecular screening of pigs and the elimination of the deleterious variant from most of the pig populations. In the 1990s, PSE incidence in US slaughter plants ranged from 6 to 33% (Kauffman et al., 1993). Following the introduction of the genetic test, the frequency of PSE loins had dropped to 0.1%–10% in 2006 (Meisinger & Berg, 2006).

This example illustrates the value of identifying deleterious and beneficial genes and pathways controlling genetic variation in sustainability-related traits. Once genes are identified, this information can be used in breeding programmes, with the expectation that the next generation will have a better performance, welfare and fewer genetic defects than the current generation. In the past, swine selection has focused on economically relevant traits, such as those related to growth, body weight and number of offspring weaned. Between 1960 and 2005, selective breeding programmes increased in litter size by 50%, lean pork percentage by 40% and feed conversion ratio by up to 100% (Tait-Burkard et al., 2018; Kumar et al., 2022). In recent years, there has been a shift in selection objectives to meet the challenges of global food security and sustainability. In 2014, research shifted to the investigation of genetic variation related to sustainable production, such as efficiency, adaptation and environmental impact (Hayes et al., 2013) and on understanding how genetics may contribute to improve animal welfare, health, longevity, environmental efficiency and resilience (Brito et al., 2021). Ongoing climate changes call for further research on adaptation to more changeable, and generally hotter, environments. Effective management procedures to enhance animal resilience are essential but offer a short-term answer to the problem. Moreover, in many developing countries, facilities and management resources are limited (Rothschild & Plastow, 2014). Genetics provides long-term solutions to improved resilience by identifying the underlying mechanisms of adaptation to stressors, either environmental or metabolic (Rothschild & Plastow, 2014). This information may then be exploited in marker-assisted and genomic selection programmes, or by gene editing, to enhance sustainability and quality in pig production system and thus the cured meat supply chain.

Before going into the details of genetic studies on sustainability-related traits in swine, we need to briefly define some basic genetic terms in the context of DNA structure, molecular markers and genomic tools used to investigate the genetic control of phenotypic variation.

1.1 Genetic Markers

DNA (deoxyribonucleic acid) contains the instructions needed for the formation and function of cells and whole organisms. It is composed of two chains winding around each other and held together by chemical bonds, forming a double helix. Each chain

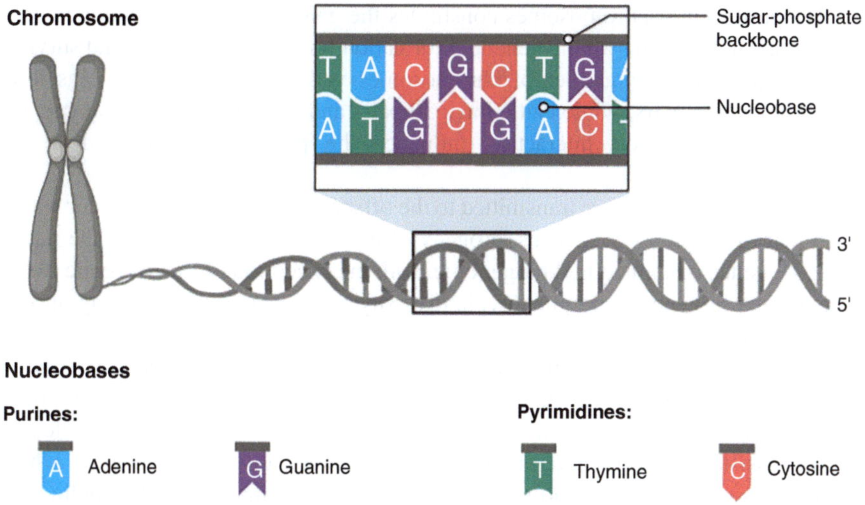

Fig. 1 DNA structure (BioRender)

is composed of building blocks, called nucleotides, consisting of a sugar, a phosphate group and one nucleobase. In DNA there are four types of nucleobases: adenine (A), guanine (G), cytosine (C) and thymine (T) (Fig. 1). DNA information held in the cell nucleus first has to be *transcribed* into ribonucleic acid (RNA), a single chain nucleic acid which reaches the cell cytoplasm where it is *translated* into an amino acid sequence and proteins are assembled. Proteins then assume a specific conformation and play their function in the organism (Travers & Muskhelishvili, 2015). Any permanent alteration in the nucleotides sequence is called mutation, and it may compromise the protein integrity and function.

In the nucleus of each cell, the DNA helix is tightly packaged in structures called chromosomes. Cells of mammals contain two copies of each chromosome and are termed *diploid*. Each chromosome of the pair codes for the same set of genes, with the genes in the same order along them and are said to be homologous. Therefore, somatic cells contain two versions of each gene. One version is inherited from the sire and the other from the dam. During the formation of gametes (sperm and oocytes), the number of chromosomes is halved by a cellular process called meiosis and gametes become *haploid*, i.e. they carry only one copy of each chromosome. When oocytes are fertilized by the sperm to form the zygote, the diploid status is reached again. In this way, DNA information is inherited across generations. There are two chromosomes that are not homologous, the sex chromosomes identified by X and Y. An XX zygotes is female, while XY is male. The two alternative DNA versions carried by an individual at the same position (locus) within a homologous pair are called alleles or variants. When the maternal allele is identical to the paternal one, the individual is homozygous at that locus. In contrast, when the two alleles are different, the individual is heterozygous.

The entire set of chromosomes constitutes the genome, which is unique to each individual and contains all the genetic information for the development and survival of an organism. The number of chromosomes varies among species; pigs have 19 chromosome pairs, while cattle have 30 pairs and humans 23. The genome, the environment and their interaction influence the phenotypes observed in the individual.

When chromosomes are transmitted to the offspring, rearrangements occur within each pair of chromosomes. Thus, progeny of the same parents differs in the nucleotide sequence contained in their genome, with the exception of monozygotic twins. This results in genetic and phenotypic diversity among individuals belonging to a same breed.

Genetic diversity is crucial for a species to cope with a wide variety of diseases and stressors and promotes adaptation and survival. Identifying the genomic positions (loci) of the genes affecting a trait of interest is the first step in developing marker-assisted breeding programmes. DNA markers are chosen to have a high degree of variation among individuals and provide information on the allelic variation at genetic loci linked to the marker along the genome. This information is obtained by observing the inheritance of the DNA markers and measuring the phenotypes of the individuals to reveal which markers are inherited with a particular phenotype, in an *association study*. When a DNA marker is associated with a phenotype (e.g. occurrence of a disease and growth rate), then it can be used as diagnostic tool or selection target to genetically select breeding individuals to improve the health and performance of the breed. Most traits of commercial interest are controlled by several genes each controlling part of the variation in the trait, which are called *quantitative traits*. The application of molecular markers facilitated the discovery of several Quantitative Trait Loci (QTL) that are genetic loci associated with variation in quantitative traits, such as growth and back-fat in pigs (Evans et al., 2003).

Over the years, several different types of molecular markers have been developed and used for research. The first molecular markers were protein variants (allozymes). However, they described DNA variation only indirectly. With the progress in DNA analysis techniques, several DNA markers have been developed. However, the original DNA markers were expensive, labour-intensive and time-consuming to use. Hence, only a few markers across the genome could be used, which limited the precision with which trait loci could be located in the genome.

The development of Next-Generation Sequencing (NGS) technologies has facilitated massive simultaneous DNA sequencing that has permitted the assembly of reference genomes for all the main livestock species. The rapid advance in technologies has greatly improved the process of genome sequencing. Early NGS technology required the genome to be fragmented into small pieces, then reassembled like a jigsaw. The latest NGS technologies can sequence very long stretches of DNA that permit the complete assembly of chromosomes from telomere to telomere (T2T). The first human genome was published in 2004 but was less than 92% complete and contained many gaps. The first complete human genome T2T was produced recently, almost 20 years later (Nurk et al. 2022). Sequencing of reference genomes included "HapMap" projects in which many individuals from a species were sequenced to identify the extent of genetic variation. At the same time, new approaches were developed, able to genotype in parallel many thousand single-nucleotide polymorphisms (SNPs). These SNP markers quickly became very popular, given their widespread presence in the genome and their potential for automated high-throughput analysis at low cost. Most SNPs are in genomic regions that do not code for a protein, but may be linked to genes and functional regions associated with phenotypes. Genome-wide SNP genotyping panels are now commercially available for the major livestock species, varying in SNP density from 5000 to 500,000 SNP and in some cases including SNP targeted to specific traits.

Sequencing the pig genome started in 2003 by the Swine Genome Sequencing Consortium (SGSC). The draft reference genome sequence was released in 2012 (Groenen et al., 2012). Since then, hundreds of pig genomes have been sequenced to study genome variation, evolution and selection, and their genomes are publicly available (Groenen, 2016). The first SNP panel commercially available for swine (PorcineSNP60 BeadChip v2, Illumina, San Diego, CA) contained approximately 60,000 SNPs covering all autosomes and the X chromosome (Ramos et al., 2009).

1.2 Genomic Tools

Livestock genetic research has primarily been focused on the identification of genetic variants associated with production traits (Sharmaa et al., 2015). Maintaining high production levels while improving sustainability-related traits is the current industry need. Because genetic changes are permanent and heritable, they provide long-term solutions for selecting resilient animal suited to various production systems and eventually better adapted to hostile environments (Berghof et al., 2019). The improvement of traits, such as efficient thermoregulation, feed use and immunity, may accelerate the development of animals more resilient to metabolic and climatic stressors.

Molecular markers can be applied to investigate genetic diversity within and between breeds and to identify genes controlling specific traits, such as those mentioned above. Several methods of data analysis and at least three approaches can be used to identify SNP markers and genes associated with target traits: genome-wide association studies, identification of selection signatures and landscape genomics.

Genome-wide association studies (GWASs) are used to identify markers associated with specific traits (Korte & Farlow, 2013). GWASs require both phenotypic records and genotypes for all the individuals involved in the study. In addition, a large cohort of individuals has to be investigated to reach a sufficient statistical power (Hayes, 2013). An example GWAS addressed boar taint, which is a problem for the pig industry (Duijvesteijn et al., 2010). In pig farms, male castration is used to avoid male sex pheromones causing pork to have an unpleasant odour. As androstenone is among the pheromones responsible for boar taint, a GWAS was conducted on androsterone levels in pigs, to explore the genetic control of this trait. Results identified a cluster of candidate genes on chromosome 6 controlling significant variation in androstenone levels, providing the opportunity to use DNA markers to accelerate genetic progress in reducing androstenone levels in sire lines.

Selection signatures are identifiable genetic features, where the level of hetrozygosity is reduced, found at genomic regions subjected to strong selection pressure (Jensen et al., 2016; Saravanan et al., 2020). The detection of selection signatures can identify genes and beneficial mutations conferring a selective advantage for the animals (Zhao et al., 2015). The advantages of using this approach are that regions under selection can be identified by genotyping a relatively small number of animals and with no need for phenotypic records. The drawback is that the selection pressure causing the signature may be difficult to identify and has to be guessed from the function of genes mapping in the genomic region identified.

A selection signatures approach was used to identify the effects of high altitude on an indigenous pig breed of the Tibet Plateau (Ai et al., 2014). Results identified a signature of selection in a genomic region encompassing genes related to hypoxia that conferred adaptation to high altitudes. Interestingly, these genes also affect pork quality traits (Gan et al., 2019).

The landscape genomics approach detects genetic adaptation related to environmental features. This approach tests the association between geo-referenced environmental data (e.g. climate, soil and topology) and the genetic information of the individuals (Dauphin et al., 2022). The application of this approach could provide insights into the genetics of swine adaptation to different environments.

The identification of genes and variants controlling a trait is now feasible using these methods. This information can then be used for marker-assisted selection (MAS), where animals carrying favourable alleles that have a large influence on the trait(s) of interest can be identified and preferentially used for breeding (Bishop & Woolliams, 2004).

The decreasing cost of sequencing and genotyping has facilitated the production of large genotype data sets. This has enabled the application of genomic selection (GS) to livestock species, suggested more than 20 years ago to decrease generation length and improve the accuracy of breeding value estimation (Meuwissen et al., 2001). GS exploits genetic markers covering the whole genome to design novel breeding programmes. Thus, it allows the prediction of the animal breeding value (GEBV) considering genomic information (Samorè & Fontanesi, 2016).

Genomics may contribute to the improvement in sustainability of swine farming at two levels as described below: (i) by characterizing the genetic diversity of pigs (local/rare breeds) that are well adapted to local climatic conditions, thus preventing the erosion of valuable genetic resources; and (ii) by genetically improving commercial breeds for traits related to sustainability, such as feed efficiency, disease resistance and welfare (Kumar et al., 2022).

2 Biodiversity

2.1 Local Breeds

Swine breeds can be classified as international, transboundary and local breeds. The first are cosmopolitan highly selected, high-performing breeds found in the intensive pig industry worldwide. Globally, pig production is mainly based on two or three-way crosses between Large White, Duroc, Landrace, Hampshire and Pietrain breeds. Pure breed sires are supplied by only few commercial companies (Rauw et al., 2020). Transboundary and local breeds are typically autochthonous of a specific region or country and are connected to local traditions and niche products (Muñoz et al., 2019). Their productivity is lower than international breeds and is often not economically sustainable. Out of the 21 Italian local breeds surveyed by the Italian National Pig Breeders Association (ANAS) the at the beginning of the twentieth century, only six are still farmed and have a national herd-book; these are Mora Romagnola, Cinta Senese, Casertana, Calabrese, Nero Siciliano and Sarda. Because of their small population size, Mora Romagnola and Sarda are listed among the endangered breeds by the Food and Agriculture Organization of the United Nations (FAO). Cinta Senese is classified as endangered maintained, while Calabrese, Casertana and Nero Siciliano are classified as vulnerable. Among the six Italian breeds, Calabrese, Casertana and Mora Romagnola have very low genetic diversity, low heterozygosity and low effective population size (Muñoz et al., 2019).

2.2 Genetic Heritage of Italian Local Breeds

Despite being less productive, local breeds display unique features that can help to face challenges of climate change and animal welfare. Local breeds are well adapted to the local agro-climatic conditions, possess high resilience and tolerance to diseases. For example, Nero Siciliano is well adapted to the unfavourable environment of Nebrodi mountains and for disease resistance (Chiofalo et al., 2003; Zumbo et al., 2020). Comparing the Nero Siciliano genome with the reference sequence of Sus scrofa, 11 million variants were only found in the Nero Siciliano (D'Alessandro et al., 2019a, b). Among these, 6747 variants were in proximity of genes related to environmental adaptation including *Vacuolar protein sorting 13 homolog A (VPS13A),* which is related to heat stress response (Groenen, 2016). *VPS13A* encodes a protein affecting blood viscosity, which is increased by heat stress and leads to a higher risk of cerebral and coronary thrombosis in humans. Mutations in *VPS13A* gene were hypothesized to reduce this risk in hot environments (Ai et al., 2015). Another variant was found in *Ligand-dependent nuclear receptor corepressor-like protein (LCORL),* which is related to body size. Body size is one of the major morphological features affecting thermoregulation (Elayadeth-Meethal et al., 2018; Berihulay et al., 2019). A variant was also identified in the

Fucosyltransferase 1 (FUT1) gene. Polymorphisms in this gene have been associated with intestinal resistance to the enterotoxigenic Escherichia coli F18, a bacterium causing post-weaning diarrhoea (PWD) in pigs (Schwartz & Teramo, 2000; Luise et al., 2019).

A recent study analysed signatures of selection in European local breeds, including the six Italian breeds (Muñoz et al., 2019). Genes related to two distinct families of olfactory receptors were found to be under selection respectively in Mora Romagnola and Calabrese breeds. The olfaction system is important for pigs which rely on their sense of smell to cope with the environment (Nguyen et al., 2012) and is associated with traits related to reproduction and behaviour, ultimately affecting fitness (McGlone et al., 2021).

Pork quality of local breeds is often different from that of cosmopolitan breeds. Most are free from the genetic variant responsible for PSS. However, in some populations, e.g. Cinta Senese and Nero Siciliano, a low frequency of the deleterious variant has been observed (Russo et al., 2004). This suggests a possible introgression of the deleterious variant from commercial breeds and shows the importance of a proper genetic management of local populations.

Another meat defect, acid meat (or "Rendement Napole", RN) is associated with a mutation in the *Protein Kinase AMP-Activated Non-Catalytic Subunit Gamma 3 gene (PRKAG3).* This deleterious variant is not found in Cinta Senese pigs (Crovetti et al., 2016). A different mutation in *PRKAG3* is associated with lower glycogen content, leading to improved pork quality (i.e. ultimate pH and pork colour). This variant was found to occur in high frequency in some local European breeds, including Casertana.

Compared to commercial breeds that have been selected for lean growth, local breeds generally have higher fat deposition (Poklukar et al., 2020). Italian local breeds have higher intramuscular fat (IMF) content compared with transboundary breeds. While IMF in Large White is lower than 1%, the Cinta Senese and Nero Siciliano have an IMF content higher than 3% in Longissimus dorsi, and in the Casertana and Mora Romagnola, the IMF content is even higher. (Franci & Pugliese, 2016). IMF content is positively correlated with organoleptic traits; therefore, local breeds are likely to produce a stronger pork taste than commercial breed. Thus, they can provide useful genetic resource to modify pork quality in highly selected breeds, particularly for cured meat supply chain.

The analysis of 48 genes related to pork quality in three transboundary breeds used in the Italian cured pork supply chain (Large White, Landrace and Duroc) and in the Nero Siciliano breed (D'Alessandro et al., 2019a, 2019b) identified 5659 SNPs that were unique to the Nero Siciliano breed. Among these SNP, five were in genes affecting fat deposition and growth: *Perilipin 1 (PLIN1), TBC1 Domain Family Member 1 (TBC1D1), Cathepsin B (CTSB), Phosphoglycerate mutase 2 (PGAM2)* and *Pancreatic Polypeptide Receptor 1 (PPYR1).*

A study of European local breeds identified a mutation in Cinta Senese in the *Alpha-2-glycoprotein 1 (AZGP1)* gene, involved in lipid mobilization (Herrero-Medrano et al., 2014) and associated with fat deposition, which was not present in commercial breeds. This variant overlaps two QTLs related respectively to abdominal fat weight and ear morphology. A different mutation in the same gene was also identified in Nero Siciliano (D'Alessandro et al., 2019a, 2019b).

2.3 Genomic Management of Local Breeds

Local breeds are a precious reservoir of genetic diversity which is importance to preserve as it is related to sustainability and provides opportunities for adaptation and improved pork quality. This genetic variability could also be important to develop genetic resistance to diseases to which high-producing genetic lines are susceptible. Genetic diversity within small breeds is threatened by inbreeding, resulting from the mating of close relatives, which leads to the loss of some genetic variants. Inbreeding depression may occur, which is associated with reduced fitness, reproduction and physiological efficiency in a population. A drop of inbreeding coefficient in the Cinta Senese breed has been observed, as it passed from 0.21 in 1996 to 0.17 in 1999 and to 0.14 in 2003 (Gandini et al., 1998; Franci et al., 2004). A recent study (Schiavo et al., 2021) used runs of homozygosity (ROH) to calculate genomic inbreeding (FROH), showing that high and worrying FROH values across all ROH classes were detected for Mora Romagnola (FROH1 = 0.41), Calabrese (FROH1 = 0.33) and Casertana (FROH1 = 0.24), whereas Nero Siciliano (FROH1 = 0.08) and Sarda (FROH1 = 0.10) displayed the lowest values. Conservation of small local breeds is needed due to their socio-cultural value, their revitalizing potential for rural communities and marginal areas and for scientific importance. Because of their unique traits, the genetic management of the Italian local breeds should aim to carefully maintain the original genetic variability present to preserve the unique features of the breed (Crovetti et al., 2013). Genetic characterization of local breeds is a preliminary and essential step for the development of appropriate breeding programmes and to add value to the breed-derived products, thus enhancing their sustainability through increased value.

2.4 How Can Genetics Valorize Local Breeds?

As all the Italian local breeds are considered "at risk", and national conservation programmes are being developed, for example, a semen cryobank has been created as genetic reserve (Moretti et al., 2022). However, a more effective strategy to maintain a breed is to associate it with a typical food product or with a specific landscape or extensive farming system. This will actively promote the use of local breeds in farms. In this way, in addition of being considered a genetic resource to be conserved, local breeds acquire value themselves, as a resource for local production and development (Lauvie et al., 2011). The link between a breed, its place of origin and its products is positively perceived by consumers in terms of food quality and contributes to improve profitability. Cinta Senese pork obtained the Protected

Denomination of Origin (PDO) label in 2011 and a protection consortium for the breed (Consorzio di Tutela della Cinta Senese) has been created. A similar consortium was established for Nero Siciliano in 2003 (Consorzio di Tutela Suino Nero Dei Nebrodi), and an official PDO request for Nero Siciliano cured pork was issued in 2011.

Safeguarding the association between a breed and its products from frauds through an effective traceability system is crucial to gain consumer trust (Ammirato & Felicetti, 2013). Traceability is defined as "the ability to access any or all information related to a product, throughout its entire life cycle, by means of recorded identifications"(Olsen & Borit, 2013). The combination of DNA variations is unique for each individual, although the pattern of variations is similar among individuals belonging to a same breed. Therefore, molecular genetic markers can be used for genetic traceability of individuals and also to assign the probability that a meat product s from a specific breed. This is important for meat products produced from a single breed.

Coat colour is one of the major traits differentiating livestock breeds (Fontanesi, 2016). Cinta Senese is morphologically characterized by black skin with a white belt surrounding the body at the shoulder level. The *KIT* gene is involved in melanin metabolism and affects coat colour and distribution in pigs. A mutation in this gene was found to cause the belted phenotype (Fontanesi et al., 2010). One SNP was identified that allows Cinta Senese pork to be identified from other non-belted breeds and thus, can be used to protect Cinta Senese products from fraud.

Melanocortin 1 Receptor (MC1R) affects brown versus white coat colour, while *Nuclear Receptor Subfamily 6 Group A Member 1 (NR6A1)* controls vertebral number in Mora Romagnola. Polymorphisms within these genes can potentially be used to protect Mora Romagnola products (Tinarelli et al., 2021).

Coat colour alone is not effective in traceability systems, e.g. for Nero Siciliano (D'Alessandro et al., 2007). Recently, a 12-SNP panel has been shown to effectively distinguished Nero Siciliano from Italian Large White, Italian Landrace, Italian Duroc, European wild boars and cosmopolitan Large White, Landrace and Duroc (Moretti et al., 2022). The addition of eight SNPs to this panel (20-SNP panel in total) also enabled Nero Siciliano purebred pigs to be distinguished from first-generation (F1) hybrids.

Overall, the conservation of genetic resources contained in local breeds is important for future breeding needs and to promote a sustainable use of rural areas. The increasing availability of genetic markers and the development of tools and techniques to analyse molecular variation are widening our capacity to characterize the genetic diversity of breeds (Bruford et al., 2015).

3 Phenotypes for Swine Sustainability

In the last two decades, new breeding goals were adopted to meet the global challenge of improving livestock system sustainability. Key breeding goals for pig farming sustainability include health (e.g. disease resistance), efficiency (feed and reproduction), adaptation (e.g. effective thermoregulation) and welfare (e.g. behaviour and no male castration) (Harlizius et al., 2004; Merks et al., 2012).

3.1 Disease Resistance and Resilience

The swine industry worldwide must cope with diseases caused by a range of pathogens, such as porcine reproductive and respiratory syndrome virus (PRRS), porcine epidemic diarrhoea virus, porcine circovirus (PCV), swine influenza virus, brachyspira-colitis (swine dysentery), Streptococcus suis septicaemia and others (VanderWaal & Deen, 2018). New pathogens and alternative strains continuously emerge (Putz et al., 2019). Besides generating financial losses for the pork industry, these diseases compromise animal welfare and increase antibiotics use. Studies that investigated opportunities to select pigs for disease resistance and resilience to pathogens have shown that phenotypes linked to disease resilience are heritable and thus improvable by genetic selection (Serão et al., 2016; Putz et al., 2019; Cheng et al., 2020; Bai & Plastow, 2022).

A successful example of genetic improvement in swine health is the marker-assisted selection against oedema disease caused by F18+ Escherichia coli. This enterotoxaemia causes diarrhoea in pigs during the first 2 weeks after weaning, and it is rapidly fatal in most of the affected individuals (Moxley, 2000). A variant of the fucosyltransferase 1 *(FUT1)* gene was identified that induces resistance to the pathogen colonization, thus providing a test to identify pigs that are resistant to oedema (Vögeli et al., 1997). Use of a genetic test based on this variant has reduced the occurrence of oedema disease from 22% to less than 1% in weaning pigs that are homozygous for the resistance allele (Mellencamp et al., 2008).

PRRS is among the most infectious diseases in swine. Efforts have been made over the years to characterize the genetic control of PRRS resistance. GWAS approaches identified a region on chromosome 4 explaining 16% of genetic variance for virus load (Boddicker et al., 2012). In this region, the interferon-induced guanylate-binding protein 5 gene (*GBP5*) was identified as the most likely candidate in several independent studies (Boddicker et al., 2014a, b). *GBP5* is involved in the immune response to bacterial and viral infection in several species (Reiner, 2016). Other studies focused on genes involved in PRRS pathogenesis, such as *cysteine-rich scavenger receptor (CD163)*, which plays a role in PRRS replication (Calvert et al., 2007). Pigs with CD163 knocked out by in gene-edited were protection from PRRSV infection (Whitworth et al., 2016). These pigs showed no clinical signs and no lung pathology, viremia or antibody response after PRRS virus inoculation.

All these studies investigated resistance to one specific disease. Cheng et al. (2022) investigated the genetic control of the response to a polymicrobial challenge through GWAS approach. The study found that the major histocompatibility complex (MHC) region (in pigs called the "swine leukocyte antigen region"—SLA) explained a substantial genetic variance for several traits related to resilience to polymicrobial challenge, such as growth rate in weaners (12.8%) and finishers (2.7%), clinical disease traits (up to 2.7%) and feeding and drinking traits (up to 4%). A significant SNP in the MHC region was identified, located in the enhancer of *Tripartite Motif Containing 39 (TRIM39)* gene, which is involved in innate immunity. The significant contribution of MHC region to genetic variance of disease resilience has been reported in many studies (Serão et al., 2014; Walker et al., 2018; Sanglard et al., 2020).

3.2 Feed Efficiency

Feed represents the largest proportion of production costs in swine farming and affects animal welfare (Galanopoulos et al., 2006). Feed efficiency is defined as the cumulative efficiency in the use of the dietary nutrients for maintenance and performance (Patience et al., 2015). Improving feed efficiency is a key objective in the pork industry, as it leads to increased animal resilience and economic sustainability. Several measures of feed efficiency have been developed, including feed conversion rate (FCR), residual feed intake (RFI), the combination of residual intake and body weight gain (RIG) and residual body weight gain (RG) (Homma et al., 2021).

Feed efficiency traits are genetically heritable, and GWAS approaches have identified key genes and genetic variants controlling feed efficiency, thus providing useful information to facilitate genomic selection to improve this trait (Do et al., 2014; Horodyska et al., 2017).

The economic impact of combining genetic selection for feed efficiency and nutrition optimization strategies in swine farming have shown that improved feed efficiency in pigs can be achieved by genetic selection and is a strategy to enhance sustainability in pork industry (Soleimani et al., 2021).

3.3 Reproduction Efficiency

Reproductive failure is the most common reason for sow culling in swine farming and mostly involves sows at low parities (Engblom et al., 2007; Stalder et al., 2003). Therefore, reproduction efficiency is a key trait to enhance sustainability on swine farming (Nonneman & Lents, 2022). Identifying genes involved in the regulation of reproductive traits is of considerable interest (Spötter & Distl, 2006). However, fertility is a complex trait, and it is generally characterized by low-to-moderate heritability (Merilä & Sheldon, 2000).

Phenotypes related to reproduction efficiency comprise ovulation rate, litter size, age at puberty and uterine capacity (Zak et al., 2017). Age at puberty has higher heritability than other fertility-related traits (Tart et al., 2013). GWASs have identified candidate genes controlling this trait, including *arginine vasopressin receptor 1A (AVPR1A)*, which is involved in sexual receptivity and olfactory response to the boar (Tart et al., 2013). The favourable allele of *AVPR1A*, associated with decreased age at puberty, is associated with increased lifetime productivity (Lucot et al., 2015).

Characterization of genotype–environment interactions is suggested to provide a better understanding of how genetic effect interacts with specific farm systems for reproduction efficiency (Zak et al., 2017).

3.4 Environmental Adaptation

The Intergovernmental Panel on Climate Change (IPCC) estimates that there will be a 1.5 °C global warming compared to the 1850–1900 baseline, and higher solar radiation will characterize the second half of the current decade (Masson-Delmotte et al., 2019). Heat stress is among the major threats to animal welfare and farm sustainability (St-Pierre et al., 2003; Mayorga et al., 2019). Heat stress effects on pigs are decrease in growth and reduced feed efficiency, reproduction efficiency and carcass quality, with an increase in mortality and morbidity (Mayorga et al., 2019). Besides infrastructure improvements, such as air cooling or evaporative pads, genetic selection can contribute to improve heat resilience by selecting animals with effective thermoregulation.

Measurements to assess thermoregulation include rectal temperature, skin temperature, respiratory rate and blood metabolites (Gourdine et al., 2021). Genetic variation of response to heat stress among different swine breeds has been reported in the scientific literature (Bloemhof et al., 2008). Differences in thermoregulation traits in Large White sows reared in a tropical climate have a heritability up to 0.35 (Gourdine et al., 2017). In addition to thermoregulation, the study of local breeds adapted to extreme environmental conditions and exposed to a range of parasites and diseases may provide information on the genetics of adaptation (Ai et al., 2015), for example pigs in Africa are often semi-feral and kept in small groups which favours natural selection for tolerance of the local conditions (Amills et al., 2013).

3.5 Animal Welfare

A poor animal welfare is unacceptable in social, economic and environmental terms (Broom, 2010). Aggressive behaviour is unsustainable in swine farming, as aggressive individuals tend to hurt pen-mates, typically tail biting, which leads to a decrease in growth rate and carcass quality. Moreover, aggressive animals are prone to be easily stressed, leading to a higher susceptibility to infectious diseases (Norris et al., 2014). The high levels of cortisol released in stressful conditions are associated with immunosuppression. Genetic selection for docility has been proposed as strategy to enhance animal welfare in swine farming (Rydhmer & Canario, 2022).

Four SNPs associated with aggressive behaviour have been identified in the monoamine oxidase A (MAOA) gene (Chen et al., 2019). Pigs carrying the wild alleles were more aggressive than mutants. The response of piglets to handling and feeding behaviour shows low-to-moderate heritability and favourable or neutral genetic correlations with production traits (Rohrer et al., 2013). This means that genetic selection could improve behaviour without detrimental effects on performance.

Another welfare issue in pork industry is related to male castration to avoid boar taint, which is mainly caused by the sex hormones androstenone and skatole. The levels of these two compounds are heritable and that genetic selection could reduce their concentration below the acceptance threshold (Robic et al., 2008; Merks et al., 2009).

4 Conclusions

Genetic selection is intrinsically sustainable as it leads to permanent and cumulative genetic progress. Selection strategies include breed choice, marker-assisted and genomic selection. New breeding goals include enhanced resilience, efficiency, adaptation and welfare, most of which show some level of heritability and so would respond to selection. The conservation of biodiversity is important, to preserve genetic variation that will secure future breeding options to adapt pigs to new management, changing consumer demands and a variety of environmental conditions. Genetic characterization and genetic traceability will help the industry to meet current and future breeding needs.

References

Ai, H., Fang, X., Yang, B., Huang, Z., Chen, H., Mao, L., Zhang, F., Zhang, L., Cui, L., He, W., et al. (2015). Adaptation and possible ancient interspecies introgression in pigs identified by whole-genome sequencing. *Nature Genetics, 47*(3), 217–225. https://doi.org/10.1038/ng.3199. [Accessed 2023 Feb 15].

Ai, H., Yang, B., Li, J., Xie, X., Chen, H., & Ren, J. (2014). Population history and genomic signatures for high-altitude adaptation in tibetan pigs. *BMC Genomics, 15*(1), 1–14. https://doi.org/10.1186/1471-2164-15-834/FIGURES/5. [Accessed 2023 Feb 16].

Amills, M., Ramírez, O., Galman-Omitogun, O., & Clop, A. (2013). Domestic pigs in Africa. *African Archaeological Review, 30*(1), 73–82. https://doi.org/10.1007/S10437-012-9111-2/TABLES/1. [Accessed 2023 Feb 17].

Ammirato, S., & Felicetti, A. M. (2013). The potential of agritourism in revitalizing rural communities: Some empirical results. *IFIP Advances in Information and Communication Technology, 408*, 489–497. https://doi.org/10.1007/978-3-642-40543-3_52/COVER. [Accessed 2023 Feb 14].

Bai, X., & Plastow, G. S. (2022). Breeding for disease resilience: Opportunities to manage polymicrobial challenge and improve commercial performance in the pig industry. *CABI Agriculture and Bioscience, 3*(1), 1–17. https://doi.org/10.1186/S43170-022-00073-Y. [Accessed 2023 Feb 16].

Berghof, T. V. L., Poppe, M., & Mulder, H. A. (2019). Opportunities to improve resilience in animal breeding programs. *Frontiers in Genetics, 9*, 1–15. https://doi.org/10.3389/fgene.2018.00692

Berihulay, H., Abied, A., He, X., Jiang, L., & Ma, Y. (2019). Adaptation mechanisms of small ruminants to environmental heat stress. *Animals, 9*(3), 75. https://doi.org/10.3390/ANI9030075. [Accessed 2023 Feb 15].

Bishop, S. C., & Woolliams, J. A. (2004). Genetic approaches and technologies for improving the sustainability of livestock production. *Journal of the Science of Food and Agriculture, 84*(9), 911–919. https://doi.org/10.1002/JSFA.1704. [Accessed 2023 Feb 17].

Bloemhof, S., van der Waaij, E. H., Merks, J. W. M., & Knol, E. F. (2008). Sow line differences in heat stress tolerance expressed in reproductive performance traits. *Journal of Animal Science, 86*(12), 3330–3337. https://doi.org/10.2527/JAS.2008-0862. [Accessed 2023 Feb 17].

Boddicker, N., Waide, E. H., Rowland, R. R. R., Lunney, J. K., Garrick, D. J., Reecy, J. M., & Dekkers, J. C. M. (2012). Evidence for a major QTL associated with host response to Porcine Reproductive and Respiratory Syndrome Virus challenge. *Journal of Animal Science, 90*(6), 1733–1746. https://doi.org/10.2527/JAS.2011-4464. [Accessed 2023 Feb 16].

Boddicker, N. J., Bjorkquist, A., Rowland, R. R., Lunney, J. K., Reecy, J. M., & Dekkers, J. C. M. (2014a). Genome-wide association and genomic prediction for host response to porcine reproductive and respiratory syndrome virus infection. *Genetics Selection Evolution, 46*(1), 1–14. https://doi.org/10.1186/1297-9686-46-18/FIGURES/6. [Accessed 2023 Feb 16].

Boddicker, N. J., Garrick, D. J., Rowland, R. R. R., Lunney, J. K., Reecy, J. M., & Dekkers, J. C. M. (2014b). Validation and further characterization of a major quantitative trait locus associated with host response to experimental infection with porcine reproductive and respiratory syndrome virus. *Animal Genetics, 45*(1), 48–58. https://doi.org/10.1111/AGE.12079. [Accessed 2023 Feb 16].

Brito, L. F., Bedere, N., Douhard, F., Oliveira, H. R., Arnal, M., Peñagaricano, F., Schinckel, A. P., Baes, C. F., & Miglior, F. (2021). Review: Genetic selection of high-yielding dairy cattle toward sustainable farming systems in a rapidly changing world. *Animal, 15*, 100292. https://doi.org/10.1016/J.ANIMAL.2021.100292

Broom, D. M. (2010). Animal welfare: An aspect of care, sustainability, and food quality required by the public. *Journal of Veterinary Medical Education, 37*(1), 83–88. https://doi.org/10.3138/JVME.37.1.83. [Accessed 2023 Feb 17].

Bruford, M. W., Ginja, C., Hoffmann, I., Joost, S., Wengel, P. O., Alberto, F. J., Amaral, A. J., Barbato, M., Biscarini, F., Colli, L., et al. (2015). Prospects and challenges for the conservation of farm animal genomic resources, 2015–2025. *Frontiers in Genetics, 6*(OCT), 314. https://doi.org/10.3389/FGENE.2015.00314/BIBTEX

Calvert, J. G., Slade, D. E., Shields, S. L., Jolie, R., Mannan, R. M., Ankenbauer, R. G., & Welch, S.-K. W. (2007). CD163 expression confers susceptibility to porcine reproductive and respiratory syndrome viruses. *Journal of Virology, 81*(14), 7371–7379. https://doi.org/10.1128/JVI.00513-07/ASSET/9299FC66-405A-4185-9651-51C9319879DD/ASSETS/GRAPHIC/ZJV0140793870008.JPEG. [Accessed 2023 Feb 16].

Chen, R., Chu, Q., Shen, C., Tong, X., Gao, S., Liu, X., Zhou, B., & Schinckel, A. P. (2019). Identification of single nucleotide polymorphisms in porcine MAOA gene associated with aggressive behavior of weaned pigs after group mixing. *Animals, 9*(11), 952. https://doi.org/10.3390/ANI9110952. [Accessed 2023 Feb 17].

Cheng, J., Fernando, R., Cheng, H., Kachman, S. D., Lim, K. S., Harding, J. C. S., Dyck, M. K., Fortin, F., Plastow, G. S., Canada, P. G., & Dekkers, J. C. M. (2022). Genome-wide association study of disease resilience traits from a natural polymicrobial disease challenge model in pigs identifies the importance of the major histocompatibility complex region. *G3 Genes|Genomes|Genetics, 12*(3). https://doi.org/10.1093/G3JOURNAL/JKAB441. [Accessed 2023 Feb 16].

Cheng, J., Putz, A. M., Harding, J. C. S., Dyck, M. K., Fortin, F., Plastow, G. S., Canada, P. G., & Dekkers, J. C. M. (2020). Genetic analysis of disease resilience in wean-to-finish pigs from a natural disease challenge model. *Journal of Animal Science, 98*(8). https://doi.org/10.1093/JAS/SKAA244. [Accessed 2023 Feb 16].

Chiofalo, B., Liotta, L., Zumbo, A., & Chiofalo, L. (2003). Seasonal variations of free fatty acids in plasma of "Nero Siciliano" pigs living in extensive conditions. *Veterinary Research Communications, 27*(SUPPL. 1), 253–255. https://doi.org/10.1023/B:VERC.0000014153.61928.EC/METRICS. [Accessed 2023 Feb 13].

Crovetti, A., Bozzi, R., Nardi, L., Franci, O., & Fontanesi, L. (2016). Assessment of variability of genes associated with meat quality traits in Cinta Senese pigs. *Italian Journal of Animal Science, 6*(sup1), 101. https://doi.org/10.4081/IJAS.2007.1S.101. [Accessed 2023 Feb 17].

Crovetti, A., Sirtori, F., Pugliese, C., Franci, O., & Bozzi, R. (2013). Pedigree analysis of Cinta Senese and Mora Romagnola breeds. In: *Acta argiculturae Slovenica*, Supplement. Vol. 4. [place unknown]; p. 41–44.

D'Alessandro, E., Fontanesi, L., Liotta, L., Davoli, R., Chiofalo, V., & Russo, V. (2007). Analysis of the MC1R gene in the nero siciliano pig breed and usefulness of this locus for breed traceability. *Veterinary Research Communications, 31*(SUPPL. 1), 389–392. https://doi.org/10.1007/S11259-007-0063-Y/METRICS. [Accessed 2023 Feb 15].

D'Alessandro, E., Giosa, D., Sapienza, I., Giuffrè, L., Cigliano, R. A., Romeo, O., & Zumbo, A. (2019a). Whole genome SNPs discovery in Nero Siciliano pig. *Genetics and Molecular Biology, 42*(3), 594–602. https://doi.org/10.1590/1678-4685-GMB-2018-0169. [Accessed 2023 Feb 15].

D'Alessandro, E., Sapienza, I., Giosa, D., Giuffrè, L., & Zumbo, A. (2019b). In silico analysis of meat quality candidate genes among Nero Siciliano, and Italian heavy pigs genomes. *Large Animal Review, 25*(4), 137–140. Accessed Feb 15, 2023, from https://www.largeanimalreview.com/index.php/lar/article/view/91

Dauphin, B., Rellstab, C., Wüest, R. O., Karger, D. N., Holderegger, R., Gugerli, F., & Manel, S. (2022). Re-thinking the environment in landscape genomics. *Trends in Ecology and Evolution, 38*(3), 261–274. https://doi.org/10.1016/j.tree.2022.10.010. [Accessed 2023 Feb 16].

Do, D. N., Strathe, A. B., Ostersen, T., Pant, S. D., & Kadarmideen, H. N. (2014). Genome-wide association and pathway analysis of feed efficiency in pigs reveal candidate genes and pathways for residual feed intake. *Frontiers in Genetics, 5*(AUG), 307. https://doi.org/10.3389/FGENE.2014.00307/

Duijvesteijn, N., Knol, E. F., Merks, J. W. M., Crooijmans, R. P. M. A., Groenen, M. A. M., Bovenhuis, H., & Harlizius, B. (2010). A genome-wide association study on androstenone levels in pigs reveals a cluster of candidate genes on chromosome 6. *BMC Genet [Internet]., 11*(1), 1–11. https://doi.org/10.1186/1471-2156-11-42/TABLES/3. [Accessed 2023 Feb 16].

Elayadeth-Meethal, M., Thazhathu Veettil, A., Maloney, S. K., Hawkins, N., Misselbrook, T. H., Sejian, V., Rivero, M. J., & Lee, M. R. F. (2018). Size does matter: Parallel evolution of adaptive thermal tolerance and body size facilitates adaptation to climate change in domestic cattle. *Ecology and Evolution, 8*(21), 10608–10620. https://doi.org/10.1002/ECE3.4550. [Accessed 2023 Feb 15].

Engblom, L., Lundeheim, N., Dalin, A. M., & Andersson, K. (2007). Sow removal in Swedish commercial herds. *Livestock Science, 106*(1), 76–86. https://doi.org/10.1016/J.LIVSCI.2006.07.002

Evans, G. J., Giuffra, E., Sanchez, A., Kerje, S., Davalos, G., Vidal, O., Illán, S., Noguera, J. L., Varona, L., Velander, I., et al. (2003). Identification of quantitative trait loci for production traits in commercial pig populations. *Genetics, 164*(2), 621–627. https://doi.org/10.1093/GENETICS/164.2.621. [Accessed 2023 Feb 16].

Fontanesi, L. (2016). Genetic authentication and traceability of food products of animal origin: new developments and perspectives. *Italian Journal of Animal Science, 8*(SUPPL. 2), 9–18. https://doi.org/10.4081/IJAS.2009.S2.9. [Accessed 2023 Feb 14].

Fontanesi, L., D'Alessandro, E., Scotti, E., Liotta, L., Crovetti, A., Chiofalo, V., & Russo, V. (2010). Genetic heterogeneity and selection signature at the KIT gene in pigs showing different coat colours and patterns. *Animal Genetics, 41*(5), 478–492. https://doi.org/10.1111/J.1365-2052.2010.02054.X. [Accessed 2023 Feb 15].

Franci, O., Gandini, G., & Bozzi, R. (2004). Why and how to select a local porcine breed: The case of the Cinta Senese. *Options Méditerranéennes*. [Accessed 2023 Feb 15]. www.anas.it

Franci, O., & Pugliese, C. (2016). Italian autochthonous pigs: progress report and research perspectives. *Italian Journal of Animal Science, 6*(SUPPL. 1), 663–671. https://doi.org/10.4081/IJAS.2007.1S.663. [Accessed 2023 Feb 15].

Fujii, J., Otsu, K., Zorzato, F., de Leon, S., Khanna, V. K., Weiler, J. E., O'Brien, P. J., & Maclennan, D. H. (1991). Identification of a mutation in porcine ryanodine receptor associated with malignant hyperthermia. *Science (1979), 253*(5018), 448–451. https://doi.org/10.1126/SCIENCE.1862346. [Accessed 2023 Feb 14].

Galanopoulos, K., Aggelopoulos, S., Kamenidou, I., & Mattas, K. (2006). Assessing the effects of managerial and production practices on the efficiency of commercial pig farming. *Agricultural Systems, 88*(2–3), 125–141. https://doi.org/10.1016/J.AGSY.2005.03.002

Gamborg, C., & Sandøe, P. (2005). Sustainability in farm animal breeding: A review. *Livestock Production Science, 92*(3), 221–231. https://doi.org/10.1016/J.LIVPRODSCI.2004.08.010

Gan, M., Shen, L., Fan, Y., Guo, Z., Liu, B., Chen, L., Tang, G., Jiang, Y., Li, X., Zhang, S., et al. (2019). High altitude adaptability and meat quality in Tibetan pigs: A reference for local pork processing and genetic improvement. *Animals, 9*(12), 1080. https://doi.org/10.3390/ANI9121080. [Accessed 2023 Feb 16].

Gandini, G., Orlandini, P., Franci, O., & Campodoni, G. (1998). Policies to decrease inbreeding in the Cinta Senese pig. *Options Méditerranéennes.* 35–37. https://om.ciheam.org/article.php?IDPDF=600110 [Accessed 2023 Feb 15]

Gourdine, J. L., Mandonnet, N., Giorgi, M., & Renaudeau, D. (2017). Genetic parameters for thermoregulation and production traits in lactating sows reared in tropical climate. *Animal, 11*(3), 365–374. https://doi.org/10.1017/S175173111600135X

Gourdine, J. L., Rauw, W. M., Gilbert, H., & Poullet, N. (2021). The genetics of thermoregulation in pigs: A review. *Frontiers in Veterinary Science, 8*, 1501. https://doi.org/10.3389/FVETS.2021.770480/BIBTEX

Groenen, M. A. M. (2016). A decade of pig genome sequencing: A window on pig domestication and evolution. *Genetics Selection Evolution, 48*(1), 1–9. https://doi.org/10.1186/S12711-016-0204-2/FIGURES/1. [Accessed 2023 Feb 15].

Groenen, M. A. M., Archibald, A. L., Uenishi, H., Tuggle, C. K., Takeuchi, Y., Rothschild, M. F., Rogel-Gaillard, C., Park, C., Milan, D., Megens, H. J., et al. (2012). Analyses of pig genomes provide insight into porcine demography and evolution. *Nature, 491*(7424), 393–398. https://doi.org/10.1038/nature11622. [Accessed 2023 Feb 15].

Harlizius, B., van Wijk, R., & Merks, J. W. M. (2004). Genomics for food safety and sustainable animal production. *Journal of Biotechnology, 113*(1–3), 33–42. https://doi.org/10.1016/J.JBIOTEC.2004.03.021

Hayes, B. (2013). Overview of statistical methods for genome-wide association studies (GWAS). *Methods in Molecular Biology, 1019*, 149–169. https://doi.org/10.1007/978-1-62703-447-0_6/FIGURES/00064. [Accessed 2022 Nov 28].

Hayes, B. J., Lewin, H. A., & Goddard, M. E. (2013). The future of livestock breeding: Genomic selection for efficiency, reduced emissions intensity, and adaptation. *Trends in Genetics, 29*(4), 206–214. https://doi.org/10.1016/J.TIG.2012.11.009

Herrero-Medrano, J. M., Megens, H. J., Groenen, M. A. M., Bosse, M., Pérez-Enciso, M., & Crooijmans, R. P. M. A. (2014). Whole-genome sequence analysis reveals differences in population management and selection of European low-input pig breeds. *BMC Genomics, 15*(1), 1–12. https://doi.org/10.1186/1471-2164-15-601/FIGURES/3. [Accessed 2023 Feb 15].

Homma, C., Hirose, K., Ito, T., Kamikawa, M., Toma, S., Nikaido, S., Satoh, M., & Uemoto, Y. (2021). Estimation of genetic parameter for feed efficiency and resilience traits in three pig breeds. *Animal, 15*(11). https://doi.org/10.1016/j.animal.2021.100384

Horodyska, J., Hamill, R. M., Varley, P. F., Reyer, H., & Wimmers, K. (2017). Genome-wide association analysis and functional annotation of positional candidate genes for feed conversion efficiency and growth rate in pigs. *PLoS One, 12*(6), e0173482. https://doi.org/10.1371/JOURNAL.PONE.0173482. [Accessed 2023 Feb 17].

Jensen, J. D., Foll, M., & Bernatchez, L. (2016). The past, present and future of genomic scans for selection. *Molecular Ecology, 25*(1), 1–4. https://doi.org/10.1111/MEC.13493. [Accessed 2023 Feb 16].

Kauffman, R. G., Cassens, R. G., Scherer, A., & Meeker, D. L. (1993). *Variation sin pork quality: History, definition, extent, resolution*. Health and Production.

Korte, A., & Farlow, A. (2013). The advantages and limitations of trait analysis with GWAS: A review. *Plant Methods, 9*(1), 1–9. https://doi.org/10.1186/1746-4811-9-29/FIGURES/4. [Accessed 2022 Nov 28].

Kumar, P., Abubakar, A. A., Verma, A. K., Umaraw, P., Adewale Ahmed, M., Mehta, N., Nizam Hayat, M., Kaka, U., & Sazili, A. Q. (2022). New insights in improving sustainability in meat production: Opportunities and challenges. https://doi.org/10.1080/10408398.2022.2096562.. [Accessed 2023 Jan 12]

Lauvie, A., Audiot, A., Couix, N., Casabianca, F., Brives, H., & Verrier, E. (2011). Diversity of rare breed management programs: Between conservation and development. *Livestock Science, 140*(1–3), 161–170. https://doi.org/10.1016/J.LIVSCI.2011.03.025

Lucot, K. L., Spangler, M. L., Trenhaile, M. D., Kachman, S. D., & Ciobanu, D. C. (2015). Evaluation of reduced subsets of single nucleotide polymorphisms for the prediction of age at puberty in sows. *Animal Genetics, 46*(4), 403–409. https://doi.org/10.1111/AGE.12310. [Accessed 2023 Feb 17].

Luise, D., Motta, V., Bertocchi, M., Salvarani, C., Clavenzani, P., Fanelli, F., Pagotto, U., Bosi, P., & Trevisi, P. (2019). Effect of Mucine 4 and Fucosyltransferase 1 genetic variants on gut homoeostasis of growing healthy pigs. *Journal of Animal Physiology and Animal Nutrition (Berlin), 103*(3), 801–812. https://doi.org/10.1111/JPN.13063. [Accessed 2023 Feb 15].

Masson-Delmotte, V., Zhai, P., Pörtner, H.-O., Roberts, D., Skea, J., Shukla, P.R., Pirani, A., Moufouma-Okia, W., Péan, C., & Pidcock, R., et al. (2019). Global warming of 1.5°C An IPCC Special Report on the impacts of global warming of 1.5°C above pre-industrial levels and related global greenhouse gas emission pathways, in the context of strengthening the global response to the threat of climate change, sustainable development, and efforts to eradicate poverty. [Accessed 2023 Feb 17]. www.environmentalgraphiti.org

Mayorga, E. J., Renaudeau, D., Ramirez, B. C., Ross, J. W., & Baumgard, L. H. (2019). Heat stress adaptations in pigs. *Animal Frontiers, 9*(1), 54–61. https://doi.org/10.1093/AF/VFY035. [Accessed 2023 Feb 17].

McGlone, J. J., Aviles-Rosa, E. O., Archer, C., Wilson, M. M., Jones, K. D., Matthews, E. M., & Reyes, E. (2021). Understanding sow sexual behavior and the application of the boar pheromone to stimulate sow reproduction. *Animal Reproduction in Veterinary Medicine*. [Accessed 2023 Feb 16].

Meade, M., & Miller, M. (1990). The use of rapid chilling to reduce pale, soft and exudative pork from highly stressed market hogs. *Journal of Animal Science.*. [Accessed 2023 Feb 14].

Meisinger, J., & Berg, E. (2006). United States pork industry quality survey. [Accessed 2023 Feb 14].

Mellencamp, M. A., Galina-Pantoja, L., Gladney, C. D., & Torremorell, M. (2008). Improving pig health through genomics: A view from the industry. *Developments in Biologicals (Basel), 132*, 35–41. https://doi.org/10.1159/000317142. [Accessed 2023 Feb 16].

Merilä, J., & Sheldon, B. C. (2000). Lifetime reproductive success and heritability in nature. *American Naturalist, 155*(3), 307–310. https://doi.org/10.1086/303330/ASSET/IMAGES/LARGE/FG3.JPEG. [Accessed 2023 Feb 17].

Merks, J. W. M., Hanenberg, E. H. A. T., Bloemhof, S., & Knol, E. F. (2009). Genetic opportunities for pork production without castration. *Animal Welfare, 18*(4), 539–544. https://doi.org/10.1017/S0962728600000968. [Accessed 2023 Feb 17].

Merks, J. W. M., Mathur, P. K., & Knol, E. F. (2012). New phenotypes for new breeding goals in pigs. *Animal, 6*(4), 535–543. https://doi.org/10.1017/S1751731111002266

Meuwissen, T. H. E., Hayes, B. J., & Goddard, M. E. (2001). Prediction of total genetic value using genome-wide dense marker maps. *Genetics, 157*(4), 1819–1829. https://doi.org/10.1093/GENETICS/157.4.1819. [Accessed 2022 Dec 21].

Moretti, R., Criscione, A., Turri, F., Bordonaro, S., Marletta, D., Castiglioni, B., & Chessa, S. (2022). A 20-SNP panel as a tool for genetic authentication and traceability of pig breeds. *Animals, 12*(11), 1335. https://doi.org/10.3390/ANI12111335/S1. [Accessed 2023 Feb 15].

Moxley, R. A. (2000). Edema disease. *Veterinary Clinics of North America: Food Animal Practice, 16*(1), 175–185. https://doi.org/10.1016/S0749-0720(15)30142-0

Muñoz, M., Bozzi, R., García-Casco, J., Núñez, Y., Ribani, A., Franci, O., García, F., Škrlep, M., Schiavo, G., Bovo, S., et al. (2019). Genomic diversity, linkage disequilibrium and selection signatures in European local pig breeds assessed with a high density SNP chip. *Scientific Reports, 9*(1). https://doi.org/10.1038/s41598-019-49830-6

Nguyen, D. T., Kyooyeol, L., Choi, H., Choi, M. K., Le, M. T., Song, N., Kim, J. H., Seo, H. G., Oh, J. W., Lee, K., et al. (2012). The complete swine olfactory subgenome: Expansion of the olfactory gene repertoire in the pig genome. *BMC Genomics, 13*(1), 1–12. https://doi.org/10.1186/1471-2164-13-584/TABLES/6. [Accessed 2023 Feb 16].

Nonneman, D. J., & Lents, C. A. (2022). Functional genomics of reproduction in pigs: Are we there yet? *Molecular Reproduction and Development*. https://doi.org/10.1002/MRD.23625.. [Accessed 2023 Feb 17]

Norris, D., Ng, J., & Olushola, J. A. (2014). Genetic selection for docility: A review. *The Journal of Animal and Plant Science, 24*(2) https://www.researchgate.net/publication/286098749 [Accessed 2023 Feb 17]

Nurk, S. et al (2022). The complete sequence of a human genome. *Science, 376*:44–53. https://doi.org/10.1126/science.abj6987

Olsen, P., & Borit, M. (2013). How to define traceability. *Trends in Food Science and Technology, 29*(2), 142–150. https://doi.org/10.1016/J.TIFS.2012.10.003

Owen, B. L., Montgomery, J. L., Ramsey, C. B., & Miller, M. F. (2000). Preslaughter resting and hot-fat trimming effects on the incidence of pale, soft and exudative (PSE) pork and ham processing characteristics. *Meat Science, 54*(3), 221–229. https://doi.org/10.1016/S0309-1740(99)00083-2. [Accessed 2023 Feb 14].

Patience, J. F., Rossoni-Serão, M. C., & Gutiérrez, N. A. (2015). A review of feed efficiency in swine: Biology and application. *Journal of Animal Science and Biotechnology, 6*(1), 1–9. https://doi.org/10.1186/S40104-015-0031-2/TABLES/4. [Accessed 2023 Feb 17].

Poklukar, K., Čandek-Potokar, M., Lukač, N. B., Tomažin, U., & Škrlep, M. (2020). Lipid deposition and metabolism in local and modern pig breeds: A review. *Animals, 10*(3), 424. https://doi.org/10.3390/ANI10030424. [Accessed 2023 Feb 16].

Putz, A. M., Harding, J. C. S., Dyck, M. K., Fortin, F., Plastow, G. S., & Dekkers, J. C. M. (2019). Novel resilience phenotypes using feed intake data from a natural disease challenge model in wean-to-finish pigs. *Frontiers in Genetics, 10*(JAN), 660. https://doi.org/10.3389/FGENE.2018.00660/BIBTEX

Ramos, A. M., Crooijmans, R. P. M. A., Affara, N. A., Amaral, A. J., Archibald, A. L., Beever, J. E., Bendixen, C., Churcher, C., Clark, R., Dehais, P., et al. (2009). Design of a high density

SNP genotyping assay in the pig using SNPs identified and characterized by next generation sequencing technology. *PLoS One, 4*(8), e6524. https://doi.org/10.1371/JOURNAL.PONE.0006524. [Accessed 2023 Feb 17].

Rauw, W. M., Rydhmer, L., Kyriazakis, I., Øverland, M., Gilbert, H., Dekkers, J. C. M., Hermesch, S., Bouquet, A., Gómez Izquierdo, E., Louveau, I., & Gomez-Raya, L. (2020). Prospects for sustainability of pig production in relation to climate change and novel feed resources. *Journal of the Science of Food and Agriculture, 100*(9), 3575–3586. https://doi.org/10.1002/jsfa.10338

Reiner, G. (2016). Genetic resistance – an alternative for controlling PRRS? *Porcine Health Management, 2*(1), 1–11. https://doi.org/10.1186/S40813-016-0045-Y. [Accessed 2023 Feb 16].

Robic, A., Larzul, C., & Bonneau, M. (2008). Genetic and metabolic aspects of androstenone and skatole deposition in pig adipose tissue: A review (Open Access publication). *Genetics Selection Evolution, 40*(1), 1–15. https://doi.org/10.1186/1297-9686-40-1-129. [Accessed 2023 Feb 17].

Rohrer, G. A., Brown-Brandl, T., Rempel, L. A., Schneider, J. F., & Holl, J. (2013). Genetic analysis of behavior traits in swine production. *Livestock Science, 157*(1), 28–37. https://doi.org/10.1016/J.LIVSCI.2013.07.002

Rothschild, M. F., & Plastow, G. S. (2014). Applications of genomics to improve livestock in the developing world. *Livestock Science, 166*(1), 76–83. https://doi.org/10.1016/J.LIVSCI.2014.03.020

Russo, V., Fontanesi, L., Davoli, R., Chiofalo, L., Liotta, L., & Zumbo, A. (2004). Analisi di alcune mutazioni puntiformi in geni maggiori e geni candidati per caratteri produttivi nella razza suina nero siciliano. *Italian Journal of Animal Science, 3*(1), 19–29. https://doi.org/10.4081/IJAS.2004.19. [Accessed 2023 Feb 13].

Rydhmer, L., & Canario, L. (2022). Behavioral genetics in pigs and relations to welfare. *Genetics and the Behavior of Domestic Animals*, 3rd ed. 325–375. https://doi.org/10.1016/B978-0-323-85752-9.00008-1.

Samorè, A. B., & Fontanesi, L. (2016). Genomic selection in pigs: State of the art and perspectives. *Italian Journal of Animal Science, 15*(2), 211–232. https://doi.org/10.1080/1828051X.2016.1172034. [Accessed 2023 Feb 17].

Sanglard, L. P., Fernando, R. L., Gray, K. A., Linhares, D. C. L., Dekkers, J. C. M., Niederwerder, M. C., & Serão, N. V. L. (2020). Genetic analysis of antibody response to porcine reproductive and respiratory syndrome vaccination as an indicator trait for reproductive performance in commercial sows. *Frontiers in Genetics, 11*, 1011. https://doi.org/10.3389/FGENE.2020.01011/BIBTEX

Saravanan, K. A., Panigrahi, M., Kumar, H., Bhushan, B., Dutt, T., & Mishra, B. P. (2020). Selection signatures in livestock genome: A review of concepts, approaches and applications. *Livestock Science, 241*, 104257. https://doi.org/10.1016/J.LIVSCI.2020.104257

Schiavo, G., Bovo, S., Muñoz, M., Ribani, A., Alves, E., Araújo, J. P., Bozzi, R., Čandek-Potokar, M., Charneca, R., Fernandez, A. I., et al. (2021). Runs of homozygosity provide a genome landscape picture of inbreeding and genetic history of European autochthonous and commercial pig breeds. *Animals Genetics, 52*(2), 155–170. https://doi.org/10.1111/AGE.13045. [Accessed 2023 Feb 15].

Schwartz, R., & Teramo, K. A. (2000). A DNA polymorphism influencing α(1,2)fucosyltransferase activity of the pig FUT1 enzyme determines susceptibility of small intestinal epithelium to Escherichia coli F18 adhesion. *Immunogenetics, 52*(1–2), 129–136. https://doi.org/10.1007/S002510000263/METRICS. [Accessed 2023 Feb 15].

Serão, N. V. L., Kemp, R. A., Mote, B. E., Willson, P., Harding, J. C. S., Bishop, S. C., Plastow, G. S., & Dekkers, J. C. M. (2016). Genetic and genomic basis of antibody response to porcine reproductive and respiratory syndrome (PRRS) in gilts and sows. *Genetics Selection Evolution, 48*(1), 1–15. https://doi.org/10.1186/S12711-016-0230-0/FIGURES/4. [Accessed 2023 Feb 16].

Serão, N. V. L., Matika, O., Kemp, R. A., Harding, J. C. S., Bishop, S. C., Plastow, G. S., & Dekkers, J. C. M. (2014). Genetic analysis of reproductive traits and antibody response in a

PRRS outbreak herd. *Journal of Animal Science, 92*(7), 2905–2921. https://doi.org/10.2527/JAS.2014-7821. [Accessed 2023 Feb 16].

Sharmaa, A., Lee, J. S., Dang, C. G., Sudrajad, P., Kim, H. C., Yeon, S. H., Kang, H. S., & Lee, S. H. (2015). Stories and challenges of genome wide association studies in livestock – A review. *Asian Australasian Journal of Animal Sciences, 28*(10), 1371. https://doi.org/10.5713/AJAS.14.0715. [Accessed 2022 Nov 28].

Soleimani, T., Hermesch, S., & Gilbert, H. (2021). Economic and environmental assessments of combined genetics and nutrition optimization strategies to improve the efficiency of sustainable pork production. *Journal of Animal Science, 99*(3), 1–14. https://doi.org/10.1093/JAS/SKAB051. [Accessed 2023 Feb 17].

Spötter, A., & Distl, O. (2006). Genetic approaches to the improvement of fertility traits in the pig. *The Veterinary Journal, 172*(2), 234–247. https://doi.org/10.1016/J.TVJL.2005.11.013

Stalder, K. J., Lacy, R. C., Cross, T. L., & Conatser, G. E. (2003). Financial impact of average parity of culled females in a breed-to-wean swine operation using replacement gilt net present value analysis. *Journal of Swine Health and Production, 11*(2), 69–74. http://www.farmdoc.uiuc.edu/marketing/livestockoutlook/0401hog_text.html [Accessed 2023 Feb 17]

St-Pierre, N. R., Cobanov, B., & Schnitkey, G. (2003). Economic losses from heat stress by US livestock industries. *Journal of Dairy Science, 86*(SUPPL. 1), E52–E77. https://doi.org/10.3168/JDS.S0022-0302(03)74040-5

Tait-Burkard, C., Doeschl-Wilson, A., McGrew, M. J., Archibald, A. L., Sang, H. M., Houston, R. D., Whitelaw, C. B., & Watson, M. (2018). Livestock 2.0 – Genome editing for fitter, healthier, and more productive farmed animals. *Genome Biology, 19*(1), 1–11. https://doi.org/10.1186/S13059-018-1583-1/TABLES/2. [Accessed 2023 Feb 13].

Tart, J. K., Johnson, R. K., Bundy, J. W., Ferdinand, N. N., McKnite, A. M., Wood, J. R., Miller, P. S., Rothschild, M. F., Spangler, M. L., Garrick, D. J., et al. (2013). Genome-wide prediction of age at puberty and reproductive longevity in sows. *Animal Genetics, 44*(4), 387–397. https://doi.org/10.1111/AGE.12028. [Accessed 2023 Feb 17].

Tinarelli, S., Ribani, A., Utzeri, V. J., Taurisano, V., Bovo, C., Dall'olio, S., Nen, F., Bovo, S., Schiavo, G., Gallo, M., & Fontanesi, L. (2021). Redefinition of the mora Romagnola pig breed herd book standard based on DNA markers useful to authenticate its "mono-breed" products: An example of sustainable conservation of a livestock genetic resource. *Animals, 11*(2), 1–16. https://doi.org/10.3390/ani11020526

Travers, A., & Muskhelishvili, G. (2015). DNA structure and function. *FEBS Journal, 282*(12), 2279–2295. https://doi.org/10.1111/FEBS.13307. [Accessed 2023 Feb 6].

Trevisan, L., & Brum, J. S. (2020). Incidence of pale, soft and exudative (PSE) pork meat in reason of extrinsic stress factors. *An Acad Bras Cienc, 92*(3), 1–9. https://doi.org/10.1590/0001-3765202020190086. [Accessed 2023 Feb 14].

VanderWaal, K., & Deen, J. (2018). Global trends in infectious diseases of swine. *Proceedings of the National Academy of Sciences, 115*(45), 11495–11500. https://doi.org/10.1073/PNAS.1806068115/SUPPL_FILE/PNAS.1806068115.SD01.CSV. [Accessed 2023 Feb 16].

Vögeli, P., Meijerink, E., Fries, R., Neuenschwander, S., Vorländer, N., Stranzinger, G., & Bertschinger, H. U. (1997). A molecular test for the detection of E. coli F18 receptors: a breakthrough in the struggle against edema disease and post-weaning diarrhea in swine. *Schweiz Arch Tierheilkd, 139*(11), 479–484. https://europepmc.org/article/med/9480539 [Accessed 2023 Feb 16]

Walker, L. R., Engle, T. B., Vu, H., Tosky, E. R., Nonneman, D. J., Smith, T. P. L., Borza, T., Burkey, T. E., Plastow, G. S., Kachman, S. D., & Ciobanu, D. C. (2018). Synaptogyrin-2 influences replication of Porcine circovirus 2. *PLoS Genet, 14*(10), e1007750. https://doi.org/10.1371/JOURNAL.PGEN.1007750. [Accessed 2023 Feb 16].

Whitworth, K. M., Rowland, R. R. R., Ewen, C. L., Trible, B. R., Kerrigan, M. A., Cino-Ozuna, A. G., Samuel, M. S., Lightner, J. E., McLaren, D. G., Mileham, A. J., et al. (2016). Gene-edited pigs are protected from porcine reproductive and respiratory syndrome virus. *Nature Biotechnology, 34*(1), 20–22. https://doi.org/10.1038/NBT.3434. [Accessed 2023 Feb 16].

Zak, L. J., Gaustad, A. H., Bolarin, A., Broekhuijse, M. L. W. J., Walling, G. A., & Knol, E. F. (2017). Genetic control of complex traits, with a focus on reproduction in pigs. *Molecular Reproduction and Development, 84*(9), 1004–1011. https://doi.org/10.1002/MRD.22875. [Accessed 2023 Feb 17].

Zhao, F., McParland, S., Kearney, F., Du, L., & Berry, D. P. (2015). Detection of selection signatures in dairy and beef cattle using high-density genomic information. *Genetics Selection Evolution, 47*(1), 1–12. https://doi.org/10.1186/S12711-015-0127-3/TABLES/4. [Accessed 2023 Feb 16].

Zumbo, A., Sutera, A. M., Tardiolo, G., & D'Alessandro, E. (2020). Sicilian black pig: An overview. *Animals, 10*(12), 2326. https://doi.org/10.3390/ANI10122326. [Accessed 2023 Feb 15].

The Quality of Heavy Pork Meat: The Role of PDO Production Specifications

Giulia Ferronato, Federico Froldi, and Aldo Prandini

1 Consumption of Pork Meat

Meat is consumed worldwide due to its relevant nutritional value as a protein source. According to population growth, meat consumption has increased over the years from 7.14E+07 tons in 1961 to 3.57E+08 tons in 2021. The share of pork has represented over the years about 37% and nowadays 34% (2021) of the total worldwide meat consumption. Major consumption was associated until the 1990s with the European continent, followed by Asia and America. Since 1994, Asian consumption has seen exponential growth to the present day, thus surpassing European consumption since 1991, which, on the other hand, along with American consumption, has seen a downward trend. Increased consumption has also characterised the African continent with steady and gradual growth to the present day. This shows how meat consumption has decreased in developed countries while it has increased in developing ones, a sign of the increasing urbanisation and ability to purchase meat. The increase in production directly reflects an increased pork meat demand and consumption level. With regard specifically to the European Union (27, EU), pork production has gone from 8.70+06 tons (1961) to 2.36E+08 tons (2021) of meat. As for Italy, production started from 3.95E+05 tons, increasing to 1.65E+06 in 2013, after which a reduction began that has settled to date with 1.35E +06 in 2021 (FAOSTAT, 2023).

Since 13/01/2022, the author is affiliated with the Department of Civil Engineering, Architecture, Environment, Land Planning, and Mathematics (DICATAM), Università degli Studi di Brescia, Brescia, Italy; email: giulia.ferronato@unibs.it

G. Ferronato (✉) · F. Froldi · A. Prandini
Department of Animal Science, Food and Nutrition (DiANA), Università Cattolica del Sacro Cuore, Piacenza, Italy

A. M. Fellegara et al. (eds.), *Sustainable Transition of Meat and Cured Meat Supply Chain*, CSR, Sustainability, Ethics & Governance,
https://doi.org/10.1007/978-3-031-34977-5_6

Currently, the average global per capita consumption of pork, expressed as carcass weight, is 16.62 kg/capita/day in 2020, ranging from 1.55 kg/capita/day in Africa to 39.21 kg/capita/day in the EU (27). Italy records, for the same year, a consumption of 32.88 kg/capita/day. Regarding the total per capita meat consumption, pork meat represents 25% globally, 39% in the EU and 36% in Italy. This corresponds at the global level to an average intake of 4.3 g/capita/day, ranging from 0.47 in Africa to 10.87 in the EU of protein and an average intake of 10.92 g/capita/day, ranging from 1.4 in Africa to 17.42 in EU (27). In Italy, it was equal to 8.59 g/capita/day of protein and 11.76 g/capita/day of fat (FAOSTAT, 2023). This is in line with the average protein requirement of about 50 g/day per capita, according to USDA (2020).

Considering the Italian national scenario, on the total meat production, expressed as live weight, pork meat represented 49% of the total share, resulting in mainly allocated to the processing industry instead of fresh consumption (about 83% of available meat due to the large production of cured products. This also influenced the export share, covering 68% of the total export value. The overall Italian meat consumption is represented by 48% of pork meat, fresh or cured (Ferronato et al., 2021).

The role of pork in culture is very strong and related to specific production conditions in the context of the Po Valley. Initially, swine were raised domestically in a semi-wild system for family subsistence by feeding the animals with waste and by-product products. After that, commercial farms began to spring up near dairy cheese factories in order to reuse by-products from the production of PDO Grana Padano, PDO Parmigiano Reggiano and other PDO cheeses, such as whey and amortise production costs. To date, the swine system is markedly more organised for each of its breeding stages. Farms are specialised and can manage large herds to optimise production performance and management costs.

2 Nutritional Value of Pork Meat

From a nutritional point of view, even if pork meat myoglobin content is lower than beef but much higher than chicken, is considered red meat. One-hundred loin meat contains about 13.32 g of protein and 27.92 g of fats, mainly monounsaturated (6.19 g) and saturated (5.23 g), and 36% and 29% of vitamin B6 and 12, respectively, of adult recommendations. Moreover, considering mineral content, 100 g of loin covers 5% of phosphorous requirements, 25% of zinc, and 7% iron. Instead, cured meat's nutritional value varies according to the single product, which turns out to be influenced mainly by the cut of meat used. For example, 100 g of PDO Parma ham contains 18 g of fats, 26 g of proteins, and 4.4 g of salts; meanwhile, PDO "Coppa piacentina", made with muscles at the back of the pig's neck, contains 30 g of fats, 24 g of proteins, and 4.8 g of salts. In general, it should be kept in mind that the nutritional value varies depending on the specific muscle (Kim et al., 2008). The anatomical location is related to a specific physiological role influencing muscles' contractile and metabolic properties (Lebret & Čandek-Potokar, 2021). Glycolytic and oxidative metabolisms influence fat's colour, exudation, quantity, and distribution and characterise white and red muscles, respectively. Moreover, the fat content and type (i.e., back-fat, intramuscular, or intermuscular), which in turn are a function of the slaughter weight, breed, sex and feeding strategy to which the animal was subjected. This then goes on to influence the specific characteristics of cured meats, which are characterised by the use of specific muscle regions.

Overwear, pork meat quality could not be intended only from a nutritional perspective but must be comprehended by a multidimensional approach that includes the commercial value of carcass and technological (i.e., suitability for processing and seasoning) attributes (Lebret & Čandek-Potokar, 2021). The achievement of both nutritional and technological attributes can be modulated during the industrial processing phase but is known to be directly influenced by the strategies adopted during the breeding phase.

In the European contest, several quality labels for pork products are registered to enhance the specificity and typicity of these products. Among them, we could find Protected Designation of Origin (PDO), Protected Geographical Indication (PGI), and Traditional Speciality Guaranteed (TSG) (European Parliament and the Council, 2012). These designations of origin serve to demonstrate the strong connection to the product's territory of origin, especially in PDO labels. This is reinforced through descriptions of farming methods (facilities and feeding), animal genetics that can be used, and meat production and processing processes. The major factors influencing commercial, organoleptic, nutritional, and technological properties are genotype, sex, age, and weight at slaughtering, rearing conditions, and diet.

3 The Role of Pork Meat Production Specification

Based on the characteristics that the final product must have and the type of product, such as cured meat or cooked meat, products made from whole pieces or cuts or sausages, the production specifications go on to regulate the animal genotypes allowed for breeding, the area of production, weight and age at slaughtering, the breeding management techniques and type of feed used, and of course, the processing and maturing stages.

For cooked products such as cooked ham, specific requirements must be reached to consider suitable meat. These depend on the quality category of the final product, which in Italy are: "prosciutto cotto", "prosciutto cotto scelto" e "prosciutto cotto di alta qualità" (Gazzetta Ufficiale, 2005). The quality indicators are represented by: (a) ham weight, (b) presence of defects (hematomas), (c) thickness and colour of subcutaneous fat (could be lower and white), (d) colour of muscles (not pale or heterogeneous), (e) ultimate pH of meat (minimal value of 5.60 for a superior quality category), and (f) presence and extent of the so-called PSE (Pale, Soft and Exudative meat) gene and destructed meat defect (Lebret & Čandek-Potokar, 2022). While in the case of cured products, such as cured ham, the specific requirements are

(a) weight of fresh ham (above 10 kg to ensure proper meat maturation and optimal fat distribution), (b) subcutaneous fat thickness (minimal of 20–30 mm to avoid excessive weight loss during seasoning and to avoid excessive salt absorption), (c) absence of defects (skin lesions and hematomas), and (d) fatty acid composition of subcutaneous fat to avoid higher lipid peroxidation (Mipaaf, 2009; Lebret & Čandek-Potokar, 2022). The specific requirements thus directly influence what breeds are allowed and how they are raised, especially in terms of feeding strategy.

Now we will focus on the specification of cured ham as one of the most important PDOs regarding pork products and that differentiates Italy in the European and world context.

3.1 Genetic

First of all, specifications regulate the genotypes allowed for the breeding of pigs because of breed and genotype are basic prerequisites for obtaining suitable animal carcasses in terms of fat mass content and localisation and lean mass content. Pigs destined for PDO production are characterised by a slaughtering weight ideally higher than 160 kg and are identified as "heavy pigs". On the other hand, pigs slaughtered at a lower weight of about 110 kg are identified as "light swine" and are mainly intended for meat production for fresh consumption.

Only genetic types able to reach before mentioned weight can therefore guarantee carcasses that fall within the U, R, O classes of the SEUROP classification (Council Regulation, 2007). This classification considers the estimated lean-meat content (percentage) of the carcass and definite classes as: S $>$ 60%, E: 55–60%, U: 50–55%, R: 45–50%, O: 40–45%, and P $<$ 40%. From this, it can be seen that carcasses suitable for PDO productions must neither exceed nor be deficient in fat coverage, with an average fat percentage of about 50% (European Parliament and of the Council, 2013).

Nowadays, offspring of boars belonging to the Italian Large White, Italian Landrace, and Italian Duroc breeds (pure or hybrid) and sows of the Italian Large White and Italian Landrace breeds (pure or hybrid) are allowed. Hybrid breeds are subject to selection and/or crossbreeding schemes of Italian Large White, Italian Landrace, and Italian Duroc breed implemented with purposes compatible with the Libro Genealogico Italiano (ANAS, Associazione Nazionale Allevatori Suini) for heavy pig production. Subjects of traditional autochthonous breeds registered with the same book are also allowed. Therefore, all subjects not belonging to these breeds and hybrids, subjects carrying stress-sensitive genes (PSS—Porcine Stress Syndrome), and boars and sows are excluded.

The ability to use only specific breeds is due to the relationship between genotype and meat's sensory properties, such as appearance, texture, and flavour. The halothane gene and RH gene influence *post-mortem* muscle glycolysis (Ciobanu et al., 2011). This directly affects pH and water-holding capacity of muscle, thus altering the future seasoning process. In fact, the breeds excluded are those carrying these genes and being breeds characterised by much leaner meat that would not be suitable for curing processes. Duroc boar is principally used for the increased presence of intramuscular fat capable of thus improving meat tenderness (Mote & Rothschild, 2020). Furthermore, within the same breed, we can find different lines of selection (i.e., Italian, Belgian), but not all are allowed as previously specified. This is because some lines have been selected for a higher percentage of muscle mass and reduced fat content, better feed conversion index, and higher growth rates, resulting in meat unsuitable for sausage production. In fact, functional parameters for cured meat production are included in the genetic selection plans of the allowed breeds (i.e., back-fat, intramuscular fat, thigh weight, water-holding capacity, thigh weight loss) (Faure et al., 2013).

These genotype-related constraints are instrumental in obtaining individuals with carcass weights between 110.1 kg and 168 kg. This carcass weight specification is newly introduced in the face of a change in the PDO Parma Ham specification; the previous version reported a live weight at the slaughter of 160 kg (±10%). This change is necessary to ensure an adequate weight of the ham legs intended specifically for the production of PDO Parma ham and with an adequate thickness of covering fat (not less than 22 mm). Genotype plays a key role in ensuring these characteristics at a specific minimum slaughter age (9 months) through a specific feeding strategy. Genetic selection of swine through the years has resulted in improvements from a production point of view, both in terms of product performance and feed and growth efficiency, in the main breeds used, which have thus distinguished themselves well from the slower-growing local native breeds. This resulted in a general improvement in carcass lean meat percentage (Bidanel et al., 2020).

3.2 Sex

In addition to genotype, it is well known how the sex of the animal can influence carcass composition since growth and fat deposition rates vary between male and female subjects. Specifically, entire male pigs are the leanest and most efficient, followed by females and castrated males (Pauly et al., 2012). On the contrary, the latter tend to be earlier in terms of growth and deposit fat mass earlier, risking exceeding the correct weight at slaughter at given age. Considering the carcass requirements and the minimum age for slaughtering 9 months, according to specifications, the choice of appropriate genetics is critical. According to PDO regulations, no sex discrimination is made except that whole males, boars, and sows are excluded at the end of their productive careers. In the specific case of the uncastrated male, this is related to the "boar odour" factor caused by hormones such as androsterone and skatole. These, accumulating in the fat layer, cause an odour in the meat that is unpleasant to the consumer. The former can be modulated through genetic selection, while the latter relates to environmental breeding conditions. However, since these are related to each other, breeding whole males is complex, considering the risk of increased aggression of such individuals towards fellow animals or human handlers (Zamaratskaia & Squires, 2009). In addition, the need for separate-sex farm management to avoid unwanted mating. The breeding at "separate sex" (female *versus* castrated males) rearing from post-weaning phase to fattening one could also be adopted to manage better animal feeding strategy and satisfy nutrient requirements to have homogeneous groups of animals by weight at slaughter time.

3.3 Production System and Housing Conditions

Pig production system and housing conditions are also factors able to impact the organoleptic profile of pork meat. Intensive or extensive systems and indoor or outdoor systems influence the pig's physical activity, which could affect the muscle texture and colour, resulting in redder meat and improved texture in extensive and/or outdoor systems. The associated environmental conditions, such as temperature, could also influence the fat content and growth rate (Lebret, 2008). The effect of environmental conditions may vary depending on the breed bred and their adaptability. Native breeds are more suitable for extensive and outdoor breeding systems than commercial hybrids that are more sensitive to extreme weather conditions (cold or heat), thus negatively affecting their growth performance.

Among breeding system techniques, the management of feeding and nutritional strategy is fundamental to preserving animal welfare conditions, explicating the production potential and obtaining meat with certain organoleptic characteristics. Each commercial hybrid or pure breed turns out to be characterised by specific energy, protein, and amino acid requirements for each growth stage. This is essential for proper morpho-functional development, fulfillment of genetic potential, and obtaining carcasses suitable for slaughter. Therefore, genetic suppliers provide manuals for proper nutritional management regulating the daily amount of food, protein, and amino acid intake, fat, fibre, and mineral and vitamin intake.

3.4 Feeding and Nutritional Strategy

The feeding strategy is a key point of PDO production regulations. These define the raw materials that can be used, their quantity, and their geographical origin. The feeds must come from the geographical breeding area, the same area where the animals can be raised. In the face of recent changes in the specification for PDO Parma Ham, it is made explicit that 100% of the raw materials must come from the designated geographical area, except for special climatic or commercial conditions. However, the link to the territory for 50% of the dry matter must be respected. The changes made included the exclusion of certain feeds from the previous version of the same specification order to increase the product's connection to the local area.

However, some were retained, although not local, due to the technical impossibility of the territory to ensure complete self-supply. Allowable raw materials and their quantity are regulated for the leaning and fattening phase, while there are no limitations during the pre- and post-weaning phases.

During the first phase of life and post-weaning time, providing adequate feeds is essential to promote correct growth and gastrointestinal tract development. The piglet goes from milk to solid feed rich in protein, fat, and fermentable carbohydrates and low in fibre. With increasing age and solid food intake, there is also a development of digestive capacity and secretion of pancreatic enzymes functional in digesting food and fibre. Feeding is at will to avoid food deficiencies. Once the weaning and growth phase has passed, there is a need for a change in feeding strategy, which changes from *ad libitum* to a rationed system. This is necessary to limit energy intake while still meeting energy needs. Diets of fattening animals are most rich in fibre with the purpose of stimulating satiety and avoiding stress on the animal and avoid excessive fattening of animals before the minimum age for slaughter.

Diet-related constraints are due to the fact that diet is the major contributing factor to body composition, carcass compliance, meat organoleptic properties, and suitability for the curing process. Observance of energy and protein requirements is critical for proper body development and respect for animal welfare. Moreover, proper dietary management is essential to the reduction of health issues and, thus, to the reduction of drug use. In addition, optimising amino acid content and using digestible protein are critical for reducing dietary protein content and nitrogen loss in feces. This has positive implications both in economic terms for the farmer and in terms of environmental sustainability.

The constraints placed by specifications are formulated to exclude the use of feeds that can change the flavour and odour of meat through either the direct transfer of flavours or absorption of love-active microbial metabolites in the gastrointestinal tract and then to modulate the amount of fat and its fatty acid composition. In swine, dietary lipids are not modified before absorption and incorporation into fat tissue so dietary fatty acids intake could predict tissue lipid composition (Scollan et al., 2017). In fact, the thickness of the fat cover of fresh ham should be about 30 mm. This is also evaluated in terms of consistency by determining iodine number and/or linoleic acid content. As per the specification, the iodine number, a generic indicator of fat unsaturation level, must not exceed values of 70, while the linoleic acid content must not exceed 15% of total fatty acids. To this end, in addition to deciding which feeds can be used, the amount is regulated to meet the maximum 5% crude fat intake and the maximum 2% linoleic acid of the diet's dry matter.

The control of diet fat content is fundamental to the animal fattening process, particularly the regulation of linoleic acid, which is functional in controlling back-fat consistency. This is a polyunsaturated fatty acid that influences the consistency of fat and oxidation. A high content of linoleic acid corresponds to a soft fat unsuitable for the curing process and may undergo rancidity processes leading to the appearance of unpleasant odours to the consumer. In addition, oxidation processes lead to a general worsening of the nutritional value of the care due to the loss of the vitamin components and the appearance of toxic molecules (Paniangvait et al., 1995; Gray et al., 1996). From the human nutritional point of view, however, high polyunsaturated fatty acid contents are preferred for their positive effects on human health, such as lowering the risk of cardiovascular problems and cholesterol levels (Caggiula & Mustad, 1997). To compensate for the negative effect of linoleic acid in the meat shelf-life, dietary antioxidant (Vitamin E and tocopherol) in swine nutrition has been investigated. Particular attention has been given to *n-3* fatty acids; however, research shows mixed results, and it is unclear what dose of this fatty acid must be supplied by food to have a significant increase in meat (Dugan et al., 2015). However, dietary strategies to increase the content of polyunsaturated fatty acids in meat for the benefit of human health cannot be adopted in the rearing of heavy pigs intended to produce cured hams. They can be used in raising pigs intended for the production of fresh meat or cooked ham.

Compared to the previous specification, the proposed changes see an increase in the amount of specific feeds to compensate for the reduction in fat mass observed in current animal genetics compared to the past. In particular, an increase in corn gluten feed has been proposed to take advantage of the protein content and digestibility of the protein. The increase of cereals such as maize, sorghum, barley, wheat, and triticale for hedging fat protection allowed the use of maize silage and threshing and distillers for fibre quality and fat source. Whole-maize mash as a substitute source of fibre over bran, the use of canola was also introduced from scratch due to the presence of new genetic varieties lacking glucosinolates and erucic acid, which were found to be anti-nutritional factors for pigs.

Cereals are the base of swine nutrition, particularly during the fattening phase. The most used are maize, followed by barley and wheat, depending on the geographical availability and market price. However, these are lower in fibre, essential to prevent digestive disease due to grain flour's higher fermentability. So fibre feeds, such as beet pulps and wheat bran, are largely used to satisfy fibre requirements (Galassi et al., 2004). The admission of maize silage could benefit animals and farmers from an economic point of view. This feed is higher in fibre content favouring satiety and preventing gastric disease (Mason et al., 2013).

Among protein sources, the major is soybean as a soybean extraction meal, which could be considered a by-product of soybean oil production. This primarily is cultivated in North and South America regions, and the transport to European countries mainly affects pork meat production's environmental sustainability. The possibility of using other co-products such as canola or corn gluten feed could ameliorate sustainability. Among meat proteins, not as much content, collagen has been investigated due to its influence on meat tenderness. This result could be modulated through correct protein and amino acid requirements, which are fundamental to the demand for glycine and proline amino acids (Li & Wu, 2018).

At last, the possibility of using minerals, additives, and vitamins was included among the foods allowed to remain excluded in the fattening phase by-products of the confectionery and bakery industry and other former foods. Considering micronutrients, pork meat could be considered a precious source of selenium for consumers. So, the Se supply has been largely investigated to improve the meat content as this trace element appears to improve meat shelf-life and antioxidant stability (Calvo et al., 2017; Silva et al., 2019; Zhang et al., 2020). Regarding the use of by-products, this could reduce food waste and improve the environmental sustainability of livestock production in terms of global warming potential (zu Ermgassen et al., 2016; Luciano et al., 2020); however, the variability of products over time and organoleptic characteristics could adversely affect the growth performance of the animals and alter the organoleptic characteristics of the meat (Luciano et al., 2022), worsening the environmental impact categories of water acidification and eutrophication (Mackenzie et al., 2016).

4 Conclusions

To obtain good-quality pork, it is essential to respect the animal's welfare through its rearing stage and during the slaughtering and meat processing stages. In particular, the rearing methods and the environmental conditions to which the animal is subjected are crucial for its proper growth and to ensure a quality end product with well-defined characteristics. For this objective, nutrition is essential to ensure its desired nutritional and technological properties, especially in the context of the designation of origin products. The specific directions given in the PDO product specifications serve to ensure the nutritional and organoleptic characteristics of the cured product and its palatability to the consumer. Obviously, this also limits the possible nutritional strategies that can be adopted to change the chemical composition of pork.

References

Bidanel, J. P., Silalahi, P., Tribout, T., Canario, L., Ducos, A., Garreau, H., Gilbert, H., Larzul, C., Milan, D., Riquet, J., Schwob, S., Mercat, M. J., Hassenfratz, C., Bouquet, A., Bazin, C., & Bidanel, J. (2020). Fifty years of pig breeding in France: Outcomes and perspectives. *Inrae Productions Animales, 33*, 1–16. https://doi.org/10.20870/productions-animales.2020.33.1.3092

Caggiula, A. W., & Mustad, V. A. (1997). Effects of dietary fat and fatty acids on coronary artery disease risk and total and lipoprotein cholesterol concentrations: Epidemiologic studies. *The American Journal of Clinical Nutrition, 65*, 1597S–1610S. https://doi.org/10.1093/AJCN/65.5.1597S

Calvo, L., Segura, J., Toldrá, F., Flores, M., Rodríguez, A. I., López-Bote, C. J., & Rey, A. I. (2017). Meat quality, free fatty acid concentration, and oxidative stability of pork from animals fed diets containing different sources of selenium. *Food Science and Technology International, 23*, 716–728. https://doi.org/10.1177/1082013217718964

Ciobanu, D. C., Lonergan, S. M., & Huff-Lonergan, E. J. (2011). Genetics of meat quality and carcass traits. *Genet Pig Second Ed*, 355–389. https://doi.org/10.1079/9781845937560.0355

Council Regulation. (2007). *Regulation N. 1234/2007 establishing a common organisation of agricultural markets and on specific provisions for certain agricultural products (Single CMO Regulation)*

Dugan, M. E. R., Vahmani, P., Turner, T. D., Mapiye, C., Juárez, M., Prieto, N., Beaulieu, A. D., Zijlstra, R. T., Patience, J. F., & Aalhus, J. L. (2015). Pork as a source of omega-3 (n-3) fatty acids. *Journal of Clinical Medicine, 4*, 1999–2011. https://doi.org/10.3390/JCM4121956

European Parliament and of the Council. (2012). *Regulation (EU) No 1151/2012 of the European Parliament and of the Council of 21 November 2012 on quality schemes for agricultural products and foodstuffs*

European Parliament and of the Council. (2013). *Regulation (EU) No 1308/2013 of the European Parliament and of the Council of 17 December 2013 establishing a common organisation of the markets in agricultural products and repealing Council Regulations (EEC)* No 922/72, (EEC) No 234/79, (EC) No 1037/2001

FAOSTAT. (2023). *Crops and livestock products*. Accessed Nov 1, 2022, from https://www.fao.org/faostat/en/#data/QCL

Faure, J., Lefaucheur, L., Bonhomme, N., Ecolan, P., Meteau, K., Coustard, S. M., Kouba, M., Gilbert, H., & Lebret, B. (2013). Consequences of divergent selection for residual feed intake in pigs on muscle energy metabolism and meat quality. *Meat Science, 93*, 37–45. https://doi.org/10.1016/J.MEATSCI.2012.07.006

Ferronato, G., Corrado, S., De Laurentiis, V., & Sala, S. (2021). The Italian meat production and consumption system assessed combining material flow analysis and life cycle assessment. *Journal of Cleaner Production, 321*, 128705. https://doi.org/10.1016/j.jclepro.2021.128705

Galassi, G., Crovetto, G. M., Rapetti, L., & Tamburini, A. (2004). Energy and nitrogen balance in heavy pigs fed different fibre sources. *Livestock Production Science, 85*, 253–262. https://doi.org/10.1016/S0301-6226(03)00124-6

Gazzetta Ufficiale. (2005). *Decreto del Ministero delle attività produttive del 21settembre 2005 sulla produzione e la vendita di alcuni salumi*

Gray, J. I., Gomaa, E. A., & Buckley, D. J. (1996). Oxidative quality and shelf life of meats. *Meat Science, 43*, 111–123. https://doi.org/10.1016/0309-1740(96)00059-9

Kim, J. H., Seong, P. N., Cho, S. H., Park, B. Y., Hah, K. H., Yu, L. H., Lim, D. G., Hwang, I. H., Kim, D. H., Lee, J. M., & Ahn, C. N. (2008). Characterization of nutritional value for twenty-one pork muscles. *Asian-Australasian Journal of Animal Sciences, 21*, 138–143. https://doi.org/10.5713/ajas.2008.70208

Lebret, B. (2008). Effects of feeding and rearing systems on growth, carcass composition and meat quality in pigs. *Animal, 2*, 1548–1558. https://doi.org/10.1017/S1751731108002796

Lebret, B., & Čandek-Potokar, M. (2021). Review: Pork quality attributes from farm to fork. Part I. Carcass and fresh meat. *Animal, 100402*. https://doi.org/10.1016/J.ANIMAL.2021.100402

Lebret, B., & Čandek-Potokar, M. (2022). Review: Pork quality attributes from farm to fork. Part II. Processed pork products. *Animal, 16*(Suppl 1). https://doi.org/10.1016/J.ANIMAL.2021.100383

Li, P., & Wu, G. (2018). Roles of dietary glycine, proline, and hydroxyproline in collagen synthesis and animal growth. *Amino Acids, 50*, 29–38. https://doi.org/10.1007/s00726-017-2490-6

Luciano, A., Espinosa, C. D., Pinotti, L., & Stein, H. H. (2022). Standardized total tract digestibility of phosphorus in bakery meal fed to pigs and effects of bakery meal on growth performance of weanling pigs. *Animal Feed Science and Technology, 284*, 115148. https://doi.org/10.1016/J.ANIFEEDSCI.2021.115148

Luciano, A., Tretola, M., Ottoboni, M., Baldi, A., Cattaneo, D., & Pinotti, L. (2020). Potentials and challenges of former food products (food leftover) as alternative feed ingredients. *Animals, 10*, 125. https://doi.org/10.3390/ANI10010125

Mackenzie, S. G., Leinonen, I., Ferguson, N., & Kyriazakis, I. (2016). Can the environmental impact of pig systems be reduced by utilising co-products as feed? *Journal of Cleaner Production, 115*, 172–181. https://doi.org/10.1016/J.JCLEPRO.2015.12.074

Mason, F., Pascotto, E., Zanfi, C., & Spanghero, M. (2013). Effect of dietary inclusion of whole ear corn silage on stomach development and gastric mucosa integrity of heavy pigs at slaughter. *Veterinary Journal, 198*, 717–719. https://doi.org/10.1016/j.tvjl.2013.09.054

Mipaaf. (2009). *Disciplinare di produzione della denominazione di origine protetta «Prosciutto di Parma»*

Mote, B. E., & Rothschild, M. F. (2020). Modern genetic and genomic improvement of the pig. *Animal Agriculture Sustainability, Challenges and Innovations*, 249–262. https://doi.org/10.1016/B978-0-12-817052-6.00014-8

Paniangvait, P., King, A. J., Jones, A. D., & German, B. G. (1995). Cholesterol oxides in foods of animal origin. *Journal of Food Science, 60*, 1159–1174. https://doi.org/10.1111/J.1365-2621.1995.TB04548.X

Pauly, C., Luginbühl, W., Ampuero, S., & Bee, G. (2012). Expected effects on carcass and pork quality when surgical castration is omitted—Results of a meta-analysis study. *Meat Science, 92*, 858–862. https://doi.org/10.1016/J.MEATSCI.2012.06.007

Scollan, N. D., Price, E. M., Morgan, S. A., Huws, S. A., & Shingfield, K. J. (2017). Can we improve the nutritional quality of meat? *The Proceedings of the Nutrition Society, 76*, 603–618. https://doi.org/10.1017/S0029665117001112

Silva, V. A., Bertechini, A. G., Clemente, A. H. S., de Freitas, L. F. V. B., Nogueira, B. R. F., de Oliveira, B. L., & Ramos, A. L. S. (2019). Different levels of selenomethionine on the meat quality and selenium deposition in tissue of finishing pigs. *Journal of Animal Physiology and Animal Nutrition (Berlin), 103*, 1866–1874. https://doi.org/10.1111/JPN.13179

USDA. (2020). *Dietary guidelines for americans make every bite count with the dietary guidelines.*

Zamaratskaia, G., & Squires, E. J. (2009). Biochemical, nutritional and genetic effects on boar taint in entire male pigs. *Animal, 3*, 1508–1521. https://doi.org/10.1017/S1751731108003674

Zhang, S., Xie, Y., Li, M., Yang, H., Li, S., Li, J., Xu, Q., Yang, W., & Jiang, S. (2020). Effects of different selenium sources on meat quality and shelf life of fattening pigs. *Animals, 10*, 615. https://doi.org/10.3390/ANI10040615

zu Ermgassen, E. K. H. J., Phalan, B., Green, R. E., & Balmford, A. (2016). Reducing the land use of EU pork production: Where there's swill, there's a way. *Food Policy, 58*, 35–48. https://doi.org/10.1016/J.FOODPOL.2015.11.001

Animal Welfare in Swine Production

Federico Froldi, Giulia Ferronato, and Aldo Prandini

1 Introduction

The last few decades have been characterised by growing public interest and concern about animal husbandry in terms of environmental sustainability and animal welfare. The latter has become increasingly important on a social and institutional level. Ensuring the protection of animals during their lives and productive careers has led to the involvement of experts from various disciplines, from veterinary medicine, humanities, sociology, economics and law, to proclaim an international measure of respect for animals.

In 1975, the Universal Declaration of Animal Rights (Unesco, 1978) was made in Paris, which paved the way for animal welfare legislation (Vipiana, 2022). Europe, in this sense, began a legislative process that aims to raise awareness in the livestock and production sectors and the entire community. Even earlier, in England, a report was published in 1965, the Brambell Report, to shed light on the conditions of both the physical and mental well-being of animals, aimed primarily at animals reared under intensive conditions (Brambell, 1965). This report is structured in five detailed freedoms.

The five freedoms are summarised as follows:

Since 13/01/2022, the author is affiliated with the Department of Civil Engineering, Architecture, Environment, Land Planning, and Mathematics (DICATAM), Università degli Studi di Brescia, Brescia, Italy; email: giulia.ferronato@unibs.it

Federico Froldi and Giulia Ferronato contributed equally with all other contributors.

F. Froldi · G. Ferronato (✉) · A. Prandini
Department of Animal Science, Food and Nutrition (DiANA), Università Cattolica del Sacro Cuore, Piacenza, Italy

A. M. Fellegara et al. (eds.), *Sustainable Transition of Meat and Cured Meat Supply Chain*, CSR, Sustainability, Ethics & Governance,
https://doi.org/10.1007/978-3-031-34977-5_7

1. Freedom from thirst, hunger and malnutrition through easy access to fresh water and a diet that promotes health;
2. Freedom from unfavourable climatic and environmental conditions, including shelter and a comfortable rest area;
3. Freedom from pain, injury and disease through prevention or prompt diagnosis and treatment;
4. Freedom to manifest natural species-specific behaviour by providing sufficient space, appropriate premises and the company of others of the same species;
5. Freedom from fear and mental distress by providing conditions that avoid mental suffering.

These freedoms were outlined to ensure a minimum level of welfare and safety for the animals. In reality, if respected, these freedoms also involve maintaining production levels and efficiency, which translates into profitability for livestock farms. In fact, the breeder's role is to raise his animals in the best possible way to avoid climatic-environmental stress as much as possible, safeguarding them from all possible adversities they may incur. Fundamental for maintaining a healthy state is to guarantee the availability of water and feedstuffs that have optimal qualitative-nutritional characteristics and avoid nutritional imbalances in the different growth phases of the reared animals.

Of the five freedoms listed, the freedom to manifest natural species-specific behaviour is the most complex to maintain and respect. Public opinion often identifies the fourth freedom as the risk that an intensive livestock farm does not have the requirements to protect and maintain sufficient animal welfare standards. In this context, the fourth freedom includes many aspects of the animal's life, such as conception in the wild, natural weaning, access to pasture and interaction with fellow animals. These aspects must be respected in organic breeding, even though situations may occur in this type of breeding that clash with other freedoms, such as stress and fear, for example, due to predation or adversity (lack of feed, water) if there is no proper management of the breeding activity. In this regard, some reflections on this are necessary.

Continuous progress in structural, nutritional, genetic, environmental and managerial matters has been made to achieve the highest possible level of welfare in animal husbandry and pig farming. European Community legislation regarding livestock facilities defines the minimum requirements in terms of space available for resting and walking, type of flooring, presence of troughs and feeders, enrichment materials and general climatic conditions of the premises. Regarding feeding arrangements, these refer to feeder access space and general satisfaction of energy needs. This ensures that the animal can express behaviour appropriate to the species, in this case, swine, and avoid stressogenic conditions that can lead to abnormal, aggressive behaviour and stereotypes.

With the increasing importance of welfare conditions on the farm and consumer attention to these, minimum standards have been implemented. Also of great importance is the role that technology plays in farming systems today. This can allow, using sensors, the continuous monitoring of the animal and the rearing conditions and thus make any necessary prompt intervention by competent personnel. To date, the main research topics aim to understand the effects of larger breeding spaces and breeding in large groups of animals, the use of enrichment materials, the introduction of immunocastration and the complete abandonment of tail docking.

2 Swine Welfare Regulations at Barns

The European Union's interest in the protection of different species and categories of livestock is based on a specific regulatory framework. For pig breeding, the reference is Directive 2008/120/EC (called *pig directive*) which establishes the minimum standards to be applied in pig breeding, transposed in Italy by Legislative Decree No. 122 of 7 July 2011. The directive's provisions on pig breeding are distinct and apply to the following categories of farmed animals: piglets and growing/fattening pigs, sows and breeding boars. Depending on the animal category referred to, breeding conditions and requirements (structures and housing), microclimatic conditions and environmental parameters are considered. Below are some of the specific characteristics defined by the regulations.

Piglets (from weaning to 10 weeks of age) and growing or fattening pigs (including gilts up to insemination) must be housed in multiple boxes in which there is a minimum and a maximum area available to them according to the number of individuals housed in the box. If there is a slatted floor in the boxes, the joists constituting it must have minimum and maximum dimensions according to the age (weeks of life) of the animals being reared. Some basic precautions are: (i) limits on the mixing of animals to avoid the establishment of hierarchies that lead to fierce fights inside the box; (ii) a simultaneous distribution and access to feed to avoid competition; (iii) the presence and possibility of access to drinking water always available; (iv) the presence of suitable environmental enrichment.

In the case of piglets from birth to weaning, referred to as piglets, as is the case for other categories of farmed animals, dimensions of floor surfaces and joists are defined. It is important to remember that part of the floor must be large enough for the animals to rest together simultaneously, filled with insulated matting or other suitable material. Piglets should be allowed to stay with their mothers until they are 28 days old, although it is possible to move piglets at 21 days of age if they are moved to specially managed all-fill/empty rooms. In the case of health problems of sows or piglets, their separation is allowed while maintaining normal welfare conditions.

In the case of sows and gilts (after insemination), they must be kept in groups, and therefore not individually, between 4 weeks after insemination and 1 week before the expected farrowing date. The regulations also stipulate a minimum box size for sows and gilts that must be respected. Minimum dimensions are also provided for both solid and slatted flooring to create an environment that is as comfortable as possible.

In the case of boars, i.e., breeding males after puberty, these must be reared in boxes with the sufficient available area as required by the regulations. It is essential to foster social relationships between the pigs through visual, auditory and olfactory contact and the possibility of turning around inside the boxes.

A number of managerial precautions must also be maintained within the barns for all categories of pigs reared. There must be a light intensity of 40 lux or more for a minimum of 8 hours/day. Animals must be able to lie down at the same time in barns that have good comfort levels, with clean and dry surfaces. In addition, there must be access to manipulable material that allows the pigs to explore and play (rooting, biting and chewing practices), recreating an environment as close as possible to the natural one. Individual boxes must be arranged where animals with pathologies, injuries or various problems can be moved to intervene with specific treatments. It is important to remember that damaging operations on pigs beyond therapeutic or diagnostic purposes are forbidden. Exceptions to this are: (i) the polishing or clipping of incisors in piglets within the first 7 days of life; (ii) the clipping of part of the tail; (iii) the castration of male pigs with instruments other than tearing tissue. These operations, which will be dealt with in more detail in subsequent paragraphs, must be carried out by competent veterinary personnel and must not, in any case, be considered routine operations on reared herds.

3 Swine Welfare Regulations During Transport and at Slaughter

They are limiting animal stress during transport, loading, unloading and waiting before slaughter is an issue that is addressed by Council Regulation (EC) No 1/2005. Maintaining minimum levels of animal welfare during handling is crucial because it affects the quality of slaughtered meat (CRPA, 2010). Negative consequences that can occur in incorrect transport situations can be: (i) weight loss at slaughter; (ii) qualitative alteration of muscle masses; (iii) increase in traumatic injuries due to incorrect loading and unloading of animals; (iv) increase in animals considered as waste and in extreme cases mortality.

Handling animals involves preparing them for transport, i.e., fasting the animals, preventing mortality during the transport and slaughter phase and preserving carcass and meat hygiene. In this regard, the specifications for PDO Parma Ham provide for the fasting of the animals for 15 hours before slaughter. When loaded onto lorries, the animals must not present injuries or wounds, physiological problems or pathologies. The use of electric prods is strongly discouraged as this action can cause stress and pain to the animals. Animals must also be separated into groups by dividers (partitions) to limit their walking on the vehicles. Passive and active ventilation must be provided during the transport, the latter being obligatory if the transport time exceeds 8 hours when the vehicle is stationary and in hot weather. Adsorbent material must be used to collect the slurry produced. If transport exceeds 8 hours, there must be the possibility for the animals to drink. In any case, transport may not exceed 24 hours, after which there must be a forced stop to unload the animals in barns and care for them for the next departure after 24 hours. Unloading procedures at the slaughterhouse must also be carried out to avoid injuries and wounds to the animals that could occur in the event of slippery floors or unsuitable unloading ramps, as defined in Council Regulation (EC) No 1099/2009. Lastly, there is the housing of animals at the slaughterhouse, which takes place in boxes of varying sizes and in which pigs are not allowed to drink. Feeding is permitted for stops longer than 12 h. Showering occurs at high temperatures, with intervals between 10 and 30 min, with the effect of immediately decreasing the animals' body temperature and reducing their aggressive behaviour (OIE, 2015).

The European Food Safety Authority (EFSA) scientific Panel on Animal Health and Welfare (AHAW) (2020) published a scientific opinion that identifies inadequate competence of slaughterhouse operators and poorly designed and constructed facilities as the primary welfare risks for pigs at slaughter. Therefore, the European Commission is working on redefining high animal welfare standards to improve animal health and food quality. Nevertheless, Council Regulation (EC) No 1099/2009, in order to ensure the protection of animal welfare at the slaughter stage (unloading, housing, handling, restraining, stunning, killing), provides for the designation of a *person responsible for the protection of animal welfare*. It is compulsory for the person in charge to acquire a certificate of competence through a specific training course. Therefore, this person's role is to minimise animals' pain, distress or suffering at the time of slaughter. The most critical issues within slaughterhouses can be found in: (i) the characteristics of the premises, conduction tunnels and routes that are not suitable for the correct passage of the animals, allowing them to reverse during the stunning phase; (ii) the incorrect functioning of the visual impediment, immobilisation and stunning systems; (iii) excessive time between the stunning and hyugulation phase. It must be remembered that the operator must be able to recognise the ineffectiveness of the animal's stunning practice to intervene promptly to avoid unnecessary suffering to the animal (Valarde & Dalmau, 2018).

4 Assessing the Welfare of Swine: The ClassyFarm Approach in Italy

To protect and guarantee the welfare of pigs, it is necessary to measure and quantify it using objective systems and indicators (Gómez et al., 2021). To be able to certify a herd in terms of animal welfare, various protocols have been proposed over the years that measure direct, i.e., animal-based, indicators. Some clarification is necessary here. Welfare indicators are divided into indirect, i.e., resource-based indicators linked to the resources provided to the animals and management-based indicators linked to farm management practices. Unlike the previous ones, animal-based indicators are direct and measured directly on animals. EFSA defines indirect indicators as systems that do not characterise animal welfare conditions but risk factors for the animals. Maximum importance is therefore given to direct indicators of ethological, physiological, pathological, productive and reproductive types.

Over the years, welfare assessment protocols applied to pig breeding have been implemented due to European projects, including Welfare Quality® (2009), covering pig categories such as sows, piglets and growing pigs. This protocol is based precisely on the evaluation of animal-based indicators without a posteriori analysis considering interrelationships between direct (i.e., physiological) and indirect indicators (Larsen et al., 2021).

At the national level, the Ministry of Health started in 2018 a monitoring approach of animal welfare and health conditions to classify farms according to their level of risk, called ClassyFarm (2018). This system, developed by the National Reference Centre for Animal Welfare, the Italian CReNBA, benefits the farmer and the entire production chain. It provides for an assessment of animal welfare through indirect and direct indicators, also including biosecurity assessment and the One Health approach (explained in the next section). The approach is based on the collection, monitoring and analysis of a series of data concerning the management, environmental and structural conditions of the farms as well as direct measurements on the animals (i.e., mortality, limb injuries, tail biting, etc.). The approach adopted by ClassyFarm is risk prevention through a scientific evaluation system that goes beyond the diagnosis of disease and subsequent treatment, including biosecurity as the cornerstone of the protocol. Four areas are considered by ClassyFarm (2021): Biosecurity, Animal Welfare, Veterinary Medicine and Environmental Impact. Data collection can occur either in the control or self-control phase by an official or company veterinarian. The company data are combined with data from the national database (BDN), official company control, slaughterhouse control and laboratory data. The aggregated data are weighted, i.e., a risk incidence on the condition to be assessed is defined. The data evaluation is done through complex algorithms that assemble the information from the four areas listed above. The interpretation of the data makes it possible to classify farms into three levels of risk of compromised animal welfare. The first level corresponds to high risk, which is an unacceptable and negative condition, a source of stress, for which there is the impossibility of living one or more of the five freedoms to the fullest, defined as a "distress" situation; the second level corresponds to controlled risk for which the animals of the herd satisfy the five freedoms without living in a stressful condition; the third level is defined as low risk, which is a positive situation and experience for the animals, in addition to living in a condition of respect for the five freedoms, defined as a "eustress" situation.

The distinction of risk conditions into different areas (managerial, structural and environmental) will also make it possible to appropriately target preventive interventions on the main factors of the weakness of the livestock system of each farm, thereby improving the living conditions of the animals. The evaluation of the data, therefore, returns numerical indicators useful for (i) making comparisons of individual farms with aggregate averages of different geographical areas or types of farms; (ii) identifying critical points within the farm; (iii) creating prerequisites for management, structural and environmental interventions in the areas most at risk;

(iv) creating support programmes for farms (Council of the European Union, 2020). Data returns are also helpful for the entire pork production chain. They serve to guarantee the ethics of pig production and to obtain a certification-valorisation of the product. To date, a pig farm is not obliged to adhere to the ClassyFarm system but could, in the future, be involved in the PDO or other supply chains (large-scale retail trade) and thus obtain a higher market valorisation of the meat.

5 One Health approach

Humans' health, animals, plants and ecosystems are closely connected. Any mutation of this interconnectedness between different spheres can risk the development and spread of new human and animal diseases. One Health is a holistic, integrated and unifying approach that aims to balance and maintain the health of people, animals and ecosystems. The One Health approach is officially recognised by the Italian Ministry of Health, the European Commission and all international organisations (EFSA, 2021).

According to the World Health Organization, about 60% of emerging infectious diseases globally originate from animals. In the last 30 years, more than 30 new human pathogens have been detected, 75% of which originated from animals (WHO, 2020). Thus, many emerging diseases are not random occurrences but are associated with the impact of human activities on natural systems. Intensification of animal husbandry and trade in live and wild animals can increase the likelihood of infectious diseases affecting people, just as the movement of people and goods can promote the spread of vector-borne diseases. Stress factors can affect ecosystems, such as land use, loss of biodiversity, contamination of natural areas, environmental pollution and climate change. Organisational, communication and coordination strategies are needed in this context. Therefore, inter-professional collaboration between different sectors helps to contain the risk of disease outbreaks through containment, prevention and surveillance plans for diseases involving humans, animals and vectors. Collaboration between human and veterinary medicine is an example of One Health applied to public health. In this regard, international organisations have developed a joint action plan entitled "Working together for the health of humans, animals, plants and the environment", which aims to strengthen states against diseases and pandemics in a cross-cutting and sustainable way (FAO, UNEP, WHO, and WOAH, 2022).

5.1 *African Swine Fever*

African Swine Fever (ASF) is a health problem now also present in Italy. At present, only a few cases have been found at the level of semi-wild reared domestic pigs and no intensive farming has been affected. The harmful potential of this disease is very high both in health and economic terms for the pig sector. ASF is a viral haemorrhagic disease with exceptionally high lethality in domestic pigs and Eurasian wild boar. The contamination pathways may be domestic pigs, wild boar, inanimate fomites (carcasses, tolls, mechanical vectors) and arthropod vectors. Nowadays, no vaccine or treatments are available, and ASF could be controlled and prevented through biosecurity farm management, but infected animals and all those present in the same production context must be killed and incinerated. Due to that, it is notifiable to the World Organization of Animal Health (OIE) (Blome et al., 2020; Sauter-Louis et al., 2021).

Every year from 2020, Italy has adopted a National Surveillance Plan of the ASF, approved and co-financed by the European Commission, which also includes eradication measures for the Sardinia region. The National Surveillance and Eradication Plan for 2023 has the objective of protecting the national pig population from ASF virus and includes: passive surveillance in wild boar populations, passive surveillance in pig holdings, management of the wild boar population, verification of the levels of application of biosecurity measures, stakeholder training and information campaign (European Commission, 2021).

It is clear how important it is to monitor and comply with the biosecurity standards included in the ClassyFarm national welfare assessment system.

6 Improvements and Available Technologies for Animal Welfare Compliance in Swine Breeding

6.1 Loose Farrowing System

Starting with breeding facilities, the most recent developments include the use of loose farrowing boxes for sows.

Farrowing crates with sow confinement are predominantly used in intensive farming systems. This system, in the face of confinement of the sow for a limited period (lactation days), avoids piglet death due to involuntary crushing by the mother during movement and allows the operator during normal routine operations. This mode preserves the welfare of the piglets more than that of the sow due to its reduced ability to move. Instead, the use of a loose farrowing system provides for the sow's movement within the box and using lockable gates to confine her to allow operations such as assistance during farrowing to take place.

The welfare of the sow at the time of farrowing is crucial because it can affect performance during lactation (Dumniem et al., 2023) and sow longevity (Kinane et al., 2022). Restriction of normal nest-making behaviour may in fact, cause stress to the sow by activating the hypothalamic–pituitary–adrenal gland axis (Jarvis et al., 2006). This stress condition could increase plasma cortisol levels, worsening milk production during lactation and, if chronic situation, negatively affecting the animal's return to estrus.

The loose farrowing system was introduced to increase the welfare of the sow. This system provides a larger box inside which the sow can move. To protect the piglets, a nest area is provided within which the piglets can stall and remain separated from their mother, avoiding the risk of being crushed while resting. In the nest area, heating lamps and/or mats are provided to create a more comfortable environment for the piglets. There are also anti-crushing bars for piglets on the walls of the box and lockable gates to limit the sow's space during farrowing and/or during routine operations on the brood in order to preserve the operator's safety. Manipulable material, such as straw or paper, is also provided in this system to support normal maternal behaviour and avoid stressful conditions in the sow in the prepartum period.

The sow's ability to move allows her to perform more of her normal maternal behaviour during farrowing and the lactation period; however, it may increase the mortality rate due to piglet crush (Kinane et al., 2022). This phenomenon may be more acute in highly prolific genetics with a high number of piglets born and a possible higher presence of underweight piglets. Underweight piglets are more likely to be devitalised and less responsive to their mother's movements especially during the first days of life (Edwards, 2002; Glencorse et al., 2019). Therefore, proper placement of heat sources within the box is also crucial. Piglets in the early stages of life need higher ambient temperatures, and in the case of uneven weather conditions inside the box, they will tend to stay close to the heat source, in this case, the sow, increasing the possibility of crushing during her movements. As a result, the loose farrowing system needs more area than the enclosed type, thus requiring more breeding area and higher construction costs from the farmer.

6.2 Tail Docking

The bite of the tail or ears is a recurring problem in swine breeding in intensive systems. Several ethological hypotheses, based on knowledge of animal behaviour, have been proposed for caudophagy. The first hypothesis indicates this behaviour as natural related to the pig's need for sucking and exploration. However, it must be maintained at low levels (Newberry et al., 1988). The increase in the incidence of the phenomenon and its frequency among pigs may be due to the occurrence of stress phenomena such as change of environment and group subjects, competition for access to food and water or lack of environmental stimuli. Factors that may affect the frequency of this phenomenon are gender, breed, stocking density, group size, flooring, air quality and light, manure handling system, feed and water, pig health and environmental enrichment (Wallgren et al., 2019).

This issue not only causes problems during the rearing phase but also can affect the suitability of the carcass intended for PDO production and the health and quality of post-slaughter meat (Scollo et al., 2023).

To prevent the problem in the preclean decades, the preventive cutting of the tail and also the filing of the incisors were carried out (Sutherland & Tucker, 2011). The current European legislation regulates these practices and allows their implementation only in a situation of proven necessity by encouraging management practices that prevent the emergence of the problem of bites (Council of the European Union, 2008). The cutting of the tail, in fact, can reduce the frequency but does not eliminate the problem because of the presence of other triggers related to the methods of breeding and management of pigs. In addition, the practice itself, which prevents the mutilation of part of the tail, involves pain to the animal if not properly carried out (i.e., first days of life, use of analgesia if adult animal), and skin injury may represent a possible site of bacterial contamination if not properly managed (i.e., clean breeding environment, disinfection and treatment of skin injury) (Schrøder-Petersen & Simonsen, 2001).

Genetic causes were also investigated to eliminate the problem and/or reduce the incidence. The incidence of tail biting varies between different breeds with the same breeding conditions and the heritability of the predisposition to biting. The most predisposed breed turns out to be Landrace (Breuer et al., 2005). Genetic selection plans have begun to include this parameter after evaluating the interaction of this with other parameters of functional selections, such as reproductive and productive performance and meat quality parameters (Breuer et al., 2005; Brunberg et al., 2013).

To control and prevent bites, the management of the breeding environment and the adaptation of the current intensive systems to conditions exceeding the minimum standards for welfare (space, feeding, enrichment materials, environmental conditions) are fundamental (D'Eath et al., 2014). The rearing of intact-tailed pigs, therefore, requires careful space management in terms of increasing the available space per head to avoid overcrowded conditions, proper microclimate management to avoid the creation of preferred and non-preferred zones (i.e., temperature, air speed, gas concentration), wide availability of suitable enrichment materials and their alternation to avoid habituation. In addition, since the tendency to bite is subjective, it is appropriate for operators to detect the presence of a biting individual in a timely manner and proceed to remove him or her from the group if necessary (Sonoda et al., 2013).

This transition is also supported by the new Community Agricultural Policy through the structuring of Eco-schemes that take into account the welfare of animals on farm (Runge et al., 2022). To date, there are already supply chains that require whole-tailed pigs to be raised as a requirement.

6.3 Enrichment Materials

Pig breeding takes place in groups of varying sizes according to the physiological stages. This strategy is critical since swine are highly social and interactive animals. However, rearing conditions can limit the animal in expressing its normal behaviour (i.e., exploration, rooting), leading to the appearance of abnormal behaviours. These include aggressive phenomena involving fighting between subjects and/or tail and ear biting. The occurrence of lesions is highly impacting animal health as it increases the state of ill health, the occurrence of disease due to the establishment of inflammation and bacterial contamination and thus the need for antimicrobial use. This also affects the general quality of the carcass and meat, and for farmers, this coincides with productive and economic losses.

In addition to improved general environmental conditions, the use of enrichment materials has been used to prevent and reduce the problem of biting in the swine industry. These are supplements consisting of manipulable, chewable, edible and safe material and possibly washable for reuse (Courboulay, 2014). Several materials are potentially usable, including straw, wood, jute ropes, chains and plastic toys. The more of the above characteristics possessed by the material, the better its enrichment value will be. In fact, the goal is to occupy most of the time of the animal's day. Considering the very curious nature of the pig, the attractiveness of the new object will be very high in the first 24 hours and will then tend to decline and lead to habituation (Carol Petherick & Blackshaw, 1987; Roy et al., 2019). Therefore, in order to avoid competition phenomena, it will also be crucial to distribute the presence of material inside the box and provide adequate amounts considering the group's size to avoid further stressful conditions and alternate the use of different materials (Roy et al., 2019). It was evaluated how the type of feeding system can also influence the effect of enrichment materials. Feeding type and accessibility to food in spatial–temporal terms directly influence herd hierarchy and aggression phenomena. This hierarchy can also be maintained in access to enrichment material and cause unequal use among animals. This problem can be overcome by means of precision feeding systems that include the use of feeders; this provides for feeding animals individually for better satisfaction of specific needs and reduction of competition for food. This also allows access to environmental enrichment materials to be deferred over time (Roy et al., 2022) and reduces as much as possible the phenomena of mixing groups to avoid the need to reestablish the internal hierarchy (Greenwood et al., 2014; Valros, 2022).

6.4 Immunocastration

Castration of male subjects is a common practice in pig breeding, as the meat of whole males, due to the presence of hormones such as androsterone and skatole, has an unpleasant smell, "boar odour", to the consumers (Wesoly & Weiler, 2012). Furthermore, from a managerial point of view, the rearing of whole males would entail a greater risk for the operator due to the potential aggressiveness of the boar and would require the rearing of pigs from the post-weaning in separate sex groups to avoid possible unwanted mating (Zamaratskaia & Squires, 2009; Holinger et al., 2015). The breeding of entire male results also correlates with a high prevalence of skin lesions (Fredriksen & Hexeberg, 2009). In order to succeed in breeding whole males, it would be necessary to define, in addition to available welfare standards, more specific and applicable breeding techniques, feeding strategies and carcass handling techniques (Holinger et al., 2015).

Surgical castration is carried out by veterinary or specialised personnel during the first 3 days of life. Animal welfare legislation foresees the use of local analgesia or total anesthesia before surgery and proper wound management in the post-implementation phase. However, the practice involves pain and stress to the animal in conjunction with the event, which, if not properly managed, can lead to the appearance of concomitant pathologies due to bacterial infections or decay of the animal (American Veterinary Medical Association, 2020).

To avoid the problems mentioned above, immunocastration has been investigated. Immunocastration involves active immunisation against GnRH in order to regulate reproductive function and postpone sexual development (Kress et al., 2019). Vaccination should be carried out between 8 and 9 weeks of the piglet's life. A second vaccination is then planned, which must take place at least 4–5 weeks before slaughter. Failure to follow the correct timing may affect the efficiency of vaccination and consequently quality, fat percentage and odour of carcass and meat. It is also possible that some individuals may not be susceptible to vaccination (0–3%) due to genetic conditions or stressful environmental conditions that may alter the effectiveness of the immune response (Batorek et al., 2012; Čandek-Potokar et al., 2017). However, studies reported even higher values, but due to the poor implementation of the practice in Europe and poor monitoring of vaccinated subjects, no firm data are available. For proper implementation of this practice, several factors must be considered. First of all, specific farm management plans need to be established to carry out vaccination at the correct age, a review of energy requirements and feeding strategy in order to have carcasses and slaughter weights corresponding to the demands and the type of final product and to manage environmental conditions (Schmidt et al., 2011; Batorek et al., 2012). Regarding the effects on meat quality, immunocastrated subjects showed no significant differences from surgically castrated subjects (Čandek-Potokar et al., 2017).

In the face of increasing consumer attention to breeding practices, the efficiency of immunocastration, its effect on meat quality and its acceptance by the final consumer and stakeholders are being investigated. This technique could benefit in terms of animal welfare, economic sustainability, but also environmental sustainability. The practice is also accepted by consumers of PDO products, and the food safety of the resulting products is proven (Mancini et al., 2017). However, to date, immunocastration is poorly adopted in Europe compared to other countries due to the high economic cost due to the lack of market competitiveness among pharmaceutical manufacturers (Kress et al., 2019).

6.5 Smart Swine Farming

Swine breeding in the last decades has strongly evolved thanks to the increased availability of technologies that can be implemented in breeding. Precision farming allows, in fact, constant monitoring of farm performance through wide data availability. This refers to automated technologies able to detect images and sound to the health status of animals (Mahfuz et al., 2022). Moreover, to these systems are added all sensors for monitoring environmental conditions such as temperature, humidity, air quality and speed, gas concentration, light and sound.

Proper management allows for an increase in production performance and improvement in production efficiency with a corresponding increase in reduction of antimicrobial use, economic sustainability for the farmer and greater environmental sustainability of the product (Racewicz et al., 2021).

The technologies available today include:

- Radio frequency identification (RFDI): to the identification of pigs and recording of individual animal data (i.e., date of birth, mortality, position) (Ariff et al., 2014; Buller et al., 2020);
- Infrared thermal imaging: to detect the animal temperature (individual or group), muscle injuries, infections, ovulation (Oh et al., 2021; Jeyakumar et al., 2022);
- Microphone, cough and/or sound detector: to detect normal or abnormal sound for sickness and behaviour of pigs (Ferrari et al., 2008; Chung et al., 2013);
- ZigBee technology: to detect environmental parameters (Zeng et al., 2021);
- Deep learning/image analysis: to detect locomotion, movement pattern, behaviour, posture, tail biting, temperature, body weight (Nasirahmadi et al., 2019);
- Two-dimensional (2D) cameras: to identify pigs based on colour, detect locomotion, behaviour, posture, environment (Riekert et al., 2020);
- Three-dimensional (3D) cameras: to detect feeding time. Body weight, posture, lameness, injuries, group behaviour (D'Eath et al., 2018);
- Accelerometers: to detect pigs' movements (standing time, posture) (Chapa et al., 2020).

The integration of these sensors in the farm is functional to more precise control of the animals, which allows the monitoring in real time in order to be able to intervene in a timely manner in case of the presence of health problems and thus reduce the problems resulting as worsening of well-being conditions and growth performance (Mahfuz et al., 2022). In addition, the use of chips or ear tags for animal identification, combined with the use of feeders, also allows, by means of precision feed, to modulate the feeding of food according to the specific needs of the animal, considering its physiological phase, weight and activity, thus reducing food waste and the excretion of undigested nutrients in the stool. This mode of management may allow animals to be managed in larger groups than common practices, such as during gestation (Anil et al., 2003; Chen et al., 2010; Roy et al., 2019).

7 Conclusions

Suitable animal welfare conditions are essential for raising pigs at all stages of growth. Respect for this condition is a foundation for obtaining healthy, quality food products and for having production systems that are efficient and less environmentally impactful. All life stages of swine breeding must be accompanied by a high overall level of welfare, which can be quantified to help farmers and the supply chain identify critical issues and implement improvements. Technology applied to animal husbandry, i.e., precision farming is the way forward to ensure respect for animal freedom, improve production efficiency and meet the increasing public awareness of welfare and sustainable animal husbandry. Respect for welfare and biosecurity standards are also key to the reduction of drug use in compliance with the principle of One Health and the reduction of the chances of occurrence of diseases such as ASF.

References

American Veterinary Medical Association, 2020. Welfare Implications of Swine Castration. Accessed Feb 8, 2023, from https://www.avma.org/resources-tools/literature-reviews/welfare-implications-swine-castration

Anil, L., Bhend, K. M. G., Baidoo, S. K., Morrison, R., & Deen, J. (2003). Comparison of injuries in sows housed in gestation stalls versus group pens with electronic sow feeders. *Journal of the American Veterinary Medical Association, 223*, 1334–1338. https://doi.org/10.2460/JAVMA.2003.223.1334

Ariff, M. H., Ismarani, I., & Shamsuddin, N. (2014). RFID based systematic livestock health management system. *Proceedings 2014 IEEE Conference on Systems, Process and Control ICSPC 2014*, pp. 111–116. https://doi.org/10.1109/SPC.2014.7086240.

Batorek, N., Čandek-Potokar, M., Bonneau, M., & Van Milgen, J. (2012). Meta-analysis of the effect of immunocastration on production performance, reproductive organs and boar taint compounds in pigs. *Animal, 6*, 1330–1338. https://doi.org/10.1017/S1751731112000146

Blome, S., Franzke, K., & Beer, M. (2020). African swine fever – A review of current knowledge. *Virus Research, 287*. https://doi.org/10.1016/J.VIRUSRES.2020.198099

Brambell, F. W. R. (1965). *Report of the technical committee to enquire into the welfare of animals kept under intensive livestock husbandry systems* (Command Rep. 2836). London: Her Majesty's Stationery Office.

Breuer, K., Sutcliffe, M. E. M., Mercer, J. T., Rance, K. A., O'Connell, N. E., Sneddon, I. A., & Edwards, S. A. (2005). Heritability of clinical tail-biting and its relation to performance traits. *Livestock Production Science, 93*, 87–94. https://doi.org/10.1016/J.LIVPRODSCI.2004.11.009

Brunberg, E., Jensen, P., Isaksson, A., & Keeling, L. J. (2013). Brain gene expression differences are associated with abnormal tail biting behavior in pigs. *Genes, Brain, and Behavior, 12*, 275–281. https://doi.org/10.1111/GBB.12002

Buller, H., Blokhuis, H., Lokhorst, K., Silberberg, M., & Veissier, I. (2020). Animal welfare management in a digital world. *Animals, 10*, 1779. https://doi.org/10.3390/ANI10101779

Čandek-Potokar, M., Škrlep, M., Zamaratskaia, G., Čandek-Potokar, M., Škrlep, M., & Zamaratskaia, G. (2017). Immunocastration as alternative to surgical castration in pigs. *Theriogenology*. https://doi.org/10.5772/INTECHOPEN.68650

Carol Petherick, J., & Blackshaw, J. K. (1987). A review of the factors influencing the aggressive and agonistic behaviour of the domestic pig. *Australian Journal of Experimental Agriculture, 27*, 605–611. https://doi.org/10.1071/EA9870605

Chapa, J. M., Maschat, K., Iwersen, M., Baumgartner, J., & Drillich, M. (2020). Accelerometer systems as tools for health and welfare assessment in cattle and pigs – A review. *Behavioural Processes, 181*, 104262. https://doi.org/10.1016/J.BEPROC.2020.104262

Chen, C. Y., Misztal, I., Tsuruta, S., Zumbach, B., Herring, W. O., Holl, J., & Culbertson, M. (2010). Estimation of genetic parameters of feed intake and daily gain in Durocs using data from electronic swine feeders. *Journal of Animal Breeding and Genetics, 127*, 230–234. https://doi.org/10.1111/J.1439-0388.2009.00833.X

Chung, Y., Oh, S., Lee, J., Park, D., Chang, H. H., & Kim, S. (2013). Automatic detection and recognition of pig wasting diseases using sound data in audio surveillance systems. *Sensors, 13*, 12929–12942. https://doi.org/10.3390/S131012929

ClassyFarm. (2018). http://www.classyfarm.it/wp-content/uploads/sites/4/2018/08/Manuale-linee-guida-rischio-taglio-coda.pdf

ClassyFarm. (2021). *Istituto Zooprofilattico Sperimentale Lombardia e Emilia-Romagna Valutazione del Rischio Taglio Coda nel Suino da Ingrasso e Svezzamento*. Accessed April 22, 2021, from https://www.classyfarm.it/wp-content/uploads/sites/4/2018/09/SUINI-Benessere-valutazione-del-rischio-Taglio-coda-3.pdf

Council Regulation (EC) No 1/2005 of 22 December 2004on the protection of animals during transport and related operations and amending Directives64/432/EEC and 93/119/EC and Regulation (EC) No 1255/97

Council of the European Union. (2008). *Council Directive 2008/120/EC laying down minimum standards for the protection of pigs*. Official Journal of the European Union L47/5–13.

Council Regulation (EC) No 1099/2009 of 24 September 2009 on the protection of animals at the time of killing

Council of the European Union. (2020). Proposal for a Regulation of the European Parliament and of the Council establishing rules on support for strategic plans to be drawn up by Member States under the Common agricultural policy (CAP Strategic Plans) and financed by the European Agricultural Guarantee Fund (EAGF) and by the European Agricultural Fund for Rural Development (EAFRD) and repealing Regulation (EU) No 1305/2013 of the European Parliament and of the Council and Regulation (EU) No 1307/2013 of the European Parliament and of the Council – General Approach (Annexes I–XIII).

Courboulay, V. (2014). Enrichment materials for fattening pigs: Summary of IFIP trials. *Cah l'IFIP, 1*, 47–56.

CRPA. (2010). *Benessere dei suini. Fasi di carico/scarico e trasporto su strada*. Opuscolo C.R.P.A. 5.54 – N. 2/2010 ISSN 0393-5094.

D'Eath, R. B., Arnott, G., Turner, S. P., Jensen, T., Lahrmann, H. P., Busch, M. E., Niemi, J. K., Lawrence, A. B., & Sandøe, P. (2014). Injurious tail biting in pigs: How can it be controlled in existing systems without tail docking? *Animal, 8*, 1479–1497. https://doi.org/10.1017/S1751731114001359

D'Eath, R. B., Jack, M., Futro, A., Talbot, D., Zhu, Q., Barclay, D., & Baxter, E. M. (2018). Automatic early warning of tail biting in pigs: 3D cameras can detect lowered tail posture before an outbreak. *PLoS One, 13*, e0194524. https://doi.org/10.1371/JOURNAL.PONE.0194524

Direttiva 2008/120/CE del Consiglio del 18 dicembre 2008 che stabilisce le norme minime per la protezione dei suini (Decreto Legislativo 7 luglio 2011, n. 122).

Dumniem, N., Boonprakob, R., Parsons, T. D., & Tummaruk, P. (2023). Pen versus crate: A comparative study on the effects of different farrowing systems on farrowing performance, colostrum yield and piglet preweaning mortality in sows under tropical conditions. *Animal, 13*, 233. https://doi.org/10.3390/ANI13020233

Edwards, S. A. (2002). Perinatal mortality in the pig: Environmental or physiological solutions? *Livestock Production Science, 78*, 3–12. https://doi.org/10.1016/S0301-6226(02)00180-X

EFSA. (2021). The European union one health 2020 Zoonoses report. *EFSA Journal, 19*, 6971. https://doi.org/10.2903/j.efsa.2021.6971

EFSA AHAW Panel (EFSA Panel on Animal Health and Welfare), Nielsen SS, Alvarez J, Bicout DJ, Calistri P, Depner K, Drewe JA, Garin-Bastuji B, Gonzales Rojas JL, Gortázar Schmidt C, Michel V, Miranda Chueca MÁ, Roberts HC, Sihvonen LH, Spoolder H, Stahl K, Viltrop A, Winckler C, Candiani D, Fabris C, Van der Stede Y and Velarde A 2020. Scientific Opinion on the welfare of pigs at slaughter. EFSA Journal 2020;18(6):6148,. 113 pp. doi:https://doi.org/10.2903/j.efsa.2020.6148.

European Commission. (2021). *Commission implementing regulation (EU) 2021/605 laying down special control measures for African Swine Fever.*

FAO, UNEP, WHO, and WOAH. (2022). One Health Joint Plan of Action (2022–2026). *Working together for the health of humans, animals, plants and the environment.* Rome. https://doi.org/10.4060/cc2289en.

Ferrari, S., Silva, M., Guarino, M., Aerts, J. M., & Berckmans, D. (2008). Cough sound analysis to identify respiratory infection in pigs. *Computers and Electronics in Agriculture, 64*, 318–325. https://doi.org/10.1016/J.COMPAG.2008.07.003

Fredriksen, B., & Hexeberg, C. (2009). The effect of removing animals for slaughter on the behaviour of the remaining male and female pigs in the pen. *Research in Veterinary Science, 86*, 368–370. https://doi.org/10.1016/J.RVSC.2008.06.005

Glencorse, D., Plush, K., Hazel, S., D'souza, D., & Hebart, M. (2019). Impact of non-confinement accommodation on farrowing performance: A systematic review and meta-analysis of farrowing crates versus pens. *Animals, 9*, 957. https://doi.org/10.3390/ANI9110957

Gómez, Y., Stygar, A. H., Boumans, I. J., Bokkers, E. A., Pedersen, L. J., Niem, J. K., et al. (2021). A systematic review on validated precision livestock farming technologies for pig production and its potential to assess animal welfare. *Frontiers in Veterinary Science, 8*, 660565.

Greenwood, E. C., Plush, K. J., van Wettere, W. H. E. J., & Hughes, P. E. (2014). Hierarchy formation in newly mixed, group housed sows and management strategies aimed at reducing its impact. *Applied Animal Behaviour Science, 160*, 1–11. https://doi.org/10.1016/J.APPLANIM.2014.09.011

Holinger, M., Früh, B., & Hillmann, E. (2015). Group composition for fattening entire male pigs under enriched housing conditions—Influences on behaviour, injuries and boar taint compounds. *Applied Animal Behaviour Science, 165*, 47–56. https://doi.org/10.1016/J.APPLANIM.2015.01.016

Jarvis, S., D'Eath, R. B., Robson, S. K., & Lawrence, A. B. (2006). The effect of confinement during lactation on the hypothalamic–pituitary–adrenal axis and behaviour of primiparous sows. *Physiology & Behavior, 87*, 345–352. https://doi.org/10.1016/J.PHYSBEH.2005.10.004

Jeyakumar, S., Kumaresan, A., Kataktalware, M. A., Manimaran, A., & Ramesha, K. P. (2022). Infrared thermal imaging and its application in animal reproduction. *Frontier Technologies in Bovine Reproduction, 47–64*. https://doi.org/10.1007/978-981-19-3072-0_3

Kinane, O., Butler, F., & O'Driscoll, K. (2022). Freedom to move: Free lactation pens improve sow welfare. *Animals, 12*, 1762. https://doi.org/10.3390/ANI12141762

Kress, K., Millet, S., Labussière, É., Weiler, U., & Stefanski, V. (2019). Sustainability of pork production with immunocastration in Europe. *Sustainability, 11*, 3335. https://doi.org/10.3390/SU11123335

Larsen, M. L. V., Wang, M., & Norton, T. (2021). Information technologies for wel-fare monitoring in pigs and their relation to welfare quality®. *Sustainability, 13*(2), 692. https://doi.org/10.3390/su13020692

Mahfuz, S., Mun, H. S., Dilawar, M. A., & Yang, C. J. (2022). Applications of smart technology as a sustainable strategy in modern swine farming. *Sustainability, 14*, 2607. https://doi.org/10.3390/SU14052607

Mancini, M. C., Menozzi, D., & Arfini, F. (2017). Immunocastration: Economic implications for the pork supply chain and consumer perception. An assessment of existing research. *Livestock Science, 203*, 10–20. https://doi.org/10.1016/J.LIVSCI.2017.06.012

Nasirahmadi, A., Sturm, B., Edwards, S., Jeppsson, K. H., Olsson, A. C., Müller, S., & Hensel, O. (2019). Deep learning and machine vision approaches for posture detection of individual pigs. *Sensors, 19*, 3738. https://doi.org/10.3390/S19173738

Newberry, R. C., Wood-Gush, D. G. M., & Hall, J. W. (1988). Playful behaviour of piglets. *Behavioural Processes, 17*, 205–216. https://doi.org/10.1016/0376-6357(88)90004-6

Oh, S. I., Lee, H. S., Bui, V. N., Dao, D. T., Bui, N. A., Le, T. D., Kieu, M. A., Nguyen, Q. H., Tran, L. H., So, K. M., Yi, S. W., Kim, E., & Hur, T. Y. (2021). Dynamic variations in infrared skin temperature of weaned pigs experimentally inoculated with the African swine fever virus: A pilot study. *Veterinary Sciences, 8*. https://doi.org/10.3390/VETSCI8100223

OIE. (2015). *Technical notes on welfare of red meat species in pre-slaughter and slaughter*. http://rpawe.oie.int/fileadmin/doc/eng/ToT_Training_material/Technical_notes_cattle_sheep_and_pigs_final.pdf

Racewicz, P., Ludwiczak, A., Skrzypczak, E., Składanowska-Baryza, J., Biesiada, H., Nowak, T., Nowaczewski, S., Zaborowicz, M., Stanisz, M., & Ślósarz, P. (2021). Welfare health and productivity in commercial pig herds. *Animals, 11*, 1176. https://doi.org/10.3390/ANI11041176

Riekert, M., Klein, A., Adrion, F., Hoffmann, C., & Gallmann, E. (2020). Automatically detecting pig position and posture by 2D camera imaging and deep learning. *Computers and Electronics in Agriculture, 174*, 105391. https://doi.org/10.1016/J.COMPAG.2020.105391

Roy, C., Kyeiwaa, V., Mancera, K. F., Seddon, Y. M., Connor, L. M., & Brown, J. A. (2022). Effects of enrichment type, presentation and social status on enrichment use and behavior of sows—Part 2: Free access stall feeding. *Animals, 12*, 1768. https://doi.org/10.3390/ANI12141768

Roy, C., Lippens, L., Kyeiwaa, V., Seddon, Y. M., Connor, L. M., & Brown, J. A. (2019). Effects of enrichment type, presentation and social status on enrichment use and behaviour of sows with electronic sow feeding. *Animals, 9*, 369. https://doi.org/10.3390/ANI9060369

Runge, T., Latacz-Lohmann, U., Schaller, L., Todorova, K., Daugbjerg, C., Termansen, M., Liira, J., Le Gloux, F., Dupraz, P., Leppanen, J., Fogarasi, J., Vigh, E. Z., Bradfield, T., Hennessy, T., Targetti, S., Viaggi, D., Berzina, I., Schulp, C., Majewski, E., Bouriaud, L., Baciu, G., Pecurul, M., Prokofieva, I., & Velazquez, F. J. B. (2022). Implementation of Eco-schemes in Fifteen European Union Member States. *EuroChoices, 21*, 19–27. https://doi.org/10.1111/1746-692X.12352

Sauter-Louis, C., Conraths, F. J., Probst, C., Blohm, U., Schulz, K., Sehl, J., Fischer, M., Forth, J. H., Zani, L., Depner, K., Mettenleiter, T. C., Beer, M., & Blome, S. (2021). African swine fever in wild boar in Europe—A review. *Viruses, 13*. https://doi.org/10.3390/V13091717

Schmidt, T., Calabrese, J. M., Grodzycki, M., Paulick, M., Pearce, M. C., Rau, F., & von Borell, E. (2011). Impact of single-sex and mixed-sex group housing of boars vaccinated against GnRF or physically castrated on body lesions, feeding behaviour and weight gain. *Applied Animal Behaviour Science, 1–2*, 42–52. https://doi.org/10.1016/J.APPLANIM.2010.11.019

Schrøder-Petersen, D. L., & Simonsen, H. B. (2001). Tail biting in pigs. *Veterinary Journal, 162*, 196–210. https://doi.org/10.1053/TVJL.2001.0605

Scollo, A., Abbas, M., Contiero, B., & Gottardo, F. (2023). Undocked tails, mycoplasma-like lesions and gastric ulcers in slaughtering pigs: What connection? *Animals, 13*, 305. https://doi.org/10.3390/ANI13020305

Sonoda, L. T., Fels, M., Oczak, M., Vranken, E., Ismayilova, G., Guarino, M., Viazzi, S., Bahr, C., Berckmans, D., & Hartung, J. (2013). Tail biting in pigs–causes and management intervention strategies to reduce the behavioural disorder. A review. *Berl Munch Tierarztl Wochenschr*. https://doi.org/10.2376/0005-9366-126-104.

Sutherland, M. A., & Tucker, C. B. (2011). The long and short of it: A review of tail docking in farm animals. *Applied Animal Behaviour Science, 135*, 179–191. https://doi.org/10.1016/J.APPLANIM.2011.10.015

Unesco. (1978). *Dichiarazione universale dei diritti dell'animale*. https://www.salute.gov.it/imgs/C_17_pagineAree_205_2_file.pdf

Valarde, A., & Dalmau, A. (2018). Slaughter of pigs. In M. Spinka (Ed.), *Advances in pig welfare* (pp. 295–322). Woodhead Publishing.

Valros, A. (2022). Review: The tale of the Finnish pig tail – how to manage non-docked pigs? *Animal, 16*, 100353. https://doi.org/10.1016/J.ANIMAL.2021.100353

Vipiana, P. (2022). *La protezione degli animali nel nuovo art. 9 Cost.* DPCE Online, [S.l.], v. 52, n. 2, July 2022. ISSN 2037–6677. Available from https://www.dpceonline.it/index.php/dpceonline/article/view/1627

Wallgren, T., Lundeheim, N., Wallenbeck, A., Westin, R., & Gunnarsson, S. (2019). Rearing pigs with intact tails—Experiences and practical solutions in Sweden. *Animals, 9*, 812. https://doi.org/10.3390/ANI9100812

Welfare Quality®. (2009). Welfare Quality® Assessment Protocol for Pigs (Sow and Piglets, Growing and Finishing Pigs). Welfare Quality® Consortium: Lelystad, The Netherlands.

Wesoly, R., & Weiler, U. (2012). Nutritional influences on skatole formation and skatole metabolism in the pig. *Animals, 2*, 221. https://doi.org/10.3390/ANI2020221

WHO. (2020). *WHO global strategy on health, environment and climate change: The transformation needed to improve lives and wellbeing sustainably through healthy environments*. Geneva, Switzerland.. https://www.who.int/publications/i/item/9789240000377.

Zamaratskaia, G., & Squires, E. J. (2009). Biochemical, nutritional and genetic effects on boar taint in entire male pigs. *Animal, 3*, 1508–1521. https://doi.org/10.1017/S1751731108003674

Zeng, Z., Zeng, F., Han, X., Elkhouchlaa, H., Yu, Q., & Lü, E. (2021). Real-time monitoring of environmental parameters in a commercial gestating sow house using a zigbee-based wireless sensor network. *Applied Sciences, 11*, 972. https://doi.org/10.3390/APP11030972

Taxation and Ecological Transition in Production Chains

Marco Allena and Andrea Purpura

1 Introduction: Enhancing the Value, for Tax Purposes, of Sustainable Production Chains

These last decades, environmental taxation and the broader approach to environmental protection have gone through profound transformations and evolutions from the regulatory, social and economic points of view. Indeed, new perspectives have surfaced in terms of human development, hinging on the affirmation of the human dignity of persons, also in relation to the environment in which they operate and live on a daily basis.

From this angle, the protection of the person as part of the environment is, at present, an unavoidable goal of any legislative action.

Hence, all entrepreneurial conducts that, by protecting the environment, are able to generate a benefit for the community do deserve to be valued and fostered.

As such, given the centrality of environmental preservation as a functional tool for protecting the entire community, national legislators are called upon to respond through the law—and also through tax rules—to modern economic and social changes, rewarding the most virtuous and sustainable production chains rather than those that are most harmful to the environment.

Specifically, while production chains are deemed to be sustainable not just for their reduced environmental impact but also their focus on community needs, tax legislators should consider the factors that determine the sustainability of a production chain as potentially conducive to a lower tax burden.

M. Allena · A. Purpura (✉)
Depatmernt of Law, Università Cattolica del Sacro Cuore, Piacenza, Italy
e-mail: marco.allena@unicatt.it; andrea.purpura@unicatt.it

A. M. Fellegara et al. (eds.), *Sustainable Transition of Meat and Cured Meat Supply Chain*, CSR, Sustainability, Ethics & Governance,
https://doi.org/10.1007/978-3-031-34977-5_8

There are at least two sets of considerations supporting the need to enhance the value, for tax purposes, of sustainable (versus environmentally harmful) production chains.

First, enhancing the value, for tax purposes, of sustainable production chains fits perfectly into those forms of widespread legal protection that environmental preservation has benefited over time through the regulatory provision of "market instruments" as applied to a broad variety of areas in the legal practice.

As a matter of fact, the expression "market instruments" is a label that covers multiple instruments with different characteristics, including cap and trade programs, subsidies and tax incentives, environmental taxes, liability cases, compensation schemes as well as, most recently, enhancement of the value, for tax purposes, of sustainable production chains.

Despite being different, while the aforementioned institutions cannot be regarded as alternatives to one another, they share a number of peculiar features:

(i). in the first place, they attribute a value to the external costs and benefits of economic activities so that economic operators can take them into account and change their behavior accordingly in order to curb environmental adverse effects and boost beneficial ones;
(ii). in addition, depending on the types of incentives, the subject matter of the measures and the way the measures operate, they may provide an incentive for enterprises to commit, in the long term, to technological innovation so as to further reduce the adverse effects on the environment and embark on a path of ecological transition.

Second, the need to value—also for tax purposes—sustainable production chains is a practical way of achieving SDG 12 of the UN's 10-year plan for a sustainable consumption and production model (United Nations, 2015). This goal highlights the need to encourage sustainable production models by incentivizing resource and energy efficiency, as well as ensuring access to basic services, decent and environmentally friendly jobs and a better quality of life for all.

This is essentially because sustainable production chains are expected to contribute towards fulfilling several goals, including:

- the reduction of future economic, environmental, and social costs;
- the improvement of economic competitiveness;
- the achievement of widespread poverty reduction.

Based on the above, the paragraphs below discuss the role of taxation in connection with environmental protection and highlight its possible contribution to the ecological transition in corporate production chains.

2 Taxation, Environmental Protection, and Sustainable Production Chains

As mentioned earlier, legislators can use a variety of instruments to implement environmentally driven legislative choices, including, in their own right, tax regulations aimed to:

(i). safeguard the healthiness of the environment;
(ii). boost companies' use of production modes that are not harmful to the environment (and, indeed, that are capable of enhancing the value of the surrounding environmental resources);
(iii). encourage the use of sustainable production chains that, as such, are capable of not wasting environmental resources while creating value for the community.

Still, the relationship between taxation and the environment has undergone a number of changes over time.

More specifically, there has been a shift away from the predominance of the so-called "Pigouvian theory" (targeting tax negative externalities and establishing a direct correlation between the damage caused to the environment and payment of a tax) and toward theories supporting the provision of benefits and reliefs capable of bolstering those production policies that are aimed at safeguarding the environment.

The purpose of this approach is essentially twofold:

(i). to steer production, and thus consumption, by abandoning the idea of tax neutrality in the economy;
(ii). to put in place more interventionist policies as a result of which such production processes as are polluting or inconsistent with reuse principles turn out to be more expensive.

In this scenario, environmental levies play a key role both for environmental protection and preservation and, more specifically, as a potential tool to accelerate the processes of ecological transition and thus a shift from polluting production chains to environmentally sustainable production mechanisms.

Hence, taxation, viewed as an instrument of environmental protection, should fulfill an additional function, i.e., it should meet the need to incentivize sustainable production chains so as to increase the benefits for businesses as well as in terms of collective welfare.

Otherwise said, taxation could be used, for example:

- to encourage use fewer resources in the production cycle;
- to reduce environmental degradation;
- to significantly mitigate, if not eliminate altogether, pollution in the entire production cycle.

Along these lines, it would seem useful to ascertain how taxation is, to date, part of the processes aimed at fostering the ecological transition of production processes, so as to subsequently verify which profiles are most worthy of attention and future intervention.

2.1 *Taxation as a Tool for Implementing Ecological Transition Processes: How Far along the Way Are We?*

In functional terms, environmental taxes, by taxing environmentally harmful processes and services, are able to "internalize" negative externalities in market prices.

Indeed, environmental damage gives rise to costs that are borne by the entire community (e.g., for protecting health or repairing the infrastructure damaged by pollution). If these costs are not borne by polluters, they are externalized, that is, borne by those who have not benefited from the polluting activity.

Since the production costs incurred by those who carry out a polluting activity do not include these "externalized" costs, the trade-off will always result in an "incorrect market signal" because it will, in a way, encourage the polluting activity beyond the "socially optimal" level for the overall economic system (Driesen, 1997).

Thus, in a nutshell, environmental taxes solve such a "market failure" by placing onto the shoulders of the so-called "polluters" the cost that would otherwise have to be borne by the entire community.

Indeed, a tax on polluting activities inevitably determines an increase in production costs, which will most likely be passed on by the entrepreneur to the final prices of traded goods.

Therefore, the effects of the introduction of the above-mentioned taxes will also be beneficial for on the demand side, as they will inevitably make disadvantageous those spending choices that relate to environmentally harmful products (Allena, 2022a, 2022b).

But there is more.

Environmental taxes are also capable of generating revenue and, on closer inspection, may prove to be a useful tool for redistributing the tax burden at different levels of taxpaying capacity.

Moreover, increasing the tax burden on polluting activities could enable national legislators to reduce the tax burden on activities that are beneficial for the economy, such as sales or labor, and pro-cyclically improve the national domestic product (Gallo & Marchetti, 1999).

In light of the above, the relationship between taxation and environmental protection turns out to be very close indeed. This is because taxation becomes a means of encouraging a shift to more environmentally friendly modes of production.

From this angle, two considerations would seem to be possible:

- first, in the three-pronged relationship among "taxation," "environmental protection," and "ecological transition," taxation is a means of achieving true sustainable economic and industrial development, that is, of bringing about a business production and growth model that enables present needs to be met, generate

beneficial effects on the company and the community without jeopardizing the ability of future generations to meet new needs that may arise over time;
- second, as will be discussed in more detail in the following section, the ecological transition necessarily entails levying environmental taxes—and, in any case, a higher tax burden—on those who, prospectively, all else being equal, do not implement an ecological conversion of their business activities.

The possibility of taxation becoming an effective tool for incentivizing a behavioral change and helping achieve strategic goals is demonstrated, for example, by some recent changes in the European system.

In the past decade, for example, the decline by about 40% in tobacco consumption in the EU can be ascribed to taxation; likewise, the sharp decline in plastic grocery bags in some countries results from the introduction of effective plastic taxes, namely the so-called *plastic tax* (which in Italy is expected to apply from January 2024).

Still, the European environmental taxation framework—and in particular energy taxation—was developed in the 1990s and last updated in 2003. For this reason, it is inadequate to accompany the environmental (energy and, as a result, ecological) transition of the future (Gherassimos, 2022).

At present, as will be highlighted in the following section, fiscal measures aimed at incentivizing green transition processes and the shift to instruments capable of enhancing the value, for tax purpose, of sustainable production chains would seem:

- on the one hand, to materialize in forms of indirect taxation aimed at internalizing negative externalities (i.e., damage to the environment and health, resulting from the production chain) in the producer's cost profiles;
- on the other hand, to be entrusted exclusively—at least from a European perspective—to the decision-making and legislative autonomy of individual Member States.

3 Fiscal Measures Supporting the Ecological Transition in the European Experience

The ecological transition is a process through which human societies relate to the physical environment, aiming for more balanced and harmonious relationships within the framework of local and global ecosystems.

In a more narrow and practical sense, it is a process of technological conversion whose purpose is to produce fewer pollutants.

The term "transition"—which, according to the literature, can have different definitions depending on the context—when applied to "ecology," takes on a quite peculiar meaning.

Indeed, it has been pointed out that, whenever the concept of "ecological transition" is referred to, it would necessarily refer to two different moments (Bennet, 2017), that is to say:

(i). the growing incorporation of nature into social culture;
(ii). the ability of the local group to meet its needs with existing resources in a given geographical area.

The ecological transition processes implemented, to date, in the European Union would appear to rely on three different taxation models:

1. the so-called "carbon taxes";
2. the taxation of car ownership;
3. energy taxation.

More precisely, according to a recent report drawn up by the European Commission (European Commission, 2020):

(i). having regard to the carbon tax, according to the sample of European countries considered for the purpose of the report, 16 out of 33 have adopted some form of carbon tax. The tax rates applied range from less than 1 euro per ton of carbon emissions (in Poland) to 110 euros in Sweden. Moreover, while some countries have had carbon taxes in place for nearly 30 years (Finland, Sweden, Denmark, Norway, Poland), others have introduced it relatively recently (Portugal, France, Spain) or are considering introducing it in the future (the Netherlands and Austria). In addition, significantly different tax rates and varying definitions of the carbon tax scope of application or of the tax base very much point to the lack of regulatory uniformity among States.
(ii). as to the taxation of car ownership, the report shows that this tax measure is widely used. And in fact, almost all of the countries considered in this piece of research do tax vehicles in one form or another. However, the report also shows that individual tax regimes differ in many ways, including, for example, depending on the types of vehicles and the tax bases considered in order to calculate tax rates;
(iii). lastly, looking at forms of energy taxation, the report points out that Directive 2003/96/EC sets forth the minimum rates of excise duty to be applied by Member States to energy products for motor fuels, heating fuels, and electricity. In principle, Member States are free to apply excise rates above these minimum taxation levels, according to their national needs and environmental ambitions.

Two extremely interesting profiles would seem to emerge from the report's data briefly referred to above.

On the one hand, it is clear that the theme of environmental protection—more so than ecological transition—is one of interest for national legislations and, specifically, tax legislations.

On the other hand, it would clearly seem that:

- first, each Member State is, in point of fact, free to adopt autonomous fiscal policies, depending on—as highlighted in the report—its national needs and environmental ambitions;
- second, the use of taxation as an instrument of environmental preservation and incentive for ecological transition works mostly downstream of the production chain (e.g. taxation of carbon emissions) rather than upstream and thus, directly inside production chains.

In this context, EU countries have embraced a further trend consisting of leveraging on ad hoc tax reliefs to foster ecological transition (and environmental protection) processes.

Here again, the European Commission report clearly points out that over 100 tax incentives are used across EU states.

Among these measures, by way of example, the following stand out:

- tax incentives to encourage the adoption of e-vehicles, which can take different forms (e.g., exemption from registration fees, road taxes, or both);
- tax incentives to improve energy efficiency and related innovation. In this regard, income or corporate tax rebates are very common when individuals or companies decide to renovate their buildings in order to bring them in line with energy efficiency standards.
- tax incentives to strengthen public transportation as a means to reduce harmful emissions in the surrounding environment.

From a "systematic" perspective, also the adoption of said tax incentives is left entirely to individual states, with the resulting effect being that:

- tax incentives could be an ideal opportunity to promote cross-border policy learning;
- the framework appears to be composite and lacks internal consistency across the European Union;
- processes of ecological transition appear to rely on tax reliefs that tend not to be included in a broader organic tax legislative framework;
- the production chain (i.e., corporate income) is not viewed as a tax handle; rather, taxation always tends to be linked to consumption and, therefore, to a stage that follows after that of production.

The profiles outlined above are extremely significant and allow for some considerations on the possible or required interventions on—and developments of—the matter under examination in the not too distant future.

3.1 *Taxation and Ecological Transition Toward Sustainable Production Chains: Is a Change of Perspective Necessary?*

In light of the preceding considerations, the current European context in which taxation is used as an instrument of environmental preservation and ecological transition would seem to be connoted by:

- a lack of regulatory uniformity among Member States (due to the current allocation of legislative powers between the States on the one hand and the European Union on the other hand);
- the application of targeted but extemporaneous (rather than systematic) tax reliefs;
- a disconnect between the determination of the tax amount and the acknowledgement, if any, of the sustainable nature of the enterprise's production chain.

Because of this, the current understanding of the relationship between taxation and ecological transition could (or should) be profoundly reconsidered.

More precisely, it would seem appropriate to go beyond just applying the well-known "polluter pays" principle and the other indirect taxation mechanisms referred to above.

Rather, action should be taken through the application of structural (rather than one-off) measures that consider the "environment" and "ecological" factors for income determination and taxation purposes, valuing sustainable production chains from a fiscal perspective.

Environmental taxes offer a number of advantages that make them a preferred option for economists specializing in environmental policy, which explains why the Academia insists on using them as well as the interest of many international organizations. These are instruments that aim to "get the right prices" while respecting the "polluter pays" principle, and they do so by leading the operators to make the appropriate decisions.

However, this principle essentially fulfills—as can be inferred from its wording—a dual function:

- on the one hand, it places an economic and/or pecuniary burden onto the operators that have engaged in environmentally harmful conduct;
- on the other hand, it serves as a means of preventing environmentally harmful conducts. This is because the economic operator, being aware of the economic risk that would arise in the event that it engages in a conduct that is harmful for the environment, will, clearly, be disincentivized from engaging in such conduct.

However, this principle would neither seem to mandate nor incentivize the adoption of ecological transition processes inside production chains.

Quite to the contrary, it would seem to place obligations to "not do something" on economic operators.

This aspect is far from ancillary, both conceptually and in terms of application; indeed, one thing is to disincentivize harmful conducts, and quite another thing is to adopt legislative policies aimed at incentivizing choices capable of producing beneficial effects on the social community.

In other words, one thing is to impose an obligation to pay aimed at restoring (if at all possible) from the damage caused by an environmentally harmful conduct, and quite another thing is to claim the willingness to consider as fiscally relevant for the purpose of determining total income such business choices as have not only forestalled damage to the environment but which, more than that, have stood out for their sustainability from an ecological and/or environmental point of view.

From this perspective, the "polluter pays" principle would seem to be only part of a broader response that taxation is called upon to give both to environmental protection processes and, more specifically, to ecological transition.

As a matter of fact, in this context, additional—rather than alternative—forms of environmental taxation should come forth that have a direct impact on the life and production phase of the businesses.

More specifically, as said earlier, environmental taxation ranges between "punitive" taxation (i.e., taxes or fees on such goods or services as harm the environment) and "incentivizing" taxation; as such, it would be necessary to steer taxation in such a way that it serves as a driver of ecological transition, along at least two lines of action:

- on the one hand, extend the scope of tax interventions to include direct taxes, especially corporate income taxes;
- on the other hand, consequently, not only sanction or prevent environmentally harmful behaviors but, rather, incentivize virtuous behaviors by companies and managers so as to improve the sustainability of their enterprises.

4 Taxation and Ecological Transition from the Italian Perspective: The "Plan for Ecological Transition"

Based on the considerations under the preceding paragraphs, which are meant to provide an overview of what seems to be the current approach in the EU to the relationship between taxation, environmental protection, and ecological transition, set out below is an analysis of this relationship from a specifically Italian perspective in relation to how the processes of ecological transition and taxation interact in the Italian body of laws and regulations.

Also in Italy, the need to continue and implement the processes necessary for an ecological transition of corporate production chains is a current and urgent theme.

This is evidenced by the recent Italian "*Plan for Ecological Transition*" of March 8, 2022, which makes it clear from the outset that "*talking about ecological transition today necessarily means broadening the perspective and evaluation criteria (...) considering the indicators of economic progress alongside environmental and social ones (...) also extending the reference horizon to future decades that will affect not only our generation, but also those who will come after us.*"

Building on the above assumption, the Italian Plan for Ecological Transition identifies three technical and economic aspects that are a must in order to achieve the Plan's goals (Quaranta, 2022), as summarized below:

- the first concerns governance and the "critical mass" of investments. In relation to this, the Plan highlights that—in order to achieve the integration and synergy of interventions and related funds earmarked for decarbonization, sustainable development and ecological transition on the basis of DNSH ("*Do not signficant harm*") in a systemic perspective of consistent policy choices—the "*largest volume of available resources (the 'critical mass,' ed.)* will be needed in order *to maximize the impact of investments and accelerate the transformation process at the national and local levels.*"
- the second concerns sustainability as a business driver for SMEs, that is to say, sustainability that "alongside the digital and technological transformations, offers unmissable opportunities for the Italian entrepreneurial fabric (mostly comprised of small- and medium-sized businesses");
- the third relates to the economic drivers for implementing the Plan. In this regard, the Plan specifies that "*one more pillar of the Ecological Transition Plan will have to be a comprehensive and structured reform of the taxation system, one that is aimed at addressing environmental issues and (...) could include a number of corrections of current market distortions (...).*"

Testifying to the very close relationship between taxation and environmental protection, among the pillars identified for steering production chains toward choices and conducts that are mindful of the ecological transition, the last pillar is specifically focused on taxation and, in particular, on a reform of the taxation system as a condition for implementing the national Plan.

In relation to this, besides the statement of intent referred to above, the Plan provides further clarifications as to how to reform the taxation system so that it is instrumental in an ecological transition plan.

In this regard, in fact, it is specified that a taxation encouraging the transition to the circular economy should be developed and implemented:

- both with the phasing out of environmentally harmful subsidies;
- and with positive forms of incentives for asset repair activities and for a more sustainable design of the same.

To this end, the Plan further specifies that new consumer education and interdisciplinary training programs should be designed for circular economy experts, while developing facilities and public–private agreements for entrepreneurial development in this new sector.

In addition, again from the perspective of reforming the tax system, the Plan for Ecological Transition proposes to tie a portion of the revenue from new forms of environmental taxation to measures that encourage sustainable investment, consumption, and production. This approach, moreover, would be in line with SDG 12, "*Ensure sustainable consumption and production patterns*," of the United Nations Agenda 2030 and the strategic choices of the National Sustainable Development Strategy.

In light of the above, the guidance under the Plan for Ecological Transition would seem to confirm the need highlighted in the previous paragraphs for a change in perspective for the purposes of environmental taxation.

And in fact, where the Plan proposes to:

- establish positive incentives for asset repair activities in view of a more sustainable design of the same;

and

- tie a portion of the revenue from new forms of environmental taxation to measures that encourage sustainable forms of production;

it would seem to be shifting the focus toward the need to use taxation not only as a punitive/reparative instrument but also to incentivize, as early as during the production of goods and conception of services, the adoption of environmentally sustainable choices in line with the need for ecological transition.

4.1 Circular Economies as a Tool for Promoting an Ecological Transition of Production Chains

Given the importance and urgency of changing the mainstream approach of tax legislators to environmental protection and ecological transition, the Italian Plan briefly referred to in the previous paragraph tries to identify which economic and production management model might be most suitable to achieve widespread decarbonization and eliminate environmentally harmful subsidies.

In this sense, the Plan for Ecological Transition identifies circular economy processes as the most suitable approach both from a strictly economic and management perspective and for assigning to taxation the function to incentivize and facilitate ecological transition toward sustainable production chains.

This is essentially because circular economies originate as a new model of production and consumption aimed to reduce waste generation by extending the life of materials and products through sharing, lending, reusing, repairing, reconditioning, and recycling of the same.

The insight in the Italian Plan for Ecological Transition would seem to be correct and consistent, first of all, with the guidance of the "*European Green Deal*" that:

- is based on European Commission Communication COM (2019) 640, which outlines an initial roadmap of key policies and measures for Europe's ecological (or green) transition;

- represents the European Union's main reference tool for ecological (or green) transition.
- is, as highlighted by the Commission itself, a new growth strategy aimed at transforming the European Union into a just and prosperous society with a modern, resource-efficient, and competitive economy that will generate no net greenhouse gas emissions in 2050 and in which economic growth will be decoupled from the use of resources.

And in fact, among the pillars that underpin the implementation of the European *Green Deal* is the use of circular economy mechanisms and thus the need to shift from an economic paradigm based on the linear economy to a new one of sustainable production aimed at reducing the exploitation of natural resources.

In this sense, the promotion of the circular economy model should also take place through the application of tax measures to encourage:

- the reuse of all raw materials, products, waste, and scrap (zero waste goal);
- the production of the maximum possible value from the company's reuse policies;
- energy savings and reduction of greenhouse gas emissions.

Secondly, the identification of circular economy mechanisms as tools to incentivize, through ad hoc tax measures, the processes of ecological transition of production chains, is also in line with the provisions of Italy's PNRR (NRRP, National Recovery and Resilience Plan).

The NRRP pays special attention to the implementation of policies designed to develop and promote "circular economy" production models.

Generally speaking, the lines of action pertain to the provision of various measures impacting different sectors, such as the relationship between circular economy and agriculture and the implementation of circular economy models at the national level.

More precisely, the Circular Economy and Sustainable Agriculture component aims to pursue a two-pronged approach to full environmental sustainability:

- on the one hand, boost waste management and circular economy by enhancing waste segregation infrastructures, modernizing or developing new waste treatment facilities and implementing highly innovative projects for strategic supply chains such as waste from electrical and electronic equipment (WEEE), paper and cardboard industry, textiles, mechanical recycling, and plastics chemistry;
- on the other hand, develop a smart and sustainable agricultural/food supply chain, reducing the environmental impact of one of Italy's best practices, through "green" supply chains.

These measures aim to achieve two, fundamental, goals: *(i)* first, full environmental sustainability; *(ii)* second, enhanced competitiveness and inclusivity of the economy, ensuring a high standard of living for people and reducing environmental impacts.

These goals should be achieved through an approach aimed at:

(i). developing a smart and sustainable agricultural/food supply chain, thus curbing the environmental impact of one of Italy's top-quality industries, through "green" supply chains;
(ii). improving waste management and circular economy by upgrading or developing new waste treatment facilities and implementing highly innovative circular economy flagship projects, e.g., for the management of electrical and electronic waste (WEEE).

In this context, two disincentivizing tax measures (Allena, 2022a, 2022b) could fit in from a strictly fiscal perspective, namely:

- the well-known "*Plastic Tax*" (which is expected to be applied in Italy from January 2024);
- the so-called "*Textile Tax*," aimed at combating product waste from fast fashion

Third, the insight in the Plan for Ecological Transition is in line with what has already matured over time, including in the tax literature: indeed, the latter has repeatedly emphasized that circular economy processes should be the focus of national legislators so that they incentivize, through specific tax measures, the implementation of sustainable production chains.

More precisely:

- the transition to a circular economy is a complex process that requires comprehensive commitment at multiple levels and from multiple members of society; as such, achieving systemic change through the use of a single policy instrument may prove to be insufficient, so that a more complex approach would be needed, developing a policy mix that addresses the multiple aspects of the transition to the circular economy (Milios, 2021).
- it has been argued that the implementation of circular-economy-driven production models is based on the concept of taxation with non-fiscal purposes (e.g. the "sin tax"). Hence, in order to use taxation as a tool to incentivize "circular taxation" processes (rather than just for raising revenue for the public budget), taxation as such should also pursue other objectives of an industrial, commercial, social, health, or environmental nature (Vence & Lòpez Pèrez, 2021).

Furthermore, looking specifically at the Italian legal practice, the literature has identified several lines of action potentially conducive to the implementation of circular economy models, as summarized below:

- the capital goods depreciation mechanism has been identified as an appropriate tool for promoting the circular economy, thus fast-tracking the possibility of enhancing the value of capital goods that comply with the canons of the circular economy (Ficari, 2016).
- it has been proposed that those profits that are reinvested for the environmental efficiency of production chains be deductible from the corporate tax base (Greggi, 2020).

Based on the policy considerations of the European "*Green Deal*" and those of the Italian plans referred to above, and considering what has also been highlighted in the specialized literature, it is clear that taxation is more and more incisively at the service of the ecological transition, thus becoming not only a tool to discourage entrepreneurial conducts that are harmful to the environment but also potentially having the ability to steer business choices toward ecologically minded attitudes even inside production chains.

To do so, however, a radical shift is necessary in the European (and Italian) approach, through forms of taxation that encourage the transition to the circular economy, by:

- strengthening the instruments that embody the Community's "polluter pays" principle;
- adopting fiscal measures that are able to incentivize the reuse, recycling and recovery of materials (i.e., the very principles on which circular economies are based) not only through indirect taxation but also impacting directly on the income of waste-reducing activities.

5 Conclusions

In light of the foregoing considerations, it is clear that taxation, as well, does play a role to help the ecological transition move forward.

As a matter of fact, taxation can—and indeed, will have to—be even more central, incentivizing the transition of public and private activities toward internationally agreed-upon sustainable and ecologically minded development goals.

This, moreover, will also help broaden, compared to the past, the operating range of the environmental tax system. Indeed, while in recent decades, as mentioned earlier, attention to radical green tax reforms has not always been encouraged (with mechanisms for internationalizing the potential costs that arise from the implementation of business conducts potentially harmful for the environment having been used instead), "green" tax reforms must now be one of the cornerstones of new regulatory proposals.

More precisely, given its cross-cutting function in directing the behavior of citizens, taxation should increasingly be considered as one of the main tools for ensuring the transition to sustainable production models. In particular, it will be up to governments (and not just the Italian one, for that matter) to implement in their body of laws and regulations such fiscal policies as are aimed at promoting ecological transition processes.

In other words, it will be necessary to incentivize—including through taxation—economic, social, cultural and, of course, environmental sustainability, by considering not just the (final) stage, i.e., consumption, but also the environmental sustainability (or otherwise) of the processes by which the goods consumed were produced.

References

Allena, M. (2022a). *Ecologia e Tributi Ambientali, Dizionario di Dottrina Sociale della Chiesa, Le cose nuove del XXI secolo*, pp. 11–12.
Allena, M. (2022b). *Circular Economy and Environmental Taxation PNRR e incentivi fiscali all'economia circolare, Green Deal e prospettive di riforma della tassazione ambientale* (p. 164). Cacucci Editore.
Bennet, J. W. (2017). *The ecological transition* (p. 6). Routledge.
Communication from the Commission to the European Parliament, the European Council, the Council, the European Economic and Social Committee and the Committee of the Region. (2019), The European Green Deal.
Driesen, D. M. (1997). The societal cost of environmental regulation: Beyond administrative cost: Benefit analysis. *Ecology Law Quarterly, 24*(3), 545–618.
European Commission. (2020). *Taxation in support of green transition: An overview and assessment of existing tax practices to reduce greenhouse gas emissions*, Final report.
Ficari, V. (2016). Nuovi elementi di capacità contributiva ed ambiente: l'alba diun nuovo giorno fiscalmente più verde?, *Riv. trim. dir. trib.*, p. 827.
Gallo, F., & Marchetti, F. (1999). I presupposti della tassazione ambientale, in *Rassegna Tributaria*, p. 115 ss.
Gherassimos, T. (2022, December 9). La transizione ecologica passa anche da un fisco attento ai comportamenti, *Il Sole 24 Ore*.
Greggi, M. (2020), L'ambiente e l'economia circolare nel diritto tributario, in *Green Deal e prospettive di riforma della tassazione ambientale*, Cacucci Editore, p. 42.
Milios, L. (2021). *Towards a circular economy taxation framework: Expectations and challenges of implementation* (p. 478). Springer.
Quaranta, A. (2022). Il Piano per la Transizione Ecologica: aspetti tecnici e culturali della svolta da imprimere al nostro Paese. *Ambiente e Sviluppo, 7*, 484.
United Nations. (2015). *Trasformare il nostro mondo: l'Agenda 2030 per lo Sviluppo Sostenibile*.
Vence, X., & Lòpez Pèrez, J. (2021). Taxation for a circular economy: New instruments, reforms, and architectural changes in the fiscal system. *Sustainability, 13*, 4581.

Protecting Farm Animal Biodiversity through Geographical Indications: A Legal Analysis

Luca Leone and Domenico Cristallo

1 Introduction

Over the last decades, increasing loss of genetic diversity in livestock farming has occurred for reasons mostly similar to those leading to the decline in plant varieties. Since the Industrial Revolution and the so-called Green Revolution started in the 1960s, in fact, deforestation and environmental degradation related to intensive forms of land use and husbandry systems have made agricultural methods incompatible with natural ecosystems, thereby compromising plant and animal biodiversity (FAO, 2019). The choice of high-productive breeds in farm management, specifically, has run hand in hand with a growing preference for products of animal origins that has been one of the main traits characterizing economic welfare in developed countries.

These changes have ended up impacting on today's knowledge-informed agricultural practices, representing a big threat for biological variety of microorganisms, flora and fauna (IPBES, 2019). According to the International Union for Conservation of Nature's (IUCN) estimates, of the 150.388 species assessed, 42.108 are considered to be threatened with extinction (IUCN, 2023).

This work expresses reflections and opinions shared by the authors. However, paragraphs 1, 2, 5 and 6 have been written by Luca Leone, while paragraphs 3 and 4 have been written by Domenico Cristallo.

L. Leone (✉)
Department of Agriculture, Food and Environment, Università di Pisa, Pisa, Italy
e-mail: luca.leone@unipi.it

D. Cristallo
Department of Juridical Sciences, Università Cattolica del Sacro Cuore, Piacenza, Italy
e-mail: domenico.cristallo@unicatt.it

A. M. Fellegara et al. (eds.), *Sustainable Transition of Meat and Cured Meat Supply Chain*, CSR, Sustainability, Ethics & Governance,
https://doi.org/10.1007/978-3-031-34977-5_9

Against this alarming scenario, the European Union (EU) has approached farm animal biodiversity with a multifaceted regulatory framework combining traditional rules with soft (i.e. non-legally binding) forms of normativity, in order to protect local and native animal breeds, while promoting sustainability of the livestock sector.

Over the years, two mutually coherent approaches have underpinned the EU biodiversity strategy (CEC, 1998; EC, 2001, 2006, 2011). On the one hand, the need for adequate gene banks useful for the conservation—in situ and ex situ—of genetic resources for food and agriculture has led to reinforce existing legislation on the matter. On the other hand, indirect forms of biodiversity preservation have prompted to act on regulations concerning quality labels, organic farming, geographical indications (GIs) and designations of origin, in the light of their potential contribution to maintain land use practices beneficial for genetic resources.

Legislation on GIs (that is, PDOs[1] and PGIs[2]), in particular, has become a tool through which to integrate, among other things, biodiversity conservation with the objectives pursued by the Common Agricultural Policy (CAP). Indeed, by relying on the relations among the product, the territory and its history, protection of GIs is supposed to help maintain a genetic pool of rustic domesticated species, thus contributing to prevent genetic erosion and foster the conservation of special agro-ecosystems that can enhance biodiversity (Arfini & Bellassen, 2019).

In 2022, in the face of the EU *Green Deal* aimed at making the agrifood realm more resilient and sustainable (EC, 2019), the GIs system has been put under normative revision. The reform is expected to increase the uptake of GIs for the benefit of rural economy, while preserving the gastronomic and cultural heritage of Member States.

For the purpose of the analysis presented here, a core question arises: Will the future GIs regulatory framework be suitable to support the protection and valorization of genetic diversity in EU livestock farming? This is the crucial query which this chapter is structured on and around. The final goal aims to explore whether and how the legislative review will be fitting with the need for a more inclusive approach that efficiently embeds and deals with the biological, ecological and social aspects pertaining to farm animal biodiversity.

2 The EU Policy Strategy on Animal Genetic Resources in Agriculture

The term 'agri-biodiversity' refers to the heritage of plant, animal and microbial genetic resources resulting from the action carried out by biological mechanisms and natural selection throughout the centuries. Agricultural biodiversity is, therefore, the

[1] Protected Denominations of Origin.

[2] Protected Geographical Indications.

outcome of interactions developing among genetic resources, scientific knowledge, management systems and traditional practices. As an excellent example of value/resource binomial, it is inextricably linked to climate and the environment, as well as to human ingenuity and cultural preferences (OECD, 2018).

The changes that animal agriculture has gone through since World War II, though, have profoundly affected and shaped the agricultural sector and the ecosystem services it delivers. While industrialization has entailed a decrease of the costs associated with the production, processing and distribution of animal products, the environmental impacts of outdoor and indoor livestock farming have spilled over into air and water quality, land use and climate. Likewise, genetic selection—phenotypic originally, genotypic in the last 40 years—has prompted a decrease in genetic diversity among animals raised for production, which in turn has led to a progressive increase in crop vulnerability and a continuing decrease in food security (Dasgupta, 2021; UNEP, 2021).

This panorama has been at the core of the EU institutions' attempt to legally preserve agri-biodiversity, by taking into account its tripartite declination in genetic diversity ('within species'), species diversity ('between species') and ecosystem diversity (the ecosystems formed by populations of species relevant to agriculture or species communities dependent on agricultural habitats) (Parris, 2001, 4).

Throughout targeted interventions, the EU has gradually implemented the guidelines that, in the global scenario, have elevated biological diversity to an autonomous conceptual category for a multifunctional agrifood model. The Convention on Biological Diversity[3] (CBD) and the institutional documents released by the Food and Agriculture Organization (FAO) and the World Organization for Animal Health (WOAH) are examples of this normative trend. In this way, the regulatory architecture has tried to tackle genetic erosion, in the face of the biunivocal relationship that correlates agriculture to the diversity of genetic resources.

The development of sectoral policies (the CAP, first and foremost) and specific initiatives of in situ and ex situ conservation has been promoted together with the establishment of a EU database of rare and endangered local animal breeds and the funding of research projects concerning the characterization and use of genetic resources in agriculture (CEC, 1998; EC, 2001, 2006, 2011). Parallelly, financial schemes have been implemented through Rural Development Programmes overseen by local breeding associations and national genetic resources monitoring actions (Brunori, 2020).

Particularly significant has been the desire to combine the sustainable use of animal genetic resources with the promotion of breeding practices supporting short supply chains and civic participation. This peculiarity has been evident since the

[3]United Nations (1992). Convention on Biological Diversity. Rio de Janeiro. https://www.cbd.int/doc/legal/cbd-en.pdf (accessed 17 January 2023).

early 1990s, when Regulation (EC) No 2078/1992[4] on agricultural production methods compatible with the requirements of the protection of the environment mentioned the need of aid schemes for the rearing of animals of local breeds in danger of extinction [Article 2, § 1, point (d)]. With the advent of the new millennium, the EU has continued on its way to guarantee on-farm conservation and ex situ collection of farm animal biodiversity. In parallel with a community programme on the characterization, collection and utilization of genetic resources in agriculture,[5] three main pieces of legislation have especially enriched the biodiversity-related legal framework.

The first one came to the light in 2014, with the adoption of compliance measures for users from the Nagoya Protocol on access to genetic resources and the fair and equitable sharing of benefits arising from their utilization in the Union.[6] The second Regulation was adopted in 2016 as regards the zootechnical and genealogical conditions for the breeding, trade in and entry into the Union of purebred breeding animals, hybrid breeding pigs and the germinal products thereof.[7] The third legislation concerned the transboundary movements of genetically modified organisms (GMOs), with the aim to establish a common system of notification and information suitable to guarantee the conservation and sustainable use of biological diversity.[8]

Yet, notwithstanding these regulatory interventions, the EU has de facto remained far from halting the intensity of drivers of agri-biodiversity loss in its territory (ECA, 2020). Some NGOs have outlined how the little progress achieved by institutions has been 'mainly due to poor strategy design, ambiguous targets, lack of national accountability and a lack of commitment to change the status quo' (Birdlife International, 2019, 7). The shortcomings stemming from new legislation and the financing and enforcement of existing legislation reflected a lack of high-level political commitment to take responsibility on delivering the objectives of the EU biodiversity strategy (EC, 2020a).

Furthermore, inadequacy of the EU measures and fundings in addressing the decline in animal genetic diversity has clearly showed how preserving genetic

[4]Council Regulation (EEC) No 2078/92 of 30 June 1992 on agricultural production methods compatible with the requirements of the protection of the environment and the maintenance of the countryside, OJ L 215/85.

[5]Council Regulation (EC) No 870/2004 of 24 April 2004 establishing a Community programme on the conservation, characterisation, collection and utilisation of genetic resources in agriculture and repealing Regulation (EC) No 1467/94, OJ L 162/18.

[6]Regulation (EU) No 511/2014 of the European Parliament and of the Council of 16 April 2014 on compliance measures for users from the Nagoya Protocol on Access to Genetic Resources and the Fair and Equitable Sharing of Benefits Arising from their Utilization in the Union, OJ L 150/59.

[7]Regulation (EU) 2016/1012 of the European Parliament and of the Council of 8 June 2016 on zootechnical and genealogical conditions for the breeding, trade in and entry into the Union of purebred breeding animals, hybrid breeding pigs and the germinal products thereof and amending Regulation (EU) No 652/2014, Council Directives 89/608/EEC and 90/425/EEC and repealing certain acts in the area of animal breeding ('Animal Breeding Regulation'), OJ L 171/66.

[8]Regulation (EC) No 1946/2003 of the European Parliament and of the Council of 15 July 2003 on transboundary movements of genetically modified organisms, OJ L 287/1.

variability goes beyond mere conservation efforts and aid schemes. It calls, rather, for a more holistic model of 'hybridized governance' (Benessia et al., 2012) where farmers' knowledge and traditions are combined with rules embedding and conveying the concepts of welfarism, quality and precaution.

In this respect, a useful contribution has come from enacting indirect forms of protection of native animal breeds. The EU legislations involved in this matter include, first, the rules on organic farming,[9] because of their references, in the choice of breeds to rear, to the capacity to adapt to local conditions and disease resistance; second, the animal health regulation,[10] in the light of the consequences that diseases affecting farm animals can have on biodiversity. In addition, the relevance that animal welfare has gained in the last decades, together with the legal acknowledgment of animal sentience in Article 13 TFEU,[11] has strongly contributed to greater consideration and attention to the issue (Leone, 2020).

Important novelties and changes have also emerged from the set of rules regarding the protection of GIs, firstly to the extent that the specifications for meats and cheeses identify the breed of origin of the raw ingredient (Gomez Ramos et al., 2006). Scholarly work has in fact showed that a significant percentage of PDO/PGI animal products in the Mediterranean countries comes from local breeds (Zjalic et al., 2012).

It is worth noticing, besides, that not only have GIs proved to play a supportive role in the conservation of several species and ecosystems (Caron et al., 2010; Evans & Blakeney, 2006), but also their link with the preservation of biodiversity can be inferred from the regulatory context. At an international level, for instance, Article 8, point (j) of the CBD regarding in situ conservation comes under the lens of observation. It does not explicitly refer to GIs; yet, an implicit reference to them derives from their being a sign that protects 'traditional lifestyles relevant for the conservation and sustainable use of biological diversity'.

In the EU normative scenario, instead, the question about the legal role that the PDO/PGI system can play in preserving local breeds and their production environments through marketing of typical products asks for a deeper analysis. Certainly, in the light of both the reform that the EU rules on quality schemes is undergoing and the novel CAP architecture entered into force, the legal relevance of GIs for the

---

[9]Regulation (EU) 2018/848 of the European Parliament and of the Council of 30 May 2018 on organic production and labelling of organic products and repealing Council Regulation (EC) No 834/2007, OJ L 150/1.

[10]Regulation (EU) 2016/429 of the European Parliament and of the Council of 9 March 2016 on transmissible animal diseases and amending and repealing certain acts in the area of animal health ('Animal Health Law'), *OJ L 84/1*.

[11]Consolidated version of the Treaty on the Functioning of the European Union—Part One—Principles—Title II—Article 13: 'In formulating and implementing the Union's agriculture, fisheries, transport, internal market, research and technological development and space policies, the Union and the Member States shall, since animals are sentient beings, pay full regard to the welfare requirements of animals, while respecting the legislative or administrative provisions and customs of the Member States relating in particular to religious rites, cultural traditions and regional heritage' (OJ C 202/54).

protection of animal genetic resources and, hence, for sustainability cannot be taken for granted (Di Lauro, 2018). As it will be shown hereinafter, sustainability depends on the quality signs' suitability to boost appropriate management practices and to influence the production system of rural areas (Flinzberger et al., 2022).

The next two sections are therefore devoted to scrutinize this intricate quandary.

3 Legislating for Food Quality: The GIs System in Europe

The plurality of meanings that the concept of food quality has acquired over the years goes hand in hand with the plethora of farmers' interests and citizens' expectations spanning from the goal of increasing the competitiveness of agricultural producers, to the need of fostering unique characteristics of specific products, which are linked to their geographical origin and to traditional know-how (Canfora, 2021). This focus on quality products and on traditional knowledge linked to them dates back to the early 1990s,[12] when the Mac Sharry reform prompted the EU policymaking to enact distinctive signs suitable to distinguish quality products with specific characteristics and protect them from unfair practices and competition.

The first Regulation on the matter was released in 1992 to prescribe a set of rules for agricultural products or foodstuffs with an identifiable geographical origin that aligned the concept of 'quality' not only with the peculiar characteristics of a given product but also with the history—human and social—of a specific territory (Trapè, 2019).

This willingness to provide farmers with legal tools that increased profitability of production and enhanced rural development was then translated into the current regulatory framework on GIs, which reflects and describes the polymorphism of quality signs (Cei et al., 2018). On the one hand, in fact, its legal basis alludes to the CAP[13] and the protection of intellectual property rights.[14] On the other hand, the objectives listed in Article 4 aim to ensure fair remuneration for product qualities and enable consumers' trust with clear and loyal information. In so doing, they give evidence of a multifaceted discipline, that is, a discipline of method, product, information and hence, of the market.

This peculiarity is highlighted by the different nature underpinning the two signs at the core of Regulation (EU) No 1151/2012. Protected Designation of Origin (PDO) is a name that identifies a product: 'a) originating in a specific place, region or, in exceptional cases, a country; b) whose quality or characteristics are essentially or exclusively due to a particular geographical environment with its inherent natural

[12] Council Regulation (EEC) No 2081/92 of 14 July 1992 on the protection of geographical indications and designations of origin for agricultural products and foodstuffs, OJ L 208/1.

[13] Art. 43(2), TFEU.

[14] Art. 118, TFEU.

and human factors; and c) the production steps of which all take place in the defined geographical area'.[15]

The close correlation between the area and the product is immediately perceivable: quality is expressed in peculiar characteristics that cannot be reproduced elsewhere and that necessarily depend on both natural and human factors. All stages of production must take place in the same geographical area, and this allows for a broader guarantee about the origin of the product. In contrast, Protected Geographical Indication (PGI) shows a weaker connection with the territory. This is because it identifies a product: 'a) originating in a specific place, region or country; b) whose given quality, reputation or other characteristic is essentially attributable to its geographical origin; and c) at least one of the production steps of which take place in the defined geographical area'.[16]

The use of the indicated distinctive signs and the protection correlated to them[17] depend on compliance with the rules contained in the specification,[18] which expresses the regulatory power of producers.[19] As a consequence, since their first adoption rules on GIs have been implemented merely as market instruments that did not embed and convey sustainability issues. Yet, Recital 23 of Reg. 1151/2012 states that, 'An agricultural product or foodstuff bearing such a geographical name must meet certain conditions laid down in a specification, such as specific requirements aimed at protecting the natural resources or landscape of the production area or improving the welfare of farm animals'.

One could observe that since recitals do not possess binding force, they represent mere descriptive and explanatory statements aimed at clarifying the normative context. It is true, instead, that these statements have acquired an increasingly significant normative value in orienting the interpretation of norms. From this perspective, they can be seen as 'prescriptive descriptions', as they shape the seemingly factual landscape legitimizing the normative provisions.

We can therefore argue that, although Recital 23 has remained mostly rhetoric, its interpretative value brings one crucial question to the forefront: In the regulatory 'storytelling' about the relationship between the product, the community and culture of a specific territory, how do PDOs and PGIs relate to sustainability and, in particular, to biodiversity conservation?

---

[15] Art. 5, Reg. 1151/2012.

[16] Ibidem.

[17] Art. 13, Reg. 1151/2012.

[18] Art. 7, Reg. 1151/2012.

[19] Only producer groups can apply for the registration of names. See Art. 49, Reg. 1151/2012.

4 The GIs Pathway Toward the Protection of Farm Animal Biodiversity

Reg. 1151/2012 never uses the term 'biodiversity' or the terms 'genetic resources' and 'genetic diversity'. The only references to animal breeds are in Articles 6 and 42: the former deals with the protection of the name; the latter provides for compliance with certain requirements when a name protected by a quality sign contains the name of an animal breed.[20]

Admittedly, associating the definition of PDOs with both specific characteristics of foodstuffs and 'natural and human factors' lays the groundwork for using such a regulatory instrument also in pursuance of biodiversity protection (Crescenzi et al., 2022). The same can be said with regard to the 'other characteristics' that, in the definition of PGIs, may guarantee the protection of animal breeds.

An indirect form of biodiversity preservation may come also from the optional quality terms scheme[21] (Cayre et al., 2018). It refers to specific horizontal characteristics, of one or more categories of products, farming methods or processing attributes which apply in specific areas, including mountain areas.[22] In this regard, legal protection addresses agricultural products in respect of which: (a) both the raw materials and the feedstuffs for farm animals come essentially from mountain areas; and (b) in the case of processed products, the processing also takes place in mountain areas.[23]

From this perspective, the role of producer groups appears of utmost interest (Cristallo, 2022). This is because they can contribute to: first, guarantee the quality, reputation and authenticity of their products on the market; second, develop promotion activities communicating the value-adding attributes of the product to consumers; and third, take measures to enhance the value of their products.[24]

After all, ensuring the quality and reputation of a food product means assuring the 'continuity of its characteristics'. This aspect is even more apparent from the reform that Regulation on PDO/PGI system is currently undergoing, where sustainability assumes relevance especially in correlation with procedural aspects. Indeed, as a direct follow-up of the *Farm to Fork* strategy (EC, 2020b), the EU Commission's proposal[25] intends to valorize the producers' initiatives that enhance the social, environmental and economic dimensions of sustainability in the product

---

[20] Art 42, Reg. 1151/2012.

[21] Art. 29, Reg. 1151/2012.

[22] Mountain areas within the Union are those delimited pursuant to Article 32(2) of Regulation (EU) No 1305/2013 of the European Parliament and of the Council of 17 December 2013 on support for rural development by the European Agricultural Fund for Rural Development (EAFRD) and repealing Council Regulation (EC) No 1698/2005, OJ L 347/487.

[23] Art. 31(1), Reg. 1151/2012.

[24] Art. 45, Reg. 1151/2012.

[25] Proposal for a Regulation of the European Parliament and of the Council on European Union geographical indications for wine, spirit drinks and agricultural products, and quality schemes for

specifications. Although the legal text lacks a normative definition of 'sustainable food', it introduces a mechanism relating to sustainability, in the face of the need for producer groups to adapt to technological, environmental and regulatory challenges (Quiñones Ruiz et al., 2018). In this vein, producers of GIs are encouraged to adhere, in the product specification, to sustainability standards higher than mandated by Union or national law and go beyond good practice in terms of social, environmental or economic undertakings.[26]

This commitment is also included among the objectives *ex* Article 4, which prescribes that, 'producers acting collectively have the necessary powers and responsibilities to manage their geographical indication, including to respond to societal demands for products resulting from sustainable production in its three dimensions of economic, environmental and social value, and to operate in the market'.

Worthy to be stressed here is that this rule alludes also to the possible recourse to private certification schemes, although with all the regulatory concerns their multiplicity poses: from the credibility of their market-driven nature, to the lack of transparency, to the added cost implications for consumers and small and medium sized enterprises and farmers (Castka & Leaman, 2016; Potts et al., 2016).

The renewed role of groups emerges, moreover, from Article 32 of the Commission's revision proposal. It states that, 'Member States may provide that public officials, and other stakeholders such as consumer groups, retailers and suppliers, also participate in the works of the producer group'. This provision reflects the Commission's desire to promote multistakeholder dialogue and cooperation, by recognizing the plurality of interests involved and the dual nature of the distinctive signs, which are meant as both market instruments and tools protecting the territory and rural community. Worthy to be mentioned, furthermore, is the Commission's power to adopt delegated acts to recognize existing sustainability standards[27] to which producers may adhere. In this vein, the proposal creates a regulatory dialogue between private autonomy and public rules.

A last novelty is the use the draft regulation makes of the term 'biodiversity'. Article 48(5) specifies in this respect that the 'other characteristics' pertaining to PGIs may include 'traditional production practices, traditional product attributes and farming practices that protect environmental value including biodiversity, habitats, nationally recognized environmental zones and landscape'.

This specification entails that the proposal, albeit lacking a direct reference to biodiversity, promotes a connection between genetic resources and geographical areas that can be translated into a sign/certificate of quality. Still, the system of animal diversity protection is totally left to the autonomy of individuals and rural communities who shall work, with the help of the authorities, to obtain the recognition and protection of animal breed.

---

agricultural products, amending Regulations (EU) No 1308/2013, (EU) 2017/1001 and (EU) 2019/787 and repealing Regulation (EU) No 1151/2012, COM(2022) 134 final, Brussels.

[26] Art. 12, Reg. 1151/2012.

[27] Art. 12(4), COM(2022) 134 final/2.

On 18 October 2022, the EU Parliament's Committee on Agriculture and Rural Development (AGRI) proposed a number of amendments to the reformed text, including references to sustainability issues.[28] It deleted, firstly, the Commission's power to define sustainability standards in different sectors. Secondly, it introduced a provision prescribing a sustainability report to be prepared by producer groups by 1 January 20206. The report should comprise 'a description of the impacts of the method of obtaining the product on sustainability, in terms of social, environmental, economic or animal health and welfare commitments, and information necessary to understand how sustainability affects the development, performance and position of the product'. In this regard, thirdly, an association of producer groups may be set up on the initiative of interested producer groups with the purpose of making recommendations to improve, inter alia, the development of GIs policies, in particular with regard to sustainability.

All these innovative and strengthened provisions proposed by the Parliament's draft report only confirm the vocation of the reform toward sustainability, as well as a revision that makes quality a concept imbued with ethical, social and environmental values. Some criticalities arise, instead, from amendments to Article 32 that concerns, as said before, the strategic role that producer groups may have in the sector. The draft text only provides for the possibility that 'a producer group may also be formed on the initiative of a Member State'. In this way, while the public relevance is formally recognized, the innovative facet of the rule is completely missed though.

With this scenario in mind, further reflections can be drown from the reformed CAP agenda, which amended Reg. 1151/2012 to simplify the GI system. In what follows, its main aspects are elucidated and discussed.

5 Which Protection from the CAP 2023–2027?

The reformed regime of the CAP *post*-2020, which generally applies from 1 January 2023, covers three Regulations establishing rules on the financing, management and monitoring of the CAP[29]; on support for national CAP strategic plans[30]; and on the

[28] European Parliament, Committee on Agriculture and Rural Development, Draft Report, 2022/0089(COD).

[29] Regulation (EU) 2021/2116 of the European Parliament and of the Council of 2 December 2021 on the financing, management and monitoring of the common agricultural policy and repealing Regulation (EU) No 1306/2013, OJ L 435/187.

[30] Regulation (EU) 2021/2115 of the European Parliament and of the Council of 2 December 2021 establishing rules on support for strategic plans to be drawn up by Member States under the common agricultural policy (CAP Strategic Plans) and financed by the European Agricultural Guarantee Fund (EAGF) and by the European Agricultural Fund for Rural Development (EAFRD) and repealing Regulations (EU) No 1305/2013 and (EU) No 1307/2013, OJ L 435/1.

common organization of the agricultural markets.[31] The new 'delivery model' proposed by the regulatory framework focuses on the performances and results achieved by Member States with respect to the objectives and targets set forth, as well as on the intention to rebalance responsibilities between the EU and national governments through enhanced subsidiarity (so-called decentralization). It is a more results-oriented CAP, whose 'environmental and climate architecture'[32] rests on a renewed model of 'enhanced conditionality', on so-called eco-schemes that are mandatory for Member States and on specific economic supports for environmental and climate commitments and other management commitments as defined under the Pillar II.

Although many doubts already surround this 'green structure', due to both the COVID-19 epidemic's impact and the Russo-Ukrainian war's repercussions on the global agrifood system (FAO, 2022), the new CAP agenda and the modalities of its implementation will be decisive for the future of PDOs and PGIs. Indeed, Regulation (EU) No 2021/2117 deals with some changes that, pending the reform of GIs, amended Reg. 1151/2012 with respect to the sustainability of these productions.

Firstly, the revision made to the objectives of Reg. 1151/2012 prescribes that quality schemes indicate or describe agricultural products with 'value-adding attributes resulting from the farming or processing methods used in their production, or from the place of their production or marketing, or from their possible contribution to sustainable development'.[33] Secondly, as regards PDOs, their product specification shall include, among other things, 'the details concerning human factors of that geographical environment may, where relevant, be limited to a description of the soil and landscape management, cultivation practices or any other relevant human contribution to the maintenance of the natural factors of the geographical environment referred to in that paragraph'.[34] Moreover, 'the product specification may contain a description of the contribution of the designation of origin or geographical indication to sustainable development'.

Specific references to animal biodiversity concern the conflicts with names of animal breeds. Article 6(2) of Reg. 1151/2012, in this regard, has been replaced by the following: 'A name may not be registered as a designation of origin or geographical indication where it conflicts with a name of a plant variety or an animal breed and is likely to mislead the consumer as to the true origin of the product or to cause confusion between products with the registered designation and the variety or breed in question. The conditions referred to in the first subparagraph shall be

[31] Regulation (EU) 2021/2117 of the European Parliament and of the Council of 2 December 2021 amending Regulations (EU) No 1308/2013 establishing a common organisation of the markets in agricultural products, (EU) No 1151/2012 on quality schemes for agricultural products and foodstuffs, (EU) No 251/2014 on the definition, description, presentation, labelling and the protection of geographical indications of aromatised wine products and (EU) No 228/2013 laying down specific measures for agriculture in the outermost regions of the Union, OJ L 435/262.

[32] Art. 109(2), Reg 2021/2115.

[33] Art. 1(2), point (b), Reg. 1151/2011 as amended by Art. 2, Reg. 2021/2117.

[34] Art. 7(1), point (f), Reg. 1151/2011 as amended by Art. 2, Reg. 2021/2117.

assessed in relation to the actual use of the names in conflict, including the use of the name of the plant variety or animal breed outside its area of origin and the use of the name of a plant variety protected by another intellectual property right'.

Although these statements could have provided a more critical overhaul of the PDO/PGI system (Di Lauro, 2022, 25), certainly they take a first step in enhancing the biodiversity-related factors inherent in local geographical areas. As known, in fact, synergies between quality schemes and sustainability vary across product types, geographical location and socio-ecological context (Flinzberger et al., 2022). This consideration entails that the recourse to PDOs or PGIs in the livestock sector depends as much on structural factors (the location of breeding facilities) as on strategies able to boost the value of fresh meat in the national contexts (the French 'Label Rouge' is an example in this regard) and the presence of structured forms of breeder associations (Belletti et al., 2008).

Additional obstacles to a policy of biodiversity valorization through GIs relate to consumer perceptions. On the one hand, the link between fresh meat and its territory is routinely recognized by consumers through the breed, which however cannot be subject to a legal protection. On the other hand, the relatively low level of processing pertaining to fresh meat seems not to allow for easy product differentiation. It is true, though, that the use of quality schemes may turn out to be advantageous for distribution enterprises. This is not only because the GI system represents both a standard of reference for breeders and a guarantee of compliance with the specification but also because it may fuel greater association of animal breeders (as it is for the Italian PGIs 'Vitellone Bianco dell'Appennino Centrale' and 'Agnello di Sardegna'), which is aimed, in turn, at triggering coordinated initiatives of promotion and commercialization of certified food products.

6 Final Remarks

The biological variability and complexity surrounding the notion of biodiversity are the result of practices, knowledge and forms of adaptation closely related to the environmental and social conditions of a given place. This presupposed, the link between food and territory is susceptible to a dual interpretation, depending on whether emphasis is put on breeding techniques, or whether the sign of quality aims at preserving local genetic resources of a given place or at reintroducing animal breeds threatened with extinction.

Affirming that GIs can strengthen biocultural diversity as an integral part of the specificity of local products seems therefore to be an agreed statement (Bérard & Marchenay, 2006). Moreover, the annotation that the indissoluble correlation with the place of origin requires the preservation of ecosystems and biodiversity is a leitmotif constantly recurring in the FAO and EU Commission's policy documents, especially when the value of GIs for the safeguarding of genetic resources through specifications targeting an ancient breed is minutely emphasized (EC, 2021; FAO, 2018).

From a legal stance, this form of support is declined into a Regulation on quality schemes that is, as this chapter has shown, framed within the CAP 'to contribute to and complement rural development policy, as well as market and income support policies'.[35] Besides, it is a legislation whose conditions laid down in the specifications constitute 'specific requirements aimed at protecting the natural resources or landscape of the production area or improving the welfare of farm animals'.[36]

Undoubtedly, such a regulatory approach needs to be coupled with the registration of animals in the herd books, so as to ensure monitoring of population trends and control of inbreeding, while strengthening the PDO/PGI certification system (Lambert-Derkimba et al., 2010). Significant is scholarly work on the selection and use of sustainability indicators for GIs as well. Against the numerous doubts that still persist on both the positive effects of GIs on all the sustainability dimensions (Dominte, 2015) and the theoretical underpinning, forms and uses of sustainability indicators in decision-making (Lehtonen et al., 2016), initiatives to ameliorate the existing structure and measurability of possible new biodiversity goals and targets under the GI framework are proliferating (Vandecandelaere et al., 2021).

It should not be overlooked, at the same time, that the reputation of some GI products could result in loss of biodiversity, because of the correlated market growth and trade internationalization that, by affecting and reshaping local ecosystems, often turn out to be detrimental for the environment (Di Lauro, 2022, 29). Likewise, linking a GI to a specific breed or rare genetic resource as a response to market demands may end up marginalizing other genetic resources that are biologically and culturally relevant, thus incentivizing loss of genetic diversity (Guerra, 2010). Further studies point out that different production needs may lead producers to modify the specification, even with reference to the plant varieties/animal breeds used, thus putting at stake the protection of autochthonous genetic resources (Arfini & Bellassen, 2019).

Such problematics testify how still numerous are the challenges that the EU legal reform needs to rigorously face to embrace GIs as a rural development strategy benefitting agri-biodiversity and local communities. The conditions of production in the specifications, together with the role of group producers and the participatory (and creative) use of traditional knowledge and practices in agriculture, are some of the aspects that the institutional debate will have to focus on and review.

The Parliament's amendments to the Commission's text seem to take an interesting avenue to address the combination of cultural and biological diversity. But undoubtedly, the Council's examination of the proposal will play its role on this matter. More critical discussion on the value of quality schemes for sustainability (and, in particular, for biodiversity conservation) will be essential to propel a normative rethinking that fosters more biodiversity-friendly husbandry systems, in

[35]Recital 4, Reg. 1151/2012.

[36]Recital 23, Reg. 1151/2012.

line with the targets on nature which the 2022 UN biodiversity conference, Cop15,[37] eventually agreed upon.

References

Arfini, F., & Bellassen, V. (Eds.). (2019). *Sustainability of European food quality schemes: Multi-performance, structure, and governance of PDO, PGI, and organic agri-food systems*. Springer.

Belletti, G., Burgassi, T., & Marescotti, A. (2008). Il ruolo delle denominazioni geografiche per la sostenibilità delle filiere zootecniche di qualità. *Agriregionieuropa, 4*(13) Accessed January 20, 2023, from https://agriregionieuropa.univpm.it/it/content/article/31/13/il-ruolo-delle-denominazioni-geografiche-la-sostenibilita-delle-filiere

Benessia, A., Funtowicz, S., Bradshaw, G., Ferri, F., Ra'ez-Luna, E. F., & Medina, C. P. (2012). Hybridizing sustainability: Towards a new praxis for the present human predicament. *Sustainability Science, 7*, 75–89.

Bérard, L., & Marchenay, P. (2006). Local products and geographical indications: Taking account of local knowledge and biodiversity. *International Social Science Journal, 58*(187), 109–116.

Birdlife International. (2019). *The EU biodiversity strategy to 2030* (Position Paper), Accessed January 23, 2023, from https://www.birdlife.org/sites/default/files/attachments/birdlife_position_biodiversity_web_01.pdf

Brunori, M. (2020). Which pathways for agrobiodiversity in the new CAP reform? *Diritto agroalimentare, 2*, 277–294.

Canfora, I. (2021). La politica della qualità dei prodotti agroalimentari dell'Ue. In P. Borghi, I. Canfora, A. Di Lauro, & L. Russo (Eds.), *Trattato di diritto alimentare italiano e dell'Unione Europea* (pp. 425–430). Milano.

Caron, A., Boisvert, V., Berthelot, C., Chambon, P., Gueringer, A. & Angeon, V. (2010). *Biodiversity conservation as a new rationale for localized and sustainable agro-food systems. The case of two French PDO mountain cheeses.* In 9th European IFSA Symposium. Vienna (Austria), Accessed January 27, 2023, from http://ifsa.boku.ac.at/cms/fileadmin/Proceeding2010/2010_WS4.1_Caron.pdf

Castka, P. & Leaman, D. (Eds) (2016). Certification and biodiversity – How voluntary certification standards impact biodiversity and human livelihoods. *Policy Matters*, Issue 21. CEESP and IUCN.

Cayre, P., Michaud, A., Theau, J., & Rigolot, C. (2018). The coexistence of multiple worldviews in livestock farming drives agroecological transition. A case study in French Protected Designation of Origin (PDO) cheese mountain areas. *Sustainability, 10*(4), 1097.

CEC. (2006). *Halting the loss of biodiversity by 2010 and beyond – Sustaining ecosystem services for human well-being*. COM (2006)216 final, Brussels.

CEC (Commission of the European Communities). (1998). *A European Community biodiversity strategy. Communication from the Commission to the Council and the European Parliament.* COM (98) 42 final, Brussels.

[37] https://www.unep.org/un-biodiversity-conference-cop-15 (accessed 27 January 2023). Convened under UN auspices, the 15th Conference of Parties to the UN Convention on Biological Diversity adopted the "Kunming Montreal Global Biodiversity Framework", including four goals and 23 targets for achievement by 2030. The global targets include, among other things: effective conservation and management of at least 30% of the world's lands, inland waters, coastal areas and oceans; reduction to near zero of the loss of areas of high biodiversity importance; positive incentives for biodiversity's conservation and sustainable use; monitoring and assessment of companies' impact on biodiversity.

Cei, L., De Francesco, E., & Stefani, G. (2018). From geographical indications to rural development: A review of the economic effects of European Union policy. *Sustainability, 10*(10), 3745.

Crescenzi, R., De Filippis, F., Giua, M., & Vaquero-Piñeiro, C. (2022). Geographical indications and local development: The strength of territorial embeddedness. *Regional Studies, 56*(3), 381–393.

Cristallo, D. (2022). Responsabilità sociale d'impresa e strumenti giuridici della filiera agroalimentare per la costruzione di un "agire responsabile". *Rivista di Diritto Agrario, 1*, 62–92.

Dasgupta, P. (2021). *The economics of biodiversity: The Dasgupta review*. HM Treasury.

Di Lauro, A. (2018). Le denominazioni d'origine protette e le indicazioni geografiche protette di fronte alla sfida dello sviluppo sostenibile. *Rivista di Diritto Agrario, 3*, 381–410.

Di Lauro, A. (2022). Gli effetti dei cambiamenti climatici sulla disciplina delle indicazioni geografiche: criticità e prospettive. *Rivista di diritto alimentare, 3*, 22–39.

Dominte, R. N. (2015). Can geographical indications bring value to environmental protection? *IUCNAEL Ejournal*, 106–110.

EC. (2011). *Communication from the Commission to the European Parliament, the Council, the European Economic and Social Committee and the Committee of the Regions – Our life insurance, our natural capital: An EU biodiversity strategy to 2020*. COM (2011) 244 final, Brussels.

EC. (2019). *Communication from the Commission to the Council, the European Parliament, the European Economic and Social Committee and the Committee of the Regions – The European Green Deal*. COM (2019) 640 final, Brussels.

EC. (2020a). *Communication from the Commission to the European Parliament, the Council, the European Economic and Social Committee and the Committee of the Regions – EU Biodiversity Strategy for 2030 – Bringing nature back into our lives*. COM (2020a) 380 final, Brussels.

EC. (2020b). *A farm to fork strategy for a fair, healthy and environmentally-friendly food system*. COM/2020/381 final, Brussels.

EC. (2021). *Evaluation support study on geographical indications and traditional specialities guaranteed protected in the EU. Directorate-General for Agriculture and Rural Development*. European Union.

EC (European Commission). (2001). *Communication from the Commission to the Council and the European Parliament – Biodiversity action plans in the areas of conservation of natural resources, agriculture, fisheries, and development and economic co-operation*. COM (2001) 162 final, Brussels.

ECA (EU Court of Auditors). (2020). *Biodiversity on farmland: CAP contribution has not halted the decline* (Special Report No 13). European Union.

Evans, G. E., & Blakeney, M. (2006). The protection of geographical indications after Doha: Quo vadis? *Journal of International Economic Law, 9*(3), 575–614.

FAO. (2019). The state of the world's biodiversity for food and agriculture. In J. Bélanger & D. Pilling (Eds.), *FAO commission on genetic resources for food and agriculture assessments*.

FAO. (2022). *Ukraine: Strategic priorities for 2023 – Restoring food systems and protecting food security*. Accessed January 22, 2023, from https://www.fao.org/3/cc3385en/cc3385en.pdf

FAO (Food and Agriculture Organization). (2018). *Strengthening sustainable food systems through geographical indications. An analysis of economic impacts*. FAO.

Flinzberger, L., Cebrián-Piqueras, M. A., Peppler-Lisbach, C., & Zinngrebe, Y. (2022). Why geographical indications can support sustainable development in European agri-food. *Frontiers in Conservation Science, 2*, 752377.

Gomez Ramos, A., Bardaji Azcarate, I., & Atance Muniz, I. (2006). The role of geographical labelling in inserting extensive cattle systems into beef marketing channels. Evidence from three Spanish case studies. *Cahiers d'économie et sociologie rurales, 78*, 82–105.

Guerra, J. L. (2010). Geographical indications, in-situ conservation and traditional knowledge. *Policy Brief, 3*, 1–11.

IPBES (Intergovernmental Science-Policy Platform on Biodiversity and Ecosystem Services). (2019). In E. S. Brondizio, J. Settele, S. Díaz, & H. T. Ngo (Eds.), *Global assessment report on biodiversity and ecosystem services of the intergovernmental science-policy platform on biodiversity and ecosystem services*. IPBES Secretariat.

IUCN (International Union for Conservation of Nature). (2023). *The IUCN red list of threatened species*. Accessed January 22, 2023, from https://www.iucnredlist.org/

Lambert-Derkimba, A., Minéry, S., Barbat, A., Casabianca, F., & Verrier, E. (2010). Consequences of the inscription of local breeds in protected designation of origin cow cheese specifications for the genetic management of the herds. *Animal, 4*, 1976–1986.

Lehtonen, M., Sébastien, L., & Bauler, T. (2016). The multiple roles of sustainability indicators in informational governance: Between intended use and unanticipated influence. *Current Opinion in Environmental Sustainability, 18*, 1–9.

Leone, L. (2020). Farm animal welfare under scrutiny: Issues unsolved by the EU legislator. *European Journal of Legal Studies, 12*(1), 47–84.

OECD (Organisation for Economic Co-operation and Development). (2018). *Mainstreaming biodiversity for sustainable development*. OECD.

Parris, K. (2001). *OECD agri-biodiversity indicators: Background paper*. Policies and Environment Division, Agriculture Directorate. OECD. Accessed January 22, 2023, from https://www.oecd.org/greengrowth/sustainable-agriculture/40350839.pdf

Potts, J., Voora, V., Lynch, M., & Mammadova, A. (2016). *Voluntary sustainability standards and biodiversity: Understanding the potential of agricultural standards for biodiversity protection*. SSI Policy Brief. International Institute for Sustainable Development.

Quiñones Ruiz, X. F., Forster, H., Penker, M., Belletti, G., Marescotti, A., Scaramuzzi, S., Broscha, K., Braito, M., & Altenbuchner, C. (2018). How are food geographical indications evolving? – An analysis of EU GI amendments. *British Food Journal, 120*(8), 1876–1887.

Trapè, A. I. (2019). Le indicazioni geografiche: un sistema plurale tra esigenze di semplificazione, diversificazione e tutela. *Rivista di Diritto Agrario, 4*, 664–695.

UNEP (United Nations Environment Programme). (2021). *Making peace with nature: A scientific blueprint to tackle the climate, biodiversity and pollution emergencies*. Accessed January 28, 2023, from https://www.unep.org/resources/making-peace-nature

Vandecandelaere, E., Samper, L. F., Rey, A., Daza, A., Mejía, P., Tartanac, F., & Vittori, M. (2021). The geographical indication pathway to sustainability: A framework to assess and monitor the contributions of geographical indications to sustainability through a participatory process. *Sustainability, 13*, 7535.

Zjalic, M., Rosati, A., Dimitriadou, A., & Murelli, E. (2012). Geographic indication of animal products and farm animal biodiversity: Case of twelve Northern and five Mediterranean Member States of the European Union. In I. Casasús, J. Rogošiç, A. Rosati, I. Štokoviç, & D. Gabina (Eds.), *Animal farming and environmental interactions in the Mediterranean region* (pp. 145–157). Wageningen Academic Publishers.

Firm Financial Performance and Growth in the Italian Meat Industry: A Longitudinal Analysis

Ilaria Galavotti and Daniele Cerrato

1 Introduction and Objectives of the Analysis

This chapter aims to offer an overview of the trends of companies operating in the Italian meat industry during the period 2017–2021, based on an in-depth analysis of the annual financial statements of 992 companies. The study has been organized in three main sections. In the first section, we introduce the industry structure by describing the companies in terms of size and geographic distribution on the Italian territory; then we develop the analysis of the performance across the three main areas of size and growth, profitability, and liquidity/financial structure. In the second section, we focus on of the major competitors in the industry, presenting data on their market shares and main indicators of economic and financial performance. Finally, in the third section, the chapter develops a picture of the firms' internationalization and modes of growth (i.e., mergers and acquisitions or strategic alliances).

Before delving into the analysis of the sampled companies, we briefly outline the methodological approach used in this study, by describing the eligibility criteria applied for the sample selection and the financial ratios and indicators that have been used to assess the performance of these firms.

I. Galavotti (✉) · D. Cerrato
Department of Economic and Social Sciences (DiSES), Università Cattolica del Sacro Cuore, Piacenza, Italy
e-mail: ilaria.galavotti@unicatt.it

A. M. Fellegara et al. (eds.), *Sustainable Transition of Meat and Cured Meat Supply Chain*, CSR, Sustainability, Ethics & Governance,
https://doi.org/10.1007/978-3-031-34977-5_10

2 Methodological Approach

The financial data and corporate information used in this analysis were collected from the AIDA database (*Analisi Informatizzata Delle Aziende*), while data on corporate growth and deals were retrieved from Zephyr, both produced by *Bureau Van Dijk*. These databases are particularly suitable for our analysis: while the former offers the company profiles and the economic and financial information on Italian corporations, the latter provides data on mergers and acquisitions and other deals executed by firms all over the world.

The companies included in this analysis have been selected based on multiple eligibility criteria:

- *Geographic location*: we focused only on Italian companies, i.e., firms having their headquarters on the Italian national territory.
- *Industry*: a selection criterion was based on the industry classification code (ATECO: 10.1—"Processing and preserving of meat and production of meat products").
- *Availability of the annual financial statements*: we set a criterion that the annual financial statements should be available for each year of observation (2017–2021).
- *Focus only on active firms*: we excluded from the analysis those companies currently under liquidation or bankruptcy procedures and kept only those firms with the last available closure date in December 2021.
- *Minimum level of revenues*: for a company to be eligible, it should have recorded at least 1 million euros revenues in at least 1 year in the observation period (2017–2021) and excluded from our sample those companies for which the time series of revenues was incomplete.

The application of the above-mentioned eligibility criteria led to the selection of a final sample of 992 companies, for which we built a panel dataset of economic and financial indicators for the 5-year period 2017–2021.

As long as the analysis of the economic-financial performance is concerned, it has been conducted based on several ratios disclosed in their annual financial statements, whose composition and meaning are outlined below.

2.1 Company Size

The firm's size is measured through three main indicators aimed at capturing both the operating and the structural aspect: number of employees; revenues (namely revenues deriving from sales and the services associated with the operating activities executed by the firm); total assets (the overall amount of the investments of the firm, including both current and non-current assets).

The number of employees registered in 2021 has been used to identify four size groups. Specifically, following the European Commission Recommendation 2003/361/EC,[1] the four size categories were defined as follows: micro (less than 10 employees); small (between 10 and 49 employees), medium (between 50 and 249 employees) and large firms (more than 250 employees).

2.2 *Profitability*

The profitability has been captured through two main indicators: EBITDA/Sales and ROA.

EBITDA/Sales (also known as *EBITDA Margin)* is a measure of the gross profitability of a firm, measured by the ratio of the gross operating margin ("Earnings before interests, taxes, depreciation, and amortization") to the firm's revenues. It indicates the firm's ability to generate income through its operating activities and hence measures the amount of operating margin that is generated for each monetary unit of sales.

ROA (Return on Assets) is the ratio between the operating income and the total assets of the firm and expresses the return on the overall firm investments. It captures the economic efficiency of the operating activities of the firm and hence measures the remuneration of the invested capital, regardless of the sources of financing being used.

In terms of interpretation of these ratios, because a firm's profitability is highly influenced by the industry in which it is active, there are normally no reference values that can be used as a benchmark in broad terms.

2.3 *Liquidity and Financial Structure*

Three indicators have been used to measure the liquidity and to assess the financial structure of the firm and the financial sustainability of firm strategy in terms of mix of the sources of financing.

Quick Ratio: this indicator measures a firm's liquidity position in the short term and thus measures the ability to meet the short-term obligations by using its liquid assets. It is calculated by dividing a firm's most liquid assets like cash, cash equivalents, marketable securities, and accounts receivables by total current liabilities.

[1] According to the European Commission Recommendation 2003/361/EC, the main indicators used to classify company size categories are: employees, annual turnover, and annual balance sheet total. In our analysis, we relied on the employee threeshold (10, 50, and 250) to identify the four groups.

The common interpretation of this indicator is that the threshold value of 1 indicates a good liquidity position, while values below 1 indicate potential difficulties in meeting short-term obligations. It should however be noted that because the composition of the liquid assets at the numerator and of current liabilities at the denominator may, more or less marginally, vary across different firms, caution should be used when interpreting the quick ratio. Therefore, observing the evolution of this ratio over time may provide richer information on the firm financial health in terms of liquidity.

Debt/Equity ratio: this indicator captures the composition of the sources of financing. Specifically, it provides information on the relationship between the external and the internal sources of funds, measuring the degree of financial dependence on external sources of financing: high values of the D/E ratio indicate that the company is highly dependent on external sources of financing, thus indicating a lower financial autonomy, while low levels of this ratio suggest that the company is able to finance its operations more through the equity from shareholders than through borrowing money. Therefore, it could also be regarded as a long-term risk assessment of the capital structure of a company.

NFP/EBITDA: it is the ratio between the net financial position (NFP) and the gross operating margin (EBITDA). The NFP is measured as follows: "Short-term bank debts + Long-term bank debts + Other short-term debts + Other long-term debts—Cash and cash equivalents." This ratio provides a measure of the extent to which the firm is able to cover their financial means through its operating margin and therefore captures the sustainability of the firm's debt position and its ability to meet its financial obligations. It can be interpreted as the number of years that will be needed to the firm to be able to repay its financial debts, given its EBITDA.

3 Companies' Profiles

The 992 Italian companies covered by our analysis collectively generated 23,677 million euros revenues in 2021 and employed 51,513 people. In terms of geographic distribution, Table 1 displays the number of companies located in each administrative region and its percentage contribution to the total. Emilia-Romagna has the highest number of registered companies (260 out of 992, corresponding to approximately 26% of the industry). Within this region, the majority of firms is located in Parma (130 companies out of 260), followed by Modena with 62 companies (24% of the region-level total). Lombardy is the region with the second higher concentration, with 191 companies (19% of the total sample). Out of these, Mantua covers the top position (39 firms, 20.42% of the region-level total), followed by Bergamo (24 companies, 12.57%) and Brescia (23 companies, 12.04%). The third region is Veneto, where 97 companies are located (almost 10% of the number of companies at the national level). Moving into the details of the towns with the highest concentration of firms in the region, the top-3 are composed of Padova (26 companies, 26.80% of the

Table 1 Distribution of companies by administrative region

Region	Number of companies	% Total
Emilia-Romagna	260	26.21%
Lombardy	191	19.25%
Veneto	97	9.78%
Piedmont	60	6.05%
Tuscany	58	5.85%
Campania	45	4.54%
Lazio	37	3.73%
Abruzzo	35	3.53%
Marches	32	3.23%
Friuli-Venezia Giulia	28	2.82%
Sicily	28	2.82%
Umbria	24	2.42%
Trentino Alto Adige	23	2.32%
Calabria	20	2.02%
Puglia	18	1.81%
Sardinia	16	1.61%
Liguria	7	0.71%
Basilicata	5	0.50%
Valle d'Aosta	5	0.50%
Molise	3	0.30%
Total	**992**	**100.00%**

Table 2 Distribution of companies by size category

Size category	Number of firms	% Total
Large	22	2.22%
Medium	126	12.70%
Small	525	52.92%
Micro	319	32.15%
Total	**992**	**100%**

region-level total), Vicenza (24 companies, 24.74%), and Verona (20 companies, 20.62%).

Moving to the size distribution, the number of firms for each size category, as defined in previous section, is reported in Table 2.

As shown in the Table 2, most of the Italian meat industry is driven by small-and medium-sized enterprises (SMEs), which account for almost 98% of the overall industry. It is also interesting to underscore the significant role played by micro-firms, which account 32% of industry players. These data are fully in line with the current landscape of the Italian industrial structure being dominated by small- and medium-sized enterprises (SMEs) (OECD, 2021).

Further focusing on employee data, information on both average and total employee expenses across the 2017–2021 by size category is shown in Table 3. Cost of employees can be considered as a proxy of employment generation. It is interesting to notice that the level of such cost across the 5 years of observation has

Table 3 Firm average and cumulative total cost of employees per year (in thousand euros, 2017–2021)

	Firm average 2017	Cumulative total 2017	Firm average 2018	Cumulative total 2018	Firm average 2019	Cumulative total 2019	Firm average 2020	Cumulative total 2020	Firm average 2021	Cumulative total 2021
Large	39′481	868′591	40′642	894′130	42′451	933′924	45′665	1′004′623	47′341	1′041′499
Medium	3′917	493′541	4′161	524′304	4′454	561′209	4′641	584′763	5′000	630′035
Small	727	381′422	770	404′444	805	422′753	789	414′223	834	437′783
Micro	204	65′152	208	66′364	211	67′356	196	62′575	201	64′145
TOTAL		**1′808′706**		**1′889′242**		**1′985′243**		**2′066′184**		**2′173′462**

constantly increased, moving from 1,808,706 thousand euros in 2017 to 2,173,462 thousand euros in 2021 (+20%).

4 Size and Growth Rates

In addition to the number of employees, which has been examined in the prior section with the aim of providing an overview of the distribution of firms by size category, the analysis of the size of firms may be carried out by exploring two additional fundamental dimensions, i.e., total assets and revenues. In terms of time distribution, Fig. 1 shows that total assets have constantly increased in the 5-year time frame of observation, with a compound annual growth rate (CAGR) of 5.87%.

Across the period, interestingly 2020 has registered the greatest growth of assets (+11.84% relative to 2019), which testifies the ability of these firms to keep growing also in crisis times during the COVID-19 pandemic, and in 2021 reached the highest value of the period, with 17 billion euros (+4.49%).

Moving to the revenues, Fig. 2 shows the aggregate revenues for each year of observation.

The revenues have steadily increased throughout the years, moving from 21,167 million euros in 2017 to 23,677 million in 2021. The compound annual growth rate (CAGR) of revenues in the 5-year period 2017–2021 is 2.84%, which confirms the maturity of the industry. As shown in Fig. 2, the annual growth rates have been relatively heterogeneous, with an overall 2.80% increase in revenues in 2019 relative to 2018, followed by a drop in the growth rate to a 0.20% in 2020. This relatively low growth rate relative to the prior year reasonably reflects the general macroeconomic contraction at both the national and international level as a consequence of the COVID-19 pandemic. However, 2021 represented an unprecedented year in terms of growth of revenues, with a + 7.72% revenues increase relative to 2020. This proves

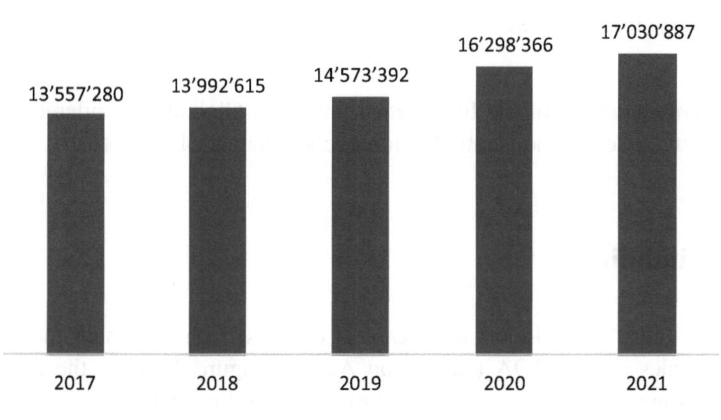

Fig. 1 Total assets per year (in thousand euros)

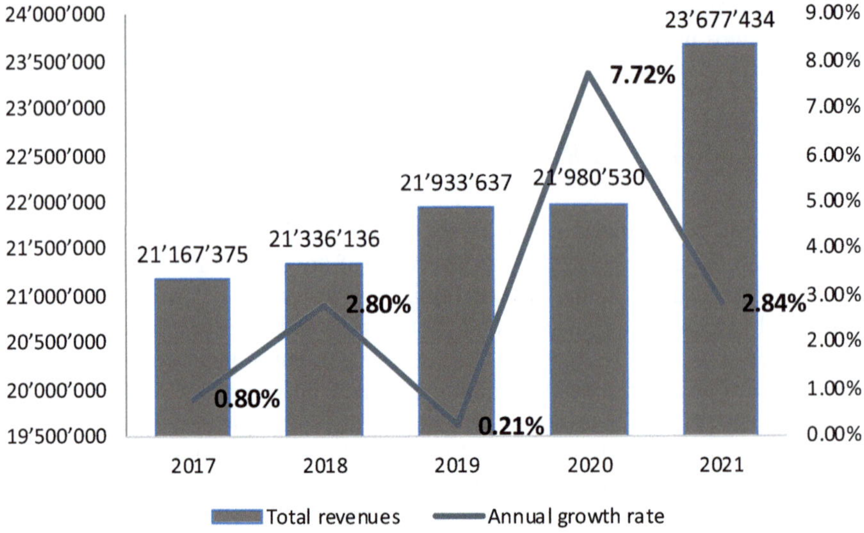

Fig. 2 Total revenues per year (in thousand euros) and annual growth rates

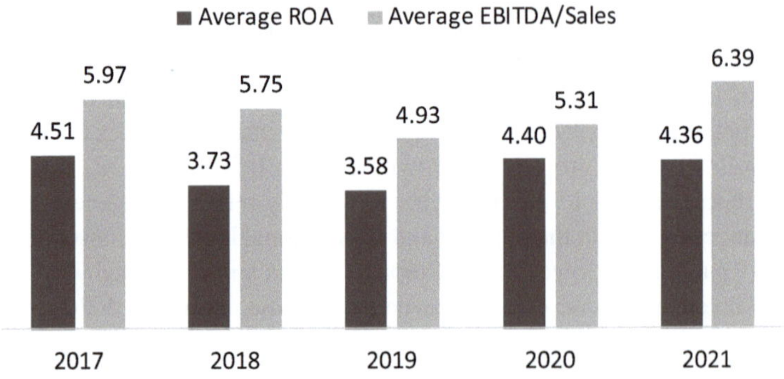

Fig. 3 Average ROA and average EBITDA/Sales (2017–2021)

the resilient capability of the Italian meat industry. Globally considered, trends of revenues and assets demonstrate the non-cyclical nature of the industry.

5 Profitability

The profitability analysis has been carried out based on two main indicators: a) EBITDA/sales and b) ROA (Return on Assets). Figure 3 shows the data on the yearly average ratios across the 5-year time frame of the analysis.

Table 4 Average ROA and EBITDA margin by size category (2017–2021)

Size groups	Average ROA	Average EBITDA/Sales
Large	2.84	3.65
Medium	3.10	4.83
Small	4.32	5.72
Micro	4.27	6.09
TOTAL SAMPLE	4.12	5.68

The yearly average EBITDA/Sales ranges from a minimum of 4.93 in 2019 to a maximum of 6.39 in 2021, with a 5.69 5-year average. In terms of variations across years, the industry registered a limited drop in the average EBITDA/Sales in 2018 and 2019, when it recorded to 5.75 and to 4.93, respectively. Interestingly, the years of the pandemic resulted in a positive effect on the profitability of the industry, as indicated by a revitalized EBITDA/Sales of 5.31 in 2020 and of 6.39 in 2021. Similar trends are shown by the return on assets (ROA), which improved from 3.58 in 2019 to 4.40 in 2020 and only slightly decreased to an average 4.36 in 2021. However, data also exhibit heterogeneity of firm performance. Indeed, average ROA for the 5-year period shows negative values for 123 companies out of 992 in the total sample (12.4% of the overall sampled firms).

Delving deeper into the analysis of profitability, we explored the distribution of ROA across the size categories (Table 4) and found that the firm size is not positively associated with profitability. Instead, the highest average EBITDA/Sales and ROA are found in SMEs, although differences among the size groups do not appear to be significant.

Data on profitability confirm that meat production is a mature, low-margin industry in which profitability does not show significant fluctuations over time.

6 Liquidity and Financial Structure

This section is dedicated to the analysis of the liquidity position and of the overall financial health of the companies analyzed. The analysis of liquidity is based on the acid test, or quick ratio, while for the examination of financial structure and sustainability, we offer an overview of two main indicators, i.e., the debt/equity ratio and the net financial position/EBITDA.

Figure 4 shows the trend of the yearly average values of the three indicators in the observed 5-year period. The quick ratio of firms in the Italian meat industry is greater than the threshold value of 1 for the entire period of observation and has remained relatively constant, with a peak in the last year (1.46 in 2021). This evidence indicates that firms in the meat industry have enough liquid assets to meet their short-term obligations and thus signals that on average these firms are in a healthy financial position.

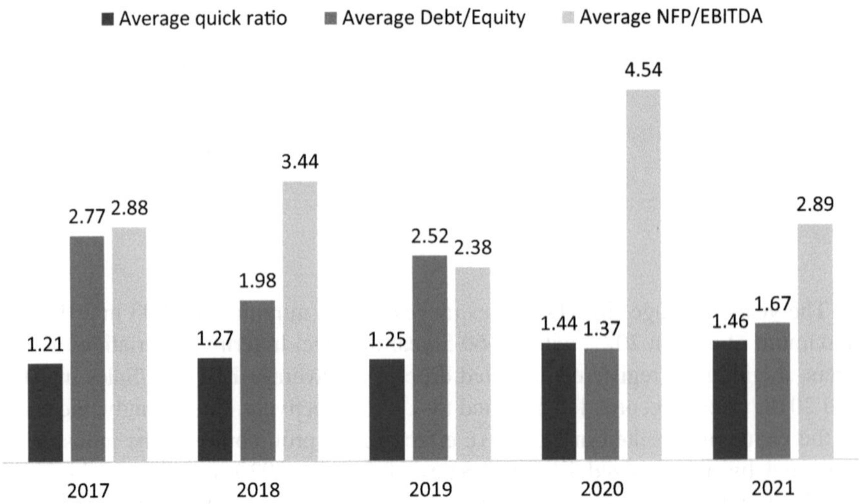

Fig. 4 Yearly average values of liquidity and financial structure indicators (2017–2021)

The average annual values of the debt/equity ratio show some fluctuations, with 2017 and 2019 representing the years where firms where comparatively more dependent on external sources of financing (average debt/equity equal to 2.77 and 2.52, respectively). It is particularly interesting to observe that during the COVID-19 pandemic years, these companies have been able to substantially increase their financial autonomy, as testified by the average debt/equity ratios of 1.37 in 2020 and 1.67 in 2021.

The second indicator used to assess the financial health of the companies is the net financial position (NFP)/EBITDA ratio. The best year of the period in terms of overall financial sustainability was 2019, as evidenced by the lowest value of the NFP/EBITDA in the period (2.38). In contrast, the indicator has reached its peak value (4.54) in 2020, which suggests that the industry may have suffered from the effects associated with the COVID-19 lockdown policies. It is however worth noticing that 2021 shows an improved average level of NFP/EBITDA.

In sum, firms in the meat industry exhibit a heterogeneous trend of liquidity and financial indicators. Overall, data indicate that companies with greater liquidity have also shown higher levels of financial autonomy in the period of observation (the correlation coefficient between quick ratio and debt/equity is −0.17). Additionally, the relatively stable levels of average liquidity have helped them in terms of sustainability of these firms' debt position and their ability to meet financial obligations.

7 Competitive Analysis: A Focus On The Top Players

Competition in an industry is substantially affected by the conditions of rivalry among incumbents. Among these conditions, the industry structure in terms of degree of concentration versus fragmentation plays a major role. In this section, we first examine the industry structure by offering an overview of firms' market shares and then outline the major growth strategies of the top players.

In terms of distribution of market shares, the industry is relatively concentrated: in 2021, the cumulative revenues of the top-10 players are 7764 million euros, accounting for 33% of the revenues of the entire sample of 992 firms. In particular, across the 5-year period, the top-10 players have generated an average of 32.34% cumulative market share. In this scenario, it is worth mentioning that the biggest firm alone has averagely contributed to 10.21% of the overall industry revenues in the period. The distribution of market shares among the top-10 players is shown in Table 5.

Delving deeper into the industry concentration in the 5-year time period, Fig. 5 displays the cumulative market shares of the top-3, top-5, and top-10 players. As shown in the figure, the market power of the top players has remained relatively stable over time.

Moving to the examination of the growth and profitability trends of these firms, data provide a relatively heterogeneous picture (Table 6): in the 2017–2021 time period, two companies—Avi.Coop. S.c.A. and Martini Alimentare S.r.l.—are growth champions, with a 9.48% and 9.68% compound annual growth rates (CAGR) of the revenues respectively. It is worth noticing that this high CAGR in

Table 5 Market shares of the top-10 competitors (2017–2021)

Companies	2017	2018	2019	2020	2021	Average 2017–2021
Agricola Tre Valli	10.34%	10.19%	10.08%	10.31%	10.14%	**10.21%**
Inalca Societa' Per Azioni	5.66%	5.50%	5.47%	5.05%	5.49%	**5.43%**
Bolton Food S.P.A.	3.73%	3.86%	3.81%	3.98%	3.78%	**3.83%**
Salumifici Granterre S.P. A.	3.03%	2.96%	3.01%	3.16%	2.98%	**3.03%**
Avi.Coop S.C.A.	2.15%	2.23%	2.22%	2.69%	2.74%	**2.41%**
Fratelli Beretta S.P.A	1.68%	1.74%	1.77%	1.88%	1.81%	**1.77%**
Martini Alimentare S.R. L.	1.33%	1.45%	1.56%	1.68%	1.72%	**1.55%**
Carnj Societa' Cooperativa Agricola	1.42%	1.45%	1.48%	1.51%	1.56%	**1.48%**
Alcar Uno S.P.A.	1.41%	1.30%	1.41%	1.39%	1.33%	**1.37%**
Giuseppe Citterio S.P.A.	1.18%	1.23%	1.26%	1.35%	1.25%	**1.25%**
Total Top-10	**31.93%**	**31.91%**	**32.07%**	**33.00%**	**32.79%**	32.34%
Others	**68.07%**	**68.09%**	**67.93%**	**67.00%**	**67.21%**	67.66%

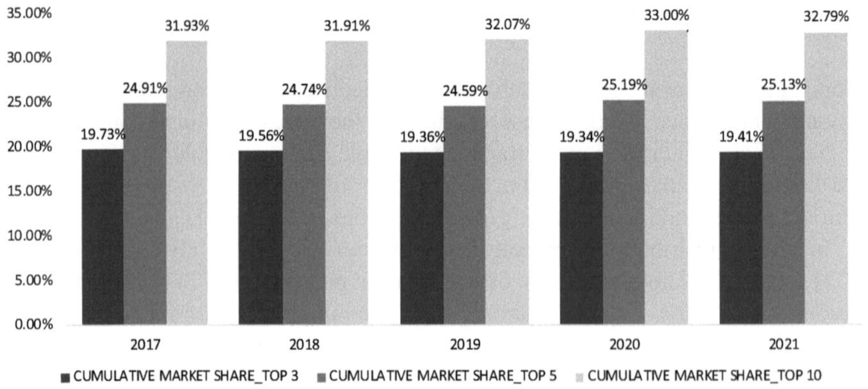

Fig. 5 Cumulative market shares (average 2017–2021)

Table 6 Average profitability CAGR of revenues of the top-10 competitors (2017–2021)

	Ebitda/Sales	ROA	CAGR revenues
Agricola Tre Valli	0.16	−0.09	2.37%
Inalca SpA	4.94	2.84	2.43%
Bolton Food SpA	11.40	10.04	3.17%
Salumifici Granterre SpA	6.52	1.87	2.49%
Avi.Coop	1.56	0.80	9.48%
Fratelli Beretta SpA	6.38	1.78	4.77%
Martini Alimentare Srl	1.92	3.74	9.68%
Carnj Società Cooperativa Agricola	1.48	0.72	5.29%
Alcar Uno SpA	1.79	1.70	1.58%
Giuseppe Citterio SpA	4.49	1.32	4.46%

the period has been mostly driven by growth in revenues registered in 2021. For instance, the 2021 revenues of Avi.Coop. S.c.A showed a + 9.87% increase relative to 2020 (moving from 590 million euros to 648 million euros); similarly, Martini Alimentare S.r.l. registered a + 10.24% increase in total revenues in 2021 vis-à-vis 2020 (moving from 369 million to 407 million euros). Bolton Food S.p.A. is the top performing firm within this group, with a double-digit profitability (as both operating margin and return on assets), followed by Salumifici Granterre SpA and Fratelli Beretta SpA, which outperform competitors in terms of EBITDA margin.

The joint examination of the growth rate of revenues and the average profitability offers an interesting overview of the competitive positioning of the main competitors. Figure 6 positions the top-10 industry players in the industry based on their cumulative average growth rate of revenues in the period 2017–2021 and average ROA. The size of the bubbles indicates firm size, measured by the 5-year average revenues of each company. The figure shows that for most of the major competitors, there is a positive association between the average growth rates of revenues and the average profitability.

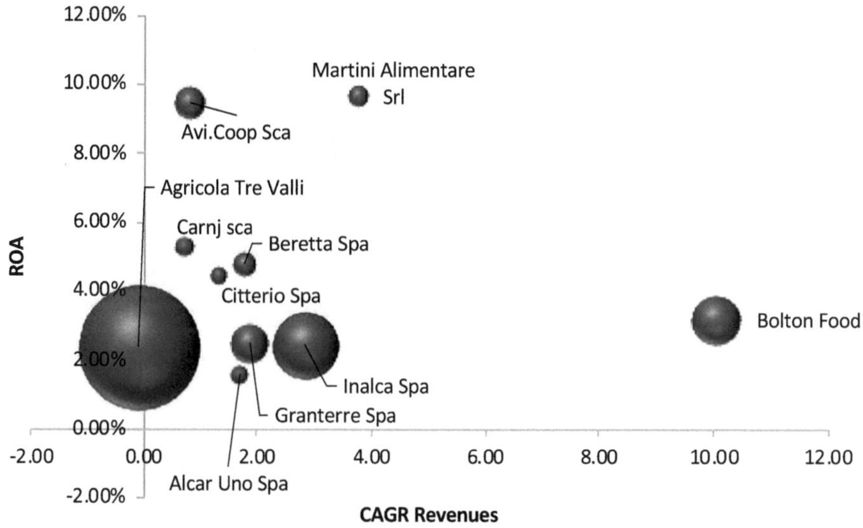

Fig. 6 CAGR revenues-ROA relationship of the top-10 players (2017–2021)

In line with the findings on the overall sample of firms in the Italian meat industry, the top-10 players also show a) a positive relationship between EBITDA/sales levels and ROA and b) a negative relationship between firm liquidity and indebtedness, i.e., higher liquidity is associated with a lower levels of debt.

8 Corporate Growth Strategies: A Focus on Internationalization Patterns

Corporate scope decisions play a crucial role for the firm's survival and sustainabile competitiveness over time. The expansion of the scope of a firm's activities can occur along either the product dimension, i.e., diversification, and the market dimension, i.e., internationalization, these being the two dominant growth strategies for firms (e.g. Hashai & Delios, 2012; Hitt et al., 1994; Kumar, 2009; Mayer et al., 2015).

In terms of diversification, companies in the meat industry show a highly focused strategic orientation and hence have prioritized their growth in the core business rather than expanding into more or less related businesses. This also suggests that the Italian meat industry is mostly driven by consolidating the firm's market power in the dominant market.

Moving to the internationalization as another crucial direction of corporate growth, we executed an analysis of the top-200 companies based on revenues. The average 2021 revenues calculated on the top-200 are 105 million euros, ranging from 2.4 billion of the largest to 18 million of the 200th firm. These companies account for

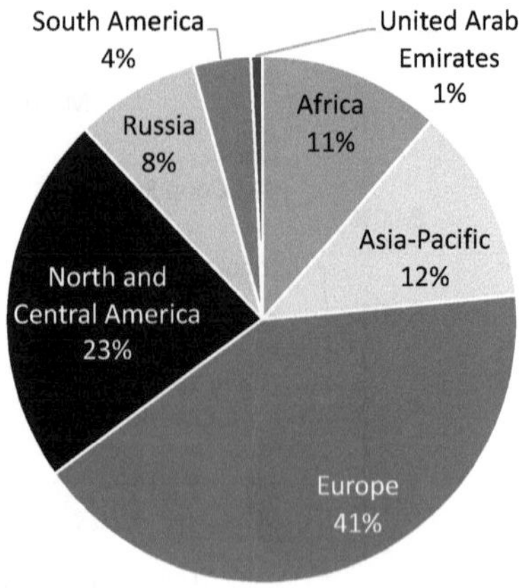

Fig. 7 Distribution of foreign subsidiaries by region

19.4 billion (82% of the cumulated revenues of the 992 sampled firms in 2021). The companies have been analyzed in terms of three key dimensions (Cerrato et al., 2016):

(a) the internationalization of resources, measured as the number of foreign subsidiaries;
(b) the geographic scope, in terms of number of foreign countries;
(c) the internationalization of sales, measured as the ratio foreign sales/total sales.

Looking at the international presence, as measured by foreign subsidiaries, purely domestic companies represent the majority: among the top-200 companies, 167 companies (83.5%) have concentrated their investment in Italy without performing foreign direct investments (FDIs), while 33 (16.5%) have established subsidiaries in foreign countries, corresponding to 76 foreign subsidiaries overall.

Delving deeper into the set of internationalized companies in terms of foreign subsidiaries, most firms (19 out of 33 of international firms) are present in one foreign market. Those firms having operations in two countries are 7 (22% of international firms), while companies having foreign subsidiaries in more than two countries are again 7 companies and only in one case, geographic diversification involves more than four countries.

In terms of geographic diversification, the top-200 Italian firms of the meat industry have located their foreign subsidiaries into 26 countries, corresponding to seven regions (Fig. 7).

Table 7 provides a more detailed picture of the distribution of foreign subsidiaries, showing the total number of subsidiaries in each region along with the specific countries included in the region.

The majority of firms exhibit an international exposure, even though to a moderate extent; however, this is mostly driven by exporting activities rather than equity commitment.

Delving deeper in the analysis of internationalization from the market side, the ratio of foreign sales on total sales in 2021 is 12.11%, ranging from a minimum of

Table 7 Geographic distribution of foreign subsidiaries

Region	Number of subsidiaries in the region	Countries
Europe	58	Austria, Croatia, France, Germany, Hungary, Great Britain, Poland, Romania, Slovakia, Spain, Switzerland
North and Central America (NAFTA)	32	Canada, Mexico, United States of America
Asia-Pacific	17	Australia, China, Kazakhstan, Malaysia, Thailand
Africa	16	Algeria, Angola, Cote d'Ivoire, Morocco, Mozambique, Nigeria
Russia	11	Russia
South America	5	Argentina, Brazil, Venezuela
United Arab Emirates	1	United Arab Emirates

0% to a maximum level of 99.12%. Specifically, for 65 out of the major 200 industry players (corresponding to the 32%), the data on foreign sales are either zero or not available from the annual reports. The remaining 135, which make part of their sales abroad, are distributed as follows: for 77 firms (38.5%), foreign sales account for less than 10% of total revenues; for 25 firms, the ratio of foreign sales to total sales is between 10% and 25%; for 27 firms, foreign sales exceed the 25% of the total revenues.

Total foreign sales of the top-200 firms in the industry equal 2.766 billion euros. In terms of size categories, large firms have on average 14.21% foreign sales/total sales, medium-sized companies display a 12.12% average value of foreign sales/total sales, while small and micro firms have a 10.85% average ratio of foreign sales on total sales. Collectively, the group of small- and medium-sized enterprises (SMEs) show a 11.58% average value of the indicator. Such data suggest that, although there is a positive relationship between the firm's size and the ratio of foreign sales on total sales (i.e., larger firms also display the greatest levels of internationalization as measured by their sales), exposure to international markets is an industry trait that characterizes the majority of firms, regardless of their size.

To better capture the overall internationalization profile of the top-200 companies, it is also worth examining the relationships between the three dimensions of internationalization being analyzed, namely subsidiaries, countries, and revenue, to identify relevant patterns of internationalization.

First, there is a positive association between the number of foreign subsidiaries and the ratio of foreign sales/total sales, indicating that firms that have more assets located abroad benefit in terms of greater foreign sales. In particular, while firms not having foreign susbsidiaries have a 9.68% average level of foreign sales/total sales, multinational firms, i.e., those firms have established subsidiaries abroad, display an average value of 22.13%. Within the latter subgroup, it is also worth noticing that the greater the number of foreign subsidiaries, the higher the average level of foreign sales/total sales. For instance, the average ratio of foreign sales to total sales is 15.16% for firms having one subsidiary abroad, 31.43% for those having two subsidiaries abroad, and 36.68% for those companies having established at least three foreign subsidiaries.

Second, the number of foreign subsidiaries is also positively related to the number of countries. This suggests that the greater the number of subsidiaries established in foreign countries, the greater the geographic scope in terms of number of countries being entered.

9 Corporate Growth Modes: A Focus on External Growth

In the current dynamic business environments, the value of existing resources is subject to erosion, and firms therefore need to upgrade their resources and capabilities by renewal, acquisition, redeployment, and recombination. Therefore, a firm's competitive positioning is increasingly based on the need to strike a balance between the competing pressures of granting continuity of the ongoing business operations and implementing strategic renewal (Haspeslagh & Jemison, 1991). In this continuous process, firms face the choice of how to implement corporate renewal. Specifically, they may choose between:

- Internal or organic growth through greenfield investments;
- External growth, including both wholly-owned subsidiaries established through mergers and acquisitions (M&As) and share-ownership modes such as joint ventures.

Between these two main options, external growth is particularly suitable to realize corporate expansion activities that deviate from the current business operations. In this scenario, mergers and acquisitions (M&A) represent a fundamental mode through which corporate expansion, redirection, and renewal are achieved. Indeed, M&As virtually impose no constraints to the kind of resources that will be internalized and to the extent to which they may be different from the resources already possessed by the firm (Kling et al., 2014; Lee & Lieberman, 2010; Nahavandi & Malekzadeh, 1988). Thus, they facilitate resources redeployment and competency transfer, while also representing a potential substitute solution in case of inefficient or absent factor markets for specialized resources (Eschen & Bresser, 2005). Despite their multiple benefits, compared to other investment decisions, they show peculiar risk characteristics as they require huge resource commitments and have considerable performance implications (Haspeslagh & Jemison, 1991).

Similarly to M&As, joint ventures are equity-based external growth modes that, however, differ from M&As in virtue of their establishment of joint ownership contracts between two or more partners. In this case, by sharing the ownership position with a partner, this mode of corporate growth enables the firm to tackle relatively new markets without bearing the entire risk.

In the period 2017–2021, Italian meat companies have been involved in 17 M&A deals, of which 15 deals had Italian firms as the acquiror and only two had Italian firms as the target of the deal. Summary data on the equity-based expansion implemented by these firms is reported in Table 8.

Focusing on those deals where the Italian companies were the acquiror, the fact that the majority of deals (14 out of 18, 77.8%) have been executed within the Italian national borders suggests that the industry tends to have a deeply rooted domestic breath. These numbers suggest that firms in the meat industry have leveraged on acquisitions primarily to increase their presence in the domestic market, rather than to expand overseas. Data on cross-border M&As indicate that one international acquisition was executed in 2019 with Parmacotto SpA acquiring the US-based Cibo Italia Llc, a key player in the US market for salami. This strategic investment enabled the acquiror to enter the US market with the newly established Parmacotto Llc.

Going deeper into the analysis of the cases in which Italian companies have been acquired by foreign investors, the deals involved the acquisition of the majority stakes and were performed in 2018 and 2021, by a German (Tonnies International Holding Gmbh) and a French (Grand Saloir Saint Nicolas Sasu) company, respectively. These two deals have represented important steps in the internationalization projects of the two Italian companies. The 2018 acquisition of a majority stake in Sinfo One SpA by the German Tonnies International Holding Gmbh was part of an already established international growth project, through which the Pomi family (owners of the Italian target) was going to strengthen the overall leadership of the firm in the German market. Similarly, the 2021 acquisition of Pio Tosini Industria Prosciutti Spa, the historical charcuterie founded in 1905 and based in Langhirano (Parma), by the French Grand Saloir Saint Nicolas Sasu, which is ultimately controlled by CA Animation, was expected to boost the overall international posture of Pio Tosini as a brand.

Looking at the time distribution of deals, 2017 has represented an inactive year in terms of contribution to the overall M&A activity. A remarkable recovery has been registered in 2018, with seven M&A deals. The trend has then gradually decreased in the following years, reaching three acquisitions in 2021.

Although the overall M&A volume registered in the period has been limited, it is worth noticing that, from an ownership stakes point of view, all acquisitions have been executed for acquiring a total or a majority controlling interest. This seems to indicate that firms in the industry that decide to execute M&A are highly committed to build a majority or full ownership position.

As a final remark, in addition to the analyzed M&A deals, one international joint venture was completed in 2018, involving an Italian and an Australian company. This demonstrates the importance of shared ownership modes in order to address greater perceived "liability of foreignness" (Zaheer, 1995), related in its turn to higher distance between countries. Indeed, shared ownership in the context of equity-based entry modes represents a vehicle through which firms can alleviate the risks and uncertainty associated with the entry in an unfamiliar market.

Table 8 Overview of the deals involving Italian firms in the meat industry (2017–2021)

Acquiror name	Acquiror country	Target name	Target country	Deal type	Year	Acquiror business description	Target business description
Inalca Spa	IT	Bf Holding Spa	IT	Capital increase 64.43%	2018	Frozen meat products manufacturer, processing and preserving services, pet food manufacturer	Farm products cultivation activities holding company
Bombieri Spa	IT	Stella 81 Spa	IT	Acquisition 100%	2018	Fresh meat and meat products manufacturer	Meat and meat products manufacturer
Principe Di San Daniele Spa	IT	Principe Salumi Australia Pty Ltd	AU	Joint venture 100%	2018	Ham manufacturer	Cured meat products manufacturer and wholesaler
Rovagnati Spa	IT	Pan B Srl	IT	Minority stake	2018	Meat and meat products manufacturer	Fast-food restaurants operator
Tonnies International Holding Gmbh	DE	Sinfo One Spa	IT	Acquisition 60%	2018	Cattle slaughtering holding company, convenience foods manufacturer holding company, logistics services holding company	Online enterprise resource planning software developer
Raspini Spa	IT	Prosciuttificio S Giacomo Srl	IT	Acquisition 100%	2018	Cured meat products manufacturer	Cured meat products manufacturer
Italia Alimentari Spa	IT	Salumi Montagna Srl	IT	Acquisition 100%	2018	Ham and processed meat products manufacturer	Ham and processed meat products manufacturer
Pini Italia Srl	IT	Ferrarini Spa	IT	Acquisition majority stake	2019	Salted and dried beef manufacturer	Cooked ham and matured ham products manufacturer
Parmacotto Spa	IT	Cibo Italia Llc	US	Acquisition 70%	2019	Prepared ham manufacturer	Cured meats wholesaler
Soc Agr Gruppo Ciemme Ss	IT	Ferrero Mangimi Spa	IT	Acquisition 70%	2019	Pigs breeding services	Animal feeds for livestock services

Rigamonti Salumificio Spa	IT	Brianza Salumi Di Vismara Luigi E C Srl	IT	Acquisition 100%	2019	Meat products manufacturer	Low-salt cured meats manufacturer
Clai Sca	IT	Zuarina Spa	IT	Acquisition 100%	2019	Ham, sausages and other meat products manufacturer	Ham, sausages and other meat products manufacturer
Clai Sca	IT	Cafaa Agricoop Sac	IT	Acquisition 100%	2019	Ham, sausages and other meat products manufacturer	Dairy products manufacturer
Inalca Spa	IT	Castelfrigo Lv Srl	IT	Acquisition 100%	2020	Frozen meat products manufacturer, processing and preserving services, pet food manufacturer	Bacon manufacturer
Mariofelice Spa	IT	Piatti Freschi Italia Spa	IT	Acquisition 50%	2020	Processed meat products manufacturer holding company	Ready meals manu-facturer and wholesaler
Veronesi Holding Spa	IT	Certosa Salumi Spa	IT	Acquisition 100%	2021	Cured meat products manufacturer	Italian cured meats manufacturer
Grand Saloir Saint Nicolas Sasu	FR	Pio Tosini Industria Pro-sciutti Spa	IT	Acquisition majority stake	2021	Pork products producer	Prosciutto manufacturer
Rigamonti Salumificio Spa	IT	King's Spa—Unipersonale	IT	Minority stake 20% and 100%	Announced in 2021 Completed in 2022	Meat products manufacturer	Cured meats producer

10 Conclusions

This chapter offers an in-depth overview of the financial performance competitiveness of the Italian firms active in the meat industry. From a methodological standpoint, a time-series analysis based on 992 companies across 5 years (2017–2021) has been conducted in order to capture the evolution of varying performance indicators, namely size and growth rates indicators, profitability ratios, liquidity, and financial sustainability. In the second part of the chapter, we delved deeper into the corporate growth of these companies in terms of both growth strategies, with a specific focus on internationalization and of expansion modes, with a detailed examination of external growth avenues through mergers and acquisitions.

Our analysis offers several interesting insights on the Italian meat industry and on the performance and the growth strategies of its players. First, the analysis of profitability indicators (EBITDA/Sales and ROA) indicates that the meat production is a mature, low-margin industry, with limited variations across years. It is worth noticing that the 2021 figures show growth trends of both revenues (+7.72%) and assets (+4.49%), which testify the resilient capability of the Italian meat industry. In contrast, more heterogeneous trends are found in terms of liquidity and financial indicators: although liquidity has remained relatively stable, the sustainability of firms' debt positions has shown more fluctuations and has also suffered at most from the Covid-19 pandemic years.

Second, in terms of corporate growth strategies, data indicate that firms in the meat industry tend to be highly focused on their core business and to pursue international expansion as their major growth direction. In line with the characteristics of the Italian industrial system, firms in the meat industry exhibit a certain international exposure and propensity to pursue commercial expansion abroad, but they primarily rely on indirect export and in general on less risky and low equity-commitment entry modes. Indeed, their propensity to make FDIs is still relatively limited, as underscored by the fact that while 165 out of 200 have foreign sales, only 33 companies have established foreign subsidiaries, although there is a growing trend in terms of establishing subsidiaries abroad.

The penetration of foreign markets through FDIs also positively affects the returns that may be accrued, as suggested by data on the positive association between the number of foreign subsidiaries and the ratio of foreign sales/total sales. This indicates that greater levels of foreign sales are driven by a deeper presence in foreign markets through subsidiaries.

Finally, in terms of modes of corporate expansion, data on deals in the last 5 years suggest that Italian companies in the industry do not extensively rely on external growth modes, as highlighted by the low number of executed deals. Overall, our analysis sheds light on important dimensions of the competitiveness of Italian firms operating in the meat industry.

References

Cerrato, D., Crosato, L., & Depperu, D. (2016). Archetypes of SME internationalization: A configurational approach. *International Business Review, 25*, 286–295.

Eschen, E., & Bresser, R. K. F. (2005). Closing resource gap: Toward a resource-based theory of advantageous mergers and acquisitions. *European Management Review, 2*, 167–178.

Hashai, N., & Delios, A. (2012). Balancing growth across geographic diversification and product diversification: A contingency approach. *International Business Review, 21*, 1052–1064.

Haspeslagh, P. C., & Jemison, D. B. (1991). *Managing acquisitions: Creating value through corporate renewal.* Free Press.

Hitt, M. A., Hoskisson, R. E., & Ireland, R. D. (1994). A mid-range theory of the interactive effects of international and product diversification on innovation and performance. *Journal of Management, 20*, 297–326.

Kling, G., Ghobadian, A., Hitt, M. A., Weitzel, U., & O'Regan, N. (2014). The effects of cross-border and cross-industry mergers and acquisitions on home-region and global multinational enterprises. *British Journal of Management, 25*, S116–S132.

Kumar, S. (2009). The relationship between product and international diversification: The effects of short-run constraints and endogeneity. *Strategic Management Journal, 30*, 99–116.

Lee, G. K., & Lieberman, M. B. (2010). Acquisition vs. internal development as modes of market entry. *Strategic Management Journal, 31*(2), 140–158.

Mayer, M. C. J., Stadler, C., & Hautz, J. (2015). The relationship between product and international diversification: The role of experience. *Strategic Management Journal, 36*, 1458–1468.

Nahavandi, A., & Malekzadeh, A. R. (1988). Acculturation in mergers and acquisitions. *Academy of Management Review, 13*, 79–90.

OECD. (2021). *Country profiles, in OECD SME and Entrepreneurship Outlook 2021*. OECD Publishing.

Zaheer, S. (1995). Overcoming the liability of foreignness. *Academy of Management Journal, 38*(2), 341–363.

References

Climate Change Risk Management and Firms' Adaptive Responses: Evidence from the Livestock Industry

Carlotta D'Este, Marcela Ciubotaru, and Marina Carabelli

1 Introduction

Risk and risk management have been extensively investigated by the academy under multiple perspectives (Heckmann et al., 2015). Although variously conceptualized, risk may be broadly defined as the likelihood of the realization of negative effects of an event or activity under uncertain conditions (Aven, 2016).

The growing levels of complexity and uncertainty characterizing the current business environment have significantly modified the breadth and scope of firms' risk, as well as risk management boundaries, prompting scholars to explore deep uncertainties and emerging risk characteristics and consequences (Ansell & Boin, 2019; Flage & Aven, 2015). Indeed, the occurrence of major disruptions in the last decades has raised concerns on the capability of traditional risk assessment and management techniques to predict and cope with severe threats. Particularly, it has been argued that the novel nature of emerging risks may hamper management's ability to identify firms' vulnerabilities as well as decision-making, thus revealing the need for organizations to develop resilient attitudes to deal with unexpected, unfavorable events calling for adaptation and amelioration strategies embedded in organizations' general risk management systems (Sejian et al., 2015).

In this scenario, increasing attention is paid to climate change, as the impact of climate shifts due to greenhouse gas emissions generates new risks for natural and human systems (Dow et al., 2013; Fawzy et al., 2020), classified by the EU Commission (2019) as physical risks, that is, risks from the physical effects of

C. D'Este (✉) · M. Ciubotaru · M. Carabelli
Department of Economic and Social Sciences (DiSES), Università Cattolica del Sacro Cuore, Piacenza, Italy
e-mail: carlotta.deste@unicatt.it

A. M. Fellegara et al. (eds.), *Sustainable Transition of Meat and Cured Meat Supply Chain*, CSR, Sustainability, Ethics & Governance,
https://doi.org/10.1007/978-3-031-34977-5_11

changing climatic conditions, and regulatory, technological, and market risks, arising from transition to a sustainable, low-carbon economy.

While firms' role in actively contributing to climate change has been widely examined and regulated at both the local and the international level (Havlík et al., 2014; Mottet et al., 2017), more recent organizational studies have started to focus on their exposure to climate-related physical risks that threaten business activities and performance (Sakhel, 2017). In this regard, extant literature reports that companies tend to overlook physical and market consequences of climate change but also that measures and actions adopted to minimize climate-related risks are sparse and diversified, depending on industry- and entity-specific characteristics (Sakhel, 2017).

Among the industrial sectors most affected by climate change, firms in the livestock supply chain are becoming a major concern not only because of the negative impact of their business activity on the natural environment (Rojas-Downing et al., 2017; Wreford & Topp, 2020) but also due to their key role in food supply and food security (Godde et al., 2021). On the one hand, the industry accounts for the 14.5% of global greenhouse gas emissions (Lazarus et al., 2022), this exposing firms to both regulatory and market risks. On the other hand, livestock companies' production processes are severely affected by climatic changes and, therefore, subject to physical risks further escalated by the strong interrelation among upstream and downstream entities of the supply chain. In this regard, while there is growing awareness on the effects of climate change on food production (IPCC, 2014)—mainly driven by natural disasters and changes in precipitations, sea, and temperature levels—poor evidence exists on livestock companies' assessment and management of climate change risks. To the best of our knowledge, research on responses of livestock supply chain firms to climate-related exposure mainly focus on mitigating strategies devoted to the reduction of emissions or on adaptation strategies undertaken by firms operating in developing countries (Rivera-Ferre et al., 2016; Thornton & Herrero, 2014), whereas little is known on entities' ability to predict, evaluate, and handle physical risks, especially in advanced countries.

Building on organizational literature on corporate risk management and emerging risks, our study aims to explore livestock firms' identification, assessment, and management of climate change risks. Specifically, prior studies testify that, although companies acknowledge climate change issues severity, they nonetheless tend to overlook and downplay climate-related risks, mainly complying with regulations and underestimating other potential negative consequences on the production process side (Manning et al., 2015). In addition, scholars point out that, among entity specificities, the firms' size may play a crucial role in shaping firms' responses due to the expensiveness of investments needed to cope with climate change threats (Pant, 2011; Sussman et al., 2014). We therefore argue that, especially for SMEs, while an adequate level of acknowledgment of climatic exposure can be expected, practices adopted to face climate change effects and reduce GHG emissions may be mainly reactive and aimed at minimizing climate-related unfavorable impacts (Ghadge et al., 2020).

We thus develop the following research questions:

RQ1: Do firms in the livestock supply chain perceive and identify climate change risks?

RQ2: Which measures are adopted by firms in the livestock supply chain to assess and manage climate change risks?

RQ3: Do firms in the livestock supply chain integrate measures against climate change risks into their risk management system?

To address our research questions, we follow an established route of investigation in climate change literature, and consistent with previous studies (Sakhel, 2017; Schuldt et al., 2015), we survey a sample of 40 Italian livestock supply chain firms operating in the supply and production stages. Supply chain downstream companies, such as abattoirs and retailers, are excluded from our sample in light of the different climate change effects impacting their business activity. We focus on the Italian livestock sector as an interesting research setting because of the effect exerted by on climatic risk management by both the supply chain high interrelatedness and the distinctive characteristics of the firms in the industry, with prevailing micro- and small-sized sole proprietorships and partnership companies (ISTAT, 2022).

Our exploratory study provides several theoretical contributions. First, we respond to the call that companies' identification, assessment, and management of climate change risk need to be explored beyond the investigation of mitigation strategies. Second, by providing evidence of livestock firms' perception of and responses to climate-related challenges, we add to the extant literature on emerging risks and adaptation strategies. Last, to the best of our knowledge, no previous study has examined climate-related risks in the Italian livestock industry: due to its peculiar characteristics in terms of company size, organizational and governance structure, and supply chain interconnectedness, we contribute to the understanding of the role of context specificities in shaping firms' reactions to uncertainties and emerging risks.

The chapter is structured as follows: Section 2 offers an overview of the extant literature. Section 3 describes our research setting and design. Section 4 presents our exploratory study results on livestock firms' identification, assessment, and management tools related to climate change risks. Section 5 provides theoretical contributions and practical implications for both livestock supply chain managers and policymakers, also suggesting future research avenues.

2 Literature Review

2.1 Deep Uncertainties and Emerging Risk

The increasing complexity and uncertainty characterizing business operations at both the corporate and the environmental levels have brought risk and risk management discourses at the core of scholars and practitioners debate over the last decades, resulting in diversified theoretical and practical approaches (Heckmann et al., 2015). In this regard, although authors report the lack of a shared definition of risk and risk-related concepts, along with the heterogeneity and multifaceted nature of the conceptualizations provided over time and across fields (Fatemi & Luft, 2002; Noy & Ellis, 2003), there is a general consensus on the nature of risk (Aven, 2016).

From a qualitative standpoint, risk is generally conceived as "the likelihood of something undesirable happening in a given time" as a result of decision making (Merna & Al-Thani, 2008, p. 11), therefore encompassing three interrelated facets, that is, adverse outcomes, the probability of their occurrence, and a link between the two (Dow et al., 2013). Accordingly, since risk relates to future actions and their potential consequences in terms of outcomes considered as negative or undesirable (Aven, 2016), the growing number of uncertainties affecting the economic environment has advanced the debate on the scope and breadth of the concept of risk (Heckmann et al., 2015). Indeed, the enhanced dynamism, globalization, and interconnection of the business environment (Slagmulder & Devoldere, 2018) have deeply transformed the landscape of risk management leading to the emergence of borderless risks, at the same time modifying risk sources, severity, and diffusion across societal, organizational, and geographic boundaries (Smith & Fischbacher, 2009).

In light of changes occurring in firms' operating context, authors have hence started to investigate the impact of deep uncertainties and emerging risks on entities' forecasting and managing ability (Cox, 2012), as well as the cascading effect of risk at increasing levels of firms' interrelations (Smith & Fischbacher, 2009). Focusing on the first, a nascent line of inquiry explores the influence of deep uncertainties on risk assessment and management (e.g., Battanti & Lanati, 2022), as the high level of complexity related to both the "known and unknown unknowns" (Ansell & Boin, 2019) hinders decision-makers' ability to effectively predict potential future scenarios and evaluate alternative outcomes based on traditional techniques, such as stochastic processes and statistical analysis (Walker et al., 2013). Besides current risks, the recurrence of black swan type of events and mega-crises such as natural disasters, Covid-19 pandemic, and terrorism (Ansell & Boin, 2019) has led the academy to explore new threats having extreme or severe consequences on both natural and human systems, introducing the notion of emerging risk, conceived as "(i) newly created risk, (ii) newly identified/noticed risk, (iii) increasing risk, or (iv) risk becoming widely known or well established" (Flage & Aven, 2015, p. 61). More specifically, emerging risk refers to "a new (novel) manifestation of risk, of a type which has never before been experienced" (Locklear, 2011, p. 5), therefore encompassing new types of risks and/or familiar risks that become apparent in new and unexpected conditions (IRGC, 2010).

By centering on experience and familiarity, emerging risk definition emphasizes the role of weak background knowledge in hampering the identification of risky events and their outcome, at the same time revealing the need for dynamic risk assessment and management systems able to incorporate knowledge developments over time (Aven, 2016). Indeed, it has been argued that emerging risks tend to fall outside firms' usual cognitive and decision-making frameworks, as outlier events are often underestimated or disregarded due to the lack of previous experience (Locklear, 2011). In this perspective, as emerging risks are the byproduct of the interaction of cognitive, interpersonal, and systemic forces (Roberto, 2002), their complexity may encounter cognitive impediments negatively affecting firms' information processing and foresight capabilities, thus calling for risk assessment and management systems based on cautionary and precautionary strategies and early risk identification methods to read signals and warnings and translate them into adaptive and resilient approaches (Aven, 2016).

This is further strengthened by the intense firms' interdependence characterizing the current business environment: while, on the one hand, such feature allows for greater efficiency through outsourcing and synergistic value creation (Cao & Zhang, 2011), on the other hand, it reduces economic systems robustness, as intercompany relationships tend to escalate and propagate the consequences of hazards to partner entities causing cascading effects on the entire network (Heckmann et al., 2015; Tang, 2006). In this regard, supply chain risk and its management have been extensively investigated, since supply chains increasing complexity and length jeopardize organizations' ability to adequately identify threats nature, likelihood, and severity and to consequently address the related containment activities (Tummala & Schoenherr, 2011), thus magnifying companies' vulnerability and the outcomes of negative events especially in a dynamic environment (Tang, 2006; Tang & Musa, 2011).

Although variously defined, supply chain risk may be interpreted as the likelihood and impact of unexpected events or conditions adversely affecting "any part of a supply chain leading to operational, tactical, or strategic level failures or irregularities" (Ho et al., 2015). While this may originate from various triggering events, it is reported that major supply chain disruptions emerge when macro-risks, described as man-made and natural catastrophic events (Sodhi et al., 2012), occur. Indeed, as emerging risks and deep uncertainties mainly materialize in globalized and complex contexts (Giddens, 1990), supply chain network characteristics appear to increase the exposure to such threats. Furthermore, existing interconnections among supply chain companies tend to decrease firms' ability to identify risk factors and causal links, thus enhancing risk opaqueness (Batsakidis & Tsigkas, 2022) and lessening organizations' risk assessment and limitation ability. Therefore, the unpredictability of emerging risks along with supply chain complexity has led scholars to underscore the role of post-disruption measures (Pyke & Tang, 2010), as the unlikelihood of identifying all emerging risks in advance calls for adaptation strategies based on information acquisition to sustain decision-making (Batsakidis & Tsigkas, 2022). Indeed, coping with emerging risks requires supply chain firms not only to adopt mitigating strategies but also to absorb and adapt to disturbances, hence developing resilience and proactive, dynamic risk management approaches (Parker & Ameen, 2018). These, in turn, should be based on knowledge development and allow for adjustments and responses to actual and expected effects of deep uncertainties and hazards arising in the business environment (Linnenluecke et al., 2013).

2.2 Climate Change Risk Management

Among the different types of emerging risks and deep uncertainties, climate change risks are gaining momentum in organizational studies (Lee & Klassen, 2016), as a growing body of literature advocates that companies will be asked to cope with changes in climate conditions to an increasing extent (Gasbarro & Pinkse, 2016; Pinkse & Gasbarro, 2019; Weinhofer & Busch, 2013). Specifically, recent developments in global climate change underscore the key contribution of firms as emitters of greenhouse gasses (Kolk et al., 2008). At the same time, it is widely recognized that firms are also potentially affected by climate change effects, which require organizations to adopt risk response measures (Goldstein et al., 2019).

According to prior research, climate-related risks may be classified into three main categories, namely, regulatory, market, and physical risk (Sakhel, 2017): while the first arises from the augmented local and international regulatory activity to reduce firms' impact on climate, market risk relates to customers' demand variations and nongovernmental entities' pressures toward a more sustainable management. Last, physical risk stems from changes in the natural environment, such as extreme meteorological events, drought, and floods (Pointner & Ritzberger-Grünwald, 2019).

Despite being aware of the potential negative consequences of climate change, companies are reported to underestimate them (Locklear, 2011) and to be far more concerned about compliance with regulatory requirements than about the exposure to market and physical risks, the latter being conceived as more distant in time and scarcely urgent (Manning et al., 2015). Particularly, previous studies testify that the number of companies adopting actions to minimize climate-related risk is relatively low (Reid & Toffel, 2009). Furthermore, it has been found that "the range of responses to climate change challenges has been very wide" (Aggarwal & Dow, 2012, p. 318), strongly depending on the type of risk as well as on industry- and entity-specific characteristics (Sakhel, 2017).

On the one hand, firms tend to handle regulatory and market risk by increasing decision-making information resources, lobbying regulatory bodies, and lowering emissions (Lazarus et al., 2022), while responses to physical risks are generally an integral part of firms' risk management approach and governed by adopting adaptation strategies (Ghadge et al., 2020), such as diversification and production relocation and insurance coverage (Berkhout et al., 2006; Martin et al., 2014).

On the other hand, it has been found that firms' perceptions of and responses to climate change risk are influenced by the industrial sector in which they operate in terms of vulnerability to primary impacts of changes in the natural environment: indeed, businesses depending on seasonal and climate conditions or those most affected by infrastructures disruptions (Winn & Kirchgeorg, 2005) are more urged to respond to climate change threats. Similar conclusions may be driven for firms in deeply interconnected supply chains, because of secondary impacts exerted by climate change exposure of upstream and downstream activities (Ghadge et al., 2020), such as resource supply and product distribution. For instance, extant literature provides evidence of the development of integrated strategies to deal with negative effects of climate change in agricultural, tourism, oil and gas, and electricity (Weinhofer & Busch, 2013), together with transportation and logistics companies (Ghadge et al., 2020). In addition, several organizational and contextual factors may foster entities' ability to deal with climate-related risks, such as directors and senior management involvement, internal audit oversight (Trotman & Trotman, 2015), resource availability, geographical location (Weinhofer & Busch, 2013), industry affiliation, and previous experiences with such risks (Lawrence et al., 2014; Sakhel, 2017).

All in all, previous evidence confirms the heterogeneity of organizations' responses to climate challenges, also due to different management's perceptions and knowledge of potential consequences arising from changes in natural environment, that in turn lead to diversified and coexisting counteractions, referred to as mitigation, adaptation, and amelioration strategies (Sejian et al., 2015). While the first may be driven by both regulations on gas emissions and corporate reputation matters (Sakhel, 2017), the second refers to actions undertaken to reduce potential adverse effects of climate changes, thus depending on management beliefs and awareness: as climate change becomes a material issue, firms will progressively move away from wait and see and/or reactive strategies in favor of proactive approaches (Weinhofer & Busch, 2013). In this perspective, an integral part of organizations' response lies in amelioration, as a reactive response aimed at minimizing the impact of already occurred climate-related disruptions.

In this scenario, while acknowledging the profitable coexistence of different and contextual measures to deal with climatic exposure, academics have outlined that greater effectiveness could result from integrating such responses into firms' risk management system (Weinhofer & Busch, 2013), according to general risk management processes based on the three subsequent stages of risk identification, risk assessment in terms of risk potential impact and probability of occurrence, and risk response in the form of risk reduction, avoidance, and transfer (Merna & Al-Thani, 2008).

2.3 *Climate Change Risk in the Livestock Food Supply Chain*

The livestock food supply chain is especially vulnerable to climate change risks along with various dimensions (Rojas-Downing et al., 2017; Sidahmed et al., 2008; Thornton & Gerber, 2010; Wreford & Topp, 2020). Indeed, the potential for climate-related impacts on livestock companies arises from the interplay between climatic hazards and the susceptibility and vulnerability of human and natural systems (Godde et al., 2021). As a result, meat industry firms play a dual role as they are both impacted by environmental issues and, in turn, they impact the natural environment due to their production processes.

On the one hand, it is widely recognized that the production processes of meat industry firms intensively affect the environment for several reasons (Djekic, 2015).

First, meat production systems are found to be inefficient in terms of nutrient and energy utilization, also having long conversion time before the meat can be transformed and distributed to retailers and consumers (Bhat et al., 2015). Second, land clearing for pasture, feed production, manure, and the methane emitted by the animals are considered to heavily contribute to greenhouse gas emissions, accounting for the 14.5% of global emissions (Lazarus et al., 2022).

On the other hand, besides meat industry's negative environmental consequences, its exposure to climate change also originates from the effects of extreme weather events on livestock activities. This is further exacerbated by the high levels of interaction of livestock supply chain stages (Golini et al., 2017), with firms showing strong interdependencies due to economic pressures toward vertical and horizontal coordination (Fearne, 1998). Consistently, not only climate change events may involve the different stages of the supply chain, but their effects may also propagate from upstream to downstream entities, thus magnifying their potential impacts. This interconnectedness can result in a cascade of negative consequences on the entire supply chain, including production, processing, distribution, and consumption of meat products, thus driving attention on the need to adopt a holistic approach to address livestock supply chain exposure and vulnerabilities (Gitz et al., 2016).

In this respect, risk identification, assessment, and management in the supply chain are made more difficult by the breadth of natural, human, and societal implications potentially arising from climate-related negative effects: indeed, the livestock industry plays a key role in food supply and food security and as a source of nutrients for poor soils together with income generation and diversification, therefore contributing to communities' wealth and resilience (Godde et al., 2021).

According to Godde et al. (2021), climate change events most impacting the livestock supply chain basically relate to four types of hazards, namely, atmospheric CO_2, tropospheric O_3, temperature, and precipitations, along with storm surges and sea level rise. Based on this, the authors analyze firms' exposure to climate change risks relating to each livestock supply chain stage, that is, fodder supply, breeding, industrial processing and distribution, and consumption (Golini et al., 2017).

Supplier and breeding firms are reported to be exposed to threats related to feed and water. Focusing on the first, while gas emissions may both positively and negatively affect livestock feed, changes in temperature and fields' dryness exert an overall adverse effect as high temperatures not only reduce crops and pastures yields but also tend to dehydrate them, thus favoring the concentration of toxic secondary compounds and lowering feed quality (Godde et al., 2021). Furthermore, warming temperatures along with drought periods, heavy rains, and greater humidity increase phytopathogens and soil contaminant concentration, while reducing pollinator availability. Similar to feed, the effects of water availability extend to the different stages of the livestock supply chain, as its use spreads from growing crops and animals to the production of fertilizers, pesticides, electricity, and fuel (Godde et al., 2021).

Focusing on animal health and production, immediate and long-lasting climate change effects relate to physiological, metabolic, and behavioral consequences (Filipe et al., 2020; Gauly & Ammer, 2020;). Warming temperatures cause animal heat stress, both on farm and during transportation, with outcomes that depend on animal species, breed, life stage, genetic potential, nutritional status, size, and level of insulation (Saeed et al., 2019). This, in turn, is found to negatively affect animals' feed intake and productivity, welfare, and survival, as well as to lower immune functions (Nardone et al., 2010) and the effectiveness of some vaccines (Godde et al., 2021), hence increasing the incidence of livestock disease.

Temperatures also negatively impact product processing, distribution, and storage, potentially causing degradation of food quality and shelf-life, along with augmented wastage, whereas extreme weather conditions may damage transportation infrastructures, hence limiting the distribution of products. This, in turn, fosters the likelihood of the proliferation of microbes, especially under humid conditions (van der Spiegel et al., 2012), making livestock products less appealing to customers, reducing meat quality, and provoking the dissemination of enteric pathogens from livestock into human food. Such consequences are further worsened by changes in dietary preferences of consumers and societal concerns on labor conditions, animal welfare, and environmental issues, especially in high-income countries that, together with physical risks and in light of livestock industry concentration and coordination, may enhance climate-related effects throughout the supply chain (Pais et al., 2020).

Despite the clear identification of climate-related risks affecting the livestock supply chain, very few studies explore the supply chain responses to climate change risks under an organizational perspective, with most contributions focusing on livestock firms' mitigation strategies in terms of reduction of greenhouse gas emissions (Chiriacò & Valentini, 2021; Havlík et al., 2014; Mottet et al., 2017). First, to the best of our knowledge, little research exists on physical risk assessment and management (Escarcha et al., 2018), as studies mainly list and analyze physical risk categories affecting the livestock industry or investigate adaptation responses in developing countries (Kabubo-Mariara, 2008; Rivera-Ferre et al., 2016; Rust & Rust, 2013; Thornton & Herrero, 2014). In this regard, extant literature testifies that adaptive responses through technical and management improvements, such as increasing feed quality, irrigation efficiency, alleviating heat effects, and changes in livestock species, are the most widespread measures enacted by livestock firms (Henry et al., 2018; Mirza, 2003; Mu et al., 2013), while systemic adaptation appears to be less common (Escarcha et al., 2018).

Second, although previous research theoretically confirms that climate variability may be managed by integrating mitigation, adaptation, and amelioration strategies, concerns arise on their actual implementations due to firms' low perception of climate change threats and limited resources as opposed to the expensiveness of such strategies (Pant, 2011; Sussman et al., 2014).

Based on the above, we develop the following research questions accordingly to the risk management system stages, that is, identification, assessment, and management (Merna & Al-Thani, 2008):

RQ1: Do firms in the livestock supply chain perceive and identify climate change risks?

RQ2: Which measures are adopted by firms in the livestock supply chain to assess and manage climate change risks?

RQ3: Do firms in the livestock supply chain integrate measures against climate change risks into their risk management system?

3 Research Setting, Methodology, and Sample

The Italian food industry is a particular interesting research setting, as it reveals several distinctive traits that influence its reputation and competitive advantage worldwide, as well as supply chain dynamics. According to Coldiretti[1] and Unione Italiana Food,[2] the agricultural and livestock industry has been recognized as: being the "greenest" agriculture in Europe, with 316 PDO/PGI/TGS[3] certified specialties recognized at the EU level; the leader in the organic sector with over 80,000 organic farms; having a varied population of both multinational enterprises and micro-, small-, and medium-sized enterprises, mutually interdependent and cooperating for production purposes (Sadeghi & Biancone, 2018); adopting innovative techniques, resilience, inventiveness, and investments in sustainability (Capitanio et al., 2009).

In this scenario, while few data on the Italian livestock supply chain have been published, several industry reports are presented by Italian trade associations and ISTAT (Italian National Institute of Statistics) on the agricultural sector. Particularly, in 2020, it comprised 1133 million firms, of which 27% in the North, 16% in Center, and 57% in the South of Italy. From an organizational standpoint, 98.3% of agricultural and livestock firms are sole proprietorships (93.5%) or partnership companies (4.8%), whereas limited liability companies and agricultural cooperatives, respectively, amount to 1% and 0.3% (ISTAT, 2022). Consistently, most of the industry entities are micro enterprises (98.6%), averagely employing up to ten workers (ISTAT, 2022) and with average total revenues of about 66,836 euros (CREA & RICA, 2020). Among agricultural companies, livestock firms account for 29% of the total national agricultural production. As of December 1, 2020, in Italy, there were 246,161 livestock firms, that is, 22% of agricultural entities. In

[1] Coldiretti—Coldiretti, is a non-profit organization, which represents agricultural enterprises, direct growers, professional agricultural entrepreneurs, agricultural companies, fish businesses and entrepreneurs, consortia, cooperatives, associations and any other entity and subject operating in the agricultural, fisheries, agri-food, environmental and rural sectors, at national, European and international level.

[2] Unione Italiana Food—Unione Italiana Food is the leading association in Italy for direct representation of food product categories and among the first in Europe. An associative "house" whose mission is the enhancement and protection of companies, products and sectors which are among the excellences of our industry, and which are called to new challenges every day on markets all over the world.

[3] PDO—protected designation of origin; PGI—protected geographical indication; TSG—traditional specialties guaranteed.

terms of firms' geographical distribution, most livestock firms are in South and North Italy (respectively, 41% and 39%), while Center-Italy regions account for 20% (CREA, 2021).

Regarding the number of animals raised, there were about 22.3 million animals raised on December 1, 2022, of which 8.7 million pigs, 1 million goats, 6.6 million sheep, and 6 million cattle and buffaloes. The largest contribution of farmed animals goes to the North-East, where half of all the registered animals is found. In this distribution, poultry and rabbits reach the highest stocks in Italy, with a good contribution also of cattle and pigs.

To address the research questions, our exploratory study relies on a survey of a sample of 40 Italian firms operating in the upstream stage of livestock supply chain, that is, fodder suppliers and breeders. This approach is consistent with previous studies (Berkhout et al., 2006; Sakhel, 2017; Schuldt et al., 2015), as questionnaires have been defined as an information gathering tool, allowing to investigate several issues simultaneously (Zammuner, 1996). Therefore, this research technique appears to be consistent with our research objective, that is, shedding light on climate change risk identification, assessment, and management practices of livestock supply chain firms. Furthermore, we excluded downstream companies, such as abattoirs, distributors, and retailers, because of the heterogeneous climate change threats affecting their businesses compared to the upstream ones.

The questionnaire was conducted on Google Forms, with a first section aimed at understanding livestock firms' identification of climate-related threats (RQ 1) and a second section investigating their climatic risk assessment and management measures (RQ 2 and RQ 3). More in detail, the first section aims to collect general information on respondents' demographic characteristics, such as the company's age, geographical location, size (in terms of employees' number and total revenues), and business activity. In addition, questions were asked on firms' risk identification in terms of awareness and perception of climatic threat materiality, aiming to provide further insight into climate risk typologies exerting greater impact on the supply chain companies. The second section of the questionnaire purposes to assess whether the sampled entities have adopted specific climatic risk assessment and management strategies and, if so, to what extent such management system distinguishes the short-term and the long-term risks, together with direct and indirect climate change impacts. Last, the survey also aims to assess companies' approach to the evaluation of the financial impact of climate change effects and to the implementation of adequate planning and control measures to counteract climate change risks. Moreover, the questionnaire also intends to understand whether livestock enterprises have identified ad hoc functions responsible for the climate change risk evaluation.

The questionnaire consists of 44 question, and it was structured using multiple choice, Likert scale, and open-ended questions. To obtain a large and varied sample, the questionnaire was sent both Confagricoltura (the Italian agricultural firms association) and AIA (the Italian association of breeders), which then proceeded to disseminate it to their members. The survey was first proposed in January 2023, and final responses were collected in February 2023, after one reminder email. Overall, 52 responses were received: following the exclusion of those sent by

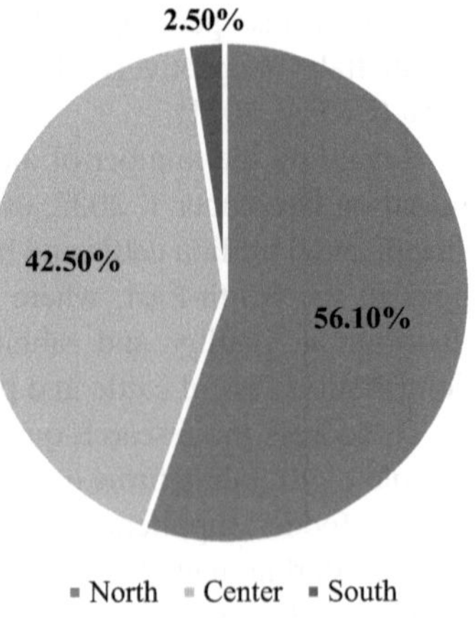

Fig. 1 Respondents' geographical distribution

firms' not operating in the livestock supply chain, our final sample consists of 41 livestock supply chain companies.

4 Findings

4.1 Sample Characteristics and Climate Change Risk Identification

In terms of demographic characteristics, respondents' geographical distribution covers the entire national territory, although not homogeneously (Fig. 1).

Nevertheless, the sample characteristics appear to mirror those of the Italian firms operating in the upstream of the livestock supply chain, where sole proprietorships and micro and small enterprises prevail, as shown in Figs. 2 and 3. This is further confirmed by respondents' average number of employees, as 85% of the sample firms employed up to ten workers during the last financial year.

In addition, 49% of the respondents are found to be long-standing firms with more than 30 years' experience (Fig. 4), thus suggesting a strong knowledge of the business environment and industry dynamics that could support them in assessing and responding to climate-related risks, as familiarity with risks is found to positively influence risk perception levels and risk management capability (Lawrence et al., 2014).

Focusing on the sample's business activity, the majority of the respondents belong to the agricultural production sector (87.8%), thus operating in the supply stage of the livestock supply chain, while only 12.2% are breeders. Despite previous studies reporting that risk identification, assessment and management approaches may be industry-specific (Sakhel, 2017), we found no significant difference in

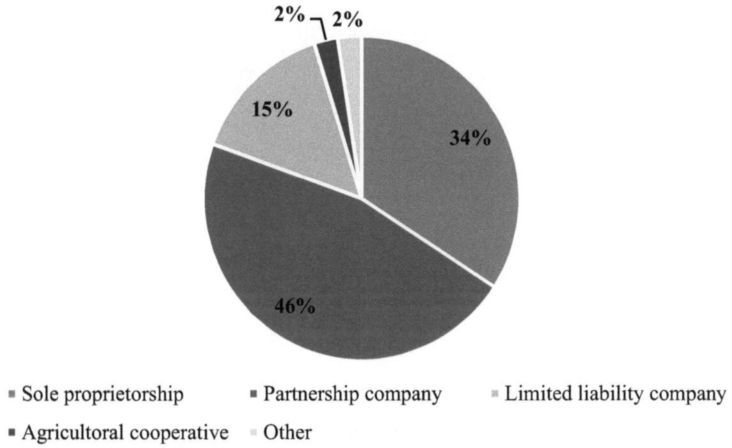

Fig. 2 Sampled firms' legal form

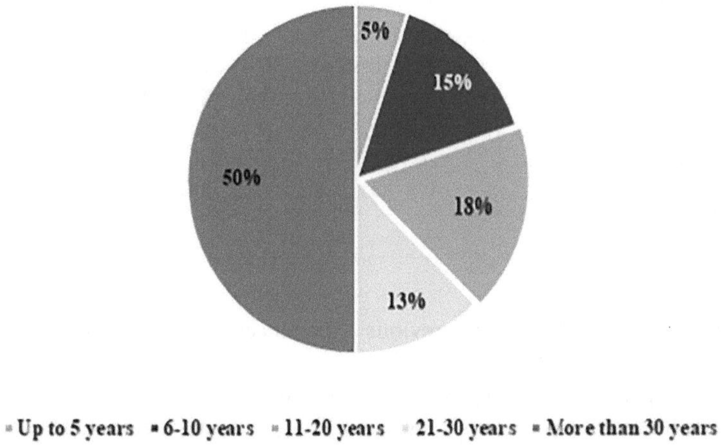

Fig. 3 Sample turnover

perceptions and responses provided by the two subgroups, perhaps due to the similarity of climatic threats affecting both of them and to the interconnectedness characterizing the supply chain (Fearne, 1998).

In terms of firms' awareness of climate-related challenges, responses provided by sampled firms reveal a widespread perception and knowledge of climate change risks that may affect their business.

Indeed, the majority of respondents (97%) perceive climate change as a current risk threatening their production processes, and more in detail, 83% conceive it as being a material issue to their business, whereas only two firms disagree on their exposure to climate-related events—namely, a poultry breeder and a soy and corn

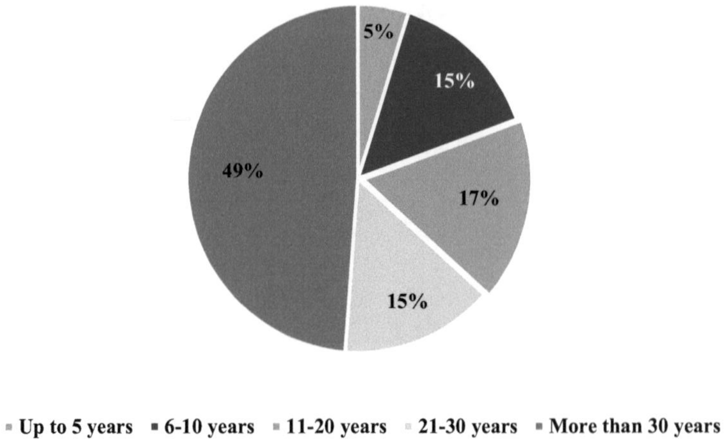

Fig. 4 Sample age

Table 1 Climate change risk perception

	Strongly disagree		Disagree		Undecided		Agree		Strongly agree	
	No.	%	No.	%	No.	%	No.	%	No.	%
Climate change may be a risk for your business activity	0	0%	2	5%	0	0%	17	43%	21	53%
Climate change risk is a material risk for your business activity	0	0%	3	8%	12	30%	20	50%	13	33%

grower—notwithstanding their previous experiences of climate negative impacts (Table 1).

On the opposite, most sampled firms appear to be aware of climate-related risks regardless of having previously suffered from climate-related negative consequences: in this regard, among those who acknowledge threats related to natural environmental changes, 78% declare to have faced earlier climate change effects, related to both draughts and rains (87%) and extreme weather events (9.7%). Specifically, most of the respondents cite Summer 2021 rise in temperatures of 1.5–2 degrees above seasonal averages and long periods of drought interrupted by violent rainfalls that destroyed crops and reduced crop yield, also causing severe stress to cows. In addition, one interviewee recalls the tragic event of the flooding in the Misa Valley, between Marche and Umbria, which last September, after six long months of drought, caused the Misa River to overflow, generating a "tsunami effect" with irreparable damage to agriculture and several victims. Furthermore, when asked about measures adopted to face these unexpected events, most entities indicate adaptation responses, such as increasing irrigations and changes in crop varieties and in seeding times, together with production activity reduction, while only two companies have opted for risk transfer through insurance coverage. Interestingly,

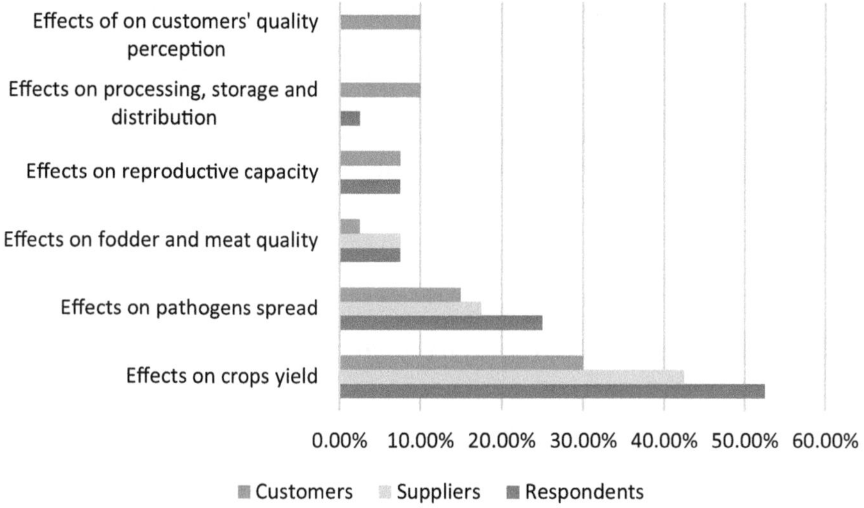

Fig. 5 Identification of climate change risks

when matching the sample's opinion on climate change risk with company's age, no relation between firms' expertise and risk perception emerges, in contrast with previous findings stating the positive impact of earlier experience on emerging risks responsiveness (Lawrence et al., 2014).

Focusing on direct risk categories identified as material to the surveyed firms' businesses, it is worth noticing that threats most recurrently cited are those related with crops yield (52.50%) and phytopathogens and microbes spread (25%), while a lower number of respondents report to expect climatic negative consequences related to fodder and meat quality (7.5%), animal stock reproductive capacity (7.5%), and product processing and storage (2.5%).

Similar results emerge when investigating major indirect risks expected to impact business activities by affecting the sample's suppliers and customers (Fig. 5). On the first, respondents are mostly concerned of climate change threats related to crop yield (42.5%), pathogens spread (17.5%), and feed quality (7.5%); regarding the second, most cited risks involve crops yield (30%), pathogens spread (15%), customers' perceptions of product quality (10%), and product processing and distribution (10%). Smaller consideration is given instead to animal stock reproductive capacity (7.5%) and feed quality (2.5%). Quite surprisingly, no mention of threats about fodder quantity, soil contamination, and pollinators' availability emerged (Godde et al., 2021).

Despite the widespread awareness arisen from questionnaire responses, only 55% firms maintain to know the European Climate Change Legislation (EEC/EU Regulation No. 1119 of 30 June 2021), which sets the binding goal of climate neutrality in the European Union by 2050, as well as the Italian regulation on climate change and greenhouse gas emissions, notwithstanding the cruciality of agricultural firms' active participation due to their role of emitters.

This is further confirmed when considering the drivers underlying the sample's increased awareness on climate-related threats over last five year, since only 5% of respondents ascribe their greater concerns to recent climate change regulation, as opposed to negative consequences of past climate-related disruptions (70%), or to both events (17.5%). Interestingly, such finding appears to contrast with the existing literature that identifies regulation on climate-related issues and greenhouse gas emissions as the key drivers of companies' responses to climate change challenges (Manning et al., 2015).

4.2 *Risk Assessment and Management*

Analyzing the questionnaire section devoted livestock firms' responses to climate change risks in terms of assessment and management systems, it is worth noticing that only about 40% of the respondents expect climate-related negative impacts to increase over the next ten years and report to have adopted measures to assess and/or manage climate-related risks.

Among the firms pertaining to this subsample, the vast majority (93.8%) relies on external sources to acquire information on climate change risks, consistently with scholars' call for compensating the lack of previous experience and the unpredictability of climatic threats (Aven, 2016) (Fig. 6). Interestingly, companies declare that the knowledge collected is then used in view of strongly diversified aims, namely, supporting mitigation and/or wait and see strategies, adjusting agricultural and breeding techniques to climate-related changes, and improving irrigation and cooling systems, along with corporate governance and strategic planning. Furthermore, one respondent specifies that knowledge acquisition is mainly aimed at

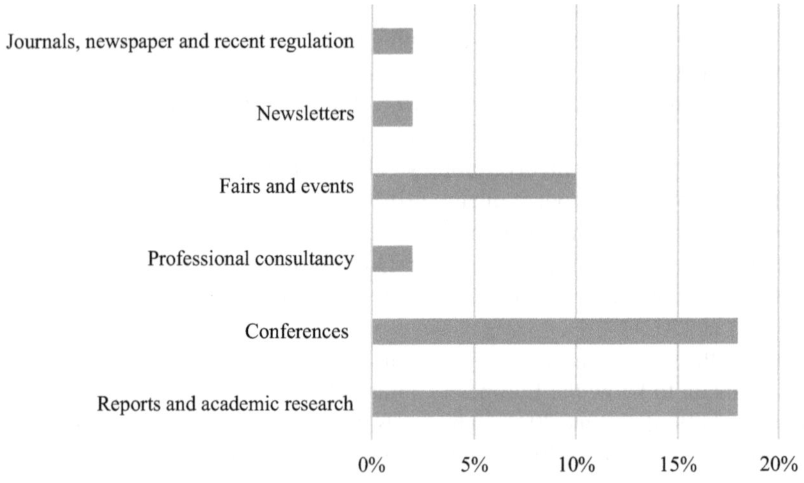

Fig. 6 Sample's external sources of information on climate change

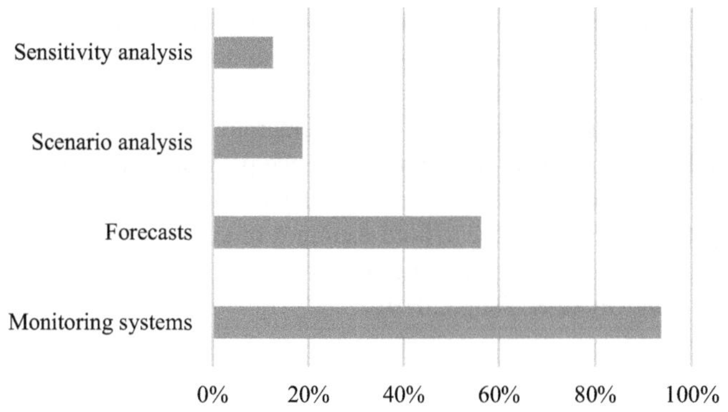

Fig. 7 Subsample's risk assessment methods

gathering information on the short medium-term climatic challenges, thus confirming the tendency to neglect long-term consequences (Manning et al., 2015). In addition, new knowledge application to the business activity is significantly restrained due to the phenomenon newness and investment expensiveness (Pant, 2011).

Although responses to the first section of the questionnaire testify firms' awareness and identification of climatic risks, answers provided to questions in the second section suggest that companies struggle to implement adequate risk assessment and management systems. In this regard, the whole subsample maintains to have adopted some forecasting method (Fig. 7), although none of them supporting the evaluation of probability of negative future events occurrence: more in detail, the monitoring system is confirmed as the most used risk assessment methods (46%), followed by forecasts (18%), scenario analysis (8%), and sensitivity analysis (4%), which appears to be in accordance with studies reporting the need for knowledge development in order to sustain the decision making process (Batsakidis & Tsigkas, 2022).

Surprisingly, only one firm reports that its monitoring system supports the estimation of potential negative impacts of climate change on financial performance and position, also allowing to distinguish between short- and long-term effects.

Regarding risk management measures, eight respondents report to have integrated climate change risk management in their risk management system, if any, and only 12.5% of them has identified a corporate function in charge of climate risk management, as 7.5% of the surveyed companies have assigned this role to the sole proprietor or a board member and two of them to an agronomist.

Consistently, 40% of the total sample have so far reacted to climate-related threats by adopting temporary measures, versus 32.5% having permanently modified some aspects of their business activity: regardless of this, firms' responses are mostly adaptive and do not differ significantly, as they mainly consist of investments in new irrigation, water storage and barn cooling systems, and drought and heat stress-resistant cultivation techniques and varieties. In addition, 56% of the sampled companies have opted for risk transfer through insurance coverage: Particularly, while 64% refers to general climatic negative events, some respondents specify that the insurance contract is related to hail (36%) or to draught and floods (18%), with seven companies not indicating insurance typology. Lastly, it should be noticed that, on the whole, companies do not plan to seek external experts' support.

As a whole, results appear to confirm evidence provided by studies on organizations' response to emerging risk, highlighting that companies tend to adopt wait-and-see and adaptation strategies due to both their lack of knowledge and the high degree of uncertainty that affects forecasting ability that in turn may hamper proactive strategic planning (Pyke & Tang, 2010).

5 Discussion and Conclusions

Our findings show that while Italian companies in the upstream livestock supply chain appear to be aware of climatic risks in the short term, they tend to perceive related future threats as impending to a lesser extent, consistently with previous findings. Indeed, responses provided by sampled firms reveal their knowledge of negative consequences potentially arising from changes in the natural environment, this being furthered by earlier experiences of unfavorable climate impacts, such as draught and floods that occurred during summer 2021. In this regard, differently from evidence emerged in prior studies (Manning et al., 2015), respondents declare to be more concerned about physical risks threatening their production processes than about regulatory requirements on greenhouse gas emissions, probably due to the strong interaction between climate-related issues and human and natural systems characterizing the industry (Godde et al., 2021), together with the intense interconnections linking firms operating at the different stages of the supply chain. Accordingly, effects on crops and livestock growth and quality have been identified as the most severe climatic consequences at both the upstream and downstream levels of the supply chain, where lower attention seems to be paid to infrastructural damages that may be caused by extreme weather events.

Despite this, a smaller number of companies appear to acknowledge potential future developments of climate-related risks, thus confirming previous findings on the perception of climatic threats as distant in time and not urgent (Godde et al., 2021). In addition, this circumstance shows consistency with existing evidence on the complexity underlying emerging risks appraisal, due to their high levels of uncertainty and to the poor predictive capabilities of firms when they lack adequate experience and knowledge (Aven, 2016), as further testified by the sample's limited awareness of both EU and national climate change regulations.

Focusing on the sample's measures enacted to cope with climatic current and future challenges, no systematic adoption of climate change risk assessment and management systems emerges. Overall, few respondents have started to collect information on climate-related threats recurring to different external sources and have implemented some assessment method, mainly a monitoring one. Nevertheless, only one company has adopted a forecasting system estimating climate-related outcomes on financial position and performance and allowing to identify short- and long-term effects. Additionally, few respondents report to have designated an internal function devoted to climatic changes management, while none of them has reported to rely on an ad hoc management system. Indeed, as shown by extant literature, sample's actions and measures undertaken or planned to face climate-related risks refer for the most part to reactive and adaptive strategies aiming at reducing, avoiding, and/or transferring negative climatic effects (Merna & Al-Thani, 2008), enabling firms to promptly adjust their business activities to climate challenges as they emerge, with enduring changes mainly introduced in irrigation and cooling systems. In this perspective, an unexpected insight arises when considering that no reference is made to external consultants' involvement.

Such results can be explained by not only firms' tendency to underestimate emerging risks and deep uncertainties (Sejian et al., 2015) but also the averagely small size of Italian agricultural and livestock firms: indeed, as declared by some interviewees, the expensiveness of investments needed to deal with climatic threats may hinder companies' ability to adequately prepare for future, unknown exposures.

Overall, our exploratory study provides several theoretical contributions and practical implications. From a theoretical standpoint, we support prior literature on emerging risks and supply chain risk management. First, the unfamiliarity and the lack of background knowledge on climate-related challenges poses questions on organizational capability to foresee and react to potential climatic threats, calling for dynamic responses that gradually incorporate past experiences to better respond to consequences of changes in the natural environment (Batsakidis & Tsigkas, 2022). Indeed, the observed cautionary, reactive, and adaptive approaches can be interpreted in light of the sampled companies' low experience as they appear to be in early stages of risk learning, in which lessons learned about risk nature and consequences, along with response strategies effectiveness, need to be stored and processed (Aven, 2016), since this "may lead to construction of more realistic risk models and more informed guesses about the future," because before and after analysis can help understanding "risk impacts and identify the reasons of success and failure" (Dikmen et al., 2008, p. 43).

Second, interconnections between firms in the livestock supply chain may foster risk identification, assessment, and management criticality, as climate change risk magnitude and unpredictability may be exacerbated by the strong links that tie upstream and downstream entities together, thus hampering their ability to identify risk drivers and causal relationships, making threats opaquer and more unexpected (Batsakidis & Tsigkas, 2022), once again eliciting adaptive approaches (Parker & Ameen, 2018).

Lastly, the peculiar characteristics of the Italian livestock supply chain confirm prior study findings on industry- and entity-specific determinants of climate-related risks responses: on the one hand, it is argued that smaller firms are less likely to implement structured risk management systems (Brustbauer, 2016); on the other hand, the industry characteristics may allow price transmission to downstream firms and customers when shocks occur (Carraro & Stefani, 2011; Cattivelli & Antonioli, 2023).

Focusing on managerial implications, livestock firms' businesses are likely to be increasingly influenced by climate-related challenges. To address them, companies need to acquire adequate knowledge about climate change and its potential effects, to increase management's perception of climatic shift potential effects (Sejian et al., 2015), and consequently, both manage physical risks and reduce the impact of production processes on greenhouse gas emissions: indeed, while mitigation and adaptation strategies can appropriately serve this purpose, shifting from a reactive to a proactive approach could lead to most effective responses to disruptive events. Given the average small size of Italian livestock firms, turning to professional consultants could be a more efficient way to develop culture of specific risk and actions to minimize climatic negative effects, together with the adoption of supply chain level responses and the reliance on agricultural and livestock consortia.

From a policy-making perspective, climate-related measures should consider Italian agricultural and livestock firm characteristics in setting incentives to foster the adoption of appropriate risk management systems, also introducing financial support to promote investments in production systems innovation and energy efficiency. Similarly, trade associations may play a crucial coordinating role in environmental effectiveness, by providing firms with regulatory and technical knowledge, collecting supply chain performance data, and participating in agreements negotiation (Bailey & Rupp, 2006).

Our study suffers from some limitations that at the same time suggest avenues for future research. First, our sample only covers the upstream stage of the livestock supply chain, while it would be interesting to investigate climate change risk assessment and management of downstream companies, such as distributors and retailers. Second, we focus on a small, Italian sample: as responses to climate-related threats are found to depend on industry-specific characteristics, more in-depth results could be reached by extending the research to other countries, with different livestock industry characteristics. Furthermore, additional insight may be provided by conducting customized interviews.

References

Aggarwal, R., & Dow, S. (2012). Corporate governance and business strategies for climate change and environmental mitigation. *The European Journal of Finance, 18*(3–4), 311–331.

Ansell, C., & Boin, A. (2019). Taming deep uncertainty: The potential of pragmatist principles for understanding and improving strategic crisis management. *Administration & Society, 51*(7), 1079–1112.

Aven, T. (2016). Risk assessment and risk management: Review of recent advances on their foundation. *European Journal of Operational Research, 253*(1), 1–13.

Bailey, I., & Rupp, S. (2006). The evolving role of trade associations in negotiated environmental agreements: The case of United Kingdom climate change agreements. *Business Strategy and the Environment, 15*(1), 40–54.

Batsakidis, A., & Tsigkas, A. (2022). Emerging risk knowledge system: An interdisciplinary approach of emerging risk in supply chain management. *American Journal of Operations Management and Information Systems, 7*(4), 34–40.

Battanti, A., & Lanati, A. (2022). A quantitative approach to risk-driven strategy formulation: A case study introducing a real-options framework. *Frontiers in Management and Business, 3*(2), 238–251.

Berkhout, F., Hertin, J., & Gann, D. M. (2006). Learning to adapt: Organisational adaptation to climate change impacts. *Climatic Change, 78*(1), 135–156.

Bhat, Z. F., Kumar, S., & Fayaz, H. (2015). In vitro meat production: Challenges and benefits over conventional meat production. *Journal of Integrative Agriculture, 14*(2), 241–248.

Brustbauer, J. (2016). Enterprise risk management in SMEs: Towards a structural model. *International Small Business Journal, 34*(1), 70–85.

Cao, M., & Zhang, Q. (2011). Supply chain collaboration: Impact on collaborative advantage and firm performance. *Journal of Operations Management, 29*(3), 163–180.

Capitanio, F., Coppola, A., & Pascucci, S. (2009). Indications for drivers of innovation in the food sector. *British Food Journal, 111*(8), 820–838.

Carraro, A., & Stefani, G. (2011). *Price transmission in three Italian food chains: A structural break approach* (No. 726-2016-49959).

Cattivelli, L., & Antonioli, F. (2023). When cointegration is interrupted: Price transmission analysis in the Italian dairy-feed industry. *Agribusiness.*

Chiriacò, M. V., & Valentini, R. (2021). A land-based approach for climate change mitigation in the livestock sector. *Journal of Cleaner Production, 283*, 124622.

Consiglio per la Ricerca in Agricoltura e l'Analisi dell'Economia Agraria (CREA) e Rete di Informazione Contabile Agricola (RICA). (2020). Le aziende agricole in Italia. Risultati economici e produttivi, caratteristiche strutturali, sociali ed ambientali. Rapporto RICA 2020, periodo 2014–2017. Available at https://rica.crea.gov.it/download.php?id=1631

Cox, L. A., Jr. (2012). Confronting deep uncertainties in risk analysis. *Risk Analysis: An International Journal, 32*(10), 1607–1629.

CREA. (2021). *The Italian agriculture in figures 2021.* Available from https://www.crea.gov.it/documents/68457/0/ITACONTA+2021_ENG+2021_WEB.pdf/25cb44ef-b254-219a-4009-c0983fc2da90?t=1653304692913

Dikmen, I., Birgonul, M. T., Anac, C., Tah, J. H. M., & Aouad, G. (2008). Learning from risks: A tool for post-project risk assessment. *Automation in Construction, 18*(1), 42–50.

Djekic, I. (2015). Environmental impact of meat industry–current status and future perspectives. *Procedia Food Science, 5*, 61–64.

Dow, K., Berkhout, F., & Preston, B. L. (2013). Limits to adaptation to climate change: A risk approach. *Current Opinion in Environmental Sustainability, 5*(3–4), 384–391.

Escarcha, J. F., Lassa, J. A., & Zander, K. K. (2018). Livestock under climate change: A systematic review of impacts and adaptation. *Climate, 6*(3), 54.

European Commission. (2019) *Guidelines on reporting climate-related information.* Available from https://ec.europa.eu/finance/docs/policy/190618-climate-related-information-reporting-guidelines_en.pdf.

Fatemi, A., & Luft, C. (2002). Corporate risk management: Costs and benefits. *Global Finance Journal, 13*(1), 29–38.

Fawzy, S., Osman, A. I., Doran, J., & Rooney, D. W. (2020). Strategies for mitigation of climate change: A review. *Environmental Chemistry Letters, 18*, 2069–2094.

Fearne, A. (1998). The evolution of partnerships in the meat supply chain: Insights from the British beef industry. *Supply Chain Management: An International Journal, 3*(4), 214–231.

Filipe, J. F., Herrera, V., Curone, G., Vigo, D., & Riva, F. (2020). Floods, hurricanes, and other catastrophes: A challenge for the immune system of livestock and other animals. *Frontiers in Veterinary Science, 7*, 16.

Flage, R., & Aven, T. (2015). Emerging risk–conceptual definition and a relation to black swan type of events. *Reliability Engineering & System Safety, 144*, 61–67.

Gasbarro, F., & Pinkse, J. (2016). Corporate adaptation behaviour to deal with climate change: The influence of firm-specific interpretations of physical climate impacts. *Corporate Social Responsibility and Environmental Management, 23*(3), 179–192.

Gauly, M., & Ammer, S. (2020). Challenges for dairy cow production systems arising from climate changes. *Animal, 14*(S1), s196–s203.

Ghadge, A., Wurtmann, H., & Seuring, S. (2020). Managing climate change risks in global supply chains: A review and research agenda. *International Journal of Production Research, 58*(1), 44–64.

Giddens, A. (1990). *The consequences of modernity*. Stanford University Press.

Gitz, V., Meybeck, A., Lipper, L., Young, C. D., & Braatz, S. (2016). Climate change and food security: Risks and responses. *Food and Agriculture Organization of the United Nations (FAO) Report, 110*, 2–4.

Godde, C. M., Mason-D'Croz, D., Mayberry, D. E., Thornton, P. K., & Herrero, M. (2021). Impacts of climate change on the livestock food supply chain; a review of the evidence. *Global Food Security, 28*, 100488.

Goldstein, A., Turner, W. R., Gladstone, J., & Hole, D. G. (2019). The private sector's climate change risk and adaptation blind spots. *Nature Climate Change, 9*(1), 18–25.

Golini, R., Moretto, A., Caniato, F., Caridi, M., & Kalchschmidt, M. (2017). Developing sustainability in the Italian meat supply chain: An empirical investigation. *International Journal of Production Research, 55*(4), 1183–1209.

Havlík, P., Valin, H., Herrero, M., Obersteiner, M., Schmid, E., Rufino, M. C., et al. (2014). Climate change mitigation through livestock system transitions. *Proceedings of the National Academy of Sciences, 111*(10), 3709–3714.

Heckmann, I., Comes, T., & Nickel, S. (2015). A critical review on supply chain risk–definition, measure and modeling. *Omega, 52*, 119–132.

Henry, B. K., Eckard, R. J., & Beauchemin, K. A. (2018). Adaptation of ruminant livestock production systems to climate changes. *Animal, 12*(s2), s445–s456.

Ho, W., Zheng, T., Yildiz, H., & Talluri, S. (2015). Supply chain risk management: A literature review. *International Journal of Production Research, 53*(16), 5031–5069.

IPCC. (2014). Summary for policymakers In: Climate change 2014: Impacts, adaptation, and vulnerability. Part A: Global and sectoral aspects. In C. B. Field et al. (Eds.), *Contribution of Working Group II to the Fifth Assessment Report of the Intergovernmental Panel on Climate Change* (pp. 1–32). Cambridge University Press.

IRGC. (2010). *The emergence of risks: Contributing factors* (Report 2010). Available from https://irgc.org/wp-content/uploads/2018/09/irgc_ER_final_07jan_web.pdf.

ISTAT. (2022). *7°Censimento generale dell'agricoltura: primi risultati.* Available from https://www.istat.it/it/archivio/272404

Kabubo-Mariara, J. (2008). Climate change adaptation and livestock activity choices in Kenya: An economic analysis. *Natural Resources Forum, 32*(2), 131–141.

Kolk, A., Levy, D., & Pinkse, J. (2008). Corporate responses in an emerging climate regime: The institutionalization and commensuration of carbon disclosure. *European Accounting Review, 17*(4), 719–745.

Lawrence, J., Quade, D., & Becker, J. (2014). Integrating the effects of flood experience on risk perception with responses to changing climate risk. *Natural Hazards, 74*, 1773–1794.

Lazarus, O., McDermid, S., & Jacquet, J. (2022). Correction: The climate responsibilities of industrial meat and dairy producers. *Climatic Change, 171*(1–2), 4.

Lee, S. Y., & Klassen, R. D. (2016). Firms' response to climate change: The interplay of business uncertainty and organizational capabilities. *Business Strategy and the Environment, 25*(8), 577–592.

Linnenluecke, M. K., Griffiths, A., & Winn, M. I. (2013). Firm and industry adaptation to climate change: A review of climate adaptation studies in the business and management field. *Wiley Interdisciplinary Reviews: Climate Change, 4*(5), 397–416.

Locklear, K. (2011). Emerging risk: an integrated framework for managing extreme events. In *2011 ERM Symposium.* Available from https://web.actuaries.ie/sites/default/files/erm-resources/CP_Extreme_Integrated_Framework_Locklear.pdf

Manning, M., Lawrence, J., King, D. N., & Chapman, R. (2015). Dealing with changing risks: A New Zealand perspective on climate change adaptation. *Regional Environmental Change, 15*, 581–594.

Martin, R., Muûls, M., De Preux, L. B., & Wagner, U. J. (2014). Industry compensation under relocation risk: A firm-level analysis of the EU emissions trading scheme. *American Economic Review, 104*(8), 2482–2508.

Merna, T., & Al-Thani, F. F. (2008). *Corporate risk management*. John Wiley & Sons.

Mirza, M. M. Q. (2003). Climate change and extreme weather events: Can developing countries adapt? *Climate Policy, 3*(3), 233–248.

Mottet, A., Henderson, B., Opio, C., Falcucci, A., Tempio, G., Silvestri, S., Chesterman, S., & Gerber, P. J. (2017). Climate change mitigation and productivity gains in livestock supply chains: Insights from regional case studies. *Regional Environmental Change, 17*(1), 129–141.

Mu, J. E., McCarl, B. A., & Wein, A. M. (2013). Adaptation to climate change: Changes in farmland use and stocking rate in the US. *Mitigation and Adaptation Strategies for Global Change, 18*, 713–730.

Nardone, A., Ronchi, B., Lacetera, N., Ranieri, M. S., & Bernabucci, U. (2010). Effects of climate changes on animal production and sustainability of livestock systems. *Livestock Science, 130*(1–3), 57–69.

Noy, E., & Ellis, S. (2003). Corporate Risk Strategy: Does it Vary Across Business Activities? *European Management Journal, 21*(1), 119–128.

Pais, D. F., Marques, A. C., & Fuinhas, J. A. (2020). Reducing meat consumption to mitigate climate change and promote health: But is it good for the economy? *Environmental Modeling & Assessment, 25*, 793–807.

Pant, K. P. (2011). Economics of climate change for smallholder farmers in Nepal: A review. *Journal of Agriculture and Environment, 12*, 113–126.

Parker, H., & Ameen, K. (2018). The role of resilience capabilities in shaping how firms respond to disruptions. *Journal of Business Research, 88*, 535–541.

Pinkse, J., & Gasbarro, F. (2019). Managing physical impacts of climate change: An attentional perspective on corporate adaptation. *Business & Society, 58*(2), 333–368.

Pointner, W., & Ritzberger-Grünwald, D. (2019). Climate change as a risk to financial stability. *Financial Stability Report, 38*, 30–45.

Pyke, D., & Tang, C. S. (2010). How to mitigate product safety risks proactively? Process, challenges and opportunities. *International Journal of Logistics: Research and Applications, 13*(4), 243–256.

Reid, E. M., & Toffel, M. W. (2009). Responding to public and private politics: Corporate disclosure of climate change strategies. *Strategic Management Journal, 30*(11), 1157–1178.

Rivera-Ferre, M. G., López-i-Gelats, F., Howden, M., Smith, P., Morton, J. F., & Herrero, M. (2016). Re-framing the climate change debate in the livestock sector: Mitigation and adaptation options. *Wiley Interdisciplinary Reviews: Climate Change, 7*(6), 869–892.

Roberto, M. A. (2002). Lessons from Everest: The interaction of cognitive bias, psychological safety, and system complexity. *California Management Review, 45*(1), 136–158.

Rojas-Downing, M. M., Nejadhashemi, A. P., Harrigan, T., & Woznicki, S. A. (2017). Climate change and livestock: Impacts, adaptation, and mitigation. *Climate Risk Management, 16*, 145–163.

Rust, J. M., & Rust, T. (2013). Climate change and livestock production: A review with emphasis on Africa. *South African Journal of Animal Science, 43*(3), 255–267.

Sadeghi, V. J., & Biancone, P. P. (2018). How micro, small and medium-sized enterprises are driven outward the superior international trade performance? A multidimensional study on Italian food sector. *Research in International Business and Finance, 45*, 597–606.

Saeed, M., Abbas, G., Alagawany, M., Kamboh, A. A., Abd El-Hack, M. E., Khafaga, A. F., & Chao, S. (2019). Heat stress management in poultry farms: A comprehensive overview. *Journal of Thermal Biology, 84*, 414–425.

Sakhel, A. (2017). Corporate climate risk management: Are European companies prepared? *Journal of Cleaner Production, 165*, 103–118.

Schuldt, J. P., Roh, S., & Schwarz, N. (2015). Questionnaire design effects in climate change surveys: Implications for the partisan divide. *The Annals of the American Academy of Political and Social Science, 658*(1), 67–85.

Sejian, V., Samal, L., Haque, N., Bagath, M., Hyder, I., Maurya, V. P., Bhatta, R., Ravindra, J. P., Prasad, C. S., & Lal, R. (2015). Overview on adaptation, mitigation and amelioration strategies to improve livestock production under the changing climatic scenario. In V. Sejian, J. Gaughan, L. Baugmard, & C. Prasad (Eds.), *Climate change impact on livestock: Adaptation and mitigation*. Springer.

Sidahmed, A. E., Nefzaoui, A., & El-Mourid, M. (2008). Livestock and climate change: Coping and risk management strategies for a sustainable future. *Livestock and Global Climate Change, 27*, 1.

Slagmulder, R., & Devoldere, B. (2018). Transforming under deep uncertainty: A strategic perspective on risk management. *Business Horizons, 61*(5), 733–743.

Smith, D., & Fischbacher, M. (2009). The changing nature of risk and risk management: The challenge of borders, uncertainty and resilience. *Risk Management, 11*, 1–12.

Sodhi, M. S., Son, B. G., & Tang, C. S. (2012). Researchers' perspectives on supply chain risk management. *Production and Operations Management, 21*(1), 1–13.

Sussman, F., Krishnan, N., Maher, K., Miller, R., Mack, C., Stewart, P., et al. (2014). Climate change adaptation cost in the US: What do we know? *Climate Policy, 14*(2), 242–282.

Tang, C. S. (2006). Perspectives in supply chain risk management. *International Journal of Production Economics, 103*(2), 451–488.

Tang, O., & Musa, S. N. (2011). Identifying risk issues and research advancements in supply chain risk management. *International Journal of Production Economics, 133*(1), 25–34.

Thornton, P. K., & Gerber, P. J. (2010). Climate change and the growth of the livestock sector in developing countries. *Mitigation and Adaptation Strategies for Global Change, 15*, 169–184.

Thornton, P. K., & Herrero, M. (2014). Climate change adaptation in mixed crop–livestock systems in developing countries. *Global Food Security, 3*(2), 99–107.

Trotman, A. J., & Trotman, K. T. (2015). Internal audit's role in GHG emissions and energy reporting: Evidence from audit committees, senior accountants, and internal auditors. *Auditing: A Journal of Practice & Theory, 34*(1), 199–230.

Tummala, R., & Schoenherr, T. (2011). Assessing and managing risks using the supply chain risk management process (SCRMP). *Supply Chain Management: An International Journal, 16*(6), 474–483.

Van der Spiegel, M., Van der Fels-Klerx, H. J., & Marvin, H. J. P. (2012). Effects of climate change on food safety hazards in the dairy production chain. *Food Research International, 46*(1), 201–208.

Walker, W. E., Haasnoot, M., & Kwakkel, J. H. (2013). Adapt or perish: A review of planning approaches for adaptation under deep uncertainty. *Sustainability, 5*(3), 955–979.

Weinhofer, G., & Busch, T. (2013). Corporate strategies for managing climate risks. *Business Strategy and the Environment, 22*(2), 121–144.

Winn, M. I., & Kirchgeorg, M. (2005). The siesta is over: A rude awakening from sustainability myopia. *Environmental Strategy and Competitive Advantage, 3, 232.*

Wreford, A., & Topp, C. F. (2020). Impacts of climate change on livestock and possible adaptations: A case study of the United Kingdom. *Agricultural Systems, 178*, 102737.

Zammuner, V. L. (1996). *Interviste e questionari: processi psicologici e qualità dei dati*. Borla.

A Specific Risk Approach to the Meat and Cured Meat Supply Chain

Anna Maria Fellegara and Andrea Lippi

1 Introduction

In December 2017, the Central Banks and Supervisors Network for Greening the Financial System (NGFS) created a working group of central banks and supervisory authorities[1] to help the financial sector manage climate change. The fundamental assumption was the recognition of environmental risk as a possible source of financial risk.[2] In fact, two main transmission channels of climate change to financial instability can be identified: physical risk and transition risk.

Physical risks were identified by Batten et al. (2016): these are the economic costs and financial losses deriving from the greater frequency and destructive force of atmospheric events (e.g., heat waves, exceptional rainfall events, tornadoes) and from the long-term effects generated by these events (e.g., ocean acidification, sea level rise, changes in rainfall frequency). The consequences of these risks can affect businesses, making them more fragile in terms of loan requests, ability to issue and repay bonds or reducing the value of their shares.

Transitional risks, on the other hand, are associated with the uncertainty at a financial level generated by rapid transition from an economy with a high consumption of fossil fuels (brown economy) to one with a low level of fossil fuel use (green

[1]To date the NGFS comprises 121 central banks and 19 supervisory authorities. https://www.ngfs.net/en/about-us/membership.

[2]"A call for action. Climate change as a source of financial risk". April, 2019. NGFS. https://www.ngfs.net/sites/default/files/medias/documents/ngfs_first_comprehensive_report_-_17042019_0.pdf.

A. M. Fellegara (✉) · A. Lippi
Department of Economic and Social Sciences (DiSES), Università Cattolica del Sacro Cuore, Piacenza, Italy
e-mail: annamaria.fellegara@unicatt.it

A. M. Fellegara et al. (eds.), *Sustainable Transition of Meat and Cured Meat Supply Chain*, CSR, Sustainability, Ethics & Governance,
https://doi.org/10.1007/978-3-031-34977-5_12

economy). These include political changes, reputational impacts, technological limitations or disruptions, and changes in market behavior. More specifically, a rapid transition toward an economy with a low consumption of fossil fuels leads to a halt in the extraction of this type of raw material, generating so-called "stranded assets." The term, coined by McGlade and Ekins (2015), is very evocative, "stranded" indicating both "blocked" and "readily available." Thus we are talking about an abundant and blocked asset that can generate systemic consequences at the financial level. McGlade and Ekins (2015) argue that in order to have at least a 50% chance of staying below a 2°C temperature rise, more than 80% of current coal reserves, 50% of natural gas reserves, and 1/3 of oil reserves should remain unused until 2050. The economic effects that could derive from this in terms of storage and/or disposal costs would be incalculable.

The combination of physical risks and transitional risks can have serious repercussions on credit risk, market risk, liquidity risk, operational risk, and insurance risk. The occurrence of physical or transition risks can, for example, lead to damage to buildings and businesses, as well as the obsolescence of entire production chains. The potential negative effects on the stability of individual intermediaries and the financial system are the reason why central banks and supervisory authorities have (for some time) included environmental sustainability in their work programs.

With specific reference to transition risk, for the financial years 2022 and 2023, banks will have to publish, among other things, the amount of their exposure toward the ten high-emission sectors defined by European legislation and toward the twenty most polluting companies at a global level. The high-emission sectors defined by the EU Commission Delegated Regulation EU/2020/1818 are as follows: (a) agriculture, forestry, and fishing; (b) mining; (c) manufacturing; (d) supply of electricity, gas, steam, and air conditioning; (e) water supply, sewerage, waste treatment, and remediation activities; (f) buildings; (g) wholesale and retail trade; (h) repairs of motor vehicles and motorcycles; (i) transport and storage; (j) accommodation and catering services[3]; and (k) the real estate business. In Italy, these sectors make up 61% of GDP, a higher value than that of the entire European Union (equal to 56%).[4] Nonetheless, the pork supply chain, examined in this work, counts as one of the sectors with the highest carbon dioxide emissions. Furthermore, from 2024, banks will have to calculate specific indicators on the alignment of counterparties' activity under European Taxonomy, such as the Green Asset Ratio (GAR), the Banking Book Taxonomy Alignment Ratio (BTAR), and greenhouse gas emissions. Specifically, the GAR measures the share of a bank's activities that are environmentally sustainable according to the European Taxonomy. The GAR is calculated as the ratio between the credit assets that finance economic activities

[3] Sector included by the EBA after discussion with experts.

[4] Angelini, P. (2022). "I rischi finanziari posti dai cambiamenti climatici: carenze informative e piani di transizione". Talk given to the Associazione nazionale per lo studio dei problemi del credito (National Association for the study of credit-related problems), Milan. https://www.bancaditalia.it/pubblicazioni/interventi-direttorio/int-dir-2022/ANGELINI-15-novembre-2022.pdf.

aligned with the taxonomy (or are invested in such activities) and total assets. In the context of business loans, the numerator includes only loans and debt securities to entities included in the scope of the Non-Financial Reporting Directive (Directive 2014/95/EU, NFRD) and in the future in the Corporate Sustainability Reporting Directive (CSRD), thus excluding SMEs. The BTAR, on the other hand, differs from the GAR since the numerator also includes exposures aligned with the Taxonomy toward companies that are not subject to the obligation of providing a nonfinancial statement (NFS), that is, SMEs.

Turning to the issue of greenhouse gas emissions, three types of calculations are highlighted. Scope 1 emissions are those generated directly by the company's production activity through the direct use of fossil fuels (e.g., gas, petroleum products, coal). Scope 2 are those emissions linked to those energy uses (such as electricity or district heating) in which the emission sources are located outside the corporate perimeter (e.g., electricity supplier companies). Scope 3 includes emissions that occur throughout the company's value chain, both downstream and upstream of its production process. It is therefore clear that banks will need to collect detailed information on the degree of alignment with the climate objectives of their customers, paying greater attention to the sustainability of the choices made by their customers. In Italy, with the approval of the CSRD (due to come into force on January 1, 2024) large companies and listed SMEs, a total of 4000–5000 companies, will be subject to the obligation to prepare a nonfinancial statement, compared with only a few hundred under the current NFRD regime.

Banks will therefore have to modify and further improve their loan investigation process, especially with reference to qualitative analysis, paying particular attention to the identification and assessment of the specific risks deriving from and generating climate change, determining the possible impacts on the value chain of every single company. In this perspective, an excessive reliance on sector data in determining individual financing and investment choices would not make sense. Indeed, sectors with extremely heterogeneous environmental footprints may coexist within a sector. For example, the "agriculture, forestry, and fishing" sector, considered to have high emissions, includes both the forestry sector and the use of forest areas, characterized by basically zero emissions, and the livestock sector, notoriously responsible for high emissions.[5]

On the basis of these premises, and without presuming to be exhaustive, in this chapter, we will present some of the most significant specific environmental footprint risks that could affect the companies that make up the pork processing chain, which banking and financial intermediaries, as well as the market, should keep in mind and consider in the credit assessment process. We will then provide a brief overview of the sustainable financial tools that can be adopted by companies in the

[5] Angelini, P. (2022). "I rischi finanziari posti dai cambiamenti climatici: carenze informative e piani di transizione". Intervento presso Associazione nazionale per lo studio dei problemi del credito, Milano. https://www.bancaditalia.it/pubblicazioni/interventi-direttorio/int-dir-2022/ANGELINI-15-novembre-2022.pdf.

supply chain to improve their carbon footprint, and finally, the role and importance of Confidi in supporting requests for funding presented by companies in the supply chain will be underlined. We recall that any company, whether large or medium-small, corporate group or sole proprietor, must decide its own financial structure, that is, the ratio between the amount of own capital: that provided by the entrepreneur and his/her family in the case of a sole proprietorship, or by the shareholders in the case of a company, and third-party capital, that is, funds raised directly from the market through the issue of bonds or other financial instruments or provided in the form of financing by banks or other financial intermediaries. A greater or lesser ease of access to credit will increasingly depend on the attention paid to climate change within the entire production process; this is thus a very important aspect that will, in many cases, determine the success or failure of a business as well as the possibility of its continuing activity over time.

2 Specific Risks of the Swine Sector and Possible Coverage

The main specific risk to which pig farmers, like all other breeders, are exposed is related to epizootics. The development of disease on the farm can lead to a significant financial loss, with repercussions on the entire supply chain as well as on the ability to repay any loans contracted with banks and financial intermediaries (e.g., mortgages, loans, leasing contracts) or directly with the market (e.g., bonds). The epizootic diseases affecting pig breeding are: foot and mouth disease, swine vesicular disease, classical swine fever, porcine brucellosis, Aujeszky disease, and trichinellosis. The occurrence of epizootics on a farm generates two further specific risks with related associated costs:

(i). Carcass disposal costs (source costs)
(ii). Loss of income due to necessary slaughter (loss of profit)

The disposal cost of carcasses is the cost incurred by the farmer for the collection and transport of dead pigs from the farm to the destruction facility, as well as the destruction costs themselves. Loss of income, on the other hand, is the total or partial loss deriving from application of orders issued by the health authority following outbreaks of epizootic diseases.

The National Agricultural Insurance Plan issued annually by Mipaaf[6] provides for a series of subsidies in order to encourage pig farmers to take out specific insurance policies. The subsidy takes the form of a contribution toward the premium paid for the insurance. It is clear that a bank, as part of its loan investigation process, must verify the existence and validity of these policies, which would enable a farmer to meet financial commitments even in the event of epidemics within the herd. In particular, insurance coverage for foot and mouth disease, swine vesicular disease,

[6] https://www.politicheagricole.it/flex/cm/pages/ServeBLOB.php/L/IT/IDPagina/8.

and classical swine fever is mandatory for pig farms. The presence of these policies and of the optional ones relating to the other epizootic diseases mentioned above facilitates the bank in determining with relative certainty a farmer's repayment capacity. As regards carcass disposal, the insured value is determined by multiplying the number of animals on the farm (on the basis of the stock register) by the so-called unitary insured value, determined each year with a specific price list issued by Mipaaf. It consists of two parts: a price for carcass removal (collection and transport) and a price for carcass destruction. If the farm is located in municipalities at an altitude of more than 600 meters, the price is increased.

Equally important is the loss of income coverage, for which the insured value is determined by multiplying the number of animals (taken from the register) by the unit insured value (€/head) established each year with a specific price list issued by Mipaaf. The unit value varies according to the type of pig. For this coverage, the compensation is determined on the basis of the number of downtime days on the farm, with a maximum limit of 180 days per year.

It should be recalled that access to the benefits of the abovementioned insurance coverage is not reserved for large companies or large farms but depends on the presence of subjective requisites such as the following:

- Being an agricultural entrepreneur in accordance with the provisions of article 2135 of the civil code, which therefore also contemplates the sole agricultural. Proprietor/entrepreneur and family-run businesses.
- Being a working farmer.
- Being the named owner of the company register in which the animals present must be detailed and those subject to insurance must be identified.
- The animals covered by the insurance must be registered in the register.

The farmer can take out insurance coverage individually or adhere to a collective policy whose policyholder is Condifesa.[7]

As an alternative to stipulating the insurance contracts mentioned above, farmers and breeders, therefore including pig farmers, can join mutual funds formally recognized by the relevant authority. It should be noted that the underwriting of several mutual insurance policies or the simultaneous activation of a mutual insurance policy and the stipulation of an insurance policy valid for the same farm (and production area) to cover the same type of risk is not permitted. With specific reference to the pig sector, the epizootic diseases already listed above are subject to mutual coverage. Like insurance policies, mutual coverage allows the bank to predict with reasonable certainty the compensation for damage suffered by the entrepreneur. Specifically, reimbursement of the value of average annual production declared by the entrepreneur and verified through the application of "Standard value" is envisaged. "Standard value" is determined by considering the production value actually obtained in the last 3 years, or in the last 5 years excluding the year with the highest production value and the one with the lowest value. This mechanism

[7] https://www.condifesa.it/.

therefore aims to stabilize the value of production towards an average, contributing to the stability of cash flows over time. However, potential lenders, banks and/or investors must take into due consideration the fact that in the event of multiple and competing requests for compensation from the fund, payouts will be limited to the actual capacity of the fund itself. This aspect represents a further element of risk not to be underestimated, but rather to be taken into due consideration in the process of qualitative analysis, in effect rewarding the presence of insurance policies.

It should be remembered that there are also specific funds for the protection of income in this sector, whose voluntary membership is subject to specific subsidies. These funds are set up with the aim of intervening in favour of agricultural entrepreneurs in the event of a market crisis causing a fall in income in the sector covered by the fund. In this case too, for purposes of eligibility for public support, farmers' membership details must report the value of each member's average annual production in the previous three-year period or the average three-year production calculated over the previous 5 years excluding the year with the lowest value and the one with the highest value. This value of average annual production also constitutes the maximum value for coverage purposes. In this case too, it should be borne in mind that in the event of multiple and competing requests for compensation from the fund, payouts will be limited to the effective capacity of the fund.

It is therefore clear that in the credit assessment process it is possible to identify a preference hierarchy with reference to the tools available to pig producers to cover their specific risks. The decision-maker will have to verify and reward the presence of insurance contracts with respect to membership of mutual funds and income protection funds which, although they represent a valid and recognized alternative, do not guarantee full coverage of damage in the case of concomitant and excessive requests for intervention by the fund.

3 Financial Contributions for the Animal Carbon Footprint

To fully understand the role of finance in the transition from a brown economy to a green economy approach and at the same time improve the environmental contribution of the pig chain, we will start by considering the global ecological footprint, which can be defined as the maximum limit of population sustainable by the planet (Kitzes et al., 2008). By analogy, the animal footprint can be defined as the ecological impact of livestock production measurable in terms of greenhouse gases (GHG) emitted, water consumed, land used and biodiversity compromised per unit (usually per kg) of a product of animal origin. In particular, the measurement of the total amount of GHG emissions linked to animal farming can be called the animal carbon footprint. By analogy, a water footprint or a soil footprint can also be defined. The term carbon footprint refers to greenhouse gas (GHG) emissions that are directly caused by an activity or are accumulated during the life cycle of a product (Wiedmann & Minx, 2008). The main sources of GHG emissions by livestock farms are:

- gaseous exchanges between biosphere and soil;
- effects of deforestation caused by livestock farming land use;
- use of mechanical equipment;
- gas (N2O) from synthetic fertilizers used for the production of livestock feed;
- enteric gas emissions from monogastrics (pigs and poultry), mainly methane (CH_4);
- breathing, and belching of gases produced during rumen fermentations of animals, mainly CH_4;
- fermentations deriving from the storage of manure from the farms themselves.

From a global point of view, pig production emits 668 Mt CO_2 equivalent, a higher quantity than poultry production (606 Mt CO_2 equivalent/year considering both meat and eggs) but significantly lower than milk and beef production (4623 Mt CO_2 equivalent/year) (McAuliffe et al., 2016). The most impacting phases of the pig chain are those related to food production and manure management (Cederberg et al., 2005; Nguyen et al., 2010; Nguyen et al., 2011; Van der Werf et al., 2005).

Life Cycle Assessment (LCA) is used in the prevailing literature for the analysis of the carbon footprint, which provides for the compilation and evaluation of input and output flows throughout the life cycle, as well as the potential environmental impacts of a product system. From the LCA analyses present in the literature, the impact of 1 kg of live weight of meat varies from a minimum value of 2.3 kg CO_2 equivalent to a maximum value of 3.4 kg CO_2 equivalent (Basset-Mens & Van der Werf, 2005; McAuliffe et al., 2016; Nguyen et al., 2011) for the breeding of pigs up to 110–120 kg. As far as heavy pig breeding in Italy is concerned, the reference data is that of Bava et al. (2017) which reports an average impact of 4.35 ± 1.03 kg CO_2 eq/kg live weight for six companies producing Parma and San Daniele ham.

These 'technical' elements must be evaluated within the bank credit investigation process. A leading international bank actively operating in the Piacenza area, for example, considering the Sustainability Accounting Standards Board (SASB),[8] carries out an ordinal quantitative assessment of the sectors (industries)/sub-sectors (sub-industries) on a scale from 0 to 5 of the overall ESG risk profile and its individual components (E, S, and G). Then, the assigned score is associated with a qualitative assessment on 5 levels (Low; Medium-low; Medium; Medium-high; High). More in detail, companies in the supply chain in question ('Agribusiness—Meats and cured meats' using the internal classification) can be disentangled in agricultural activities (Pig breeding, ATECO 01.46.00), manufacturing (food industry—Processing and preservation of meat and production of meat-based products, ATECO 10.11.00 and ATECO 10.13.00) or commercial (Wholesale of delicatessen products, ATECO 46.32.20; Retail trade of meat and meat-based products in specialized establishments, ATECO 47.22). In the SASB classification, the activities of pig breeding and the processing, transformation, and preservation of meat are attributed to the Food and Beverage Industry and to the Meat, Poultry, and

[8] www.sasb.org.

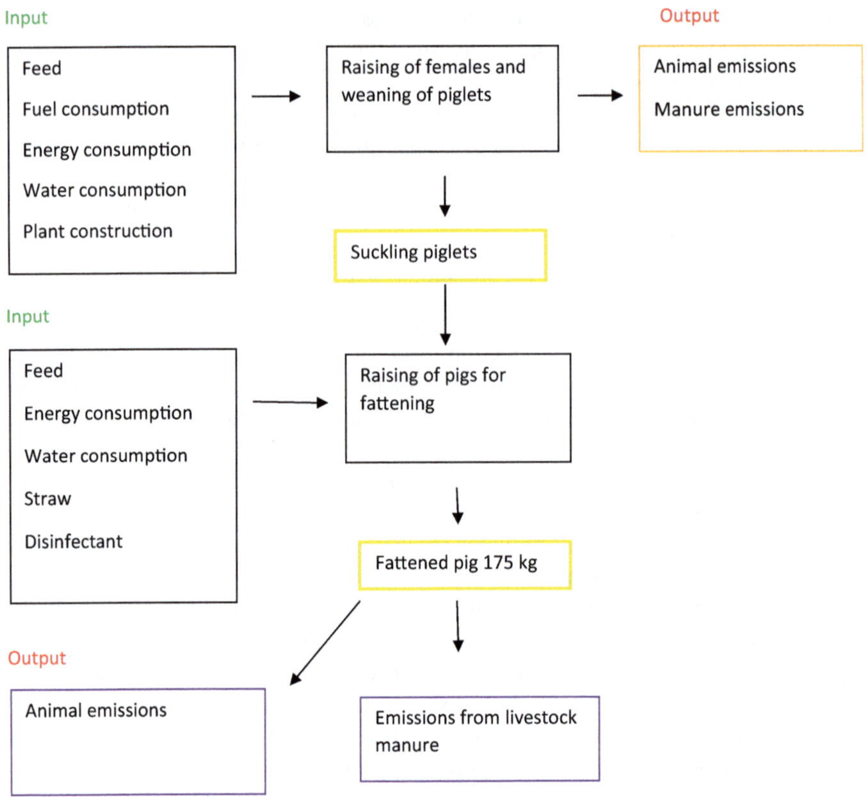

Fig. 1 Flow chart of a traditional pig production chain. Source: Centro Ricerche Produzioni Animali (CRPA)

Dairy sub-industry. The credit risk analysis provided by the bank in our example (based on the algorithm that processes the data provided by SASB) attributes a score of 3.6 (on a scale from 0 to 5) to the ESG risk of the sub-sector in question and an overall qualitative risk assessment of "medium-high."

Nguyen et al. (2010) identify the use of pig manure in energy production as a key measure to reduce greenhouse gas emissions and at the same time to limit consumption of fossil fuels.

Figure 1 is a flow chart showing a traditional pig production chain, that is, without any specific intervention oriented toward environmental sustainability.

Figure 2 shows Fig. 1 but considers specific interventions linked to environmental sustainability. In particular, as suggested by Nguyen et al. (2010), the presence of a biogas plant and two photovoltaic plants is hypothesized.

A comparison of the two different approaches shown in Figs. 1 and 2 makes it possible to calculate that the decision to use renewable resources in the pig

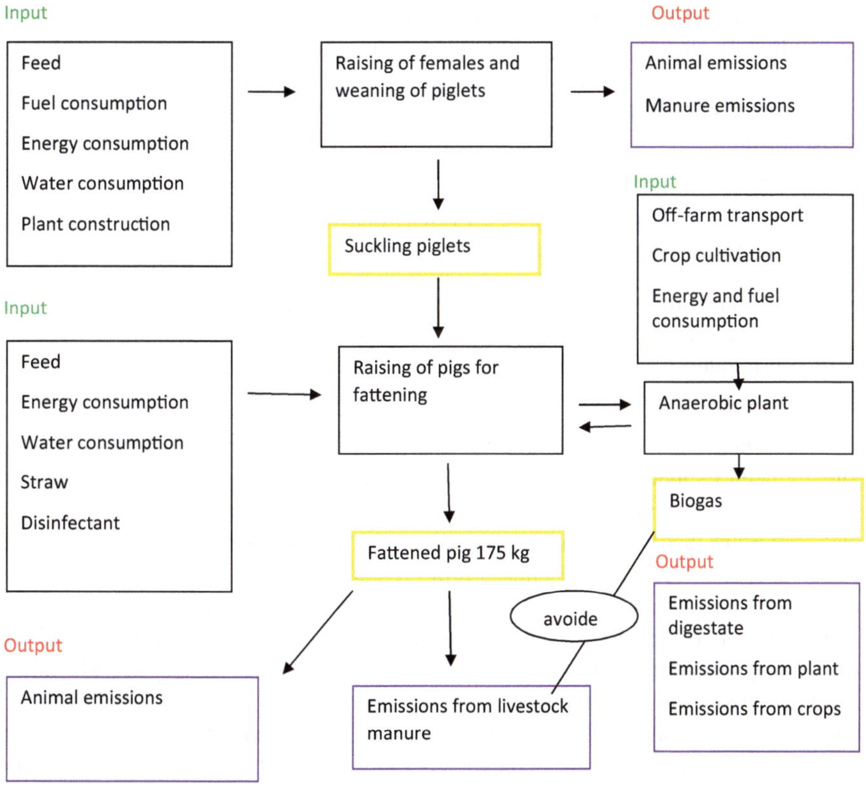

Fig. 2 Flow chart of a sustainable pig production chain. Source: Centro Ricerche Produzioni Animali (CRPA)

production process generates a lower carbon footprint, which decreases from 5.08 to 1.06 kg CO_2 equivalent/kg of live weight.

The achievement of the above result, significant in environmental terms as has been described, involves the construction of specific plant requiring much capital. As well as through traditional banking channels, this can be obtained through the use of market instruments also able to involve the final consumer more, raising awareness of the achievement of these important results in terms of animal carbon footprint. We are here referring to the possibility of pig chain companies issuing Sustainability Linked Bonds (SLB). These are bonds for which the financial and/or structural characteristics can vary depending on the achievement or otherwise of a predefined objective in terms of sustainability. The International Capital Market Association (ICMA)[9] has issued specific principles, the adoption of which is voluntary, which permit objective and unequivocal identification of an SLB. These Sustainability Linked Bond Principles (SLBP) cover five points:

[9] https://www.icmagroup.org/.

1. Selection of Key Performance Indicators (KPIs)
2. Calibration of objectives (Calibration of Sustainability Performance Targets—SPTs)
3. Characteristics of the bond
4. Reporting
5. Verification

KPIs are objectives (internal or external) that must be identified by the issuer. They must be credible goals and should:

- Involve a central and material element of the strategic activity of the issuer
- Be measurable and quantifiable objectively
- Be verifiable by a person external to the issuer
- Be comparable against a publicly observable benchmark

Where possible, issuers should consider as target parameter elements that have already been included in the past in their annual reports (e.g., nonfinancial reports; sustainability reports) so as to allow the investor to observe changes over time. It is also important that the issuer clearly states what the targets are and how they were selected. It is evident that the emission of GHG (but also, e.g., a reduction in water consumption) by the pig chain respects all the points listed above.

Calibration of the SPTs serves to establish the level of achievement of the objectives, which must have an effective impact on the issuer's business. The target level declared should be ambitious, should be consistent with the issuer's sustainability strategy, and should represent a material improvement to be pursued in a predefined period of time. The achievement of the pre-established objectives must be objectively demonstrable on a scientific basis and comparable with an adequate peer group. The starting point must be clear, and the environmental strategy adopted and how this can contribute to the achievement of the objectives must be described, also declaring any other factor that could have a negative impact on the achievement of the individual objectives. Furthermore, the nomination of a suitable person for providing a Second Party Opinion is recommended, that is, an independent expert, external to the issuer, who is able to express an authoritative opinion on the SLB and specifically on the targets achieved and to be achieved.

The most important elements of an SLB are the structural and/or financial characteristics of the bond, which must change when the target objectives are achieved. The most common example is that of bonds incorporating a change in the amount of coupon paid periodically upon the occurrence of a certain event or the achievement of a certain target level. It is recommended that the modification of the bond be proportionate to the size of the target achieved. In this sense, reporting takes on an important role: it must be extremely clear and detailed and be published regularly at least once a year and in any case upon the occurrence of events relevant to the issuer.

It is evident that a pig producer can define ambitious objectives for the reduction of the animal carbon footprint, to be achieved by means of the construction of special plant financed through the emission of SLBs. Upon the achievement of specifically predefined intermediate objectives, one could envisage modification, specifically an increase, in the coupon rate for the holders of these SLBs so that the final consumer can penalize by means of his/her purchasing behavior, those operators who do not concretely work to improve their environmental impact. By way of example, an SLB issued for a duration of 10 years and aimed at the construction of biogas plant for the reduction of CO_2 emissions could provide for an annual coupon of 0.5% for the first 2 years. At the end of the 2 years, upon achieving a consistent reduction, appropriately measured, in the CO_2 emitted, the coupon could rise to 1% for the next 3 years and so on until the natural maturity of the bond.

Structuring an SLB could be particularly complex. However, to support companies wishing to face the transition from a brown to a green economy, the financial system provides specific simpler financial instruments, defined as transition bonds. These are bonds that can be issued by companies that intend to proceed with a gradual transition toward a more environmentally sustainable business model. They are particularly useful in helping transition not only for pig farmers but also for all other parties involved in the pig chain, such as transporters. As an example, we can consider transport companies with fleets of vehicles equipped with diesel engines. The complete replacement of these fleets with electrically powered vans would not only be expensive but, in the short term, could also cause delays to business operations. In order to financially support this important investment aimed at reducing CO_2 emissions from vehicles, transport companies could raise money by issuing transition bonds explicitly intended for the replacement of their vehicle fleets not only when necessary (the vehicles could in fact still be fully functional and serviceable) but to pursue an effective and progressive reduction of CO_2 emissions. The same goes for shipping companies, should the product be marketed internationally; switching from heavy marine diesel to liquefied natural gas propulsion is currently the most effective solution for reducing emissions from large-scale commercial shipping. In this case too, issuing transition bonds could be a valid way to face this important financial commitment.

If the objective of the loan is not ecological transition but the realization of a specific project with an environmental impact, the issue of green bonds would also be possible. Green bonds are in fact any type of bond instrument whose proceeds are used to finance new and/or pre-existing environmental projects or to finance activities that generate a positive environmental impact. To date, there is still no official and shared definition of green bonds, but only voluntary guidelines (principles and standards) issued by:

- Public bodies (e.g., Technical Expert Group on sustainable finance—TEG)
- Market operators (e.g., International Capital Market Association—ICMA or Bloomberg)
- Nongovernmental organizations (NGOs) active in the "sustainability" ecosystem (e.g., Climate Bond Initiative[10])

[10]https://www.climatebonds.net/.

Although the nature and origin of the bodies mentioned above are different, the principles issued by them are convergent. For this reason, in this case too, we will make explicit reference to the Green Bond Principles (GBPs) issued by ICMA in July 2018. For a bond to be defined as green on the basis of these principles, it must make reference to five elements:

- Use of proceeds
- Evaluation and selection of the project
- Income management
- Reporting
- External review/audit

The proceeds deriving from the issue of the bond must be used, entirely or in part, to finance or refinance eligible "green" projects, with the aim of clear and documentable benefits. Eligible green projects include those falling within the so-called green taxonomy as defined by EU Regulation 2020/852, that is, projects aimed at mitigating climate change, adapting to climate change, conserving water and marine resources, transition to a circular economy, biodiversity conservation, and pollution prevention and control. With specific reference to the pig sector and without claiming to provide a full list, projects involving the development of renewable energy sources, energy efficiency, pollution prevention and control, sustainable management of natural resources and soil, clean transport, sustainable water and wastewater management, sustainable construction, and the adoption of eco-efficient and circular processes and technologies could therefore be financed by issuing green bonds. The issuer must communicate clearly to investors the environmental sustainability objectives to be achieved, the process according to which project compatibility with eligible categories is assessed and the specific eligibility criteria examined to identify risks of negative impact.

It will be very important to define a formal internal procedure for the tracking and allocation of proceeds, with the provision of separate accreditation methods (e.g., dedicated current account, allocation to a sub-portfolio, etc.). Investors must also be notified of the temporary placement arrangements for the portion of net proceeds not yet allocated to the project in question. Each year, or more frequently in the event of significant developments, the issuer of the green bond must provide investors with detailed information on the use of the proceeds. In particular, it will be necessary to draw up a list and description of the projects to which the proceeds have been allocated, to quantify the sums allocated and to describe the expected impacts, and to include quantification based on consolidated performance metrics. Finally, GBPs also require formal control (review/audit) by external and independent experts in order to guarantee and protect investors.[11]

---

[11] Four types of review/audit are possible:

- Second party opinion: the auditor must express an opinion on the objectives declared by the issuer and on the internal procedures on sustainability and on the environmental characteristics of the financed projects.

4 The Role of Confidi

The companies making up the pig chain include micro or small and medium enterprises, that is, small-scale breeders (including single proprietor companies), owners of vehicles used for the transport of the finished product, and retailers, including the many small shops still present in Italy. Each of these may need financing to support and improve their business, including in terms of ecological sustainability and very often encounter problems regarding access to credit, especially where they are clients of national and international rather than local banks. These companies are able to approach banks for credit more easily thanks to the presence of collective credit guarantee consortia, known as Confidi. Generally speaking, these are consortia that provide guarantees to facilitate companies in accessing loans, both short-, medium-, and long-term, intended for economic and productive activities. Confidi are divided into two macro categories: major Confidi and minor Confidi. The former are registered in the "Single register of financial intermediaries" held by the Bank of Italy and governed by Article 106 of the Consolidated Banking Act. The prerequisite for registration is that the volume of financial assets of these intermediaries should exceed 150 million euros on an annual basis, while below this level, the Confidi are automatically registered as minor Confidi (art. 112 of the TUB). The distinction between major and minor Confidi concerns their activities as well as their asset volume. Legislation permits major Confidi a wider breakdown of activities:

I. *Main activity*: collective credit guaranteeing, which on the basis of the Bank of Italy's regulatory provisions, consists in the use of resources deriving in whole or in part from member companies for entrepreneurial support and the provision of guarantees, in favor of the same consortium or member companies, in order to facilitate their financing by banks and other entities operating in the financial sector (Bank of Italy Circular No. 288)[12].
II. *Complementary activities*: these are related to the main activities and concern: the provision of guarantees for the State financial administration, for the purpose of providing tax refunds to consortium or member companies; the management of public subsidy funds; the signing of contracts with banks that

- Verification: the auditor must express an opinion on the environmental criteria adopted in the selection of the financed projects, on the environmental characteristics of the financed activities, on the tracking and allocation systems for the proceeds and on the impact report.
- Certification: the auditor must judge the green bond as a whole or some of its fundamental characteristics.
- Scoring/rating: the auditor must express the sustainability rating to be attributed to the green bond.

[12]The prevalence requirement is satisfied when the following two conditions are jointly met: the amount of revenues deriving from the collective credit guarantee activity and related and technical activities exceeds 50% of total revenues; the nominal amount of the collective credit guarantees exceeds 50% of total balance sheet assets.

are assignees of public guarantee funds. These complementary activities must be aimed primarily at consortium or member companies.

III. *Residual activities*: these are other forms of financing in accordance with article 106 of the TUB, paragraph 1, provided that it is within a limit which, until the recent enactment of the "Cura Italia" Decree (Law no. 18/2020), was 20% of total assets. Currently, however, this threshold has been raised to 49%. Within this overall limit, the consortia can also guarantee the issuing of debt (such as, e.g., the aforementioned green bonds, transition bonds, and sustainable linked bonds) by member small- and medium-sized enterprises.

IV. *Related and technical activities*: "related activities" cover ancillary services, which make it possible to develop the collective credit guarantee activity and have purposes, which are consistent with it (e.g., consultancy services in the field of company finance for the improvement of financial management carried out for member companies; the signing of agreements with banks, financial intermediaries, and others operating in the financial sector aimed at facilitating access to credit for member companies); "technical activities: are essentially services auxiliary to the activity carried out, such as: (i) study, research, and analysis of economic and financial matters; (ii) the purchase of properties, exclusively used for the carrying out of the main activity or intended for and rented to employees (also including properties acquired for debt recovery, which can be held for the time strictly necessary for their sale); (iii) the acquisition of shareholdings exclusively in other consortia or collective guarantee banks, that is, in other financial intermediaries which, on the basis of specific agreements, issue guarantees to their shareholders, or in companies set up for the provision of technical services.

The list of minor Confidi is held by a specific supervisory body, the Organismo Confidi Minori (OCM). This type of credit guarantee consortia is solely responsible for carrying out the collective credit guarantee activity for member and associated companies and related and technical services. The related and technical activities that can be carried out by minor Confidi are almost the same as those of major Confidi. The main difference lies in the type of beneficiaries: while minor Confidi can carry out these activities only for member companies, major Confidi can carry out related and technical activities for nonmembers too provided that this is for the development of the prevailing activity, that is, the collective guarantee of credit lines or the residual activity of disbursement of other forms of financing[13] and/or providing guarantees for the issuance of debt instruments by member SMEs.

On December 31, 2021, at the national level, there were 210 Italian Confidi, 33 major Confidi registered in the register pursuant to art. 106 TUB and subject to the supervision of the Bank of Italy, and 177 minor Confidi pursuant to art. 112 legislative decree 1 September 1993 number 385, registered in the OCM list, subject to the supervision of the minor Confidi body. The major Confidi are present

[13] Art. 106, paragraph 1 of the TUB.

only in 15 Italian Regions and are mainly concentrated in the north (64% of the total, 21 Confidi out of 33); less than half the major Confidi are located in the regions of central and southern Italy (18% of the total in both areas, six in the central and six in the southern regions). The minor Confidi are instead distributed throughout Italy, and at least one is present in each Region, demonstrating their close links with their local context and with the micro-, small-, and medium-sized enterprises operating in Italy. In particular, the majority of minor Confidi are located in the southern Regions (58% of the total, 103 minor Confidi out of 177), followed by the northern Regions (49 minor Confidi, 28% of the total) and the center (25 minor Confidi, 14% of the total).

From analyzing the company names, it emerges that of these 177 minor Confidi, eight have "agri" in their name, testifying to their "agricultural nature," fundamental for their being able to evaluate farms in order to approve guarantees to companies in this sector. The regional distribution of these eight Confidi is as follows: three in Emilia Romagna, three in Valle d'Aosta, one in Lombardy, one in Sardinia, one in Calabria, and one in Sicily. It should be noted that the other 169 minor Confidi can also deal with agriculture. Of the major Confidi, two are based in Emilia Romagna (Cooperfidi and Fider) and are also involved in agriculture even if they do not expressly refer to this in their company names.

Some summary data highlight the role and importance of Confidi in the Italian context. Cooperfidi, one of the largest, during 2021 provided guarantees for 44,574,000 euros, against loans of 74,830,000 euros, of which 20,800,000 euros in Emilia Romagna. Of the more than 44,000,000 euros of guarantees issued, 19,100,000 euros (about 42.85%) was for agriculture, forestry, and fishing and 3,915,000 euros (about 8.78%) for transport and warehousing.[14] Figures for the minor Confidi are equally significant: Agrifidi Uno Emilia Romagna, which had 5124 members at the end of 2021, guaranteed loans of 56,000,000 euros, all intended for the agricultural sector.[15]

The contribution and support of Confidi to the agricultural sector, including in terms of support for sustainability, is therefore evident.

5 Conclusions

The livestock industry, especially the pig production chain, is particularly aware of the animal carbon footprint issue due to the high level of climate-changing gas emissions deriving from it. The reduction of these emissions and therefore transition to a more sustainable production process is a major challenge that necessarily involves incurring high transition costs. When granting credit, the financial market in all its forms, banks foremost, must necessarily bear in mind the specific risks that

[14]Cooperfidi—Financial statements at 31-12-2021.

[15]Agrifidi—Financial statements at 31-12-2021.

characterize the production and distribution processes of companies in this supply chain. However, the mere identification of such risks cannot be an end in itself; the financial system offers financial instruments and possible support solutions in order to facilitate transition from a brown economy to a green economy. In this chapter, we have presented some of these, which render necessary specific consultancy by experts who must be suitably trained as regards the transversal issues of finance and environmental sustainability.

References

Angelini, P. (2022). *I rischi finanziari posti dai cambiamenti climatici: carenze informative e piani di transizione*. Intervento presso Associazione nazionale per lo studio dei problemi del credito. https://www.bancaditalia.it/pubblicazioni/interventi-direttorio/int-dir-2022/ANGELINI-15-novembre-2022.pdf

Basset-Mens, C., & Van der Werf, H. M. (2005). Scenario-based environmental assessment of farming systems: The case of pig production in France. *Agriculture, Ecosystems & Environment, 105*(1–2), 127–144.

Batten, S., Sowerbutts, R., & Tanaka, M. (2016). *Let's talk about the weather: The impact of climate change on central banks* (Working Paper).

Bava, L., Zucali, M., Sandrucci, A., & Tamburini, A. (2017). Environmental impact of the typical heavy pig production in Italy. *Journal of Cleaner Production, 140*, 685–691.

Cederberg, C., Wivstad, M., Bergkvist, P., Mattsson, B., & Ivarsson, K. (2005). Environmental assessment of plant protection strategies using scenarios for pig feed production. *AMBIO: A Journal of the Human Environment, 34*(4), 408–413.

Kitzes, J., Wackernagel, M., Loh, J., Peller, A., Goldfinger, S., Cheng, D., & Tea, K. (2008). Shrink and share: humanity's present and future ecological footprint. *Philosophical Transactions of the Royal Society B: Biological Sciences, 363*(1491), 467–475.

McAuliffe, G. A., Chapman, D. V., & Sage, C. L. (2016). A thematic review of life cycle assessment (LCA) applied to pig production. *Environmental Impact Assessment Review, 56*, 12–22.

McGlade, C., & Ekins, P. (2015). The geographical distribution of fossil fuels unused when limiting global warming to 2 C. *Nature, 517*(7533), 187–190.

Nguyen, T. L. T., Hermansen, J. E., & Mogensen, L. (2010). Fossil energy and GHG saving potentials of pig farming in the EU. *Energy Policy, 38*(5), 2561–2571.

Nguyen, T. L. T., Hermansen, J. E., & Mogensen, L. I. S. B. E. T. H. (2011). *Environmental assessment of Danish pork*. Aarhus University.

Van der Werf, H. M., Petit, J., & Sanders, J. (2005). The environmental impacts of the production of concentrated feed: The case of pig feed in Bretagne. *Agricultural Systems, 83*(2), 153–177.

Wiedmann, T., & Minx, J. (2008). A definition of 'carbon footprint'. *Ecological Economics Research Trends, 1*(2008), 1–11.

Managing Generational Handover in Family Business: Some Case Studies in the Charcuterie Factories

Barbara Barabaschi, Roberta Virtuani, and Franca Cantoni

1 Introduction

The main challenges that arise when it comes to generational handover, especially in SME, are widely covered by the scientific literature and essentially concern the difficult coexistence of different goals/expectations/values and personalities, the lack of role formalization, and work ethic that tends to differ significantly as the family business moves through its generations (Barabaschi et al., 2021).

The dynamics that characterize the generational transition are anything but linear and differ across generations. The model we use identifies four types of succession behavior (evaded, postponed, scheduled, and instant) for the present generation, while other types of succession are adopted (claimed, conflicting, psychological, collaborative) if we consider the emerging generation. Interweaving the two perspectives results in a particularly interesting pattern of analysis as it is possible to identify different main possible areas of intergenerational coexistence in family business.

In this far from easy context, recent studies concerning the generational transition in family businesses have highlighted the role that new generations of entrepreneurs recognize in sustainability, an element neglected by the predecessors or at least not adequately considered (Chiang et al., 2022). Being the central topic of our analysis, the charcuterie industry that processes and converts agricultural raw materials into to high-quality food products, key issues such as energy use, greenhouse gas emissions, resource and waste management, water and wastewater management, and packaging are indispensable parts of sustainable food. Some studies have proven that

B. Barabaschi (✉) · R. Virtuani · F. Cantoni
Department of Economic and Social Sciences, Università Cattolica del Sacro Cuore, Piacenza, Italy
e-mail: barbara.barabaschi@unicatt.it

A. M. Fellegara et al. (eds.), *Sustainable Transition of Meat and Cured Meat Supply Chain*, CSR, Sustainability, Ethics & Governance,
https://doi.org/10.1007/978-3-031-34977-5_13

new entrepreneurial generations are prone to invest more than the older ones in environmental, economic, and social sustainability (e.g., by increasing investment in new machineries to create safer workplaces, in training sessions for HR development) (Ferreira et al., 2021). This represents a trait not yet sufficiently explored in the scientific literature concerning the generational transition (Clauß et al., 2021)

To understand if a succession process has been sustainable from the social/relational and economic/organizational point of view, we studied the following factors of family business: succession planning, corporate governance, and leadership.

The chapter is organized as follows: in the first paragraph, we try to understand the dynamics of succession; the second paragraph is dedicated to understanding how sustainability applies in generational handover; paragraph 3 explains the methodology adopted, while the results are described in paragraph 4. Some conclusions and implications are depicted in paragraph 5.

2 Family Business and the Challenge of Generational Handover: Understanding the Dynamics

When it comes to generational handover, it is necessary to understand behavioral dynamics that could affect generational handover. The literature proposes Piantoni's matrix (1990), which consider jointly the behavior of the generations involved, the present and the emerging ones.

With reference to the perspective of successors and predecessors, this model identifies different types of succession.

About the present generation behavior, the model identifies four types of succession: evaded, postponed, scheduled, and instant.

Evaded succession is characterized by a real or apparent disinterest in the succession on the part of the entrepreneur who does not accept the idea of planning the directive transition. It is a situation that occurs in cases where the entrepreneur has an extreme tendency toward centralization, a strong propensity to act rather than to plan, or when he is so involved in operational management that he does not have the time to devote to the succession.

Postponed succession, in which the present generation belongs, is inclined to involve the new generation in the decision-making process and to favor shared management but is pushed by operational commitments and the surrounding environment, to postpone the real transfer of power and to delay the succession process, without proper planning.

Planned succession is already in advance of the moment of insertion; there is a constant effort toward a gradual transfer of power, in the search for a participatory leadership style.

Instant succession, a form of centralized and nonparticipatory management, although the entrepreneur is well prepared to plan the handover, he exercises full

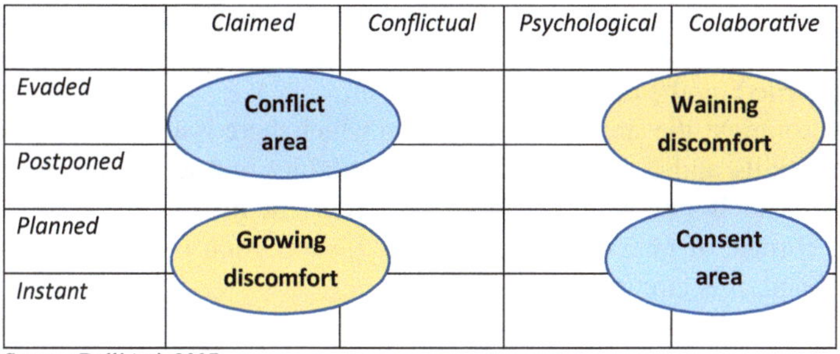

Source: Dell'Atti, 2007

Fig. 1 Areas of intergenerational coexistence. Source: Dell'Atti (2007)

power and has full responsibility for management up to the day of the inevitable handover.

Considering the emerging generation, the model identifies other types of succession: claimed, conflicting, psychological, and collaborative.

Claimed succession is the case of an emerging generation which, by virtue of the position occupied in the family clan, is eager to occupy leadership positions. Therefore, the strategy it implements is usually opportunistic with little will to introduce improvements.

In conflicting succession, there is an excessive impatience of the successor to play roles of responsibility, without sharing decisions with the present generation.

In physiological succession, the nontraumatic entry of the new generation pushes them to seek a lasting balance with the existing management. The business conduct guidelines are tacitly approved, as the successor lacks a determination to take over the company to cover positions of responsibility.

In collaborative succession, the emerging generation succeeds, through effective communication, in proposing innovations, involving them in development projects.

Interweaving the two perspectives results in a particularly interesting pattern of analysis as it is possible to identify three main possible areas of intergenerational coexistence in family business: an area of conflict, an area of discomfort (being overcome or growing), and an area of consensus (Dell'Atti, 2007) (Fig. 1).

A representative of the present generation unwilling to delegate the entrepreneurial role (evaded succession) and a representative of the emerging generation who is restless and unable to consciously assume this role (claimed succession) determine a climate of conflict. Both protagonists are aggressive, emotional, and disinclined to rationality.

In area of consent, it occurs in the case of the available attitude of the present generation, on the one hand, and the concrete and positive qualities developed by the emerging generation on the other.

Area of discomfort can in turn be divided into two sub-areas: that of growing discomfort and that of waning discomfort. In particular, a present generation representative attentive to the problem of succession and an emerging generation representative who is not up to the task lead to an increasing situation of unease. On the one hand, the succession is planned, while on the other hand, it is claimed. Clearly, it is easy to fall into the *area of conflict* since the experiences of the present generation are not inherited by the children.

On the contrary, the situation may arise in which there is an emerging generation with good skills and a sense of business continuity and a centralizing a present generation who is not willing to leave the reins of his company, so there is a declining climate of unease. On the one hand, succession is collaborative, and on the other hand, it is circumvented.

3 Family Business and Sustainability

The new generation of entrepreneurs seems to pay increasing attention to sustainability issues (Chiang et al., 2022). The World Commission on Environment and Development (1987) defines business sustainability as meeting current needs without compromising the next generation's ability to meet its needs. Ward (1987) has emphasized that each family business should have a plan for sustaining the business through the generations that will serve both the needs of the business and the needs of the family, thus setting both the family and the business onto the right path.

The main interest of the charcuterie industry is processing and converting raw materials into to high-quality food and beverage products. Key issues such as energy use, greenhouse gas emissions, resource and waste management, water and waste water management, and packaging are indispensable parts of sustainable food. Some studies have proven that new entrepreneurial generations are prone to invest more than the older ones in environmental, economic, and social sustainability (e.g., by increasing investment in new machineries and to make safer workplaces, in training session for the human resources development).

To understand if a succession process has been sustainable from the social/relational and economic/organizational point of view, we studied the following factors of family business: succession planning, corporate governance, and leadership.

Compared to other businesses, family businesses exhibit different features in many respects. Some of these features are advantages, whereas some pose disadvantages. These disadvantages and risks can be turned into opportunities through sustainable development activities. Sustainable development shows what areas businesses should focus to ensure sustainable development and allows businesses, governments, and civil society to create and realize common objectives in terms of social and economic sustainability.

The process of transitioning a family-owned business is a crucial phase to assure firm continuity and may represent an opportunity to introduce or reinforce sustainability among firm's goals and values. Every business and every family is unique, and the right solution, the right path through sustainability, for each business is likely to be unique. Nevertheless, focusing on the generational handover, Scholars (Corona, 2021; Barabaschi, 2019; Barabaschi et al., 2021) have identified some common factors in successful succession processes accompanied by the development of sustainability and innovation strategies.

3.1 Succession Planning

Succession planning is a structured approach to plan ahead for leadership positions in the family business; it can improve a potential leader's skills through experience and the assignment of appropriate tasks to individuals who will one day lead the family business.

Hence, prior studies highlighted the importance of succession planning to ensure the success of the generation transition and family business continuity. To continue to prepare for the next generation, the succession plan must be initiated by the business's founder and continuously updated even after a successful business transition. According to Sharma et al. (2003a, 2003b), the succession process can be successful only in the presence of family commitment to the firm, a desire to keep the firm in the family and the ability of a trusted successor to assume control, thanks to a collaborative intergenerational coexistence before the generational handover. Succession planning is strongly interconnected to the strategic planning (i.e., different from strategic planning for nonfamily-owned firms because it considers family issues and goals), which helps in extending the business lifespan and is based on family commitment and goals to continue the business into the future.

3.2 Governance Structure

Family firms depend on solid governance for the longevity of both the family and the firm (Pieper, 2003). Family business governance differs from nonfamily business governance because:

> (1) the family has a long-term relationship with the business; (2) the family has its own cultural views and norms that are implemented in the business and perpetuated by the successive generations; and (3) the stakeholders and board members are genetically related to each other (Ward, 2003). According to Rosenblatt et al. (1985) conflicts that arise in the family and business environment include the following: difficulty in separating family matters from business matters and vice versa, difficulty in making decisions, legacy and leadership. The risk, especially when family business are small, is that of a single decision-making owner avoiding a collaborative leadership style and, as a consequence, losing the opportunities of innovation. In this case, the collaboration with third parties, also external to the family (consultant, sector associations, consortium, for example), may favor changes.

3.3 Leadership

Researchers acknowledge leadership as a major factor in a business's survival and success (Gersick et al., 1997; Fiedler, 1996; Van Der Westhuizen & Garnett, 2014). In a family business, achieving competent family leadership through the generations is one of the greatest challenges to business continuity (Le Breton-Miller et al., 2004). It is difficult to achieve competent family leadership without a willing successor or leadership skills that affect the business's continuity (Lansberg, 1988). Therefore, the sub-criteria for leadership considered in this study are competent family member leadership and effective leadership skills. In particular, a relevant role in firm longevity has assumed skills such as vision and sustainable mindset.

Sustainable leadership is a style of management that drives solutions for environmental, social, and economic challenges. Sustainable leaders understand and face complexity, becoming more adaptable as a result; they are long-term thinkers who see business as deeply interwoven with people and the environment, not as individual entities. Driven by their strong values, they make bold moves that focus on the impact of the organization on the next three generations, rather than the next quarter. With these skills embedded in their management style, sustainable leaders, when coincide with the emerging generation, prepare the organization to flourish and expand long into the future.

In this regard, the founder or incumbent leader plays a vital role in teaching and training his or her successor so that he or she has the knowledge and skills required to lead and continue the business in the next generation (Cater & Justis, 2010; Dyck et al., 2002).

3.4 Family Business Values

Family business values contribute to the longevity of the family business by configuring a common vision and creating a code of work (Aronoff & Ward, 2000; Tapies & Moya, 2012). Given that there are often conflicts of interest between business and family goals, family business values should be well known and serve as a common ground between the business and the family to achieve their goals (Koiranen, 2002). Family business values are key elements in sustaining the family firm; when both generations work together, values are successfully transferred to and embedded in the next generation (Erdem & Baser, 2010).

Tapies and Moya (2012) reported quality, honesty, and hard work as the most important family values that highly contribute to the family firm longevity. Miller and Le Breton-Miller (2005) identify value-driven employees as a fundamental condition for the continuity of family business. Today, sustainability, from an environmental, economic, and social sustainability, may become a crucial part of family business philosophy and strategy.

4 Methodology

The methodology followed is the case study that allows to deep qualitative aspects through structured interviews. The intention was to derive some preliminary information that will be tested with a further investigation phase with an expansion of the sample investigated. Therefore, this research intends to lay the foundations for further and subsequent investigations. For the preliminary study, four companies with production certified by the Protected Designation of Origin (PDO) where initially engaged and both the first- and second-generation interviewed but separately. The text of the interview as well as the objective was anticipated so that the interviewees could adequately prepare. Aim of the interviews—lasting in average 1 hour—was to understand the main difficulties encountered in the succession process and the different management styles adopted by the successor. Particular attention was dedicated to understanding stakeholder relations and the focus on sustainable projects.

This methodology has been chosen basically for two reasons: the first aspect is that such practice will progress the knowledge and understanding of specific situations still not adequately explored in the literature; secondly, it is because of its duality of being both situationally grounded and generalizable. Moreover, the case study method facilitates the collection of more extensive amounts of information than other methodologies: this provides for more comprehensive data and a greater understanding of the phenomenon. Due to the nature of the investigation, most of the questions were open questions.

The companies chosen are in the Piacenza area, particularly recognized and famous to produce the highest-quality cured meats. We analyzed four companies of the sector that is characterized by craft and small family business. The companies are as follows: Salumificio San Carlo, Salumificio Gagliardi, Salumificio Giordano, and Salumificio Grossetti.

5 Research Results

The subject of our analysis is family businesses with production certified by the Protected Designation of Origin (PDO) . The PDO-certified productions concern three products: salame piacentino, coppa piacentina, and pancetta piacentina. Piacenza and its province are the only ones in Europe to have three PDOs. PDOs originated in Europe as an idea in 1992 with EC Regulation 2081 updated in 2012 with EU Regulation 1151/2012. These regulations were established in order to protect the traditional products of the various European countries from imitative phenomena and to satisfy the ever-increasing search by consumers for quality foodstuffs linked to tradition and with an identifiable geographical origin. Each product is generated by the territory that expresses it: it is unique. It is made recognizable by the European identification symbols. With the PDO, the entire process of obtaining the product, from the raw material to the final processing, refers to the area of the designation. In order to bear the symbol, foodstuffs must follow a precise and strict recognition process at first national and then European level. Before being placed on the market, they must undergo strict controls by Certification Bodies, which operate under the supervision of the Ministry of Agriculture.

Companies in Piacenza chose to enter the certification path on July 1996 with the aim of offering the consumer a great guarantee in terms of quality. The high costs incurred at the time were not matched by the certainty of a successful certification process. Certainly, manufacturers would have had to bear higher costs and stricter controls without knowing in advance the reaction from the market.

The old entrepreneurs invested in their companies with great gradualness and prudence to innovation.

In the 1950s, 1960s, and 1970s, the lever of success was the production of quantity, while quality was secondary. Only later quality become diriment to success in the marketplace. It was at that time that the companies that had invested in certification were repaid: adapting to the rules to obtain PDO certification proved to be the right move, the result of entrepreneurs' strategic vision.

It is a niche sector where demand is still growing. Almost all the companies are investing in expansions to have new and very modern plants. The first reference market is the domestic one, while exports are still weak. Investments are being made to open up sales in Germany, France, the United States, Canada, and Japan.

The companies with PDO cured meats are united in the Consorzio di Tutela Salumi DOP Piacentini, which is the association of the 12 companies that produce PDO-cured meats. They consist of ten family business and two cooperative companies. The companies are led by the second generation, and almost all of them have a third generation that is committed to charcuterie. Hence, there is a justification for the investments that are being made based on family continuation. The biggest investments are being made in the slicing lines, which represent an important innovation. To support the investments being made, the Consortium is participating in specific calls for tenders from the Ministry of Agricultural Policies and the Emilia Romagna Region.

Case are analyzed under different aspects: succession planning, governance, changes, leadership, and values.

Succession Planning

Salumificio San Carlo is the largest company followed by Salumificio La Rocca. All the companies in the Piacenza area have gone through the succession process, which is underway and at an advanced stage. In two of the four companies analyzed, the succession process has been completed with the exit of the incumbent, establishing the second and third generation, with the fourth generation having just started to work in the company. In the other two cases, the generations coexist. In all the companies interviewed, the successors have completely substituted the incumbents for the management of the company. In a case (Salumificio San Carlo), the successor is the new CEO. San Carlo's board is participated by a large national company that holds a minority stake in the sausage factory. San Carlo benefits strategically from this participation in all areas of management. The incumbent is still present as Chairman of the Board. The two generations, incumbent and successor, share the strategic vision of the company.

In the Salumificio Giordano, as result of the generational transition, the son took over the leadership and management. The succession was not planned, and it saw a temporary entry of a partner from outside the family. At Salumificio Gagliardi, the transition happened from the father (who succeeded his grandfather) to the two sons. In both companies, the process was completed with the exit of the previous generations. There was no real planning, as there was a coexistence between generations that lasted many years.

The Grossetti charcuterie is in its fifth generation. Governance is currently in the hands of the grandson (son of the incumbent's brother), with the recent takeover of the youngest son. The administrative responsibilities are entrusted to the nephew while the production and commercial areas to the son. The incumbent is still present in the company, but not involved in the operational management. He is gradually making room for the new generation to develop its own strategic vision. In Salumificio Grossetti, the succession wasn't planned. The new generation was gradually introduced to the management of the company. The entry took place after a shared family decision, due to management needs.

Sustainability of succession planning is inspired by firm continuity. All family members present a high level of commitment, share the same values, and cooperate to transit the firm over the different phases of the life cycle, also when not completely aligned on the same ideas. They show the attitude to negotiate and overcome divergencies in a relative spontaneous way, thanks to the strong affective involvement into the family and due to the close relations among all the family members.

Governance

The governance of the San Carlo charcuterie is shared between father (chairman of the board) and daughter, who is responsible for the operational management.

Also in this case, it is not possible to identify a succession plan. The daughter's entry came after her experience in another sector, making herself available to take on responsibilities in the family's charcuterie business.

San Carlo is the only charcuterie that works also for foreign markets. It is the biggest company in the area, and thanks to its size, it has developed the sales in Europe and the United States. It participates to many trade fairs helped by the intermediation of the Consortium for the protection of Piacenza DOP-cured meats.

In other companies, the governance is characterized by a concentration of strategic decisions in the person of the owners (second or third generation). They oversee the administrative as well as the production and commercial sector.

In general, the governance reflects values and norms perpetrated by the different generations through the family business history. The governance structure is designed to maintain positive social relations especially among family members actively involved in the business and not. In all analyzed cases, governance only considers members who work within the firm. The family members not working in the firm don't participate to its governance. The aim is to reduce the risk of increasing complexity in the governance structure during and after the succession process. This approach appears to be successful in ensuring the sustainability of succession, even from a social perspective.

Changes

All companies have introduced changes and innovations in response to the needs of their environment. The management areas most affected by the changes relate to the expansion of production facilities, digitalization, and facilities for environmental and social sustainability. In all the cases, investigated investments made are aimed at guaranteeing the high quality of the product (e.g., those for the ripening cells and cellars) and making management more efficient. Plants for the complete recovery of water from production and photovoltaic systems were installed with both environmental and economic benefits. As far as San Carlo, for example, the photovoltaic system has made the company independent for 20% of its annual energy needs. It is now benefiting of the advantages of these investments facing the increase of energy costs of the last year.

To meet consumer taste, a further area of investment concerns the facilities to offer the sliced and packaged product.

The new generation has made decisions on certifications, starting with the DOP, which places the quality of the product at a higher level of quality. Other certifications concern the efficiency of production systems. Certifications are favoring relations with large-scale distribution increasingly sensitive to the issue of sustainability to follow market demands and to comply with regulatory obligations.

New generations have also reinforced the collaborations with external actors, in particular, the local Consortium, with sector associations as well as with other firms according to a coopetition approach. They don't see other firms as mere competitors. They are considered agents sharing the same problems and limits, especially for what concern the possibility to access financing or training. Firms cooperate on certain business areas when it's convenient, to preserve economic sustainability.

Leadership

The new generations adopt leadership styles that, in some cases, can be defined as directive without hierarchical levels, also in relation to the small size of the workforce. The largest charcuterie is organized with functional area managers and department heads. There is a strong focus on health, safety, and hygiene in the workplace, formally certified. There is a strong focus on creating working conditions that support collaboration, including benefits such as meal vouchers, fuel vouchers, and company welfare.

In the sector, there is a strong difficulty in recruiting new personnel, especially in the production area, which, in some cases, has led to outsourcing strategies.

In general, a collaborative leadership style focused on social sustainability seems to be prevalent. Some companies have adopted a top-down approach to management, with the successor or incumbent taking charge. However, in all cases, there is a strong focus on managing human resources to maintain positive, and sometimes friendly, relationships with both old and new employees. These employees are seen as collaborators whose loyalty plays a strategic role in ensuring continuity and quality in the production process.

Values

The new generations show that they have absorbed the values, principles, and ethical codes of the previous ones. The entrepreneurial vision is strong as demonstrated by the investments planned and implemented to grow the company.

Critical issues in the sector are linked to ensuring a high-end product, offered on the market at a higher price than that of non-PDO competitors. Consumer health safety is a value that is also pursued and defended through compliance with production and workplace hygiene standards.

The strong focus on these values is one of the factors that has contributed to the strong growth of the sector in the past years. Today, the sector is going through a consolidation phase with moderate growth.

This sector is also suffering from the sharp rise in raw material and energy costs, which on the one hand require more prudent management and on the other stimulate investments in sustainability.

In this sense, we can affirm that, although every firm has its own development path, all the family businesses investigated present a tension through sustainability. This tension is stimulated by good results obtained by investments in safer workplaces and organic waste recycling. The focus on sustainability has produced higher employees' motivation and loyalty, higher products quality, an increase in the number of clients, and better economic returns. These elements seem to open-up the way to more consolidated sustainability strategies that, added to the more traditional values of the family business model (respect, sacrifice, cooperation), may lead to assume sustainability as a real philosophy in all activities.

6 Conclusion and Implications

The generational handover in family businesses of the charcuterie sector in the Piacenza territory presents similar characteristics to those of businesses in other sectors (Barabaschi et al., 2021) with reference to the primary desire to preserve the economic, social, and affective heritage developed in the family business.

Focusing on succession, it takes place through processes rooted in family history, which, in the case of Piacenza's salumi, sometimes involved up to five generations. We noted that the transition took place naturally without any particular conflict. The successor is easily identified as these families are not very numerous, and in some cases, the successor started working in the company at a very young age (see Salumificio Gagliardi).

From the perspective of the successor behavior, succession processes have been postponed in two cases, in which the generation governing the charcuterie involved the new generation in the decision-making process but remained pushed by operational commitments and the surrounding environment, finally postponing the real transfer of power. In two cases, the succession may be defined as partially scheduled, since the generational handover has been represented by a long-run process, with a long period of coexistence of the two generations into the business. This has favored a peaceful handover of strategic functions to the new generation.

Considering the new generation behavior, the succession may be defined as both *physiological and collaborative,* since in two cases the nontraumatic entry of the new generation pushes them to seek a lasting balance with the existing management. The business conduct guidelines were tacitly approved, as the successor was too young to take over the company to cover positions of responsibility. These two processes ended in a collaborative and peaceful generational handover. In the cases of *collaborative succession*, the emerging generation succeeded through effective communication, in proposing innovations, involving all the firm stakeholders in development projects.

Finally, if we try to interpret jointly the behavior of the different generations involved in succession processes, we observed a prevalent convergence in the area of a reduced discomfort and an increased consent, since the eventual conflicts generating from the coexistence of different personalities have been overcame thanks to clear roles for each family member and the strong sharing of family values and responsibility. The common goal is to assure family business continuity overtime. This latter is always the priority leading to the resolution of every dispute by all generations involved.

The characteristics of the sector favor succession orientation, as it is a healthy sector with growth prospects, despite the criticalities posed by the socioeconomic context, such as rising energy costs and changes in consumption styles. Critical issues are faced thanks to the strong spirit of collaboration and association that finds expression in the Consortium for the Protection of PDO Piacenza Salumi. The 12 members took decisions unanimously, demonstrating the will to act at system level.

Key instruments to face the challenges of the sector and promote its growth are the numerous quality certifications, first and foremost the PDO, a guarantee of healthy production processes to protect the quality of the product and the working environment, as well as the health of the consumer.

New generations are seizing the opportunities related to investments in sustainability, also to follow the new sensitivity at the level of the economic system.

The "passing of the baton" takes the form of the transmission of the attitude to entrepreneurship, with its principles and values, such as the spirit of sacrifice, responsibility, optimism, and risk-taking. In this sense, the present study confirms the literature (which is, moreover, underdeveloped with reference to family businesses in the food and meat sector) that identifies hard work and humility as the principles characterizing the enterprises under examination. They could be more sustainable with application of human resources development and professional management. Meanwhile attractive factors of the FBs were the food quality, human service, and affordable food price.

The positive results of succession processes also seem to be linked to the ability of previous generations to promote peaceful and fruitful coexistence in favor of the new generations, leaving them the space they need to express and make the most of their skills, through flanking and support activities. On the other hand, the new generations show that they identify with the values of the family tradition and believe in the business project implemented by the generations that preceded them, contributing to its future and renewing its principles. This last aspect is particularly strong and characterizing the specific reality investigated.

From the managerial implications point of view in the realities observed, the success factors identified are a balanced relationship between generations and a passion for the business project, for which the new generations are willing to face responsibilities and develop opportunities. These are factors that is difficult to replicate in other contexts. The PDO-cured meat sector is a niche with successful companies whose stakeholders have strong ties with the territory and tradition. The new generations, represented by the successors, are following in the footsteps of their fathers and grandfathers by adapting their businesses to the most modern management systems. Values, vision, and passion for the business project transmitted from one generation to the next are the success factors of entrepreneurial realities such as those analyzed.

A critical factor seems to be the low investment in communication, with particular reference to marketing. More business development strategies were needed, such as website marketing. This is a common fact among delicatessen companies, which is, however, related to being B2B and not B2C companies.

References

Aronoff, C., & Ward, J. (2000). *Family business values: How to assure a legacy of continuity and success*. Business Owner Resources.

Barabaschi, B. (2019). Management for Stakeholders Approach for a socially sustainable governance of megaprojects. In F. Cantoni & E. Favari (Eds.), *Megaproject management: A multidisciplinary approach to embrace complexity and sustainability* (Vol. 2020, pp. 27–41). Springer.

Barabaschi, B., Cantoni, F., & Virtuani, R. (2021). Managing generational handover in family business: A multistakeholders' perspective focusing on HR role. In G. Flamini & L. Gnan (Eds.), *Designing and implementing HR Management Systems in Family Businesses* (pp. 244–263). IGI Global.

Cater, J. J., & Justis, R. T. (2010). The development and implementation of shared leadership in multi-generational family firms. *Management Research Review, 33*, 563–585.

Chiang, H., He, L.-J., & Yu, H. J. (2022). Family Firm's succession and Firm's sustainability. *Journal of Family and Economic Issues, 43*(3), 637–646.

Clauß, T., Jones, P., & Kraus, S. (2021). Sustainability in family business: Mechanisms, technologies and business models for achieving economic prosperity, environmental quality and social equity. *Technological Forecasting and Social Change, 176*(Special Issue), 121450.

Corona, J. (2021). Succession in the family business: The great challenge for the family. *European Journal of Family Business, 11*, 64–70.

Dell'Atti, A. (2007). *Il passaggio generazionale nelle imprese familiari*. Cacucci.

Dyck, B., Mauws, M., Strake, F. A., & Mischle, G. A. (2002). Passing the baton: The importance of sequence, timing, technique and communication in executive sucession. *Journal of Business Venturing, 17*, 143–162.
Erdem, F., & Baser, G. G. (2010). Family and business values of reginal family firms: A qualitative research. *International Journal of Islamic and Middle Eastern Finance and Management, 3*, 47–64.
Ferreira, J. J., Fernandes, C. I., Schiavone, F., & Mahto, R. V. (2021). Sustainability in family business – A bibliometric study and a research agenda. *Technological Forecasting and Social Change, 173*, 121077.
Fiedler, F. E. (1996). Research on leadership selection and training: One view of the future. *Administration Science Quarterly, 41*, 241–250.
Gersick, K., Davis, J., Hampton, M., & Lansberg, I. (1997). *Generation to generation: Life cycle of family business*. Harvard Business School.
Koiranen, M. (2002). Over 100 years of age but still entrepreneurially active in business: Exploring the values and family characteristics of old Finnish family firms. *Family Business Review, 15*, 175–187.
Lansberg, I. (1988). The succession conspiracy. In C. E. Anroff, J. H. Astrachan, & J. L. Ward (Eds.), *Family business sourcebook II* (Vol. 1, pp. 70–86). Business Owner Resources.
Le Breton-Miller, I., Miller, D., & Steier, L. P. (2004). Toward an integrative model of effective FOB succession. *Entrepreneurship Theory and Practice, 28*, 305–328.
Miller, D., & Le Breton-Miller, I. (2005). *Managing for the long run: Lessons in competitive advantage from great family businesses*. Harvard Business School Press.
Piantoni, G. (1990). *La successione familiare in azienda. Continuità dell'impresa e ricambio generazionale*. Etas.
Pieper, T. M. (2003). *Corporate governance in family firms: A literature review*. INSEAD Initiative for Family Enterprise.
Rosenblatt, P. C., De Mik, L., Anderson, R. M., & Johnson, P. A. (1985). *The family in business*. Jossey-Bass.
Sharma, P., Chrisman, J. J., & Chua, J. H. (2003a). Predictors of satisfaction with the succession process in family firms. *Journal of Business Venturing, 18*, 667–687.
Sharma, P., Chrisman, J., & Chua, J. (2003b). Succession planning as planned behavior: Some empirical results. *Family Business Review, 16*, 1–15.
Tapies, J., & Moya, M. F. (2012). Values and longevity in family business: Evidence from a cross-cultural analysis. *Journal of Family Business Management, 2*, 130–146.
Van Der Westhuizen, J., & Garnett, A. (2014). The correlation of leadership practices of first and second generation family business owners to business performance. *Mediterranean Journal of Social Sciences, 5*, 323–338.
Ward, J. (1987). *Keeping the family business healthy: How to plan for continuing growth, profitability, and family leadership*. Jossey-Bass.
Ward, J. L. (1988). The special role of strategic planning for family businesses. *Family Business Review, 1*(2), 105–117.
Ward, J. L. (2003). *Good governance is different for family firms* (pp. 84–85). Family Business.
World Commission on Environment and Development. (1987). *Our common future. The Brundland report*. Oxford University Press.

Generation Z, Consumption of Cured Meats, and Lifestyles

Antonio Molinari and Elisa Zane

1 Introduction

"2022 is the European Year of Youth. It is time to give back to a generation that has shown so much solidarity, and lost so much, in the pandemic. I want Europe to work for the next generation. Young Europeans, make your voice heard. This is your Europe." It is with these words that, at the start of the new year, the President of the European Commission, Ursula von der Leyen, launched the initiatives marking the "European Year of Youth," aimed at focusing on the new generations as drivers of change, toward a more sustainable and inclusive future: "2022 is the European Year of Youth, shining a light on the importance of European youth to build a better future—greener, more inclusive and digital. With plenty of opportunities to learn, share your vision, meet people and engage in activities all over Europe, the European Year of Youth is the moment to move forward with confidence and hope in a post-pandemic perspective. Find out what the Year has in store for you and join in the #EYY2022" (https://youth.europa.eu/year-of-youth). The questionnaire, "THE CONSUMPTION OF DELI MEATS BY GENERATION Z," is part of a broader interest in future generations. Its aim is to survey the consumption habits of deli meat by young people, specifically those aged between 15 and 25. The survey will look into their knowledge of the product, how they consume it, their preferences, and what influences their purchasing decisions. The age group surveyed is defined as "Generation Z," that is, people born between 1995 and 2010—an era characterized by rapid social and technological change. Gen Z currently comprises adolescents and young people, that is, those approaching adulthood and who are experiencing the first forms of commitment, responsibility, and autonomy outside the contexts of the

A. Molinari · E. Zane (✉)
Alta Scuola per l'Ambiente, Università Cattolica del Sacro Cuore, Brescia, Italy
e-mail: antonio.molinari@unicatt.it; elisa.zane@unicatt.it

A. M. Fellegara et al. (eds.), *Sustainable Transition of Meat and Cured Meat Supply Chain*, CSR, Sustainability, Ethics & Governance,
https://doi.org/10.1007/978-3-031-34977-5_14

family and the school environment, taking into account the historical events that are shaping their life. The new generations are heavily influenced by ever-changing and increasingly persuasive technological innovation. This makes them more aware of the benefits and risks associated to living in a world of continuous technological transformation. For Gen Z, being able to manage change is key in becoming an effective adult: "training and reinforcing knowledge and skills for managing change is crucial for a generation, whose life expectancy is over 90; a generation that has to lay the foundations of adulthood in a world that will be very different from today one that will have to design a whole new concept of 'old age'" (Rosina, 2018, p. 14). The researcher also emphasizes Gen Z is a relatively small group in Italy. Being able to monitor them and get them to reflect on their lifestyle from a young age will not only allow us to get to know them but will also help prepare them for a challenging and complex future: "identifying this new generation and helping them improve both their own quality of life and a common future is the task of the outgoing generations" (Rosina, p. 16).

For the new generations, the complexity of current times translates into multiple paths with seemingly infinite possibilities of choice. This array of scenarios and contexts creates a fragmented outlook for Gen Z, which offers both a myriad of opportunities but also many uncertainties: "Looking into their biographies reveals a generation that belongs to multiple contexts and experiences, which, however, also indicates superficial and discontinuous experimentation. This inevitably leads to uncertain, rootless identities" (Amadini, 2018, p. 144).

The scenario indicates a crisis resulting not only from the period of transition to adulthood but also caused by the myriad of choices. This difficulty, however, can enable adolescents to test their limits and construct their own identity. Speaking about "new generations" often risks lapsing into rhetoric and paternalistic alarmism through generalization that often reveals more about the fear of adults rather than the reality of youth: "generalising this reading to an entire generation, using this part for the whole, prevents us from appreciating the heterogeneity of the world of adolescents, their resources and talents. It also risks penalising and disempowering an entire generation" (Ellena & Marta, 2022, p. 16). The activism shown by Gen Z is a strong, visible sign of their quest for involvement. This eagerness to be involved is not limited to climate issues, which, rightly, gets a lot of media coverage. However, it also translates into participation in voluntary activities, social and solidarity commitment, and the desire to be an active part of society by making one's voice heard and sharing one's stories and ideas (Alfieri, 2021). To be able to provide the tools necessary to develop the skills to respond to the challenges posed by the complexity of the social and environmental realty, the issues facing young people also need to be considered at institutional level. The National Recovery and Resilience Plan provides funding for initiatives aimed at tackling issues such as NEET (Not in Education, Employment or Training) and youth unemployment. The plan also seeks to promote institutional and business development to support the growth and inclusion of younger generations: "The plan has set transversal objectives for young people, which include investing in initiatives for ecological transition, implementing digitalization, and improving the entire education and research process" (Malavasi, 2022, p. 31). The creation of institutional and financial mechanisms marks a necessary involvement by the public and private sectors, but without the contribution of educational support that prepares Gen Z to face the challenges at hand, it can only be a limited process that risks becoming ineffective. Young people must be given the tools to understand and operate within their reality and must be willing to contribute toward their community. New skills and new creative outlooks can generate innovation and entrepreneurship by renewing corporate contexts: "ongoing organisational changes are a positive expression of the younger generations only if they are prepared to be challenged, allow creativity to find new ways of expression and if they are able to enrich the common good in line with their time" (Mazzoli, 2021, p. 12). In addition to being able to express their potential, therefore, there needs to be an educational outlook that directs their actions within the reality that they understand: "the younger generations must be helped to acquire adequate tools to understand reality with which they can express their interests, values and skills and, thus, embark on an emancipatory path to give new directions of meaning to the communities in which they live" (Bornatici, 2020, p. 13).

2 New Generations: Consumption and Lifestyles

"Food serves more than just a purpose of providing us with the nutrients we need to survive. It also plays a crucial role in shaping our social interactions and our sense of identity" (Birbes, 2012, p. 11).

Asking about the worth of food requires more than just considering its economic value. It involves deeper reflection and analysis. To better understand the consumers of tomorrow, it is important to read and interpret the food behavior and consumption habits of the new generations through a pedagogical gaze. "Understanding the small daily habits and generalised attitudes of entire societies towards nutrition can help to identify certain social rules of thought and behaviour that guide our planet's communities towards dialectics of prosperity or poverty, altruism or individualism, towards the safeguarding of creation or indiscriminate exploitation of resources" (Righettini, 2020, p. 229). By using an educational approach to interpret data, we can not only trigger reflexive processes but also create fertile ground for the construction of good educational practices and food education projects. In today's modernity, characterized by strong inequalities—both quantitative and qualitative—food education is becoming a necessity. This requires us to consider the growing connection between lifestyles and marketing. As Bornatici (2017, p. 45) explains, "recognising food as an element of identity and belonging is a path that guides the search for the meaning of educating, generates unprecedented modes of social interaction and participation in the construction of shared scenarios, and urges the activation of processes of change in a transformative perspective." The social and value dimensions of food reach beyond the individual and extend to the collective, meaning that pedagogical research must be projected toward future generations in order to influence changes in consumption and promote the necessary ecological conversion.

Adolescents and young adults represent a segment of the population that is beginning to buy independently but often has a fragmented and confused approach to consumption, oscillating between self-expression and homologation with their peer group.

Recognizing this, the "Human Development" research unit decided to focus on this segment of the population by involving them in the administration of a semi-structured survey questionnaire to investigate how the new generations relate to the consumption and purchase of deli meats.

In order to investigate the connections between sustainability and the consumption of deli meat in the imagination of Generation Z, the focus group tool was chosen, the results of which are discussed in more detail in the contribution of Prof. Birbes and Prof. Bornatici.

Pedagogical research historically prefers qualitative methods to develop its reflections, using data collection and analysis techniques that focus on investigating experience with a peculiar approach: "a philosophy that has as its first principle the search for heuristic procedures capable of accessing the complexity of the phenomena of reality, in particular those classifiable as 'experiences' and the 'construction of the meaning' of such experiences" (Mortari & Zannini, 2017, p. 14).

Making use of qualitative research methods does not exclude the use of quantitative instruments. In fact, combining both approaches allows the researcher to trace new scenarios of reflection with greater depth (Mortari, Zannini).

Educational research must also be accompanied by an in-depth and critical interpretation of empirical data, as "the human sciences, even those that study the processes and problems of education, considered as a whole, cannot exempt themselves from the need to pursue a systematic knowledge of reality, qualified by a form of empirical validity, that is, by an effort of objectivation and distinction between true and false" (Viganò, 2003, p. 35).

Following extensive reflection, it was decided to use a quantitative methodological approach for the survey, which included a semi-structured questionnaire consisting of 18 questions—17 closed-ended questions, using the Likert scale, and one open-ended question.

The survey focused on the consumption of deli meats by Generation Z, exploring the imagery it evokes in young people, the relationships underlying the moments of consumption, and the relationship with educational agencies such as the family in the purchase and consumption of the product. The context of consumption is a valuable area of investigation, as it is constantly changing, partly due to companies becoming increasingly attentive to consumer opinion in relation to the issue of supply chain sustainability and corporate social responsibility. As Fellegara (2015, p. 183) highlights, "the choice of increasing disclosure levels through integrated reporting choices appears, therefore, as a means of expression of the progressive awareness of corporate bodies to sustainability aspects that look beyond the traditional boundaries of the economic subject." The meat and cured meat industry has become a subject of great consideration in terms of sustainability, both in terms of environmental impacts and nutrition. Moreover, it is important to consider the need to safeguard traditional and professional cultures related to them (Bernardi et al., 2018).

3 Data Analysis

A random survey was administered within the school-university context to members of Generation Z. No pre-selection of participants was made prior to survey administration.

The survey was administered with guidance only in the informational and explanatory portion to allow participants to complete it independently. Ninety-four percent of the youth involved completed the questionnaire, and all questions were answered at least once. During the survey, the administration of the questionnaires was closely monitored to ensure the homogeneity of the Generation Z age groups. The age groups most represented were 14–19 years and 20–24 years, due to the contexts chosen for the survey.

In total, 339 youth were surveyed; 53% were born between 2007 and 2002 (14–19 years), 37% were born between 2001 and 1997 (20–24), and the remaining percentages were distributed between those born before 1997 and after 2007. Seventy-seven percent of the respondents were female, while 23% were male.

The territory involved was intentionally limited to the Lombardy region, the Italian leader for swine breeding, with more than 4 million heads (Basile, 2022). The survey covered almost all provinces, revealing a predominance of young residents in the province of Brescia (68%), followed by Bergamo, Cremona, Mantua, Lodi, and Varese; the provinces of Piacenza, Trento, and Verona complete the territorial composition.

It is interesting to highlight the size by population of the municipalities of residence. This data raises the initial research question of whether there is a correlation between the origin or residence of participants and their consumption of deli meats in Generation Z.

More than half of the young people (64%) live or reside in a medium-small municipality (population of less than 15,000 inhabitants); just under a quarter (23%) of the respondents come from provincial capitals (cities of more than 100,000 inhabitants) while a few (13%) in large towns or small cities (between 15,000 and 100,000 inhabitants).

In regard to the course of studies attended, the percentages are subject to the context chosen to administer the survey (schools and universities); 37% of the youth attended secondary school, while 62% attended university, with the remaining 1% split between primary school and postgraduate training. Even before investigating whether young people are consumers of deli meat or not, they were asked to express up to a maximum of three words associated with deli meat, also indicating the order of priority.

In absolute terms, "salami" is the concept most frequently associated with deli meat as well as being the first word mentioned; other recurring words initially

Fig. 1 Word cloud "What three words come to mind when you think of deli meats"

mentioned were related to the type of cured meat (ham, bresaola, coppa, speck, bacon), the category of animal (pig), macronutrients contained in deli meat (protein, fat), taste and flavor (good, disgust), places of production or consumption (farms, butcher's shop, bar, family), and traditions (Fig. 1).

In response to the question, "Do you eat deli meat?," 91% answered in the affirmative. If we investigate this percentage within the different age groups of Generation Z, we do not notice any particular deviations.

Of the total number of respondents, 9% were young people who said that they did not eat deli meat; of these, just under half (46% of nonconsumers) gave ethical reasons, mostly related to environmental and animal sensitivities, vegetarian diets, and other (37%) cited health reasons.

The same absolute percentage ratios were found within the different age groups of Generation Z. It is also noteworthy that the youngest participants expressed ethical motivations in their choice of consumption, which opposed family conditioning, as will be discussed further.

There was another question aimed at detecting the frequency of consumption.

The distribution of the answers is noteworthy: 29% eat deli meats once a week, 26% eat up to three times a week, and another 26% do not pay attention to the frequency of consumption; only 13% of the sample consume deli meats daily.

By far, the preferred point of sale for the purchase of deli meat is the supermarket of the large-scale retail trade (GDO) surveyed by 54% of the total answers given by young consumers (up to three answers were possible in the specific question); a significant part (30%) of the answers expressed their reliance on a trusted shop, while 8% of the answers relate to the purchase directly from the breeder.

Buying from organic shops or in bulk as a group of consumers did not reach significant percentages (between 2% and 5%).

It was considered whether there was a relationship between the place of purchase and the size of the municipality of residence; the specific research question was whether in small- and medium-sized municipalities (population below 15,000 inhabitants) people referred more to trustworthy shops or buying groups and vice versa in large municipalities and cities (population above 15,000); large-scale retail outlets are exclusive. No specific correlation was found, that is, the absolute percentages were also found in the different territorial bands.

This would also seem to reveal an amount of mobility from small towns to areas better served by outlets.

The daily occasions of consumption of deli meats refer to main meals for 55% of the respondents; this indication becomes more significant considering that up to three answers could be expressed and, therefore, at least one out of two of the respondents associated the consumption of deli meats with ordinary events. Slightly more than one in four (29%) of the surveyed Generation Z said they consumed deli meats at social occasions while 18% at special events.

It is interesting to note the correlation of information with the results of the following question, which reveals who deli meats are consumed with.

In absolute terms, almost all those surveyed said they consumed deli meat with family (91%), more than half (62%) also with friends, and alone (36%).

Those who consume deli meat on a daily basis (55% of the total) of which a small portion (9%) consume them on social occasions indicate a preference for the family context (42% of the restricted cluster "daily"). Those who consume deli meat alone on a daily basis (32% of the restricted cluster "daily") increase; friends and partner in this subcategory are in line with the overall figure.

The consumption of deli meats once a week is still favored within the family (62%), but as can be assumed, about half also share it with friends (49%).

Another question in the survey that we wanted to highlight is the type of deli meats typically bought. Non-sausage-style deli meats prevail by far, with a particular preference for raw ham. More specifically speck, bacon, raw ham, bresaola, pancetta, lard, and others are the types mentioned by over 80% of respondents, followed by 75% of those who also prefer cooked ham, cooked turkey breast, and chicken breast.

Salami, sausage, and cotechino, that is, the category that is immediately associated with the word "deli meat," are chosen by about one in two respondents (48%); less common are frankfurters, pig's trotter, and mortadella.

In relation to the choice of deli meat, it emerges that young people of Generation Z take the lead; the majority (38%) delegate the purchase to others and do not feel involved in the choice.

However, there is another fair proportion of young people (33%) who said they paid attention to the provenance and quality of the products.

Price is identified as the third discriminating criterion for choosing one deli meat over another (30%).

A second tier, so to speak, of criteria for selection belongs to the category related to health: around one in four (25%) choose leaner, healthier deli meats and change type or try not to always consume the same food.

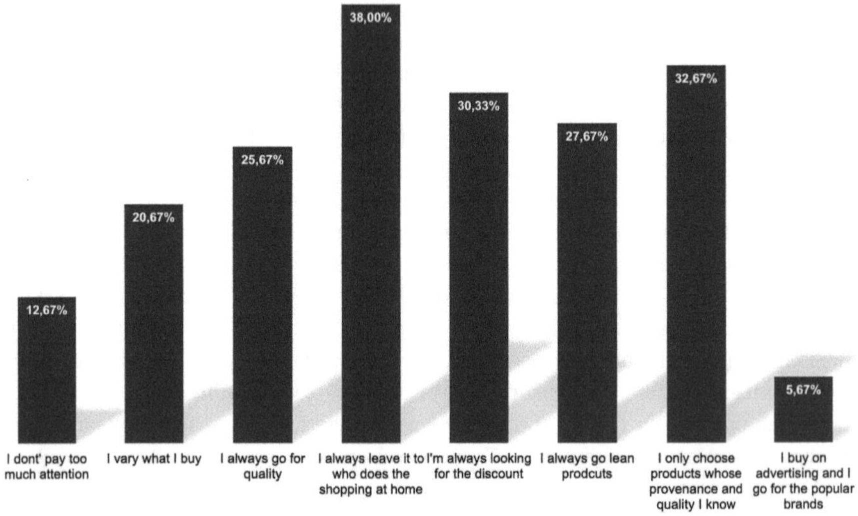

Fig. 2 The three main criteria for choosing deli meats (%)

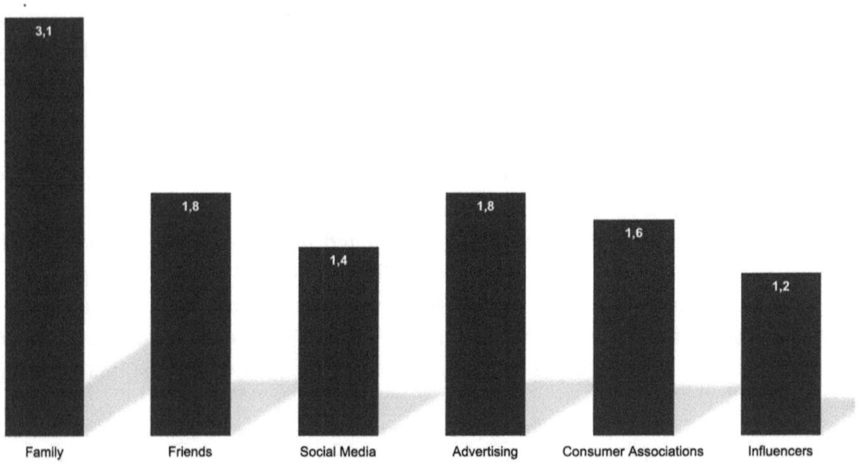

Fig. 3 Context of purchasing influence

A small part of the sample pays no special attention (12%), and even fewer seems to be influenced by advertising or well-known brands (5%) (Figs. 2 and 3).

The family appears to be the main context for purchasing and consuming deli meats (weighted average 3.6 score on the scale 1 = none; 5 = very much), followed by friends, social media, advertising, consumer associations, and influencers.

Three-quarters of Generation Z youth are inclined to research or are active in discovering the provenance of deli meat; one in four shows no particular interest in learning more about the provenance of deli meat. More specifically, 35% of the respondents expressed their unpreparedness but exhibited an inclination toward seeking information, whereas 38% of the participants claimed they were already well informed.

When selecting and consuming deli meat, consumers place high emphasis on sensory attributes, such as the visual appearance of the product, including its color. Color is a particularly important factor in the decision-making process, receiving a weighted average score of 3.5 on a scale from 1 (none) to 5 (very much). Attention to the provenance of the meat (3.2 weighted average) as well as the price of the cured meat (3 weighted average) is also worth mentioning.

Factors linked in some way to health, animal welfare, and the typicity of an area are given little consideration in the motivations for choosing deli meat (average less than 1.5).

Lastly, the "most famous" deli meat was investigated, that is, the one most known among the types of Indication Geographical Protected (IGP) and Protected Designation of Origin (PDO) Italian deli meats.

Parma ham is the best-known cured meat (91%), followed by San Daniele ham (75%). Some typical regional deli meats, such as speck from Alto Adige, bresaola from Valtellina, coppa from Parma, mortadella from Bologna, and Modena ham, complete the array of deli meats known to at least one out of two Generation Z youth. Deli meats from the Po Valley and Piacenza area (coppa, salami, cotechino, pancetta) are gradually gaining popularity (one out of every two respondents claims to know and eat them).

4 Concluding Remarks

The purpose of this essay is to present the findings of an exploratory survey that aimed to investigate the consumption patterns of deli meat among the young Generation Z demographic. The reflections presented herein provide an introductory overview of the research outcomes.

Members of Generation Z exhibit a strong sense of familial ties and possess the ability to uphold ethical and well-being values and is keenly interested in gaining a deeper understanding of the cured meat supply chain.

This could be an initial snapshot that the research has revealed.

The survey revealed that the food consumed on a daily basis depends to a large extent on family choices: from purchase to consumption, these are decisions that young people are not generally involved in.

This underscores the need for comprehensive educational interventions that emphasize the significance of food, particularly deli meat, in promoting eating habits that align with an environmentally conscious, health-oriented, and locally focused developmental model. However, the trend among young people to delegate food choices warrants further scrutiny, including an examination of intergenerational and parent-child relationships.

To avoid routine consumption, it is essential to discourage the daily intake of deli meats. Educating young people about their own values and ethical convictions is important to help them understand the broader implications of what they are eating, including considerations related to health and culture.

The survey results suggest a partial discrepancy between the idealized image of cured meats, particularly salami, and the types of deli meats that are actually consumed. Despite the popular perception of salami as the quintessential cured meat, cooked or raw non-salted meats are actually more commonly consumed.

Notably, this perception is not heavily influenced by mass media, marketing, or advertising, underscoring the need for information and education on the topic.

Comprehensive education on the consumption of deli meats is crucial to address all the dimensions involved, including dietary, cultural, social, and territorial considerations.

Possible developments of this preliminary investigation into the consumption of deli meats in Generation Z could be the following:

- The contribution of school curricular disciplines, including civic education, should be examined to promote greater environmental and food awareness.
- It is important to preserve the culinary traditions of the local area.
- The role of technology, especially social media, in shaping attitudes toward deli meat consumption should be investigated.

This research has also highlighted the tendency of Generation Z to prioritize responsible consumption but they are seldom the decision-maker when it comes to choice of deli meats, leaving that decision to others.

The younger members of Generation Z appear to be less optimistic than their Millennial counterparts regarding their ability to effect meaningful change. On one hand, it is worth noting that the younger generation will undergo the crucial phase of transitioning into adulthood during a period of economic recovery from the crisis. This presents an opportunity for them to be the driving force behind a new phase of growth, should conditions continue to improve. However, this will require a reimagining of social and developmental models (which they will need to actively participate in defining and building). On the other hand, they live in a modern world that is becoming increasingly complex and experiencing a rapid rate of change (Rosina, 2018, p. 13).

The demands of Generation Z can be seen as a sign of a difficult journey ahead, one that will require growth and the development of autonomy.

Many have called for the establishment of a "global educational pact"—an alliance between educators worldwide to educate the younger generations on their role in protecting the environment. This should start with listening to children, adolescents, and young people. An appeal that embraces all disciplines and even religious denominations; Pope Francis, in his latest messages to young people, asks them to be "generative young people, capable of generating new ideas, new visions of the world, the economy, politics and social coexistence to make conscious, significant choices" (2022). Generation Z appears to be able to answer this call and help promote a culture of deli meat that values and supports the local area, evident in their consumption decisions.

References

Alfieri, S. (2021). Quarta fermata: la partecipazione. In E. Marta, P. Bignardi, & S. Alfieri (Eds.), *Adolescenti e partecipazione. Indagine Generazione Z 2019–2020* (pp. 3–11). Vita e Pensiero.

Amadini, M. (2018). Generazione Z: uno sguardo pedagogico. In E. Marta, P. Bignardi, & S. Alfieri (Eds.), *Generazione Z. Guardare il mondo con fiducia e speranza* (pp. 143–151). Vita e Pensiero.

Basile C. G. (Ed). (2022). Il mercato dei suini. Produzione e consumo 2021. In *Osservatorio agroalimentare lombardo, 30*. ERSAF.

Bernardi, E., Capri, E., & Pulina, G. (2018). *La sostenibilità delle carni e dei salumi in Italia. Salute, sicurezza, ambiente benessere animale, economia circolare e lotta allo spreco*. Franco Angeli.

Birbes, C. (2012). *Nutrirsi di relazione. Una riflessione pedagogica tra cibo e educazione*. Pensa MultiMedia.

Bornatici, S. (2017). *Dal banco alla tavola. Percorsi educativi, spreco alimentare, didattica sociale*. Pensa MultiMedia.

Bornatici, S. (2020). *Pedagogia e impegno solidale. A scuola di service-learning*. Vita e Pensiero.

Ellena, A. M., & Marta, E. (2022). Leggere la Generazione Z attraverso il positive youth development. In C. Pasqualini, E. Marta, F. Introini, & A. M. Ellena (Eds.), *Relazioni, comunità, fede. Le generazioni Z a Otranto* (pp. 15–26). Vita e Pensiero.

Fellegara, A. M. (2015). Considerazioni conclusive. In A. M. Fellegara, C. D'Este, & D. Galli (Eds.), *Livelli di disclosure e scelte di integrated reporting nelle grandi imprese italiane. L'informativa aziendale tra globalizzazione e identità territoriale*. Franco Angeli.

Malavasi, P. (2022). *PNRR e formazione. La via della transizione ecologica*. Vita e Pensiero.

Mazzoli, S. (2021). *Riflessione pedagogica, pratiche lavorative, generazioni. Questioni emblematiche*. Pensa MultiMedia.

Mortari, L., & Zannini, L. (2017). Introduzione. In L. Mortari & L. Zannini (Eds.), *La ricerca qualitativa in ambito sanitario* (pp. 9–17). Carocci.

Pope Francis. (2022). Messaggio ai partecipanti alla conferenza europea dei giovani, Praga.

Righettini, C. (2020). Eredità. Laudato si', riflessioni pedagogiche, alimentazione. In S. Bornatici, P. Galeri, Y. Gaspar, P. Malavasi, & O. Vacchelli (Eds.), *Laudato si' +5, Fratelli tutti. Human Development. A great cultural, spiritual political, economic, educational challenge* (pp. 221–234). Pensa MultiMedia.

Rosina, A. (2018). Zeta: un'incognita ancora da decifrare. In E. Marta, P. Bignardi, & S. Alfieri (Eds.), *Generazione Z. Guardare il mondo con fiducia e speranza* (pp. 11–16). Vita e Pensiero.

Viganò, R. (2003). *Professionalità pedagogica e ricerca*. Vita e Pensiero.

The Sustainability of Meat and Cured Meat Supply Chain: Where Are we Now?

Andrea Caccialanza, Andrea Sartori, Stella Gubelli, Francesca Romana Giannini, and Ettore Capri

1 Introduction

The world's growing population (United Nations, 2021) is forcing a progressive increase in attention to the ability to meet food demand in order to assure food to 9,7 billion of people in 2050 (FAO, 2018). Food production and consumption will also have to face with the responsible use of environmental and economic resources (European Commission, 2020; Hilborn et al., 2018; Sala et al., 2017), as well as socially equitable distribution of impacts on local communities. In addition, diets play a crucial role for the nutritional and health dimension (Green et al., 2020; Mele et al., 2015), while preserving cultural and local traditions (Atkins and Bowler, 2016). Prior analysis described the key role planyed by agricultural step of food production (ALTIS, 2021a) or for the final stage of distribution and consumption (ALTIS, 2021b; BEUC, 2022). This chapter will focus mainly on the trasformation phase of one of the most diffused protein sources.

Protein sources represent a well-known pillar for a balanced diet, even though not fairly distributed in different continent and regions (Macdiarmid et al., 2021). Europe has the leadership in terms of proteins per-capita consumption of protein per year (Henchion et al., 2021). In Western countries, diet composition meat and

A. Caccialanza (✉)
Department of Economic and Social Sciences (DiSES), Università Cattolica del Sacro Cuore, Piacenza, Italy
e-mail: andrea.caccialanza@unicatt.it

A. Sartori · S. Gubelli · F. R. Giannini
ALTIS – Alta Scuola Impresa e Società - Università Cattolica del Sacro Cuore, Milan, Italy

E. Capri
Department for Sustainable Food Process (DiSTAS), Università Cattolica del Sacro Cuore, Piacenza, Italy

A. M. Fellegara et al. (eds.), *Sustainable Transition of Meat and Cured Meat Supply Chain*, CSR, Sustainability, Ethics & Governance,
https://doi.org/10.1007/978-3-031-34977-5_15

cured meat products represent a significant part of protein sources (WHO, 2020), while the cultural determinants in meat consumption change over different areas (Mathijs, 2015; Nam et al., 2010).

Sustainability of the meat and cured meat supply chain is growing attention of consumers (Cappelli et al., 2020; Tait et al., 2016) (see for more details Chapter "Managing Generational Handover in Family Business: Some Case Studies in the Charcuterie Factories"), companies, research centres and policymakers, especially from an environmental perspective and in the context of growing concerns regarding human and animal welfare (see for more detail Chapter "Animal Welfare in Swine Production"). Numerous scientific studies (Cesari et al., 2017; Clark et al., 2019; Djekic and Tomasevic, 2016; Tukker et al., 2011) and surveys carried out by interest groups (Carni sostenibili, 2016; Greenpeace Italy, 2020; Demetra – Lav, 2021; Nomisma, 2020; WWF, 2021) (see for more details also Chapter "Generation Z and Sustainable Cured Meat Consumption: Educational Challenges and Pedagogical Perspectives") have examined the environmental, health and welfare impacts (Godfray et al., 2018; Mele et al., 2015).

Recently, the EAT-Lancet Commission (Willett et al., 2019) concluded that the '*Great Food Transformation will only be achieved through widespread, multisector, multilevel action that includes a substantial global shift towards healthy dietary patterns, large reductions in food loss and waste, and major improvements in food production practices*'.

This awareness calls for a sense of urgency in understanding what changes are taking place in the strategic orientation of companies operating in this sector. A better understanding of the dynamics of increased awareness, monitoring and disclosure areas is the central.

While the previous chapter analysed disclosure propensities in the broader context of the Italian agribusiness, this section of the book will explore individual areas and topics of analysis related to managerial practices.

As anticipated priorly in other contributions, the meat supply chain consists of three macro-levels of analysis that traditionally coincide with the breeding, slaughtering and processing, distribution and consumption phases (Taylor, 2005). This contribution aims to highlight, with an exploratory study, the central phase of this chain, playing the role of link between the livestock farm and the final consumer.

The main goal of this chapter is the investigation on the diffusion of sustainability practices and accountability principles at the transformation tier of meat and cured Italian meat supply chain.

The Italian context is of interest precisely because it belongs to the European area—with high-content protein diets (Henchion et al., 2021; IPCC, 2019)—and has a limited level of direct environmental and social impact compared to other areas, as well as encompassing 49 Protected Designation of Origin (PDO) and Protected Geographical Indication (PGI) meat products (ISMEA – Qualivita, 2022; e-Ambrosia – European Commission, 2022).

Literature shows how the attribution of environmental impacts in the meat supply chain in Italy is a complex issue. Analyses of the positive evolution of feed conversion indices suggest an increasing efficiency of feed (Assalzoo, 2021) and a greater overall sustainability of feed, especially for the protein part (FEFAC, 2021). The concomitant decrease in the use of antibiotics suggests an improvement in animal welfare conditions and standards (European Commission, 2022), while the analysis on the impacts of carbon emissions attributes only 7.1% to the agricultural sector, of which just over 5% to livestock farming (ISPRA, 2021). This 'over performance' of the Italian context would suggest a better propensity to communicate results and an overall better accountability.

On the other hand, studies on social impacts of meat farming and processing activities produce outcomes that are not always comparable (Aranda et al., 2021). This prevents the possibility of carrying out comparative studies of the effects on the environment, communities, products, consumers and supply chain tiers other than the one analysed with a holistic perspective (Alemayehu, 2011; Golini et al., 2017). Most of these analyses identify the meat sector as a whole or the value chain as the field of investigation, favouring an industry perspective, but without examining the role of processing companies and the strategies they adopt to integrate sustainability in their activities in order to meet a demand for more sustainable food products.

At the processing level, there has been a development in terms of technological innovation, aimed at increasing both production efficiency and food safety. In addition to the progressive implementation of traceability systems and controls along the supply chain, there has also been an enhancement of the craft techniques that are integrated in this production processes. In particular, with reference to PDO and PGI products, the processed meat segment recognises a higher average price in the protected pork circuits (Ferrer-Perez et al., 2020). The Italian context also stands out for the adoption of high standards on process and quality control throughout the supply chain, as well as the need to promote forms of product protection.

This effort is awarded with a distinctive positioning and competitive advantage in terms of exports, particularly evident in the peak recorded in 2020 (Assica, 2021).

On basis of these assumptions, this research explores Italian meat processors' sustainability disclosure in order to identify different attitudes towards the management of environmental, social and governance (ESG) factors. To our knowledge, this is one of the few scientific studies on the transformation tier of the meat supply chain and with Italian data showing evidence on distinct patterns towards sustainability communication practices.

This study is articulated in four further sections. The first aims to present the material and methods applied, then the stages of Corporate Social Responsibility (CSR) development in the meat supply chain firms are discussed, thirdly the discussion of results are proposed and, finally, conclusions and further research directions are drawn.

2 Material and Methods

The survey sample was selected from Italian companies operating in the processing and preservation of meat and production of meat products (NACE Code C.10.1).

Of the 7678 companies registered in the Aida database (Bureau van Dijk),[1] 3757 are active and with a published balance sheet in the two-year period 2019–2020. Within this list of companies, the number of companies that exceed at least two of the three reference size thresholds for the obligation to prepare a non-financial statement under the regulations currently in force (Directive 2014/95/EU and Legislative Decree 254/2016) was identified. This cross-analysis showed that in the two consecutive years 46 companies simultaneously exceeded at least two of the three requirements. For companies belonging to a group, the reporting documents published by the holding company were assessed if present.

The methodology for analysing and assessing companies is divided into two sections.

The *general section* assesses the presence of a structured approach to sustainability, through the analysis of the sustainability communication and reporting tools adopted by the companies. The documents analysed include company websites, social media, blogs or magazines and sustainability reports in the most recent edition as of February 2022 if applicable. In this sense, the section also intends to examine the readiness of the companies in light of the planned extension of sustainability reporting obligations under the Corporate Social Reporting Directive (CSRD) approved in November 2022 by the European Parliament.

The *thematic section* analyses and evaluates the sustainability practices adopted and reported by the companies. The analysis is based on a sectoral materiality matrix, which groups the ESG topics that are most relevant for the meat supply chain since they are associated with significant negative or positive impacts on stakeholders or the environment, as identified on the basis of an analysis of the abovementioned scientific literature, of the main international sustainability reporting standards—Global Reporting Initiative (GRI) Standard and Sustainability Accounting Standards Board (SASB) Materiality Map©—and of the sustainability reports published by the companies themselves, as analysed with an inductive approach. The matrix includes 14 material topics that were further grouped into six macro-areas on grounds of thematic consistency.

Each material topic is associated to a variable number from two to five of possible management practices, including the formalisation of company policies, the presence of certified management systems and the activation of specific projects or actions aimed at improving ESG performance.

The practices are associated with a score between 1 and 2 depending on the degree of evolution of the management approach they denote, as established by the researchers' expertise in the field. The overall score for the specific section is calculated as the weighted average of the score obtained for the individual material topics, weighted by a percentage factor of topic materiality. The overall assessment of the companies gives a weight of 30% to the score for the general section and the remaining 70% to the score for the specific section of the topics presented in Fig. 1.

[1] Data extracted on 10 January 2022.

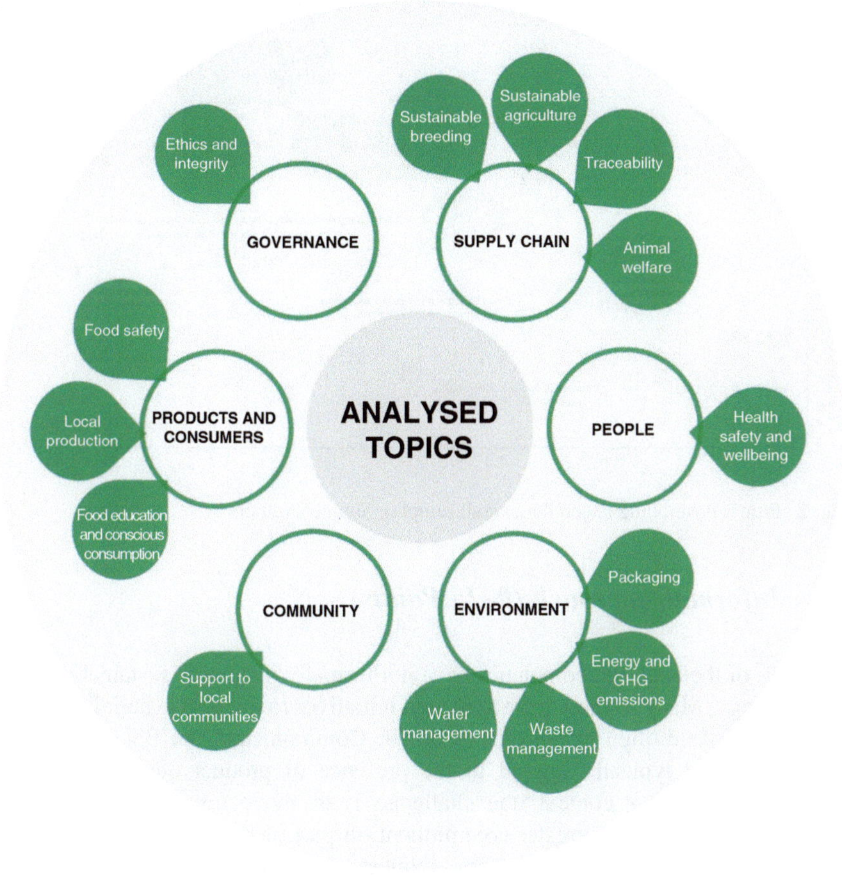

Fig. 1 Analysed topics of the thematic section. Source: Authors' representation

The score obtained by each company was associated with one of the stages of sustainability evolution identified by the model proposed by Molteni (2007): informal, current, systematic, innovative and dominant.

3 The Stages of CSR Development in Meat Supply Chain Transformation Firms

As anticipated in the previous section, the 46 companies analysed were classified according to the stages of the Molteni (2007) model. Based on the methodology described above, the distribution is presented in the following paragraphs (Fig. 2).

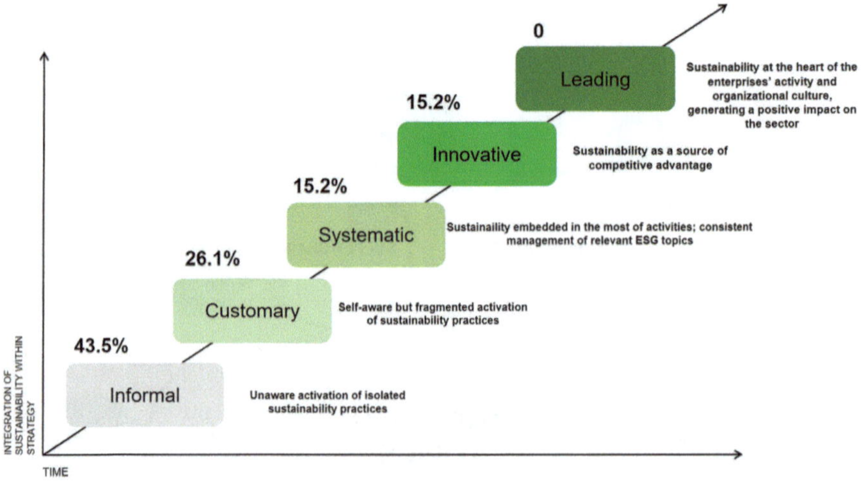

Fig. 2 Firm's positioning (% on the overall sample). Source: Authors

3.1 *Informal Approach (0–25 Points)*

The 43% of the analysed companies have not formally integrated sustainability into their strategy. Many of these have activated initiatives to manage material issues but in a sporadic and often unconscious manner. Communication of ESG practices is still partial and typically limited to the presence of product quality and safety certifications. In this context, the challenge is to move towards a fully aware sustainability, through a greater commitment on part of the top management, also in response to the emergence of requests or pressure from stakeholders (e.g. consumers, employees, institutions, suppliers, competitors, etc.).

3.2 *Current Approach (25–45 Points)*

Just over a quarter of the companies (12) in the panel fall into the second stage, distinguished by the implementation of some initial formal social responsibility initiatives, including the adoption of a code of ethics and/or social and environmental policies. Virtuous practices, more or less numerous, are well communicated and valorised, even if focused only on certain sustainability issues, typically related to the supply chain and product quality. The current stage of sustainability should only be seen as a transitory moment: the 'natural' evolution, once the effectiveness of sustainable practices in the company has been ascertained, is to initiate a process of critical analysis of the company's products and activities aimed at defining a strategic plan and sustainability reporting, creating the conditions to move on to the systematic stage.

3.3 Systematic Approach (45–60 Points)

This stage includes seven companies that have implemented numerous initiatives relating to all the different aspects of sustainability: supply chain, product quality, environment, employees and community. In addition to the presence of social and environmental policies, there are the first attempts at sustainability performance reporting and the communication of strategic, qualitative or quantitative objectives. At this stage of development, top management has become fully familiar with social and environmental responsibility issues, implementing ongoing stakeholder engagement initiatives in order to monitor the results achieved with respect to the objectives defined during strategic planning.

3.4 Innovative Approach (More than 60 Points)

The seven companies in the innovative stage see the sustainable approach as a real opportunity for competitive advantage and a source of innovation. Therefore, the companies are committed to communicating their numerous sustainability initiatives, actively involving stakeholders and publishing reporting documents and strategies with clear and challenging objectives.

In the meat sector, the innovative stage is also characterised by the launch of initiatives that mobilise different stakeholders, changing the cooperation/competition modes to favour value sharing along the entire value chain. Within the sample, the innovative stage appears to be more easily accessible to large companies: four of the seven companies identified, in fact, exceed 500 employees, beside three significant cases of medium-sized companies, one of which belongs to a larger group, which have made sustainability a distinctive element of their strategy.

3.5 Dominant Approach

The transition to the final stage of the path, the dominant one, is of a purely cultural nature: top management comes, in fact, to consider sustainability as the cornerstone of the company mission and its strategic vision, thus assuming a driving function for the entire sector and setting itself up as a model to be emulated. In the present survey, it was not possible to identify companies at this stage, since sustainability does not yet seem to represent the primary driver of development for companies in the sector, but rather a lateral and complementary aspect—however relevant—with respect to product quality. By analysing the paths taken by some innovative companies, however, it is possible to grasp the first expressions of a new concept of 'sustainable quality', the concrete declination of which may guide the future growth of the entire sector.

4 Discussion

This section aims to identify the communication and reporting strategies widespread in the slaughterhouse and processing phase. This section will be subdivided to present the results of the analysis conducted on both the general section and the thematic session, as anticipated in methodology.

4.1 General Section

In the analysed sample, nine companies presented a publicly available sustainability or environmental report, representing 19.6%.

Of the nine publicly available reports:

- Only one is prepared in accordance with the currently applicable regulatory obligations (Legislative Decree 254/2016).
- All adopt the GRI international standards according to the different compliance options.
- Four were subject to an assurance review by an external auditing firm.
- Three reports were published in their first edition in 2021, demonstrating significant growth in the uptake of these tools.

It should be emphasised that the adoption of GRI Standards entails carrying out a materiality analysis, that is, the identification of the ESG topics that are most relevant to the company and its stakeholders. This process of analysis implies the activation, by the company, of a direct dialogue with its stakeholders, aimed at identifying their requests, expectations and possible concerns about its activities and development strategies, thus avoiding the risk of self-referential communication and favouring a proactive approach to critical perceptions affecting the supply chain.

There are also nine companies that report their contribution to the pursuit of the Sustainable Development Goals (SDGs) promoted by the United Nations, either in their sustainability report (eight companies) or on their institutional website (1). This reporting practice aligns and connects the company's commitment to the goals and orientations of international policy makers, denoting an awareness of the global challenges involving the supply chain—first and foremost that of the sustainability of agrifood production systems expressed by Target 2.17 (see for comparison with others food categories the previous chapter).

Of the sample of 46 companies, almost half (22) have a section of their website dedicated to sustainability. The percentage of 47.8% makes clear a widespread interest in sustainability issues, as well as a propensity to include these principles in corporate communication and positioning strategies. This evidence is confirmed by the fact that, even in the absence of a unified section, all the companies analysed disclose information on their sites on certain ESG issues, albeit with very different levels of breadth and detail.

The propensity to publish ESG objectives was another of the parameters taken into consideration to analyse the strategic orientation of companies towards sustainability.

- A total of 59.6% of the companies in the sample indicate qualitative objectives in their public reports or on the institutional website, expressed in the form of explicit commitments with respect to certain material topics.
- A total of 39.6% of the sample publishes quantitative objectives, with the adoption of numerical indicators and/or objective criteria and the identification of specific targets to be achieved within a defined time frame.

From the point of view of communication, the presence in the sustainability report or on the institutional website of references to the topics covered by this survey is quite varied:

- Twenty consider less than 50% of the topics identified.
- Fourteen present between 50% and 75% of the contents considered.
- Twelve include more than 75% of the topics.

4.2 *Thematic Section*

This section will open up the discussion around the six different thematic sessions: governance, people, supply chain, products and consumers, environment and community. For each topic, a summary of the criteria involved has been listed in the following tables.

Corporate **governance** is of interest in the analysis of sustainability orientation. This section is, therefore, mainly focused on the relevance of the issue of business ethics and integrity, linked to the publication of two documents: the Code of Ethics (44.7%) and the Organisation and Management Model pursuant to Legislative Decree 231/2001 (40.4%). In Table 1 is proposed a list of the key criteria adopted for the analysis of health (HS), safety (HSE) and welfare of workers.

The topic of sustainability cannot disregard the consideration of the role of **people** who work along the supply chain and the companies within it. The analysis of this pillar has been declined according to the presence of various criteria relating to both the protection of workers' rights, with specific reference to occupational health and

Table 1 People: Health, safety and well-being

Practice	Percentage of companies
HS or HSE policy	57.4%
ISO 45001 (or equivalent)	19.1%
OHS training hours per employee disclosure	19.1%
OHS incident reporting	17.0%
Employee welfare measures	14,9%

Source: Authors

Table 2 Supply Chain: Sustainable breeding

Practice	Percentage of companies
Policy or statement	70.2%
Certified organic product	38.3%
Breeder selection practices based on environmental criteria	29.8%
Breeder selection practices based on social criteria	19.1%
Training for breeders on sustainability	17.0%

Source: Authors

Table 3 Supply Chain: Sustainable agriculture and feed

Practice	Percentage of companies
Assessment and management of environmental and food risks	34.0%
Traceability of raw materials	29.8%
Circular economy practices	21.3%
Adherence to sustainability standards	21.3%

Source: Authors

safety, and to the active promotion of well-being and skills development. While most companies state that they are explicitly committed to protecting their employees, reporting on the actions and practices undertaken shows significant room for improvement.

Overall, it emerges that worker protection and human capital development policies are reported almost exclusively in the context of sustainability reports, only rarely finding space in web-based communication, suggesting a low perception of relevance of people-related issues by companies in the sector (Table 2).

The **supply chain** issue has been analysed through five dimensions: sustainable breeding, sustainable agriculture, traceability and animal welfare.

The breeding phase is decisive in assessing the overall sustainability of the supply chain, representing its first level. However, the implementation of selection practices that consider environmental and social criteria is still limited, or at least its communication. This also applies to the issue of training farmers on sustainability, which is addressed by eight companies, often in the context of interventions promoted within controlled supply chain paths, with distinctive positioning or because they own shares in processing companies. On the other hand, the diffusion of communication of product lines certified as organic is wider, in response to the growing demand (Table 3).

Italy is dependent on foreign cereal supplies for almost half of the raw materials that form the basis of formulations and according to varying percentage shares: 46.5% for maize, 82.3% for soybean meal and 86.1% for sunflower meal (Assalzoo, 2021). This deficit in terms of imports in recent decades has been influenced both by the loss of arable land areas and by the allocation of part of the national production to the feeding of biogas plants, which are also used for the valorisation of livestock manure. This is also the context of the research promoted to study the development

Table 4 Supply Chain: Traceability

Practice	Percentage of companies
Policy or statement	87.2%
Technological systems for the traceability of the supply chain	59.6%
ISO 22005 or equivalent	40.4%

Source: Authors

Table 5 Supply Chain: Animal Welfare

Practice	Percentage of companies
Policy or statement	72.3%
Decent living conditions in transports and at slaughter	46.8%
Use of drugs limitations	38.3%
Measures to ensure adequate living spaces	36.2%
Limitation of mutilations	12.8%

Source: Authors

of feed conversion indices over time, highlighting improved efficiency of livestock production and the environmental impact of different formulations (Assalzoo, 2021).

It is a well-established fact that there is, in the breeding phase in particular, a historical propensity to use by-products and co-products, thus valorising volumes of products that represent waste in the context of other food production chains (see for more details Chapter "Sustainability of Swine Breeding: Future Challenges and Opportunities") (Table 4).

The issue of traceability is important in any manufacturing context, but it finds one of its highest levels of expression precisely in the Italian agri-food sector. In this production context, in fact, it is emphasised that product and consumer quality protection systems are promoted at an operational level in each of the contexts analysed (Sacchettini et al., 2021). The criteria used to observe the communication of this attention, in fact, emphasise this attention at a transversal level.

Almost all companies explicitly emphasise their dedication to promoting the full traceability policy of their product in their corporate documents and media. This statement is often accompanied by specific certifications of international importance, such as ISO 22005 or DTP 035, to assure the quality of the product, as well as the traceability of the raw material processed, also to guarantee PDO and PGI branded products. A small group of companies make an explicit reference to technological systems for traceability (Table 5).

Animal welfare transversally involves all three groups of actors in the supply chain in different ways. In fact, this issue personally involves the breeder who invests in the modernisation of structures and facilities, as well as the downstream stages of the chain (slaughterhouse, processing and distribution) through the implemented control system. As regards the focus of this analysis, most processors belonging to the sample explicitly declare themselves attentive to the respect and protection of animal welfare in their supply chain policies. This broad declaration of sensitivity is followed by the analysis conducted of the practices and criteria that

Table 6 Products and consumer: Local Production

Practice	Percentage of companies
Use of 100% Italian meats	87.2%
At least one PGI or PDO-labelled product	76.6%
Choice of native or rare breeds	6.4%

Source: Authors

Table 7 Products and consumer: Food safety

Practice	Percentage of companies
BRC or IFS certification	80.9%
Policy or statement	78.7%
GMO free products (at least one)	46.8%
Nitrite free products (at least one)	31.9%

Source: Authors

contextualise and operationalise this commitment, especially in relation to the European Farm to Fork strategy and national legislation (EC Regulation 429/2016; EC Regulation 625/2017; Legislative decree. n°27/2021). Decent condition in transport and at slaughter represents a criterion that is closer to the direct operation and control of processors, and it is therefore mentioned in the communication by almost half of the sample. The limitation with respect to the use of drugs is an interesting topic especially with respect to the promotion of references with limited or no use of antibiotics in the life of the animal. The main references on the market are the voluntary standards DT 35 and DT 109 for the pig sector (Table 6).

The topic of **products and consumers** has been articulated in the valorisation of local production, food safety and the education to a conscious consumption. The provenance of raw materials and of the products themselves is one of the main elements of consumer interest, both for meat and cured meat products, and is the focus of recent regulatory interventions on labelling (see for more details Chapter "Protecting Farm Animal Biodiversity through Geographical Indications: A Legal Analysis"). The sample shows a strong preference for the use of meat from Italian farms, at least limited to specific product lines, which finds ample space in environmental communication. Equally pervasive is the presence of PGI- or PDO-labelled articles, especially in the production of cured meat: this element confirms the role of the territory and production traditions as a central asset of the sector, also from a sustainability point of view (see also Chapters "The Quality of Heavy Pork Meat: The Role of PDO Production Specifications" and "Protecting Farm Animal Biodiversity through Geographical Indications: A legal Analysis").

On the other hand, the proposal of product lines from local or rare breeds appears to be a minority, which finds a structural limitation in the reduced production volumes but meets with strong consumer interest, both for qualitative and sustainability factors, such as the frequent use of extensive farming practices and the contribution to the protection of zootechnical biodiversity (Table 7).

Table 8 Products and consumer: Food education and conscious consumption

Practice	Percentage of companies
Communication of the products' nutritional values via web	44.7%
Sustainability claims on social channels	29.8%
Communication practices for responsible consumption	27.7%
Initiatives to raise awareness and fight against food waste	23.4%
Support for food education campaigns	17.0%
Information on the environmental impact of products	12.8%

Source: Authors

Consistent with market perceptions, companies in the supply chain appear to be particularly active in communicating their food safety practices, regardless of the publication of a sustainability report or the presence of a dedicated section on the website: food safety is, in this sense, a cornerstone of corporate communication.

Focusing on practices beyond compliance with regulations on self-control and risk analysis, the spread of formal policies and affirmations of commitments and objectives undertaken by the company and, above all, the presence of international food safety certifications, such as British Retail Consortium (BRC) and International Food Standard (IFS), stand out. These are not limited to third-party audits of the Hazard Analysis & Critical Control Points (HACCP) system, but also include the adoption of good management requirements and practices in product processing, analysis laboratories and hygiene protection, requiring the structuring of advanced management systems (Table 8).

While companies in the supply chain effectively monitor food safety with a preventive approach, they are not as committed to active consumer communication to address concerns about product sustainability and health impacts.

A predominantly passive approach also emerges when analysing communication practices regarding the environmental sustainability profiles of production. Also emerging is the potential for developing participation in initiatives to combat food waste, which is responsible for a significant part of the industry's environmental impacts.

These results seem to confirm the prevalence of communication strategies still focused mainly on product quality, which also emerges from the analysis of sustainability reporting and communication practices (Table 9).

The **environment** topic in the meat industry has been analysed also with the concern of greenhouse gas emissions that arise mainly from energy consumption and fuel consumption for company fleets. The results of the analysis reflect the growing sensitivity of public opinion towards climate change. The most widespread concrete initiatives concern the purchase or self-production of electricity from renewable sources, implemented by almost half of the panel. In particular, the companies that opted for self-production mainly invested in photovoltaic systems, often taking advantage of the ample availability of space on farms and/or production sites. Initiatives for upgrading or installing modern energy-efficient systems were

Table 9 Environment: Energy and GHG emissions

Practice	Percentage of companies
Use or self-production of energy from renewable sources	46.8%
Environmental policy with reference to energy consumption and emissions	42.6%
ISO 14001 or Eco-Management and Audit Scheme (EMAS)	38.3%
Installation or upgrading of energy systems in the last 2 years	19.1%
ISO 50001 (or equivalent)	10.6%
Logistics optimization initiatives	6.4%

Source: Authors

Table 10 Environment: Water management

Practice	Percentage of companies
Environmental policy with reference to water consumption	38.3%
Water purification plants	29.8%
Installation or requalification in the last 2 years of high efficiency water systems or with water recycling	14.9%

Source: Authors

Table 11 Environment: Waste management

Practice	Percentage of companies
Environmental policy with reference to waste management	36.2%
Food waste reduction and/or recovery actions	27.7%
Cogeneration powered by waste	23.4%

Source: Authors

apparently less widespread and, perhaps, considered less impactful than actions related to the use of energy from renewable sources (Table 10).

Concerning water consumption, as for all environmental aspects, this analysis only considers the impacts of the industrial phases of meat and cured meat production, which represent a marginal component of the water footprint in comparison to the breeding and feed cultivation phase. For beef products, for example, water consumption from processing is estimated to contribute 6% of the total water footprint (Carni Sostenibili, 2016). Within the analysed panel, the topic does not seem to be perceived as particularly relevant: only 38% of companies, in fact, include a reference to water consumption in their environmental policies. Focusing on communication and the development of concrete initiatives, the percentages drop even further (Table 11).

Like almost all agricultural raw material processes, meat processing generates different types of waste and discards, consisting mainly of animal by-products (EC Regulation 1069/2009). Some by-products are therefore compulsorily destined for incineration, while others can be fed into new production processes (for more

Table 12 Environment: Packaging

Practice	Percentage of companies
Recyclable packaging	42.6%
Reduction in packaging weight	29.8%
Environmental policy with reference to packaging	27.7%
Packaging from recycled raw materials	19.1%

Source: Authors

Table 13 Community: Support to local communities

Practice	Percentage of companies
Support to environmental projects	55.3%
Support to social projects	45.7%
Support to cultural projects	17.0%

Source: Authors

details, see Chapter "The Quality of Heavy Pork Meat: The Role of PDO Production Specifications"). Despite the relevance of the topic, a small percentage of the companies analysed address waste management in their communication and through formalised policies, and even fewer affirm that they have promoted actions aimed at reducing or recovering their food waste, which essentially take the form of transferring by-products to companies dedicated to the production of pet food, animal feed or fertilisers (Table 12).

In the agri-food sector, the use of packaging with a lower environmental impact is becoming increasingly widespread. This run-up seems easy to share at a strategic level in the light of some data: according to a Nomisma study, 33% of Italian consumers see packaging characteristics as a fundamental aspect in the definition and perception of the sustainability of a food product, and for one Italian in four, the presence of sustainable packaging is the main purchase driver (Nomisma, 2021). These new trends are reflected in the results of the analysis, from which emerges a particular interest in fully recyclable packaging, usually made of several easily separable materials (paper/plastic laminates) or more rarely in mono-material such as PE and PET. Less consistent, but still interesting, is the group of companies that opted for a reduction in packaging weight, at the same time gaining environmental and economic advantages due to the lower use of resources and reduced transport costs. On the other hand, a still small proportion has introduced the use of recycled raw materials, a result justified by the economic efforts involved, which are generally greater than the other practices mentioned (Table 13).

Business activity does not limit its sphere of influence to the narrow group of stakeholders such as shareholders, employees and suppliers, but also has an impact on the social fabric, the surrounding environment and the **local community** that hosts it.

This relationship between the local community and business activity is evident and tangible in the ability to valorise and promote products that are typical of the territory or fall within the protection circuit of the numerous consortia. This kind of impact has repercussions on qualitative and quantitative variables (production and sales volumes, prices and territorial diffusion) that have already been effectively monitored for some time by other studies such as the annual ISMEA—Qualivita report (2022). What is complex to map to date is the set of initiatives that individual companies promote that have positive environmental as well as social and cultural impacts. For the selected sample of companies, this type of commitment was also mapped.

The environmental sphere includes all the projects promoted by companies with the aim of having a direct positive impact on the local area, as for instance reforestation, biodiversity conservation or food waste projects. The figure on social projects consists of initiatives promoted in collaboration with non-profit associations, local administrations and initiatives implemented for the fight against Covid-19.

It is also worth mentioning the projects developed in the cultural sphere, such as the creation of educational and training courses in the gastronomic sphere, as well as the promotion of spaces dedicated to the product and tradition' story telling.

5 Conclusions

Analysing the macro-areas on which reporting and communication focus the most, it is possible to identify a significant differentiation within the sample. While a very high proportion of the companies surveyed communicate sustainability-relevant practices in the areas of supply chain and products, fewer companies communicate in the remaining topic areas, reaching percentages of less than 50% for environmental and governance topics. Figure 3 graphically synthesise the areas of communication and reporting covered by the sample of companies.

From the analysis, companies in the sector seem to adopt rather selective sustainability communication and reporting practices, focusing on a relatively narrow range of topics. Considering the macro-areas within which the individual companies report at least one practice, topics relating to the supply chain (87.2%) and to products and consumer relations (80.9%) prevail decisively over the rest, indicating a communication focused primarily on the production dimension and a vision of sustainability strongly anchored to products, processes and to territorial identity.

On the other hand, the environmental area (46.8%) and the governance dimension (44.7%), to which the companies in the sample seem to assign less relevance, are less attended to. As far as the environmental dimension is concerned, although some aspects related to the sustainability of livestock and feed are dealt with under the supply chain area, the companies express a perception of urgency that is misaligned with that of public opinion, the media and NGOs. Similarly, a substantial part of the sample apparently tends to take for granted areas related to people and communities, despite the fact that these include issues that are indispensable for a comprehensive and effective approach to sustainability, such as occupational health and safety and business ethics.

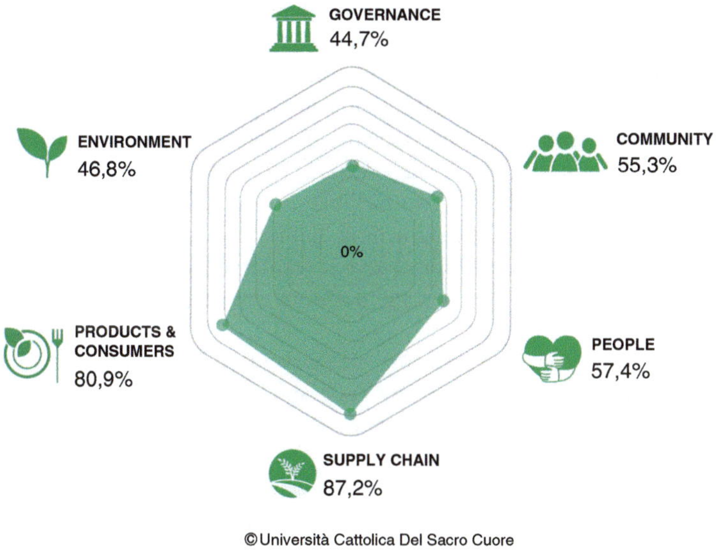

Fig. 3 Areas of communication and reporting. Source: Authors representation

An effective response by the supply chain as a whole to the challenge of sustainable development cannot disregard, in any case, an acceleration of the path by the small- and medium-sized enterprises (SMEs) that make up the vast majority of the sector: an objective that appears ambitious in the current context of turbulence on the raw materials and energy markets aggravated by the war in Ukraine jeopardises the economic sustainability of livestock farming activities and may lead to postponing significant investments in the environmental and social field. Given the benefits, including economic ones, that sustainability practices such as energy and water saving, the rational use of raw materials and the reuse of waste can bring to businesses, a vicious circle risks being set in motion that could jeopardise the sustainable transition and the very sustainability of the supply chain as a whole. It is therefore necessary to reflect on the incentives that can be activated to encourage SMEs to adopt a more strategic and systematic approach to sustainability.

With regard to regulatory developments, the approval of the CSRD and the consequent lowering of the size thresholds for the reporting obligation will lead to a greater spread of such practices, presumably including the 46 companies analysed. If this extension considered in isolation does not appear sufficient to bring about a qualitative leap in the sector, since it affects only a small portion of the sector, it would however be able to exert a significant 'push' to the extent that it is seized as an opportunity for strategic reflection, and not only for narration, triggering emulation by SMEs. Still in the regulatory sphere, we can expect from the introduction of the Corporate Sustainability Due Diligence and the related obligations for large companies to identify and mitigate the environmental and social impacts of the supply chain, a consolidation of the supplier assessment practices based on ESG criteria already implemented by large industrial groups and many large-scale distribution players, with a contribution to the spread of systems for monitoring socio-environmental performance (see for more detail previous chapter). However, legislative interventions run the risk of legitimising a perception of sustainability as a mere compliance constraint, overshadowing the competitive opportunities it opens up for companies. In this sense, the potential impact of public or public-private policies to support the visibility of sustainable products and companies, through the creation of new labels or the strengthening and rationalisation of labels already on the market, should not be underestimated, but accompanied by a stronger investment in food education programmes and the development of critical consumer analysis skills.

Further research could broaden the category of products involved or propose comparative analyses between different geographical contexts (other EU countries) or groups of companies relevant to other product classifications in the context of agri-food manufacturing.

Given the sector's limited financial resources, however, a decisive driver will be the ability to allocate a sufficient volume of public and private investment to support the sustainable transition of the agri-food sector.

References

Alemayehu, K. (2011). Value chain assessment of beef cattle production and marketing in Ethiopia: Challenges and opportunities of linking smallholder farmers to the markets. *Livestock Research for Rural Development, 23*(12), 255–265.

ALTIS. (2021a). *Lo stato dell'arte della sostenibilità nella GDO alimentare*. Report di ricerca 2021/01. https://altis.unicatt.it/altis-2021-partnership-gdo-settore-agroalimentare-filiera-sostenibile

ALTIS. (2021b). *Il paradosso dell'olio d'oliva: prodotto sostenibile, comunicazione acerba*. Report di ricerca 2021/02. Retrieved from https://altis.unicatt.it/altis-2021-olio-oliva-sostenibilita

Aranda, J., Zambrana-Vásquez, D., Del-Busto, F., & Círez, F. (2021). Social impact analysis of products under a holistic approach: A case study in the meat product supply chain. *Sustainability, 13*(21), 12163.

Assalzoo. (2021). *Report ambientale* 2020. Retrived from https://www.assalzoo.it/wp-content/uploads/2021/06/ASSALZOO_Report_Ambientale_2020.pdf

Assica. (2021). *Rapporto annuale 2020*. Retrived from https://www.assica.it/it/pubblicazioni/rapporto-annuale.php

Atkins, P., & Bowler, I. (2016). *Food in society: Economy, culture, geography*. Routledge.

BEUC - Bureau Européen des Unions de Consommateurs. (2022). *One bite at a time: consumers and the transition to sustainable food*. Retrieved from https://www.beuc.eu/publications/beuc-x-2020-042_consumers_and_the_transition_to_sustainable_food.pdf

Cappelli, L., D'Ascenzo, F., Arezzo, M. F., Ruggieri, R., & Gorelova, I. (2020). The willingness to pay in the food sector. Testing the hypothesis of consumer preferences for some made in Italy products. *Sustainability, 12*(15), 6275.

Carni sostenibili. (2016). *La sostenibilità delle carni e dei salumi in Italia*. Franco Angeli.

Cesari, V., Zucali, M., Sandrucci, A., Tamburini, A., Bava, L., & Toschi, I. (2017). Environmental impact assessment of an Italian vertically integrated broiler system through a life cycle approach. *Journal of Cleaner Production, 143*, 904–911.

Clark, M. A., Springmann, M., Hill, J., & Tilman, D. (2019). Multiple health and environmental impacts of foods. *Proceedings of the National Academy of Sciences, 116*(46), 23357–23362.

Demetra – Lav. (2021). *Il costo nascosto del consumo di carne in Italia: impatti ambientali e sanitari.* Retrieved from https://www.lav.it/cpanelav/js/ckeditor/kcfinder/upload/files/files/RICERCA_INTEGRALE_DEMETRA%281%29.pdf

Djekic, I., & Tomasevic, I. (2016). Environmental impacts of the meat chain – Current status and future perspectives. *Trends in Food Science & Technology, 54*, 94–102.

e-Ambrosia – European Commission. (2022). *Database: last access 16/06/2022.* Retrieved from: https://ec.europa.eu/info/food-farming-fisheries/food-safety-and-quality/certification/quality-labels/geographical-indications-register/

European Commision. (2022). *Study on Animal Welfare Labelling.* Retrieved from: https://op.europa.eu/en/publication-detail/-/publication/49b6b125-b0a3-11ec-83e1-01aa75ed71a1/language-en

European Commission. (2020). Farm to fork strategy: For a fair, healthy and environmentally-friendly food system. DG SANTE/unit 'food information and composition, food waste'. Retrieved on 14 April 2021 from https://ec.europa.eu/food/sites/food/files/safety/docs/f2f_action-plan_2020_strategy-info_en.pdf.

FAO. (2018). *The future of food and agriculture—Alternative pathways to 2050.* Food and Agriculture Organization of the United Nations.

FEFAC. (2021). *Soy Sourcing Giudelines.* Retrieved from https://fefac.eu/wp-content/uploads/2021/02/FEFAC-Soy-Sourcing-Guidelines-2021.pdf

Ferrer-Pérez, H., Abdelradi, F., & Gil, J. M. (2020). Geographical indications and price volatility dynamics of lamb prices in Spain. *Sustainability, 12*(7), 3048.

Godfray, H. C. J., Aveyard, P., Garnett, T., Hall, J. W., Key, T. J., Lorimer, J., et al. (2018). Meat consumption, health, and the environment. *Science, 361*(6399), eaam5324.

Golini, R., Moretto, A., Caniato, F., Caridi, M., & Kalchschmidt, M. (2017). Developing sustainability in the Italian meat supply chain: An empirical investigation. *International Journal of Production Research, 55*(4), 1183–1209.

Green, A., Nemecek, T., Chaudhary, A., & Mathys, A. (2020). Assessing nutritional, health, and environmental sustainability dimensions of Agri-food production. *Global Food Security, 26*, 100406.

Greenpeace Italia. (2020). *Il peso della carne.* https://www.greenpeace.org/static/planet4-italy-stateless/2020/10/b3ee8b89-report-il-peso-della-carne.pdf

Henchion, M., Moloney, A. P., Hyland, J., Zimmermann, J., & McCarthy, S. (2021). Trends for meat, milk and egg consumption for the next decades and the role played by livestock systems in the global production of proteins. *Animal, 15*, 100287.

Hilborn, R., Banobi, J., Hall, S. J., Pucylowski, T., & Walsworth, T. E. (2018). The environmental cost of animal source foods. *Frontiers in Ecology and the Environment, 16*(6), 329–335.

IPCC (2019), Intergovernmental Panel on Climate Change, Report 2019, (last access: january 2023) retrived from: https://www.ipcc.ch/site/assets/uploads/2019/11/SRCCL-Full-Report-Compiled-191128.pdf

ISMEA – Qualivita. (2022). *Rapporto 2021 sulle produizioni agroalimentari e vinicole italiane DOP, IGP e STG.* https://www.qualivita.it/scarica-il-rapporto-ismea-qualivita-2021/.

ISPRA (2021), Istituto Superiore per la Protezione e la Ricerca Ambientale, Report: Le emissioni di gas serra in Italia: obiettivi di riduzione e scenari emissivi, (last access: january 2023) retrived from: https://www.isprambiente.gov.it/files2023/pubblicazioni/rapporti/rapporto_384_2023_le-emissioni-di-gas-serra-initalia.pdf

Macdiarmid, J. I., Cerroni, S., Kalentakis, D., & Reynolds, C. (2021). How important is healthiness, carbon footprint and meat content when purchasing a ready meal? Evidence from a non-hypothetical discrete choice experiment. *Journal of Cleaner Production, 282*, 124510.

Mathijs, E. (2015). Exploring future patterns of meat consumption. *Meat Science, 109*, 112–116.
Mele, M., Nudda, A., Pauselli, M., Roscini, V., Casarosa, L., Secchiari, P., & Pulina, G. (2015). Consumo di carne e salute umana. In *Alimenti di Origine Animale e Salute*. Franco Angeli.
Molteni, M. (2007). Gli stadi di sviluppo della CSR nella strategia aziendale. *Impresa Progetto-Electronic Journal of Management*, (2).
Nam, K. C., Jo, C., & Lee, M. (2010). Meat products and consumption culture in the east. *Meat Science, 86*(1), 95–102.
Nomisma. (2020). *Osservatorio the world after lockdown*. Consumer Survey per Fileni.
Nomisma. (2021). *Osservatorio Packaging del Largo Consumo*. Consumer Survey.
Sacchettini, G., Castellini, G., Graffigna, G., Hung, Y., Lambri, M., Marques, A., et al. (2021). Assessing consumers' attitudes, expectations and intentions towards health and sustainability regarding seafood consumption in Italy. *Science of the Total Environment, 789*, 148049.
Sala, S., McLaren, S. J., Notarnicola, B., Saouter, E., & Sonesson, U. (2017). In quest of reducing the environmental impacts of food production and consumption. *Journal of Cleaner Production, 140*, 387–398.
Tait, P., Saunders, C., Guenther, M., & Rutherford, P. (2016). Emerging versus developed economy consumer willingness to pay for environmentally sustainable food production: A choice experiment approach comparing Indian, Chinese and United Kingdom lamb consumers. *Journal of Cleaner Production, 124*, 65–72.
Taylor, D. H. (2005). Value chain analysis: An approach to supply chain improvement in Agri-food chains. *International Journal of Physical Distribution & Logistics Management., 35*, 744.
Tukker, A., Goldbohm, R. A., De Koning, A., Verheijden, M., Kleijn, R., Wolf, O., et al. (2011). Environmental impacts of changes to healthier diets in Europe. *Ecological Economics, 70*(10), 1776–1788.
UNITED NATIONS DEPARTMENT FOR ECONOMIC AND SOCIAL AFFAIRS. (2021). *WORLD POPULATION PROSPECTS 2017-VOLUME I: Comprehensive tables*. UN.
WHO. (2020). *World health statistics 2020: Monitoring health for the SDGs, sustainable development goals*. World Health Organization.
Willett, W., Rockström, J., Loken, B., Springmann, M., Lang, T., Vermeulen, S., et al. (2019). Food in the Anthropocene: The EAT–lancet commission on healthy diets from sustainable food systems. *The Lancet, 393*(10170), 447–492.
WWF. (2021). Dalle pandemie alla perdita di biodiversità. Dove ci sta portando il consumo di carne, Retrieved from: https://www.wwf.it/uploads/Report-Allevamenti-e-Zoonosi_21lug21.pdf

The Spread of Sustainability Reporting in the Italian Food Manufacturing Context

Andrea Caccialanza and Marco Marinoni

1 Introduction

The search for a renewed balance between modern food systems and the growing food demand is continually challenging current production systems in order to achieve more sustainable development models (Adams et al., 2021). This challenge is being met by both policy makers and production systems with an awareness of the need to set ambitious targets for the ecological transition of production chains (Caiado et al., 2017; Lai & Stacchezzini, 2021). This awareness has been further consolidated and promoted by various plans, both national and international, for combating the anthropogenic effects on the climate and its alterations (Adams & Mueller, 2022; Ernstberger & Grüning, 2013). In this regard, one of the best known and most widespread programmes is the one promoted by the United Nations (UN) through the 17 Social Development Goals (SDGs) of 2030 Agenda. The progressive increase of the world population represents in this context an additional element of stress for the achievement of these objectives by the production systems (Statista, 2021). In this context, it is therefore interesting to understand how agrifood production systems can be able to meet the growing food demand by triggering, at the same time, a more integrated strategic approach linked to the pursuit of 17 SDGs targets in the medium and long term (Garner & Ayala, 2018). For this purpose, it must necessarily be associated with processes and tools capable of effectively measuring the overall performance and learning effects of individual production units and their supply chains (Derchi et al., 2021) and engage a forward-looking perspective (León-Bravo et al., 2019). In particular, the publication of a

A. Caccialanza (✉) · M. Marinoni
Department of Economic and Social Sciences, Università Cattolica del Sacro Cuore, Piacenza, Italy
e-mail: andrea.caccialanza@unicatt.it

A. M. Fellegara et al. (eds.), *Sustainable Transition of Meat and Cured Meat Supply Chain*, CSR, Sustainability, Ethics & Governance,
https://doi.org/10.1007/978-3-031-34977-5_16

sustainability report (SR) suggests a significant interest in the disclosure of performance achieved (Abela, 2022; Erin et al., 2022).

Previous studies have confirmed the emergence of a progressive circularity in agrifood systems (Morea et al., 2022; Westerholz & Höhler, 2022), as well as the impact of digital technologies (Secundo et al., 2022) and performance assessment (Kumar et al., 2022) in promoting the SDGs.

The purpose of this chapter therefore is twofold: at first, it has been mapped the presence of the ESG dimensions and the spread of the 17 SDGs identified by the 2030 Agenda (RQ1); then, it is presented the investigation of sustainability reporting for the Italian context of the Italian food manufacturing sector in order to contextualise the current level of disclosure for each category of food products (RQ2).

The analysis of drivers that trigger a greater propensity to report on the performance achieved in companies is a topic widely debated in the literature, but that has not yet exhausted the examination of the most influential types of factors for each productive context (Carnegie & Napier, 1996; Dienes et al., 2016; Jensen & Berg, 2012). In the context of the different types of indicators, it is of interest for this chapter the deepening of the level of adherence by companies to macro-objectives set by the 2030 Agenda SDGs, as well as the extension of their implementation in performance measurement systems and SR (Ordonez-Ponce et al., 2021). Similarly, for each context, the propensities to identify objectives and to the subsequent disclosure of their performance may be different (Waheed & Zhang, 2020; Agostini et al., 2022). This chapter, apart from the effective ability of the individual companies to achieve the self-proposed or the embraced objectives, aims to understand if SDGs are at least a discussed issue in the institutional communication and included in the SR (Weber & Saunders-Hogberg, 2018). This decision can be seen as a proxy anticipating or confirming a greater strategic, systemic and integrated commitment to a sustainability orientation leading to an effective transition to a sustainable production model (Moldavska & Welo, 2019). This integrated and systemic sustainability-oriented approach has proved even more crucial in times of crisis and disruption such as Covid-19 (Leoni et al., 2021; Leoni et al., 2022). Correia et al. (2017) have previously shown how there can be a progressive approach to sustainability and that there are stages – more or less defined – in the life of the company, which then lead to an integrated approach to sustainability and the verifiability of what has been declared. These elements included in the present analysis through the verified presence of external assurance, the presence of a code of conduct and the publication of Italian organisational model 231 (Legislative Decree 231/2001). In this context, there has been a positive response to the corporate implementation of external certifications (Farooq et al., 2021), which are particularly significant in large companies and internationally structured groups (Gangi et al., 2020).

The structure of the chapter is thus proposed as follows. The second section presents the methodologies for the selection and analysis of the sample. The third section will examine the levels of disclosure related to the ESG dimension, as well as the inclusion of the 2030 Agenda objectives in the strategies of the sampled companies. In the fourth section, an analysis of the SR' dissemination in the Italian agrifood companies is proposed as well as the implementation of the reporting model proposed by both the GRI and qualitative-quantitative indicators. The last section summarises the concluding considerations.

2 Material and Methods

The methodological approach adopted is based on a qualitative-quantitative perspective aimed at mapping both the engagement with the 17 SDGs (RQ1) and the disclosure of non-financial performance through the drafting and publication of SRs (RQ2). The analysis process proposed in the chapter includes the desk analysis of a sample of companies operating in Italy in the agrifood manufacturing sector. The sample used for the analysis included the use of the Aida-Bureau van Dijk – database (sample extraction date: 17/11/2022) and used for the extraction of accounting and dimensional data of all the companies with headquarters in Italy and belonging to the following ATECO (2007) product categories: *101: Processing and preservation of meat and production of meat products, 102: Processing and preservation of fish, crustaceans and molluscs, 10: Processing and preservation of fruit and vegetables, 104: Production of vegetable and animal oils and fats, 105: Dairy industry, 106: Grain processing, production of starches and starch products, 107: Production of bakery and farinaceous products*. The grouping related to coding *108 Production of other food products* was removed as it was related to too many different types of food products that did not allow clear identification of causes and/or contextual factors for the RQs. Similarly, the coding *109 Production of animal feeding products* was removed because production is not for human consumption, which is the subject of the RQs. This sampling criteria was pursuit in the awareness of the relevance of a comparison within the same group of food processing activities and to optimise the assessment on the integration of sustainability in similar business contexts (Ryberg et al., 2018).

The sample selection process involved analysing only recognised companies with legally active status (10′189) and had a minimum threshold of declared revenues of more than €10,000 in the fiscal year 2021 (7′611). This dimensional filter has been applied in order to ensure the minimum level of consistency of the company's economic information data and foster the homogeneity within the sample (Segarra & Teruel, 2012). Variables as firm size, industry sector and country of operation are suggested by prior study as relevant also in the agrifood industry in order to determine the sustainable innovation propensity (Nybakk et al., 2011).

Accordingly, with Doni et al. (2020), reference was then made for the selection of two groups of analyses belonging to the selected sample to the EU Directive 2014/95, which in turn represents a European regulatory intervention with significant impacts with respect to the issues of: transparency of companies towards stakeholders, high and comparable level of non-financial disclosure and incentive for the introduction of non-financial performance indicators. This legislation, transposed in Italy through Legislative Decree No. 256/2016, is to be applied to *'public interest*

Table 1 Number of enterprises and dimension

Group	101	102	103	104	105	106	107
Total number of legally active enterprises by group	1318	211	856	509	1143	361	3192
Dimension of legally active enterprises by group:							
Turnover (mln €)	1411	10,893	11,251	9767	12,295	16,893	3283
Total asset (mln €)	11,327	7961	11,719	9156	11,896	15,442	3931
Employees	29	23	33	10	23	25	16
Of which, according to the Directive 2014/95/UE and Legislative Decree 254/2016:							
– with more than 20 mln € in turnover	168	22	142	50	157	62	119
– with more than 40 mln € in total asset	105	16	63	36	68	35	61
– with more than 500 employees	12	0	10	1	6	2	7
Number of sustainability reports by group	**9**	**2**	**11**	**8**	**9**	**3**	**9**
Dimension of legally active enterprises that publish sustainability reports by group:							
Turnover (mln €)	584,353	93,592	221,703	380,224	462,822	162,586	501,37
Total asset (mln €)	246,178	81,728	283,725	236,155	874,822	322,388	500,217
Employees	1754	156	497	171	789	413	879

entities', that is, taking as reference the distinction based on three main indicators: (1) the number of employees exceeding 500 and at least one of the other two thresholds (2) the balance sheet total exceeding € 20 mln or (3) the net turnover exceeding € 40 mln.

These discriminating parameters are supported by the recent intervention of the European legislator, which has recently proposed to extend the non-financial performance reporting obligations to all companies covered by the Corporate Social Responsibility Directive (CSRD) in 2022 (entered into force on 2023 January fifth amending the previous ones, as regards corporate sustainability reporting). In Table 1 is proposed a synthesis of the distribution within the sample of the firms belonging to the sample overall, with higher dimensional parameters and the number of published reports for each product category.

In the next section, a more detailed analysis of the non-financial reporting in Italian agrifood systems is proposed.

3 Non-financial Reporting in Italian Agrifood Systems

This section will be devoted to the discussion of three aspects related to non-financial reporting evolution in the analysed context: first, the growing reference to ESG dimensions in the assessment of corporate performance is analysed and then relates this aspect to the involvement of stakeholders in the evaluation process, thirdly evaluating other documentary resources for the assessment of the formalisation of a commitment to the integrity of conduct.

3.1 References to ESG and SDGs/Agenda 2030

The environmental and social sustainability of business activity has been at the centre of the international agenda for almost two decades and spreads fundamentally from voluntary initiatives that reflect the joint efforts of international organisations, states and the entrepreneurship world (Aureli et al., 2020). These initiatives have progressively allowed the development of standards and best practices that have had an increasingly direct impact on the organisation of business (Neumayer & Perkins, 2004), through the precise definition of voluntary rules that firms have implemented for the prevention, management and mitigation of environmental and social risks related to business activities (Derchi et al., 2021). However, the issue of reporting sustainability strategies and performance is inextricably linked to multiple factors and conditions, such as the age of the company, its governance, its economic and organisational size, its profitability and solidity, its geographical and cultural reference context and the historical and temporal context in which it operates (Dalton, 2020; Dienes et al., 2016). Within the EU agrifood context, there is evidence of this hypothesis (Hingley & Sodanoa, 2018). Accordingly, with Conca et al. (2021), the ESG propensity to disclosure sustainability practices has a direct impact on corporate profitability. More specifically, their evidence provides the existence of a positive relationship between profitability and disclosure practices of environmental and social issues and, conversely, a negative effect between company market value and disclosure practices relating to governance (Figge & Hahn, 2004). These considerations are equally valid when analysing the Italian agrifood sector, based mostly on many SMEs (Fiandrino et al., 2019).

The European regulatory framework and its forthcoming evolutions are outlining a new dimension for the European large enterprise (Melissen et al., 2018). However, it should not be thought that the issue only affects few large companies, despite the fact that the regime of mandatory only concerns large companies and with the exception of reporting obligations for listed small- and medium-sized enterprises (SMEs). The changes also affect SMEs, due to the growing demand for sustainability information for access to traditional financing channels and participation in value chains of large companies (Baudot & Cooper, 2022; Drempetic et al., 2020).

In this context, there are two important innovations at the European level: (*a*) Directive (EU) 2022/2464 on the new sustainability reporting obligation, which replaces the directive on non-financial information and extends both its scope and the content of the information to be provided and (*b*) the proposal for a directive of 23 February 2022 on companies' duties of care for sustainability purposes, which introduces (1) general duties of care for directors, (2) obligations for companies in the fight against climate change and (3) behavioural obligations relating to negative impacts on human rights and the environment that may arise from the activities not only of companies but also of their value chains.

The main innovations with respect to the current framework are: the expansion of the subjects covered by the disclosure obligations, a broadening of the information to be provided and greater harmonisation of the reporting criteria and the introduction of the obligation to review the information provided.

Underlying this change was the consideration expressed by the European authorities that the existing framework did not guarantee the information needs of users in several respects: information deficits, unreliable information and information that was not comparable, difficult to find, not available in digital format, not enough information on intangible assets (Secundo et al., 2022).

In particular, the EU directive also specifies the content that the standards must provide on environmental, social and governance issues. Those information are provided at the level of the individual company or at the level of the group. At individual company level, the discipline applies to large companies (listed and unlisted)—large companies are those companies that exceed, for at least two consecutive financial years, at least two of the following parameters: 250 average number of employees, € 20 mln balance sheet total, € 40 mln in revenues and SMEs with securities listed on European markets—SMEs include those companies that have exceeded, in the previous two financial years, two of the following size limits: (*1*) balance sheet total: € 350.000; (*2*) net revenues from sales and services: € 700.000; (c) average number of employees during the financial year: 10. At the group level, the disclosure requirements concern the parent companies of large groups. These dimensional thresholds are also similar to those applied in the sample' selection phase.

Information must also be provided on intangibles, understood as those intangible factors that are not recognised in financial statements and that contribute to value creation.

The information must consider the short, medium and long term and must be qualitative and quantitative, prospective and actual (see also Fig. 4).

The information should cover the company's business relationships and value chains. With regard to the information to be provided on the value chain, Directive (EU) 2022/2464 lays down a principle of proportionality with regard to the information that the company required to publish the sustainability report may request from SMEs.

This complex scope of information must be fulfilled by following the reporting standards adopted by the European Commission, based on a proposal formulated by

EFRAG. Simplified reporting standards are to be adopted for SMEs listed on regulated markets.

Based on the international reporting standards, performance measurement ESG rating has arisen (Pizzi et al., 2021). It is a numerical assessment of companies' commitment to environmental, social and governance issues. The approach used in calculating the score is defined as 'data-driven'; only public information, typically provided by the companies themselves, is processed on an ongoing basis (Zira et al., 2021). This approach avoids the *ex-ante* definition of an evaluation paradigm. In fact, the valuation is standardised on the basis of industry and country data. The methodological principles underlying the calculation of the ESG rating are as follows (Cooper & Michelon, 2022; Cort & Esty, 2020):

- Principle of *materiality*: the aspects assessed and the weight given to them depend on the reference sector.
- Principle of *transparency*: great importance is given to the quantity and quality of the information provided by the companies themselves, so as to assess not only the effort made on the various areas assessed but also their ability to communicate them.
- *Standardisation* of the evaluation against national and sectoral benchmarks.
- Numerical *quantification* of the score: attribution of a numerical value (e.g. 0–100), to the assessment, in such a way as to facilitate its immediate and easy comprehension.

Although the process is 'data-driven' and therefore based on algorithms, the judgement provided by experts in the field remains essential, to maximise the quality of the information assessed and to capture the effort made by the company as a whole (Larrinaga & Bebbington, 2021).

The ESG rating is calculated from a lot of parameters, which refer to three fundamental pillars that are environmental, social and governance aspects. The weight given to the environmental and social pillars varies depending on the analysed sector, while the weight given to the governance pillar is fixed (Giner & Luque-Vílchez, 2022). The steps of the assessment process are as follows:

- *ESG category scores*, first numerical analysis of the data.
- *Materiality matrix*: the information is filtered according to the type of company evaluated.
- *Overall ESG Score Calculation and Pillar Score*: the information is processed to calculate the score for the individual pillars and then the final score.

The risk that corporate non-financial reports is purely formal and does not reflect a real commitment to taking responsibility for the organisation's activities on the environment, and society can be reduced by the possibility of certifying the implementation process of non-financial reporting or the quality of the information reported in corporate documents (Naidoo & Gasparatos, 2018).

Also for this reason, the information is to be provided in an electronic format, and there is to be (*or could be for voluntary one*) a review on it in the form of limited assurance. The form of the review may change over time, however, with a view to a progressive strengthening of the review, which should come closer to that provided for financial information. The main purpose is to promote the role of the external auditor in improving the process of general compliance with international sustainability standards and the logic and methodologies for the asseveration of documents (required by Legislative Decree 14/2019).

The topics subject to asseveration concern the policies adopted by the organisation, the main risks and the results achieved in relation to environmental and social data, information concerning personnel, actions taken to ensure respect for human rights and the fight against corruption, disclosing the situation in which the company finds itself and the impact of its activities.

Previous analyses have already contributed to systematically mapping the dissemination and integration of SDG-related objectives into strategies at the level of different supply chains (Pizzi et al., 2020).

Also, within the agrifood studies, the diffusion of this transversal commitment to SDGs has been mapped in other international contexts, both with an environmental (Tanveer et al., 2021) or social (Ali & Gölgeci, 2020) perspective.

Recently, with regard to the Italian context, the contribution to the objectives related to the SDGs focused on bibliometric studies with respect to references in the documents of agrifood companies (Agnusdei & Coluccia, 2022) and the role of digitisation in the implementation of processes (Secundo et al., 2022).

In this chapter, the contribution to each of the 17 SDGs has been mapped in relation to the product category group and represented in Fig. 1 as absolute frequency of the SDG target by single sustainability report published. The group 102 seems under-represented due to the presence of only two sustainability reports disclosed while, in other groups, the distribution. The distribution is sustainably uniform for the other groups and with a slightly higher frequency of SDGs 2 (*Zero Hunger*), 8 (*Decent Work and Economic Growth*), 12 (*Responsible Consumption and Production*) and 13 (*Climate Action*).

3.2 The Impact of ESG Dimensions on Stakeholders

It has already been discussed that the information contained in a sustainability report must reflect the significant impacts of a social, environmental, human rights and respectful nature and that could condition the decisions of any category of stakeholder (Braun et al., 2021).

Stakeholder expectations of companies have undergone a change over time as a result of an increased focus on sustainability aspects, and the issue of corporate social responsibility has emerged as a driving force that has contributed to the adoption of new forms of reporting aimed at showing how the company's activities affect the environment and society itself (García-Sánchez et al., 2019).

The spread of non-financial reporting has been dictated not so much by the willingness of companies to report, but by the demand for accountability raised by the complex system of stakeholders with which organisations are called upon to

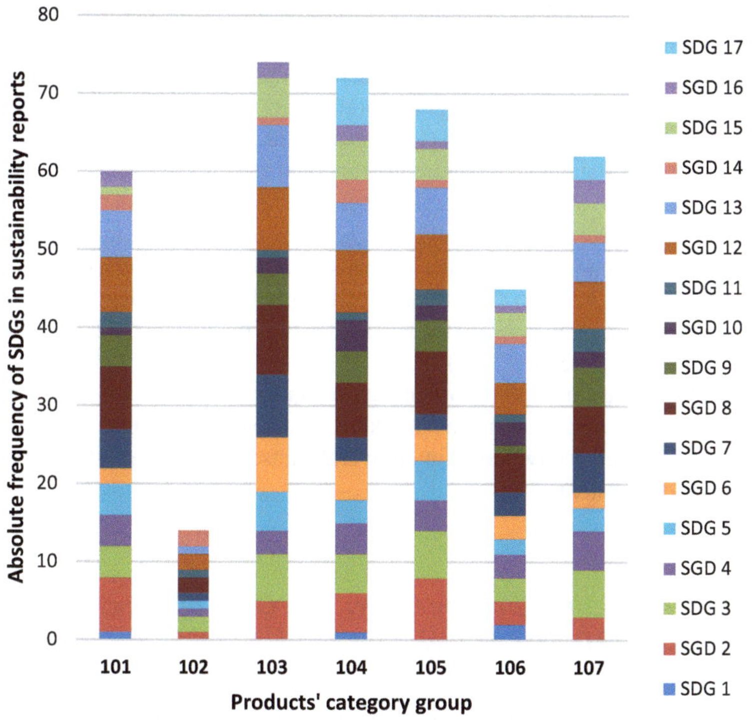

Fig. 1 SDGs' frequency by agrifood category group. Source: Authors

interact (Cooper et al., 1989). This kind of reporting, in its most recent approach, has led to so-called integrated reporting, that is, an evolved reporting system that combines financial, economic, environmental and governance data in a single document. This new form of reporting aims to provide a comprehensive representation of corporate performance, complementing financial reporting with non-financial reporting.

As recently pointed out by Agostini et al. (2022) for the Italian context of listed companies, it was noted that Directive (EU) 2014/95 has actually improved the amount of non-financial disclosure, but only non-financial disclosure quality was positively associate with corporate financial performance.

The abovementioned changes therefore also affect companies that are not directly affected by the regulations, due to the growing demand for sustainability expressed by business financiers, both from the banking channel and from the market; due to the participation of small- or medium-sized companies in value or supply chains of large companies; due to pressure from stakeholders other than shareholders who enter into relations with companies; and due to the thrust of civil society (Spence & Rinaldi, 2014). This condition is verified for various supply chains in which a dominant role of a great enterprise – called 'focal firms' – is involved in paths of transition towards more sustainable or certifiable models of product or processes

(Seuring & Müller, 2008). This trend is confirmed internationally also for agrifood chains (Pohlmann et al., 2020).

Company's alignment with its stakeholders' system of moral and ethical values is also a fundamental factor in the legitimisation of its activities by the community in which an organisation is embedded (Herremans et al., 2016). In particular, corporate sociality, later translated into the more international stakeholder theory, envisages an approach according to a new ethical perspective whereby companies must adopt decision-making processes that take into account not only the interests of those stakeholders most interested in its performance (mainly shareholders, employees and public institutions) but also the interests of the public and the legitimacy that the company finds in it, in response to the expectations of the social context in which it is embedded (Soewarno et al., 2019).

These disciplines are bound to generate a significant impact for large and very large companies, conditioning their market choices, organisational structures, risk and opportunity perspectives and, in an overall sense, the business strategies of the entire economic system.

3.3 Business Ethics and Integrity: The Code of Conduct and the 231/2001 Model

The introduction of integrated reporting practices and the representation of the performance related to them can be read as the result of a conditioning determined by the institutions that are present in the companies' environment (Vitolla et al., 2019). The behaviour of the latter is conditioned by the particular norms and ethical-moral principles that characterise the environment in which they are embedded (Contrafatto, 2014).

With regard to the contents of the non-financial declaration, Article 3, paragraph 1 of Legislative Decree 254/2016 attributes as its purpose that of ensuring the understanding of the business activity, its performance, its results and the impact produced by it, covering environmental, social, personnel-related, human rights issues, and the fight against active and passive corruption, which are relevant taking into account the activities and characteristics of the business. In particular, paragraph 1 of Art. 3 defines the areas to be addressed by the non-financial statement, such as the following:

- The company's business management and organisation model, including any organisation and management models adopted pursuant to Article 6(1)(a) of Legislative Decree No. 231 of 8 June 2001, also with reference to the management of the aforementioned issues
- The policies practised by the company, including those of due diligence, the results achieved through them and the relevant non-financial key performance indicators

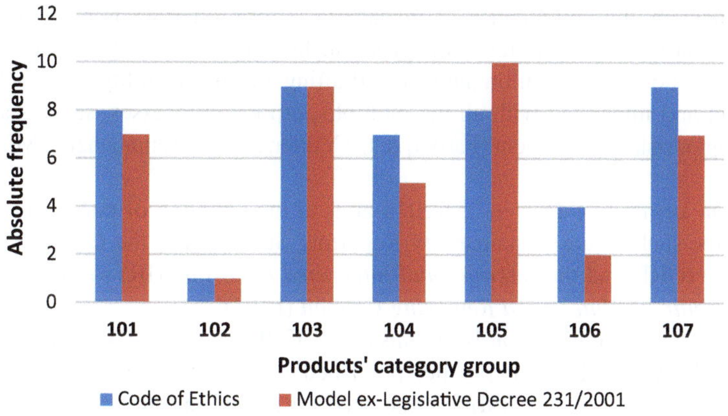

Fig. 2 Code of Ethics and Model ex-Legislative Decree 231/2001 frequency by agrifood category group. Source: Authors

- The main risks, generated or suffered, related to the above issues and arising from the company's activities, products, services or business relationships, including, where relevant, supply chains and subcontracting

According to Maggio (2021), the Italian legislative regulation is innovative in nature and goes beyond the constitutional and conventional principles on procedural guarantees in the fight of briberies, but at the same time, the perception of legal security and persecution of irregularities must be promoted actively. In this chapter, therefore, it has been mapped for the agrifood context the different propensities to disclosure and publish the code of ethics and the 231 model, judged as proxies for a greater formalisation of processes and commitment by companies (Cavotta & Dalpiaz, 2022). Within the sample, it was noted that companies publishing the sustainability report are equally inclined to publish these additional documents, as shown in Fig. 2. This condition was not found in the remaining part of the sample, which is also limited to exhibiting certifications (e.g. British Retail Consortium (BRC) and International Food Standard (IFS)) or designation of origin, which are a prerequisite or source of competitive advantage for the export of the finished product (De Chiara, 2020).

4 Global Reporting Initiative and Performance Metrics

Progress in the harmonisation of sustainability reporting standards and definitions has evolved substantially over the last decade (de Villiers et al., 2022). Today, more than in the past, it is therefore relevant to set ourselves the audit objective of understanding whether the term materiality can also be used to refer to sustainability compliance. In this key, the concept of materiality can be interpreted as an assessment of the significance of managerial efforts on ESG issues, which then translate into shared corporate strategies, satisfaction of the needs of corporate and other stakeholders and, ultimately, the drafting of sustainability reports that are coherent and integrated with all the multiple corporate processes, such as strategic planning or risk management (Farooq & De Villiers, 2019; Tettamanzi & Minutiello, 2022).

Italian Legislative Decree 254/2016 aims at the adoption of common reporting standards, such as the Sustainability Reporting Standards of the *Global Reporting Initiative* (GRI) and the *International Integrated Reporting* (IR) *Framework 1.0 of the International Integrated Reporting Council* (IIRC).

The five reporting standards organisations, CDP, CDSB, GRI, IIRC and SASB (so-called Group of Five), in parallel, published the joint statement in 2020, in which they describe materiality, affirming the need for a new reporting approach that can nestle into the management culture and guide the decision-making processes of corporate value creation, with a broad meaning of the term (CDP, 2020).

GRI defines materiality as the threshold for influencing the economic decisions of users of an organisation's financial statements, in particular investors. In the GRI approach, the threshold concept is also taken up for sustainability reporting but in a broader sense, since it refers to a wider range of impacts and a wider audience of stakeholders (GRI 4, 2022).

The choice of the reporting standard to be adopted is reflected in the performance indicators used for monitoring and evaluating activities, as these must be those indicated by the chosen standard but also representative of the different areas and consistent with the activity carried out and the impacts generated on stakeholders (Helfaya & Whittington, 2019; Humphrey et al., 2017; Torelli et al., 2020). The legislator has therefore adhered to the provisions of the European Directive, without introducing further specifications regarding the area, indicators and calculation methods to be followed during the production of the report. This choice is justified by the desire not to burden organisations with renovated dimensional caps for mandatory non-financial disclosure, in order to stimulate them to draw up a reliable and useful report to represent the social and environmental performance achieved during the financial year (Christensen et al., 2021), as well as with the intention of allowing them to select the performance indicators most suitable to illustrate the activity carried out (e.g. CSRD). However, it is necessary to highlight how a decision of this nature leads to inhomogeneity between reports and therefore makes it difficult to compare different organisations that choose to disclose non-financial information.

In this context, corporate reporting has evolved, emphasising not only the historical-consumptive disclosure of what and how has been done, but also future perspectives, that is, moving away from a static logic of business communication and opening up to a forward-looking approach that primarily concerns what the company's stakeholders of tomorrow will be, what the future (qualitative-quantitative) objectives will be, what actions will be taken to deal with risks and uncertainties and so on. Here is the concept of double (Baumüller & Sopp, 2022) and dynamic materiality (Zeisel, 2020), that is, the recognition of a flexible decision-making and planning process, which must be able to be continually remodelled to external changes in the environment, which affect the company's value, both from the point of view of the economic and financial equilibrium, for management, investors, employees and creditors, but also from the point of view of the keys to success in terms of ESG, more generally for the community and citizens.

In conclusion, differences in the determination of the materiality of information within the non-financial discipline could also generate information asymmetries with reference to the relevance of the same topic for organisations operating in the same sector, calling into question the comparability of companies' sustainability reporting (Schoeneborn et al., 2020).

The aim is to support organisations that, faced with a wide choice of potential issues to report on, must select those that are significant and, therefore, suitable to reflect their impact at an economic, social and environmental level.

The ability of an enterprise to develop in-house performance measurement systems further pushes it to adopt international standards of process and non-financial reporting gradually and increasingly (Yacob et al., 2019). This stage in turn matures in the propensity to proceed with the external assurance of the results achieved (Ioannou & Serafeim, 2017).

As remarked by Hassan et al. (2020), it can be seen as an additional form of transparency the implementation of external assurance of the evidences presented in the sustainability reports. The augmented perceived quality on the external-stakeholders side relies on the higher credibility and reliability of EGS performances, in particular on certain supply chains of weak normative contexts.

However, part of the literature points out that assurance-related schemes is in fact disconnected from the reporting process, criticising the effectiveness of controls (Boiral & Heras-Saizarbitoria, 2020).

Within the observed sample, as shown in Fig. 3, it is noted that the propensity for assurance is limited overall, with the sole exception of meat (101) and fish (102) products' groups.

4.1 Sustainability Reporting

Forms of corporate disclosure based on integrated reporting, while potentially beneficial in terms of decision-making, external communication and stakeholder relations, may be less effective if used primarily with a view to adhering to guidelines (Mahmood & Uddin, 2021). From the point of view of corporate transparency, the main critical issues concern the ability to interpret the data reported in the integrated report, their comparability and the potential misalignment between stakeholder expectations and the contents offered (Cho et al., 2015; Cho, 2020). In this regard, the need to manage these elements leads to a rethinking of the organisations reporting and external communication processes, in virtue of the increased importance attributed to the issue of sustainability (Ibáñez-Forés et al., 2023).

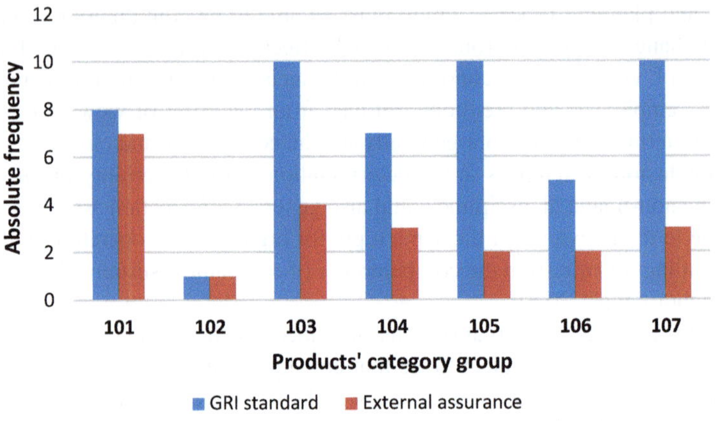

Fig. 3 GRI standard and external assurance' frequency by agrifood category group. Source: Authors

The implementation of the integrated reporting process by companies envisages the creation of a report capable of presenting stakeholders with an analysis of the company's relationships, internal and external resources and the repercussions these have on the company's ability to create value, based on a concept of sustainability (Bellucci et al., 2019).

It is intended to be a document that is easy to read and that allows stakeholders to come into possession, in an easy way, of information that they deem useful in order to have an assessment of the company as a whole, thanks to the co-presence of information concerning different aspects of its business, that is, economic-financial, social, environmental and governance, in order to have a balanced representation of these aspects, in line also with the relations that companies assume with the external environment and the community (Leoni et al., 2022).

In this sense, a company's disclosure policies, with the adoption of 'sustainability reports', allow it to respond to the information requests of both the most direct stakeholders and the other actors that play an important role in the value creation process over time.

4.2 The Emerge of GRI 4 Framework and the Evolution of Performance Indicators

The GRI Sustainability Reporting Standards represent the most widely used reporting tool for companies and constitute a modular and interconnected system of standards as a global benchmark for sustainability reporting (Jain et al., 2022).

In fact, these standards can be used by any organisation that intends to identify and report on its impacts, thereby communicating its contribution to sustainable development. In the ongoing process of harmonisation and endorsement of GRI, the new GRI standards (revised version 2022, October 5th) came into force on 1 January 2023, aiming at greater transparency and accountability, aiming at the new CSRD and the International Financial Reporting Standards (IFRS).

The most substantial update relates to the following three Universal Standards, with the aim of making reporting more comprehensive and adherent to international principles of (a) responsible governance, (b) due diligence (identifying, preventing and mitigating negative impacts) and (c) respect for human rights:

- GRI 1 Foundation 2021
- GRI 2 General Disclosures 2021 (explains how to report the organisation's context information)
- GRI 3 Material Topics 2021 (practical guide for identifying and managing material topics)

In addition to the abovementioned new Universal Standards, each organisation will have to refer to the relevant 'Sector Standards' based on its industry sector. The new Sector Standards are designed to increase the quality, completeness and consistency of the information reported, describing the contexts within which the different sectors are developed and listing the specific aspects to be reported.

It should be emphasised, however, that the adoption of the Sector Standards does not replace the process that each organisation has to undertake to identify its own 'material topics', but rather represents a guide to understanding and addressing the challenges shared by operators in the same supply chain (Lai et al., 2019).

The first Sector Standard to be published was the Oil & Gas Sector Standard (GRI 11), followed by those for coal and agriculture-aquaculture-fisheries.

Finally, the Topic Standards (revised in form, rather than substance) guide organisations in reporting on the impacts related to specific topics with appropriate qualitative and quantitative indicators and on the basis of the results highlighted by the materiality analysis.

The new version of the standards provides a new approach to materiality that incorporates the concept of 'due diligence' and reinforces that of 'impact', helping to paint a complete picture of business risks and long-term value creation. Considering the context, activities and business relationships of a given organisation, an issue is defined as material when it reflects the organisation's most significant impact on aspects such as the economy, the environment, people and their human rights. For this reason, stakeholders are actively involved (engagement) throughout the analysis and management process to create a complete view of the organisation (see GRI 1, page 10).

Universal, sector-specific and topic-specific standards are to be used as one interconnected set of modular reporting.

In methodological terms, there will no longer be a difference between adopting standards in *core* or *comprehensive* mode, but one can report one's impacts exclusively through the following options:

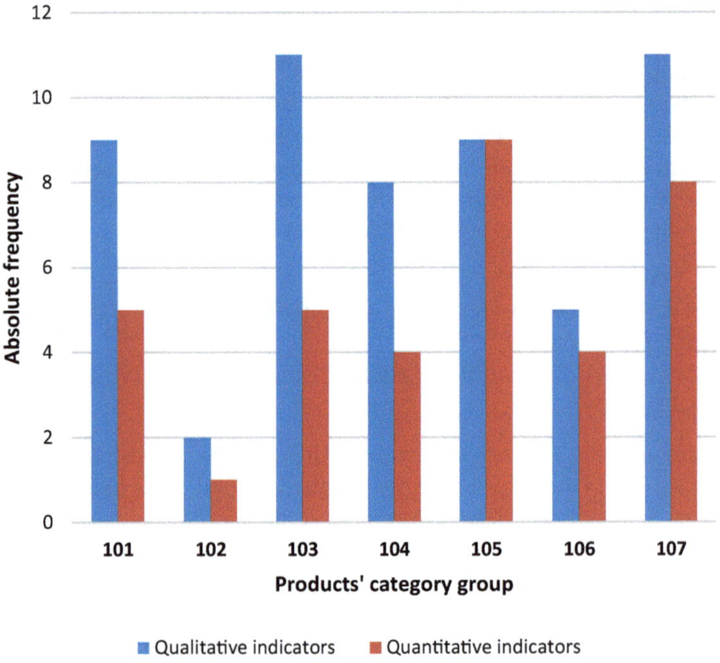

Fig. 4 Indicators, standards and certifications' frequency by agrifood category group. Source: Authors

- *With reference to* (GRI Standards) when an organisation is unable to meet the mandatory requirements of the GRI standard or wishes to report only specific information
- *In accordance with* (GRI Standards) when an organisation is able to meet all nine mandatory requirements of the standard

As priorly discussed, the implementation of ESG measures in the accounting standards is something that companies tend to adopt progressively and therefore develop, internally or in parallel, in the information system. Therefore, it is quite common for a company to first adopt a report *with reference to* GRI standards and then proceed to implement all mandatory requirements. At a still more generic level, we could emphasise that at first occurs the identification of a qualitative objective, then of any quantitative supporting measures. The identification of purely qualitative objectives in fact prevails in all food categories, generally followed in subsequent editions by the definition of quantitative objectives as well. In order to understand the development of this trend, therefore, these aspects were mapped in Fig. 4. A further in-depth analysis on the context of group 101 (meat and meat products) is offered in the next chapter.

5 Conclusions

This study was conducted with the aim of mapping and discussing non-financial reporting practices in the context of Italian agribusiness processing companies, representing the first recent study of each product category analysed in this area.

This chapter focused on at least three elements of attention regarding financial reporting in the context of the Italian agrifood chains.

First of all, the impact that the evolution of European and Italian legislation has had in influencing and conditioning the propensity to report non-financial performance. Other elements linked to the conditions of the evolution of international reporting frameworks have further contributed to consolidating the focus on sustainability performance. These frameworks have sometimes also provided elements of innovation that have anticipated legislative interventions or have influenced the content requirements.

Second, consistent with this prospective reading, a further increase in the propensity for ESG performance reporting and disclosure is expected. The growing number of agribusiness companies that have published their first sustainability report recently suggests a further confirmation for the Italian context.

Thirdly, in this context of increasing ESG reporting, the GRI framework is confirmed as the one adopted by the vast majority of companies. As further underlined by the comparison of the values represented in Table 1 and Fig. 3, almost all companies that report according to an international standard choose the GRI. Within the Italian agrifood context therefore is confirmed what has been observed by previous studies in other sectors at international level.

These observations to further developments in future studies in relation to the implementation and application of both European legislation and the new GRI 4 guidelines. This chapter can also feed the debate on the evaluation of business performance from a perspective that integrates the principles of sustainable development.

References

Abela, M. (2022). A new direction? The "mainstreaming" of sustainability reporting. *Sustainability Accounting, Management and Policy Journal, 13*(6), 1261–1283.

Adams, D., Donovan, J., & Topple, C. (2021). Achieving sustainability in food manufacturing operations and their supply chains: Key insights from a systematic literature review. *Sustainable Production and Consumption, 28*, 1491–1499.

Adams, C. A., & Mueller, F. (2022). Academics and policymakers at odds: The case of the IFRS foundation trustees' consultation paper on sustainability reporting. *Sustainability Accounting, Management and Policy Journal, 13*(6), 1310–1333.

Agnusdei, G. P., & Coluccia, B. (2022). Sustainable agrifood supply chains: Bibliometric, network and content analyses. *Science of the Total Environment, 824*, 153704.

Agostini, M., Costa, E., & Korca, B. (2022). Non-financial disclosure and corporate financial performance under directive 2014/95/EU: Evidence from Italian listed companies. *Accounting in Europe, 19*(1), 78–109.
Ali, I., & Gölgeci, I. (2020). Managing climate risks through social capital in agrifood supply chains. *Supply Chain Management: An International Journal, 26*(1), 1–16.
Aureli, S., Del Baldo, M., Lombardi, R., & Nappo, F. (2020). Nonfinancial reporting regulation and challenges in sustainability disclosure and corporate governance practices. *Business Strategy and the Environment, 29*(6), 2392–2403.
Baudot, L., & Cooper, D. J. (2022). Regulatory mandates and responses to uncomfortable knowledge: The case of country-by-country reporting in the extractive sector. *Accounting, Organizations and Society, 99*, 101308.
Baumüller, J., & Sopp, K. (2022). Double materiality and the shift from non-financial to European sustainability reporting: Review, outlook and implications. *Journal of Applied Accounting Research, 23*(1), 8–28.
Bellucci, M., Simoni, L., Acuti, D., & Manetti, G. (2019). Stakeholder engagement and dialogic accounting: Empirical evidence in sustainability reporting. *Accounting, Auditing & Accountability Journal., 32, 1467.*
Boiral, O., & Heras-Saizarbitoria, I. (2020). Sustainability reporting assurance: Creating stakeholder accountability through hyperreality? *Journal of Cleaner Production, 243*, 118596.
Braun, A. B., Visentin, C., da Silva Trentin, A. W., & Thomé, A. (2021). List of relevant sustainability indicators in remediation processes and their validation by stakeholders. *Journal of Cleaner Production, 317*, 128440.
Caiado, R. G. G., de Freitas Dias, R., Mattos, L. V., Quelhas, O. L. G., & Leal Filho, W. (2017). Towards sustainable development through the perspective of eco-efficiency-a systematic literature review. *Journal of Cleaner Production, 165*, 890–904.
Carnegie, G. D., & Napier, C. J. (1996). Critical and interpretive histories: Insights into accounting's present and future through its past. *Accounting, Auditing & Accountability Journal, 9*(3), 7–39.
Cavotta, V., & Dalpiaz, E. (2022). Good apples in spoiled barrels: A temporal model of firm formalization in a field characterized by widespread informality. *Journal of Business Venturing, 37*(2), 106188.
CDP. (2020). Five global organisations, whose frameworks, standards and platforms guide the majority of sustainability and integrated reporting, announce a shared vision of what is needed for progress towards comprehensive corporate reporting – and the intent to work together to achieve it. Retrieved from: https://www.cdp.net/en/articles/media/comprehensive-corporate-reporting
Cho, C. H. (2020). CSR accounting 'new wave'researchers:'step up to the plate'... or 'stay out of the game'. *Journal of Accounting and Management Information Systems, 19*(4), 626–650.
Cho, C. H., Laine, M., Roberts, R. W., & Rodrigue, M. (2015). Organized hypocrisy, organizational façades, and sustainability reporting. *Accounting, Organizations and Society, 40*, 78–94.
Christensen, H. B., Hail, L., & Leuz, C. (2021). Mandatory CSR and sustainability reporting: Economic analysis and literature review. *Review of Accounting Studies, 26*(3), 1176–1248.
Conca, L., Manta, F., Morrone, D., & Toma, P. (2021). The impact of direct environmental, social, and governance reporting: Empirical evidence in European-listed companies in the agri-food sector. *Business Strategy and the Environment, 30*(2), 1080–1093.
Contrafatto, M. (2014). The institutionalization of social and environmental reporting: An Italian narrative. *Accounting, Organizations and Society, 39*(6), 414–432.
Cooper, S., & Michelon, G. (2022). Conceptions of materiality in sustainability reporting frameworks: Commonalities, differences and possibilities. In *Handbook of accounting and sustainability* (pp. 44–66). Edward Elgar Publishing.
Cooper, D., Puxty, T., Lowe, T., & Willmott, H. (1989). *The accounting profession, corporatism and the state* (pp. 245–270). Palgrave Macmillan UK.

Correia, E., Carvalho, H., Azevedo, S. G., & Govindan, K. (2017). Maturity models in supply chain sustainability: A systematic literature review. *Sustainability, 9*(1), 64.

Cort, T., & Esty, D. (2020). ESG standards: Looming challenges and pathways forward. *Organization & Environment, 33*(4), 491–510.

Dalton, V. (2020). The challenge of engaging with and reporting against the SDGs for SMEs such as Sydney theatre company. *Journal of Management & Organization, 26*(6), 975–994.

De Chiara, A. (2020). Sustainable business model innovation vs. "Made in" for international performance of Italian food companies. *Agriculture 2021, 11*, 17.

de Villiers, C., La Torre, M., & Molinari, M. (2022). The global reporting Initiative's (GRI) past, present and future: Critical reflections and a research agenda on sustainability reporting (standard-setting). *Pacific Accounting Review, 34*(5), 728–747.

Derchi, G. B., Zoni, L., & Dossi, A. (2021). Corporate social responsibility performance, incentives, and learning effects. *Journal of Business Ethics, 173*(3), 617–641.

Dienes, D., Sassen, R., & Fischer, J. (2016). What are the drivers of sustainability reporting? A systematic review. *Sustainability Accounting, Management and Policy Journal., 7, 154.*

Doni, F., Bianchi Martini, S., Corvino, A., & Mazzoni, M. (2020). Voluntary versus mandatory non-financial disclosure: EU directive 95/2014 and sustainability reporting practices based on empirical evidence from Italy. *Meditari Accountancy Research, 28*(5), 781–802.

Drempetic, S., Klein, C., & Zwergel, B. (2020). The influence of firm size on the ESG score: Corporate sustainability ratings under review. *Journal of Business Ethics, 167*, 333–360.

Erin, O. A., Bamigboye, O. A., & Oyewo, B. (2022). Sustainable development goals (SDG) reporting: An analysis of disclosure. *Journal of Accounting in Emerging Economies, 12, 761.*

Ernstberger, J., & Grüning, M. (2013). How do firm-and country-level governance mechanisms affect firms' disclosure? *Journal of Accounting and Public Policy, 32*(3), 50–67.

Farooq, M. B., & De Villiers, C. (2019). Understanding how managers institutionalise sustainability reporting: Evidence from Australia and New Zealand. *Accounting, Auditing & Accountability Journal, 32*(5), 1240–1269.

Farooq, M. B., Zaman, R., & Nadeem, M. (2021). Account Ability's AA1000AP standard: A framework for integrating sustainability into organisations. *Sustainability Accounting, Management and Policy Journal, 12*, 1108.

Fiandrino, S., Busso, D., & Vrontis, D. (2019). Sustainable responsible conduct beyond the boundaries of compliance: Lessons from Italian listed food and beverage companies. *British Food Journal, 121*(5), 1035–1049.

Figge, F., & Hahn, T. (2004). Sustainable value added—Measuring corporate contributions to sustainability beyond eco-efficiency. *Ecological Economics, 48*(2), 173–187.

Gangi, F., Meles, A., Monferrà, S., & Mustilli, M. (2020). Does corporate social responsibility help the survivorship of SMEs and large firms? *Global Finance Journal, 43*, 100402.

García-Sánchez, I. M., Gómez-Miranda, M. E., David, F., & Rodríguez-Ariza, L. (2019). Analyst coverage and forecast accuracy when CSR reports improve stakeholder engagement: The global reporting initiative-international finance corporation disclosure strategy. *Corporate Social Responsibility and Environmental Management, 26*(6), 1392–1406.

Garner, B., & Ayala, C. (2018). Consumer supply-chain demands and challenges at farmers' markets. *British Food Journal, 120*, 2734.

Giner, B., & Luque-Vílchez, M. (2022). A commentary on the "new" institutional actors in sustainability reporting standard-setting: A European perspective. *Sustainability Accounting, Management and Policy Journal, 13*(6), 1284–1309.

GRI - Global Reporting Initiative. (2022). *Understanding materiality can unlock accountability.* Retrieved online at: https://www.globalreporting.org/news/news-center/understanding-materiality-can-unlock-accountability/

Hassan, A., Elamer, A. A., Fletcher, M., & Sobhan, N. (2020). Voluntary assurance of sustainability reporting: Evidence from an emerging economy. *Accounting Research Journal, 33*(2), 391–410.

Helfaya, A., & Whittington, M. (2019). Does designing environmental sustainability disclosure quality measures make a difference? *Business Strategy and the Environment, 28*(4), 525–541.
Herremans, I. M., Nazari, J. A., & Mahmoudian, F. (2016). Stakeholder relationships, engagement, and sustainability reporting. *Journal of Business Ethics, 138*, 417–435.
Hingley, M., & Sodanoa, V. (2018). Corporate social responsibility reporting: The case of the Agri-food sector. Corporate social responsibility reporting: the case of the agri-food sector, 93–120.
Humphrey, C., O'Dwyer, B., & Unerman, J. (2017). Re-theorizing the configuration of organizational fields: The IIRC and the pursuit of 'Enlightened'corporate reporting. *Accounting and Business Research, 47*(1), 30–63.
Ibáñez-Forés, V., Martínez-Sánchez, V., Valls-Val, K., & Bovea, M. D. (2023). How do organisations communicate aspects related to their social performance? A proposed set of indicators and metrics for sustainability reporting. *Sustainable Production and Consumption, 35*, 157–172.
Ioannou, I., & Serafeim, G. (2017). The consequences of mandatory corporate sustainability reporting. Harvard Business School research working paper, (11–100).
Jain, A., Islam, M. A., Keneley, M., & Kansal, M. (2022). Social contagion and the institutionalisation of GRI-based sustainability reporting practices. *Meditari Accountancy Research, 30*(5), 1291–1308.
Jensen, J. C., & Berg, N. (2012). Determinants of traditional sustainability reporting versus integrated reporting. An institutionalist approach. *Business Strategy and the Environment, 21*(5), 299–316.
Kumar, M., Sharma, M., Raut, R. D., Mangla, S. K., & Choubey, V. K. (2022). Performance assessment of circular driven sustainable Agri-food supply chain towards achieving sustainable consumption and production. *Journal of Cleaner Production, 372*, 133698.
Lai, A., Panfilo, S., & Stacchezzini, R. (2019). The governmentality of corporate (un) sustainability: The case of the ILVA steel plant in Taranto (Italy). *Journal of Management and Governance, 23*, 67–109.
Lai, A., & Stacchezzini, R. (2021). Organisational and professional challenges amid the evolution of sustainability reporting: A theoretical framework and an agenda for future research. *Meditari Accountancy Research, 29*(3), 405–429.
Larrinaga, C., & Bebbington, J. (2021). The pre-history of sustainability reporting: A constructivist reading. *Accounting, Auditing & Accountability Journal, 34*(9), 162–181.
León-Bravo, V., Moretto, A., Cagliano, R., & Caniato, F. (2019). Innovation for sustainable development in the food industry: Retro and forward-looking innovation approaches to improve quality and healthiness. *Corporate Social Responsibility and Environmental Management, 26*(5), 1049–1062.
Leoni, G., Lai, A., Stacchezzini, R., Steccolini, I., Brammer, S., Linnenluecke, M., & Demirag, I. (2021). Accounting, management and accountability in times of crisis: Lessons from the COVID-19 pandemic. *Accounting, Auditing & Accountability Journal, 34*(6), 1305–1319.
Leoni, G., Lai, A., Stacchezzini, R., Steccolini, I., Brammer, S., Linnenluecke, M., & Demirag, I. (2022). The pervasive role of accounting and accountability during the COVID-19 emergency. *Accounting, Auditing & Accountability Journal, 35*(1), 1–19.
Maggio, P. (2021). A critical analysis of corruption and anti-corruption policies in Italy. *Journal of Financial Crime, 28*(2), 513–530.
Mahmood, Z., & Uddin, S. (2021). Institutional logics and practice variations in sustainability reporting: Evidence from an emerging field. *Accounting, Auditing & Accountability Journal, 34*(5), 1163–1189.
Melissen, F., Mzembe, A. N., Idemudia, U., & Novakovic, Y. (2018). Institutional antecedents of the corporate social responsibility narrative in the developing world context: Implications for sustainable development. *Business Strategy and the Environment, 27*(6), 657–676.
Moldavska, A., & Welo, T. (2019). A holistic approach to corporate sustainability assessment: Incorporating sustainable development goals into sustainable manufacturing performance evaluation. *Journal of Manufacturing Systems, 50*, 53–68.

Morea, D., Fortunati, S., Cappa, F., & Oriani, R. (2022). Corporate social responsibility as a catalyst of circular economy? A case study perspective in Agri-food. *Journal of Knowledge Management*, (ahead-of-print).

Naidoo, M., & Gasparatos, A. (2018). Corporate environmental sustainability in the retail sector: Drivers, strategies and performance measurement. *Journal of Cleaner Production, 203*, 125–142.

Neumayer, E., & Perkins, R. (2004). What explains the uneven take-up of ISO 14001 at the global level? A panel-data analysis. *Environment and Planning A, 36*(5), 823–839.

Nybakk, E., Crespell, P., & Hansen, E. (2011). Climate for innovation and innovation strategy as drivers for success in the wood industry: moderation effects of firm size, industry sector, and country of operation. *Silva Fennica, 45*(3), 415–430.

Ordonez-Ponce, E., Clarke, A., & MacDonald, A. (2021). Business contributions to the sustainable development goals through community sustainability partnerships. *Sustainability Accounting, Management and Policy Journal, 12*, 1239.

Pizzi, S., Caputo, A., Corvino, A., & Venturelli, A. (2020). Management research and the UN sustainable development goals (SDGs): A bibliometric investigation and systematic review. *Journal of Cleaner Production, 276*, 124033.

Pizzi, S., Rosati, F., & Venturelli, A. (2021). The determinants of business contribution to the 2030 agenda: Introducing the SDG reporting score. *Business Strategy and the Environment, 30*(1), 404–421.

Pohlmann, C. R., Scavarda, A. J., Alves, M. B., & Korzenowski, A. L. (2020). The role of the focal company in sustainable development goals: A Brazilian food poultry supply chain case study. *Journal of Cleaner Production, 245*, 118798.

Ryberg, M. W., Owsianiak, M., Clavreul, J., Mueller, C., Sim, S., King, H., & Hauschild, M. Z. (2018). How to bring absolute sustainability into decision-making: An industry case study using a planetary boundary-based methodology. *Science of the Total Environment, 634*, 1406–1416.

Schoeneborn, D., Morsing, M., & Crane, A. (2020). Formative perspectives on the relation between CSR communication and CSR practices: Pathways for walking, talking, and T(w)alking. *Business and Society, 59*(1), 5–33.

Secundo, G., Schena, R., Russo, A., Schiavone, F., & Shams, R. (2022). The impact of digital technologies on the achievement of the sustainable development goals: Evidence from the Agri-food sector. *Total Quality Management & Business Excellence*, 1–17.

Segarra, A., & Teruel, M. (2012). An appraisal of firm size distribution: Does sample size matter? *Journal of Economic Behavior & Organization, 82*(1), 314–328.

Seuring, S., & Müller, M. (2008). From a literature review to a conceptual framework for sustainable supply chain management. *Journal of Cleaner Production, 16*(15), 1699–1710.

Soewarno, N., Tjahjadi, B., & Fithrianti, F. (2019). Green innovation strategy and green innovation: The roles of green organizational identity and environmental organizational legitimacy. *Management Decision, 57*(11), 3061–3078.

Spence, L. J., & Rinaldi, L. (2014). Governmentality in accounting and accountability: A case study of embedding sustainability in a supply chain. *Accounting, Organizations and Society, 39*(6), 433–452.

Statista. (2021). Per capita meat consumption forecast in European countries from 2015 to 2022 (in kilograms) [Graph]. In Statista. Retrieved from: https://www.statista.com/forecasts/679528/per-capita-meat-consumption-european-union-eu

Tanveer, U., Ishaq, S., & Gough, A. (2021). Circular economy in Agri-food sector: Food waste management perspective. Challenges and Opportunities of Circular Economy in Agri-Food Sector*:* Rethinking Waste, 55–75.

Tettamanzi, P., & Minutiello, P. (2022). *ESG: Bilancio di sostenibilita'e integrated reporting*. IPSOA.

Torelli, R., Balluchi, F., & Furlotti, K. (2020). The materiality assessment and stakeholder engagement: A content analysis of sustainability reports. *Corporate Social Responsibility and Environmental Management, 27*(2), 470–484.

Vitolla, F., Raimo, N., & Rubino, M. (2019). Appreciations, criticisms, determinants, and effects of integrated reporting: A systematic literature review. *Corporate Social Responsibility and Environmental Management, 26*(2), 518–528.

Waheed, A., & Zhang, Q. (2020). Effect of CSR and ethical practices on sustainable competitive performance: A case of emerging markets from stakeholder theory perspective. *Journal of Business Ethics*, 1–19.

Weber, O., & Saunders-Hogberg, G. (2018). Water management and corporate social performance in the food and beverage industry. *Journal of Cleaner Production, 195*, 963–977.

Westerholz, H. K., & Höhler, J. (2022). Corporate social responsibility reporting in the food industry—Comparison of co-operatives and investor-owned dairies. *Corporate Social Responsibility and Environmental Management, 29*(1), 211–222.

Yacob, P., Wong, L. S., & Khor, S. C. (2019). An empirical investigation of green initiatives and environmental sustainability for manufacturing SMEs. *Journal of Manufacturing Technology Management, 30*(1), 2–25.

Zeisel, S. (2020). Is sustainability a moving target? A methodology for measuring CSR dynamics. *Corporate Social Responsibility and Environmental Management, 27*(1), 283–296.

Zira, S., Rydhmer, L., Ivarsson, E., Hoffmann, R., & Röös, E. (2021). A life cycle sustainability assessment of organic and conventional pork supply chains in Sweden. *Sustainable Production and Consumption, 28*, 21–38.

The VIS Assessment Tool for the Cured Meat Italian Supply Chain: Fostering Accountability for Sustainability through a FAO SAFA-Based Framework

Davide Galli, Riccardo Torelli, and Andrea Caccialanza

1 Introduction

In the previous two chapters, the topic of reporting and communication of nonfinancial performance within the context of agri-food supply chains was discussed. In particular, it has emerged that there has been a differentiated approach to the issues of reporting on international targets (e.g., SDGs), as well as with regard to the definition of internal firms' targets and communication of overall firm performance. A varied picture emerged, composed of different, more or less integrated approaches, which outline a differentiated level of maturity in the awareness of firm's impacts. For this purpose, and as a complement to the themes and contents proposed, this chapter aims to focus on the assessment of impacts according to an integrated and structured approach for the entire supply chain.

The choice of the agri-food chain as the object of analysis poses an even higher level of possible interactions to be included and evaluated (Adams et al., 2021; Helfaya & Whittington, 2019; Hingley & Sodanoa, 2018). Accordingly with Kamble et al. (2020), there are significant issues that need to be addressed to achieve sustainability transparency in agri-food supply chains globally, namely, the lack of involvement of the small farmers, norms to control food safety and quality, inhomogeneous levels of automatization of processes, and information inaccuracy. Through an integrated approach on several levels of the supply chain, however, it is possible to partially overcome the mentioned barriers, thanks to the possibility of tracking and reporting on the actual efforts undertaken in individual business contexts (Aureli et al., 2020; Jensen & Berg, 2012).

D. Galli · R. Torelli (✉) · A. Caccialanza
Department of Economic and Social Sciences (DiSES), Università Cattolica del Sacro Cuore, Piacenza, Italy
e-mail: riccardo.torelli2@unicatt.it

A. M. Fellegara et al. (eds.), *Sustainable Transition of Meat and Cured Meat Supply Chain*, CSR, Sustainability, Ethics & Governance,
https://doi.org/10.1007/978-3-031-34977-5_17

The aim of this chapter is to propose an assessment tool for the cured meat supply chain that addresses the need to set a benchmark level for companies at both the farming and processing levels.

This study does not aim to systematize an ex novo model of analysis, but rather is part of a strand of literature that has already experimented with various levels of in-depth analysis in different agri-food contexts.

Previous studies (Demartini et al., 2016; De Olde et al., 2016; Talukder & Blay-Palmer, 2017) have helped to map and systematize various schemes already available for an assessment of performance from a corporate perspective, identifying different frameworks according to the focus and perspectives of the investigation (e.g., IDEA, RISE, SAFE. SOSTARE and MOTIFS). Many of these, however, did not offer the possibility of including the corporate governance dimension as an influencing factor within the same analysis model. Consistent with the dynamic and prospective perspective that these measurement systems require, however, it would be reductive to exclude it a priori (Melissen et al., 2018; Schneider & Meins, 2012; Ssebunya et al., 2017). In the search for a suitable framework, therefore, it was verified that it was suitable for cross-county application (Paraskevopoulou et al., 2020) and that it considered the sustainability drivers on the level of the different company dimensions involved (Ernstberger & Grüning, 2013). In addition, it is a prerequisite that the Assessment of Food and Agriculture systems (SAFA) Framework proposed by the Food and Agriculture Organization (FAO) of the United Nations (FAO, 2013a) is able to pursuit. In particular, it allows comparisons on a time scale both in terms of the performance development of the enterprises along the supply chain and with respect to a supply chain benchmark. Moreover, as supported by the analysis of Schader et al. (2014) between 35 assessment tools, SAFA framework is the best fitting for this purpose in terms of scope and precision.

In addition, accordingly with also Bonisoli et al. (2019), SAFA framework reveals relevant advantages: (1) *flexibility*, the capability of being adapted for multiple users and purposes; (2) *high credibility*, being developed and validated by UN organization with the contribution of nongovernmental organizations; (3) *user-friendly*, thanks to the easiness of the implementation; (4) *comprehensiveness* of the themes and indicators involved; and (5) *compatibility* with others quality certifications and assessment tools.

The SAFA model is applied in many contexts and in different approaches more or less complete in terms of information and selected indicators (FAO, 2013b, FAO, 2014). As pointed out by Marchand et al. (2014), in fact, the scalability of the level of detail required makes this tool also suitable for smaller contexts.

Table 1 provides a summary of the main applications of the SAFA model, divided by the completeness of the application, geographical framework, focus and type of stakeholders involved.

Among these proposed, in particular, Hřebíček et al. (2013) and Kassem et al. (2017) proposed a conjoint application of the model with the reporting scheme proposed by the Global Reporting Initiative (GRI).

Following on from what Gasso et al. (2015) has proposed, it has therefore proceeded to identify in the Italian context of cured meat those elements that, in

Table 1 Prior applications of the SAFA framework

Group	References	Countries	Focus
Complete sustainability assessment using SAFA	Gayatri et al. (2016)	Indonesia	Beef meat in small producers supply chain
	Ssebunya et al. (2017)	Uganda	Coffee supply chain
	Landert et al. (2017)	Switzerland	Urban food systems
	Butti Al Shamsi et al. (2018)	United Arab Emirates and Italy	Organic products
	Cammarata et al. (2021)	Italy	Agroecology and organic farming in Sicily
	Pérez-Lombardini et al. (2021)	Mexico	Compares three types of production systems
Partial sustainability assessment using SAFA	Theurl et al. (2017)	Austria and Italy	Winter vegetables
	Bonisoli et al. (2019)	Organic and conventional bananas	Brazil
Sustainability assessment using some of the SAFA indicators	Hřebíček et al. (2013)	Czech Republic	Czech food products
	Kassem et al. (2017)	Czech Republic	Czech agriculture companies
	Gaviglio et al. (2017)	Italy	Evaluation of farm assessment tools
SAFA applied in synergy with other frameworks	Hřebíček et al. (2015)	Czech Republic	Analysis of determinants for the application of GRI and SAFA frameworks
	Gasso et al. (2015)	Germany and Denmark	Biogas sustainability assessment
	Dabkienė (2016)	European countries	Scope of farms sustainability using FADN Data
	Soldi et al. (2019)	Paraguay	Assessment of different classes of agricultural systems
	Havardi-Burger et al. (2021)	Germany	Flowering potted plants supply chain

addition to the transversality of the environmental dimension at international level, respond to the social and economic peculiarities of this sector.

The chapter is structured proposing the applied methods, the discussion of the dimensions involved in the VIS model, as well as an overview of the applicative potentialities, and the conclusions.

2 Methodology

This section of the chapter aims to describe the process implemented in the selection of themes, sub-themes, and indicators; the type of indicators; the scale adopted for scores; and the management of feedback received in the field test phase.

Following the review of the literature carried out in the first phase of the project and summarized in Table 1 of the introduction, we proceeded with the comparison of the themes proposed in each of the four dimensions of the SAFA model: governance, environment, economy, and social. Prior analysis on meat supply chains was applied to developing countries (Gayatri et al., 2016), so that a re-prioritization of material themes occurred.

At first, an individual analysis of the compatibility and significance of the sub-themes and indicators for the Italian context was carried out. A first version of the self-assessment tool was drawn up following the comparison. In a second phase, it has been circulated to six trade associations of the sector, preparing for this purpose a series of moments of comparison. The omission of some sub-themes has never been motivated for necessity of synthesis of the self-assessment tool but due to the inconsistency compared to the context of the chain of the Italian meat and cured meat supply chains (e.g., exploitation of child labor).

In a second phase aimed at receiving feedback, it was forwarded to two farms and processing. At this stage, additional feedback was collected for the drafting of the sections of the document aimed at the operational guide for completion. This section has also been enriched by providing definitions for the dimensions involved, as well as how to calculate the required indicators. This additional request has been implemented for model performance indicators only. Table 2 proposes a comparison between the width of the SAFA model in terms of themes, sub-themes, and indicators covered, compared to those selected within the VIS model.

Once the proposal was drowned, the coverage of the issues and indicators was continued with the definition of a rating system that would be adequate to exploit not only the commitment in terms of reporting the result. This choice may have prejudiced the group of companies that already published sustainability reports (less than ten, as emerged and discussed in the previous chapter) regardless of the performance or investments undertaken or planned. This type of evaluation is shared

Table 2 Comparison within SAFA and VIS models

	SAFA Framework			VIS Framework		
Dimension	Themes	Sub-themes	Indicators	Themes	Sub-themes	Indicators
Good Governance	5	14	19	3	5	9
Environmental Integrity	6	14	52	6	9	31
Economic Resilience	4	14	26	4	11	29
Social Well-being	6	16	19	4	5	11
Total	**21**	**58**	**116**	**17**	**30**	**80**

Table 3 VIS model scoring methodology

	Typology of the VIS model indicator		
Rating	Target	Practice	Performance
0	No specific targets	No specific practices	No specific indicator
1	One specific target	A managerial practice is summarily described	There is a non-quantitative proxy or another indicator
2	Target is associated with an indicator	Are widely described more managerial practices	There is the indicator for at least one year

at the level of the literature also from previous studies on the validation of new methodologies of assessment (Singh et al., 2009). Like the SAFA model, the VIS model also has three types of indicators: target, practices, and performance. In the selection of the typology of indicators, therefore it has been always held in consideration the decision to propose the topic as important or less to level of corporate governance through the typology of pointers target. The actual development and implementation of practices in business processes has been enhanced with practice indicators. Finally, the quantitative measurement of impacts has been enhanced by performance indicators.

Table 3 proposes an outline of the incremental qualitative scoring methodology adopted in the VIS model for each of the types of metrics implemented: target, practices, and performance.

In order to constitute a first nucleus of historical series of data at the first compilation, it should be required the inclusion of the performance of the previous two years (at least, depending on firm data availability). This additional request has been implemented for model performance indicators only.

In the next section will be presented and discussed the four dimensions of the VIS model: governance, environmental, economic, and social.

3 Dimensions of the VIS Model

3.1 Governance

Governance is the process through which decisions are made and implemented (UNESCAP, 2009) in the economic, environmental, and social spheres. In addition, a good governance system addresses aspects of business ethics, accountability, stakeholder participation, and involvement, as well as making commitments in terms of sustainability (Spence & Rinaldi, 2014). The weight given to the issue of governance by various UN agencies is in line with other international approaches, such as the UN Principles for Responsible Investment, the UN Global Compact (UNGC/IFC, 2009), and the GRI Guidelines (GRI, 2013). The governance issue revolves around an understanding of Good Corporate Governance (GCG) that explicitly takes into consideration all relevant stakeholders. A company committed to sustainable development needs a governance structure in which the company's content, values, and responsibilities are clearly stated and through which transparency and accountability are ensured.

The area of governance is a focal point in sustainability studies, particularly when analyzing the entire supply chain in the agri-food industry. Several studies have focused attention on governance mechanisms able of promoting virtuous behaviors, including those with a view to a sustainable transition, and paying particular attention to processes able of influencing the entire supply chain and to cases of the presence of products of protected origin (Fernández-Barcala et al., 2017; Martins et al., 2017; Ouma et al., 2017; Poponi et al., 2021; van der Merwe et al., 2019).

The area of governance (G) in the VIS assessment model is made explicit through three themes (divided into five sub-themes and nine indicators) that, respectively, relate to: company commitment (the mission) (G.1), corporate responsibility (G.2), and integrated planning (G.3). The theme of company commitment is explored through the analysis of the effective Statement of Intent (G.1.1) by the company. The Statement of Intent is the declaration by the highest-level manager and should contain a commitment to sustainability. To show that it is truly committed to sustainability, the company must demonstrate that this commitment is evident in the company's codes and policies. In addition, in reporting its results, the company must demonstrate the influence that its commitment to sustainability has had in informing and developing the company's implemented policies and practices. It is important to understand that including sustainability principles in one's mission is not a sufficient item in itself; actions and results are needed beyond statements of intent. This deepening is done through the measure of the company's explicit commitment to making explicit and securing involvement of all corporate stakeholders (G.1.1.1); the measure of relevant commitment embodied in the actual impact of the mission statement on corporate practices, processes, and strategies (G.1.1.2); and the measure of sustainability training dedicated to corporate personnel (G.1.1.3). The theme of accountability is explored through the subtopics of monitoring (G.2.1) and evaluation (G.2.2). Undergoing a genuine sustainability audit is important evidence that sustainability values are embedded in organizational governance and culture. Institutionalized sustainability reporting and auditing tools are developed and adopted by many larger companies, while smaller companies and those at the beginning of a sustainability journey may find less prescriptive approaches, such as Social Auditing, more accessible as they can make efficient use of all the organization's existing data systems (Dalton, 2020; Gangi et al., 2020). The highly customizable approach has proven effective in diverse cultures where reporting methods can be differentiated using a wider range of means than just paper or electronic documents. With this in mind, the VIS model has included a measure of reporting on the company's sustainability performance (G.2.1.1) and the tools of the same reporting (G.2.1.2). Turning to the topic of evaluation where the company's performance is found to be deficient, the governing body takes responsibility for improving performance and involving stakeholders in the monitoring of performance improvement plans. Organizations with more articulated governance will find this easier to accept and institute than smaller, emerging organizations;

however, some small, traditional companies have a very solid understanding of the leadership responsibilities that can translate into this goal. In order to measure this, it was chosen to assess the company's transparency regarding practices for monitoring, evaluating, and correcting sustainability performance (G.2.2.1). Finally, the topic of integrated planning is assessed through the sub-themes programming (G.3.1) and cost configuration (G.3.2). Sustainability plans are a relatively recent phenomenon, used by organizations to provide good governance guidance for their sustainability efforts and to help incorporate values and aspirations for sustainability to be formally included in business planning. Sustainability planning is rapidly spreading; however, it is necessary to ensure that these plans are integrated and cover each of the four pillars of sustainability. In order to measure the concreteness of this planning, it was decided to assess the company's performance through the analysis of the presence and diffusion/sharing of the sustainability plan (G.3.1.1 and G.3.1.2). As consumers, shareholders, and other stakeholders become more aware of and concerned about the potential environmental and social impacts of companies, they demand better information about performance in these areas (Garner & Ayala, 2018). Social auditing and environmental accounting have contributed to an emerging field of work that seeks to improve the accuracy and use of full-cost accounting (FCA). It is believed that these initiatives will enable companies to make better decisions because they more fully understand the full impact of those decisions. The FCA process makes transparent both direct and indirect subsidies received, as well as direct and indirect outsourced costs. There is still no international consensus on an all-encompassing standard for FCA. However, good experiences with comparable tools for some aspects of accounts, such as measuring an organization's carbon footprint, are emerging. In this view, the company is assessed on the presence of any full-costing systems capable of also considering direct or indirect costs generated by economic activity on society and the environment (G.3.2.1).

3.2 Environment

As human activities are exceeding planetary boundaries (Rockström et al., 2009), protecting the integrity of the Earth system is a precondition of any development. Environmental integrity is about maintaining life-support systems essential for human survival, minimizing negative environmental impacts on the environment and promoting positive impacts. The state of the world's ecosystems, assessed again this year by the IPCC (2023), is irreversibly affected by human actions that are changing the diversity of life on Earth and the integrity of the environment. Critical ecosystem services on which development depends, including air and water purification, soil formation, disease control, pollination, and reduced vulnerability to natural disasters such as floods, droughts, and landslides, are being compromised. The Convention on Biological Diversity believes that a general application of an ecosystem approach will help to achieve the balance of three goals, namely, conservation, sustainable use, and fair and equitable sharing of the benefits arising from the use of natural genetic resources.

In the agri-food sector, and especially in the meat and cured meat sector, the environmental issue is the focus of public opinion, stakeholders, and even the academic world. Numerous researches in this area have investigated aspects of great relevance to the current challenges of the sector, such as life cycle assessment (LCA) (Zira et al. 2021), carbon footprint, consumer perception, environmental impacts of different stages of the supply chain and resource use of livestock farms (Jacobsen et al., 2014; López-Andrés et al., 2018; Navarrete-Molina et al., 2019; Skunca et al., 2018; Tait et al., 2016; Vergé et al., 2016; Wiedemann et al., 2017).

The area of environment (A) in the VIS assessment model is analyze through six themes (then explored through 9 sub-themes and 31 specific indicators): atmosphere (A.1), water (A.2), soil (A.3), biodiversity (A.4), materials and energy (A.5), and animal welfare (A.6). The topic of the atmosphere is explored through a focus on greenhouse gas (GHG) emission (A.1.1). This in-depth analysis looks at a company's commitment toward curbing GHG emissions. Whether a company meets this goal can be determined by GHG balance calculation and, if difficult to assess, by using the estimated impact of GHG emissions and sequestration practices. The greenhouse gas budget is the difference between direct (and indirect) greenhouse gas emissions and on-site sequestration from the enterprise. The measurement of this commitment is done through three different indicators on targets, practices, and emissions balancing (A.1.1.1, A.1.1.2, A.1.1.3). The topic of water, on the other hand, is explored through the analysis of water withdrawal and use from the ground (A.2.1). An analysis is made of how an enterprise's supply contributes to problems to ecosystems or water for human use in any of the sites in which it operates (Weber & Saunders-Hogberg, 2018). This assessment also needs to be linked to the regional context, other land uses, and cumulative effects. The indicators that have been selected relate to the presence of declared targets, activated practices, and annual withdrawal effects (A.2.1.1, A.2.1.2, A.2.1.3). The topic of soil is approached through the focus on the subtopic of soil degradation (A.3.1). This is a major issue for which conservation and land recovery practices aim to prevent the loss of productive land and the recovery of degraded land. The analysis again is made by measuring the presence of stated objectives, substantive practices, and the ratio of rehabilitated land-to-land degraded by the enterprise (A.3.1.1, A.3.1.2, A.3.1.3). The theme of biodiversity is analyzed through the sub-theme of genetic variety (A.4.1). The importance of species abundance and diversity cannot be underestimated in both agriculture and livestock species. There are a wide range of strategies that can be adopted to improve genetic diversity, including using locally adapted breeds and protecting and preserving native or rare breeds. In this sense, we went to investigate the presence of objectives related to the preservation of traditional and/or rare breeds, practices to improve genetic diversity, the share of production from local and rare breeds, and the share of production from locally adapted breeds (respectively A.4.1.1, A.4.1.2, A.4.1.3, A.4.1.4). With regard to the topic of materials and energy, three specific subtopics have been explored, such as materials use (A.5.1), energy use (A.5.2), and waste reduction and disposal (A.5.3). Achieving efficiency gains in material use results in a wide range of environmental, social, and economic benefits. Several materials that are vital to the operation of food supply chains are produced from nonrenewable sources. Dependence on these finite sources should be gradually reduced by restoring renewable alternatives and recycling nonrenewables. Replacing virgin nonrenewable materials with recycled or renewable materials and reducing the material intensity of production (as a measure of eco-efficiency) are central pillars of a green economy. With this in mind, nutrient balance targets (nitrogen and phosphorus), practices for using recycled or renewable materials, and the annual share of materials used from re-cycled sources were analyzed (A.5.1.1, A.5.1.2, A.5.1.3). If switching from nonrenewable to renewable and sustainable energy sources improves sustainability from the food supply chain, energy efficiency and reduction of energy consumption are the other necessary pillars on the road to a sustainable energy system. Five different indicators were used on the topic concerning the presence of targets for the use of renewable energy (A.5.2.1), energy-saving practices (A.5.2.2), quantification of the total energy consumption of the business (A.5.2.3), quantification of the land area covered and used by the business (A.5.2.4), and the amount of renewable energy purchases (A.5.2.5). The generation of waste, and particularly hazardous waste, creates disposal problems that can cause social problems (e.g., health risks, noxious odors), environmental pollution (e.g., leaching from improper disposal, gaseous emissions), and economic damage (e.g., cost of disposal). The adoption of waste reduction plans and safe disposal practices is the basis sustainable production of supply chains. Three indicators were used in this regard regarding the presence of targets related to waste reduction, active practices in this regard, measurement of solid waste generated, and waste reused, recycled, or recovered (A.5.3.1, A.5.3.2, A.5.3.3, A.5.3.4). On the last topic of animal welfare, we focused on two distinct elements, the health of farm animals (A.6.1) and their freedom from stress (A.6.2). Animal health is a state of physical and environmental well-being. For simplicity, it can also be understood as the absence of disease and injury. It encompasses the activities that support animal health, including good nutrition, health care and the absence of stress, the presence of factors that reduce the need for veterinary treatment, and undesirable animal losses. Four different indicators were used on these elements concerning the objectives set regarding animal welfare in the supply chain (A.6.1.1), active animal welfare practices (A.6.1.2), practices to reduce losses among animals (A.6.1.3), and the percentage of animals raised without the use of antibiotics or products from such animals (A.6.1.4). Proper animal handling practices aim to ensure that animals can enjoy the "five freedoms," namely, freedom: from hunger and thirst, from discomfort and pain, from injury and disease, from fear and distress, and freedom to express normal behavior. Freedom from stress increases animal health as well as the quality of animal products. This element was further explored through analysis of the presence of controls on stocking density (A.6.2.1) and active practices toward reduced risk of injury and animal suffering (A.6.2.2).

3.3 Economy

Economic activity involves the use of labor, natural resources, and capital to produce goods and services to meet people's needs. This dimension of sustainability is directly linked to the satisfaction of needs, a pillar of sustainable development as defined by the World Commission on Environment and Development (WCED, 1987). Sustainability in the social and environmental fields is supported by functioning economies and institutions. Although interconnected, it is critical to assess economic sustainability as a dimension of sustainability in its own right. To be considered economically sustainable, a business should be able to pay all its debts, generate positive cash flow, offset negative externalities, be able to generate profits, and adequately remunerate workers and shareholders. In addition, it should have reserve mechanisms (savings, assets) to cope with changes and shocks beyond its control, for example, economic crises, adverse weather, or catastrophic accidents. In essence, it must be economically resilient. In the present self-assessment system, the macro-economic issue of growth rates is overcome in favor of a micro-economic approach that focuses on the resilience of the business and the local community.

This area, while less focused on and less discussed than the environmental, social, and governance areas, is of equal relevance. Previous studies focused on agri-food supply chains have deepened the economic area by analyzing possible alternative approaches to the economic, financial, and managerial management of an enterprise, able of generating fewer negative impacts and promoting virtuous and positive practices. In particular, studies on the possible applications of circular economy models and their possible effects and consequences are highlighted (Poponi et al., 2021; Roos Lindgreen et al., 2022; Sani et al., 2021).

The area of economy (E) in the VIS assessment model is analyzed through four themes (then explored through 11 sub-themes and 29 indicators): vulnerability (E.1), product and information quality (E.2), local economy (E.3), and development network and territorial planning (E.4). The theme of vulnerability was touched upon through five sub-themes: production stability (E.1.1), supply stability (E.1.2) market stability (E.1.3), liquidity (E.1.4), and risk management (E.1.5). As part of its risk management strategy, an enterprise must reduce as much as possible the negative impact caused by production shortfalls due to economic, social, and environmental shocks and ensure that the volume and quality of production are met. This element was analyzed through the analysis of the presence of production-related risk analysis tools and the quantification of turnover attributable to supply chain products (E.1.1.1 and E.1.1.2). The stability of supply is influenced by the channels of procurement, or the ways in which the enterprise procures the inputs needed to produce the product(s) to be sold in the market or to offer the main enterprise's service(s) to customers. Three indicators were used on this subtopic focusing, respectively, on mechanisms for reducing the risk from supply shortages (E.1.2.1), the percentage of suppliers with whom there are long-standing relationships (E.1.2.2), and the percentage of purchases from the main firm supplier (E.1.2.3). For the purpose of target market stability, the ultimate goal of marketing channels is to ensure that products or goods are sold in an appropriate moment and that the firm receives revenue. Market risk could be significantly reduced through the institution of stable business relationships with a certain number of buyers. In addition, it could be minimized through the identification of alternative marketing channels that could be accessible when contracts, agreements, or relationships are interrupted. The strategies implemented to diversify the product portfolio and sales channels (E.1.3.1) and the percentage of purchases absorbed by the three main customers (E.1.3.2) were considered with regard to this risk. The ability to sustain appropriate levels of financial liquidity against economic, environmental, and social risks is critical to a sustainable enterprise. Safety nets—which could be programs, institutions, networks, social relations, and mechanisms—support the enterprise to withstand any kind of systemic shock. The need for access to safety nets is critical, especially in times of crisis, when, for example, the enterprise faces a lack of cash flow and is unable to meet its short-term financial obligations. On the liquidity element in the VIS model, two different indicators were selected focusing, respectively, on net cash flow generation and formal or informal financial sources for liquidity crisis response (E.1.4.1 and E.1.4.2). Enterprise risk management includes risks related to: price, production, market, and credit re-risk, unstable labor relations, unavailability of labor force, conflicts with community and other stakeholders, natural disasters, disease, and climate change. With regard to the management of these risks, an analysis of tools to ensure a determined qualitative-quantitative level of production was carried out (E.1.5.1). The topic of product quality and information was deepened through three sub-themes: food safety (E.2.1), food quality (E.2.2), and product information (E.2.3). A food safety hazard is a biological, chemical, or physical agent present in food commodities with the potential to cause an adverse health effect. Food safety hazard management includes awareness and management of control measures, that is, actions that the enterprise can take to reduce the potential for exposure to food hazards or to reduce the probability of risk of exposure to hazards. In this context, two specific indicators were selected with regard to food hazard control measures and detection of cases of contamination of food goods (E.2.1.1 and E.2.1.2). Food standards with regard to quality are a body of rules or legislation that defines certain criteria, such as composition, appearance, freshness, origin, wholesomeness, and purity, that food must meet to be suitable for distribution or sale. The enterprise implements quality control measures to ensure that the expected level of product quality and nutritional standards are met. Through the survey of the existence of quality controls carried out by the enterprise (E.2.2.1), the presence of dedicated quality control staff (E.2.2.2), and the proportion of the production volume that conforms to quality standards (E.2.2.3), one goes into the VIS model to investigate this aspect of particular relevance to the supply chain. The information usually provides details not only on product content and composition but also on particular aspects of the product, such as its origin and production method. Increasingly, mechanisms and procedures ensure traceability at all stages of the food chain, so that products can be easily and correctly identified and, if necessary, re-claimed. Traceability systems improve the management of risks related to food safety and ensure the authenticity of products in the case of specific claims (e.g., organic), thus providing reliable information to customers. On these elements, it was chosen to analyze the presence of traceability systems (E.2.3.1), the percentage of products in which there is information in addition to that required by the regulations (E.2.3.2), the presence of an objective regarding the supplier selection based on quality/sustainability certifications (E.2.3.3), and the percentage of suppliers that have quality/sustainability certifications (E.2.3.4). On the topic of local economy, on the other hand, the sub-themes of value creation (E.3.1) and local procurement (E.3.2) were explored. The enterprise can support value creation in a local economy through employment opportunities and tax contributions. Employees as employed by the enterprise who come from the community, municipality, or region where operations are based create a regional workforce. The enterprise's contribution to the local economy through the employment of local professionals and technicians is a significant component of sustainable development and could benefit the long-term viability of the enterprise. This subtopic was worked on by going to survey the priority given to hiring regional candidates (E.3.1.1), the percentage of new hires residing in the local area (E.3.1.2), and the percentage of new hires with university degrees residing in the local area (E.3.1.3). Local sourcing refers to the company's commitment and effective realization to benefit local economies through purchasing from local suppliers. Purchasing from local suppliers contributes to a more dynamic economy. Stakeholders in the supply chain grow and could generate value through employment, community investment, and skills development. On this specific topic, the use of procurement policies in favor of local suppliers (E.3.2.1), the percentage of purchases from local suppliers (E.3.2.2), and the percentage of purchases from local suppliers by type (E.3.2.3) were explored. Finally, on the topic of development and spatial planning networks, a specific subtopic, that of local networks (E.4.1), was worked on. The enterprise can actively participate both in the development and innovation of the product and its supply chain through participation in consortiums and business networks and in the strategic planning of the reference territory through adherence to plans promoted by local public bodies. In this sense, indicators were chosen regarding the number of consulting and collaboration contracts with universities and research centers in the area (E.4.1.1), participation in quality consortia (E.4.1.2), participation in enterprise networks (E.4.1.3), and participation in forms of strategic territorial planning (E.4.1.4).

3.4 Society

Social sustainability concerns the satisfaction of basic human needs and the right and freedom to fulfill one's aspirations for a better life (WCED, 1987). This applies as long as the satisfaction of one's own needs does not compromise the ability of others, or future generations, to do the same. Basic human needs and rights are defined in the International Bill of Human Rights, which consists of the Universal Declaration of Human Rights (UN, 1948), the International Covenant on Civil and

Political Rights (UN, 1966), and the International Covenant on Economic, Social and Cultural Rights (UN, 1966). Human rights are further specified for workplaces in the Declaration of Fundamental Principles and Rights at Work (ILO, 1998). Business enterprises are responsible for the respect of human rights, both in their business activities and when human rights impacts are "directly related to their operations, products and services generated by their business relations" (UNHCR, 2011).

In the context of the agri-food supply chain and particularly in the Italian cured meats sector, the focus on social issues appears to be directed toward issues related to consumer choices and perceptions (especially regarding product quality and safety) and the potential impacts on the context and community of reference that business choices and practices, especially from a supply chain perspective, can create, promote, or limit (Conca et al., 2021; Farooq et al., 2016; Farooq et al., 2021; Heise & Theuvsen, 2017; Jarzębowski et al., 2020; Veser et al., 2015).

The area of society (S) in the VIS assessment model was touched upon through four different themes (then divided into 5 sub-themes and 11 indicators): decent living conditions (S.1), equity (S.2), safety and health (S.3), and fair business behavior (S.4). The topic of decent living conditions was analyzed through the sub-theme of quality of life (S.1.1). Corporate employees are entitled to a quality of life that provides time to spend with family and for recreation, adequate rest from work, voluntary overtime, and educational opportunities for themselves and their families. On this subtopic, practices for supporting employees' work-life balance and the percentage of change in the average wage level (S.1.1.1 and S.1.1.2) were analyzed. In contrast, the theme of equity was investigated according to two different sub-themes, nondiscrimination (S.2.1) and gender equality (S.2.2). Sustainable enterprises shall not discriminate against any employee or potential employee or on the basis of race, creed, color, national or ethnic origin, sex, age, handicap or disability, union or political activity, immigration status, citizenship, marital status, or sexual orientation in hiring, training, advancement, layoff, or dismissal. On these highly relevant and topical issues, an indicator was used to detect the presence of nondiscrimination goals mentioned in recruitment and human resource management policies (S.2.1.1) and a second indicator for practices adopted for nondiscrimination in promotion, dismissal, and contract and job assignment policies (S.2.1.2). The sub-theme on gender equality aims to focus on whether there are barriers to women's employment, women's pay, and opportunities for training and advancement. This is analyzed by surveying equal opportunity goals, practices for reducing the risk of discrimination of women, and the per-centage of women working in the enterprise (S.2.2.1, S.2.2.2, and S.2.2.3). The issue of safety and health is analyzed through the sub-theme of workplace safety and health provisions (S.3.1). The provision of a safe and healthy workplace for all staff and employees begins by providing work facilities that are healthy, adequately ventilated, structurally sound, and meet or exceed local building codes, as well as necessary and safe equipment. Through specific indicators, we chose to survey the hours of training employees receive on health and safety (S.3.1.1), the presence of goals pertaining to workplace safety and health (S.3.1.2), and the presence of incidents of in-house injuries (S.3.1.3). The topic of fair-trade behavior was deepened through the subtopic of fair-trade contract and market (S.4.1). For sustainable trade relationships to exist, buyers must pay primary producer prices for their products that reflect the true cost of the entire process of sustaining a regenerative ecological system: a regenerative ecological system. This also supports a living wage and a right to a decent livelihood for primary producers, their families, and workers, as well as covering the producer's costs. This topic has been analyzed through an indicator inherent in the recognition of fair prices, transparent contracts, and rights of workers (S.4.1.1).

4 Conclusions

Starting from the identification of a gap in the literature concerning the quantification of the real impacts of the cured meat supply chain, this trans-disciplinary approach contributes to the determination of the distribution of value between the categories of stakeholders involved.

Therefore, this study represents the preliminary development of the field validation of a self-assessment tool that can be of significant impact in the self-assessment of sustainability performance at firm level, as well as with respect to the evaluation of the appropriateness of managerial practices and processes.

There are several advantages that such a thorough analysis can bring to the company.

First, this tool allows a comparison of performance in a time perspective, both regarding internal performance evolution and to the potential comparison with what has been implemented by other competitors.

Secondly, this logic linked to the comparability of data (and therefore of information) makes it possible to develop within the organization an orientation of decision-making processes toward a data-driven approach. A positive implication from the perspective of the supply chain is the overall reduction of information asymmetries between stakeholder categories.

Thirdly, the company that implement this model can be oriented to a holistic approach to sustainability and, therefore, encourages it to consider dimensions and themes that would otherwise not be considered in a long-term planning phase of strategic objectives. This partial approach, limited to a few areas of sustainability, is therefore discouraged both from the perspective of enhancing internal resources and in view of the ever more pressing push toward transparent production systems.

Given the clarity of managerial implications, from the point of view of theoretical implications, it can also be emphasized how this model can also be used in the future for the comparison of different production contexts that already report on their own performance and that cannot address further comparisons on the disclosure of single dimensions or themes.

This study presents limitations in terms of the limited production context analyzed both from the geographical point of view and the category of products analyzed in the food industry. Further studies will further expand the categories of products involved with further tool developments in the context of other categories of agri-food products or compared to other geographical areas.

References

Adams, D., Donovan, J., & Topple, C. (2021). Achieving sustainability in food manufacturing operations and their supply chains: Key insights from a systematic literature review. *Sustainable Production and Consumption, 28*, 1491–1499.

Aureli, S., Del Baldo, M., Lombardi, R., & Nappo, F. (2020). Nonfinancial reporting regulation and challenges in sustainability disclosure and corporate governance practices. *Business Strategy and the Environment, 29*(6), 2392–2403.

Bonisoli, L., Galdeano-Gómez, E., Piedra-Muñoz, L., & Pérez-Mesa, J. C. (2019). Benchmarking Agri-food sustainability certifications: Evidences from applying SAFA in the Ecuadorian banana Agri-system. *Journal of Cleaner Production, 236*, 117579.

Butti Al Shamsi, K., Compagnoni, A., Timpanaro, G., Cosentino, S. L., & Guarnaccia, P. (2018). A sustainable organic production model for "food sovereignty" in The United Arab Emirates and Sicily-Italy. *Sustainability, 10*(3), 620.

Cammarata, M., Timpanaro, G., & Scuderi, A. (2021). Assessing sustainability of organic livestock farming in Sicily: A case study using the Fao Safa framework. *Agriculture, 11*(3), 274.

Conca, L., Manta, F., Morrone, D., & Toma, P. (2021). The impact of direct environmental, social, and governance reporting: Empirical evidence in European-listed companies in the Agri-food sector. *Business Strategy and the Environment, 30*(2), 1080–1093.

Dabkienė, V. (2016). The scope of farms sustainability tools based on FADN data. *Scientific Papers Series Management, Economic Engineering in Agriculture and Rural Development, 16*(1), 121–128.

Dalton, V. (2020). The challenge of engaging with and reporting against the SDGs for SMEs such as Sydney theatre company. *Journal of Management & Organization, 26*(6), 975–994.

De Olde, E. M., Oudshoorn, F. W., Bokkers, E. A., Stubsgaard, A., Sørensen, C. A., & De Boer, I. J. (2016). Assessing the sustainability performance of organic farms in Denmark. *Sustainability, 8*(9), 957.

Demartini, E., Gaviglio, A., & Bertocchi, M. (2016). Lessons learned from a process of farm sustainability assessment: Literature review, methodology and governance opportunities. *Rivista di studi sulla sostenibilità, 2*, 129–139.

Ernstberger, J., & Grüning, M. (2013). How do firm-and country-level governance mechanisms affect firms' disclosure? *Journal of Accounting and Public Policy, 32*(3), 50–67.

FAO. (2013a). *Sustainability assessment of food and agriculture systems: User manual version 2.2.40*. Food and Agriculture Organization of the United Nations. Retrieved from: http://www.fao.org/3/a-i4113e.pdf

FAO. (2013b). *Sustainability assessment of food and agriculture systems: SAFA tool, beta version 2.1.50*. Food and Agriculture Organization of the United Nations. Retrieved from: http://www.fao.org/fileadmin/templates/nr/sustainability_pathways/docs/SAFA_Tool_User_Manual_2.1.50.pdf

FAO. (2014). *Sustainability assessment of food and agriculture systems: SAFA guidelines, version 3.0*. Food and Agriculture Organization of the United Nations. Retrieved from: https://www.fao.org/3/i3957e/i3957e.pdf

Farooq, U., Tao, W., Alfian, G., Kang, Y. S., & Rhee, J. (2016). ePedigree traceability system for the agricultural food supply chain to ensure consumer health. *Sustainability, 8*(9), 839.

Farooq, M. B., Zaman, R., & Nadeem, M. (2021). Account Ability's AA1000AP standard: A framework for integrating sustainability into organisations. *Sustainability Accounting, Management and Policy Journal, 12, 1108*.

Fernández-Barcala, M., González-Díaz, M., & Raynaud, E. (2017). Contrasting the governance of supply chains with and without geographical indications: Complementarity between levels. *Supply Chain Management: An International Journal, 22*(4), 305–320.

Gangi, F., Meles, A., Monferrà, S., & Mustilli, M. (2020). Does corporate social responsibility help the survivorship of SMEs and large firms? *Global Finance Journal, 43*, 100402.

Garner, B., & Ayala, C. (2018). Consumer supply-chain demands and challenges at farmers' markets. *British Food Journal., 120*, 2734.

Gasso, V., Oudshoorn, F. W., De Olde, E., & Sørensen, C. A. (2015). Generic sustainability assessment themes and the role of context: The case of Danish maize for German biogas. *Ecological Indicators, 49*, 143–153.

Gaviglio, A., Bertocchi, M., & Demartini, E. (2017). A tool for the sustainability assessment of farms: selection, adaptation and use of indicators for an Italian case study. *Resources, 6*(4), 60.

Gayatri, S., Gasso-tortajada, V., & Vaarst, M. (2016). Assessing sustainability of smallholder beef cattle farming in Indonesia: A case study using the FAO SAFA framework. *Journal of Sustainable Development, 9*(3), 1755–1315.

Global Reporting Initiative (GRI) index (2013). World Bank Group, Washington, DC.

Havardi-Burger, N., Mempel, H., & Bitsch, V. (2021). Framework for sustainability assessment of the value chain of flowering potted plants for the German market. *Journal of Cleaner Production, 329*, 129684.

Heise, H., & Theuvsen, L. (2017). What do consumers think about farm animal welfare in modern agriculture? Attitudes and shopping behaviour. *International Food and Agribusiness Management Review, 20*(3), 379–399.

Helfaya, A., & Whittington, M. (2019). Does designing environmental sustainability disclosure quality measures make a difference? *Business Strategy and the Environment, 28*(4), 525–541.

Hingley, M., & Sodanoa, V. (2018). Corporate social responsibility reporting: The case of the Agri-food sector. Corporate social responsibility reporting: the case of the agri-food sector, 93–120.

Hřebíček, J., Trenz, O., & Vernerová, E. (2013). Optimal set of Agri-environmental indicators for the agricultural sector of Czech Republic. *Acta Universitatis Agriculturae et Silviculturae Mendelianae Brunensis, 61*(7), 2171–2181.

Hřebíček, J., Faldík, O., Kasem, E., & Trenz, O. (2015). Determinants of sustainability reporting in food and agriculture sectors. *Acta universitatis agriculturae et silviculturae Mendelianae Brunensis, 63*(2), 539–552.

ILO. (1998). *Declaration on fundamental principles and rights at work.*

Intergovernmental Panel on Climate Change (IPCC). (2023). *Climate Change 2023: AR6 Rapporto di sintesi.*

Jacobsen, R., Vandermeulen, V., Van Huylenbroeck, G., & Gellynck, X. (2014). Carbon footprint of pigmeat in Flanders. *International Journal of Agricultural Sustainability, 12*(1), 54–70.

Jarzębowski, S., Bourlakis, M., & Bezat-Jarzębowska, A. (2020). Short food supply chains (SFSC) as local and sustainable systems. *Sustainability, 12*(11), 4715.

Jensen, J. C., & Berg, N. (2012). Determinants of traditional sustainability reporting versus integrated reporting. An institutionalist approach. *Business Strategy and the Environment, 21*(5), 299–316.

Kamble, S. S., Gunasekaran, A., & Gawankar, S. A. (2020). Achieving sustainable performance in a data-driven agriculture supply chain: A review for research and applications. *International Journal of Production Economics, 219*, 179–194.

Kassem, E., Trenz, O., Hřebíček, J., & Faldík, O. (2017). Sustainability assessment & reporting in agriculture sector. *Acta Universitatis Agriculturae et Silviculturae Mendelianae Brunensis., 65*, 1359.

Landert, J., Schader, C., Moschitz, H., & Stolze, M. (2017). A holistic sustainability assessment method for urban food system governance. *Sustainability, 9*(4), 490.

López-Andrés, J. J., Aguilar-Lasserre, A. A., Morales-Mendoza, L. F., Azzaro-Pantel, C., Pérez-Gallardo, J. R., & Rico-Contreras, J. O. (2018). Environmental impact assessment of chicken meat production via an integrated methodology based on LCA, simulation and genetic algorithms. *Journal of Cleaner Production, 174*, 477–491.

Marchand, F., Debruyne, L., Triste, L., Gerrard, C., Padel, S., & Lauwers, L. (2014). Key characteristics for tool choice in indicator-based sustainability assessment at farm level. *Ecology and Society, 19*(3).

Martins, F. M., Trienekens, J., & Omta, O. (2017). Governance structures and coordination mechanisms in the Brazilian pork chain–diversity of arrangements to support the supply of piglets. *International Food and Agribusiness Management Review, 20*(4), 511–532.

Melissen, F., Mzembe, A. N., Idemudia, U., & Novakovic, Y. (2018). Institutional antecedents of the corporate social responsibility narrative in the developing world context: Implications for sustainable development. *Business Strategy and the Environment, 27*(6), 657–676.

Navarrete-Molina, C., Meza-Herrera, C. A., Herrera-Machuca, M. A., Lopez-Villalobos, N., Lopez-Santos, A., & Veliz-Deras, F. G. (2019). To beef or not to beef: Unveiling the economic environmental impact generated by the intensive beef cattle industry in an arid region. *Journal of Cleaner Production, 231*, 1027–1035.

Ouma, E., Ochieng, J., Dione, M., & Pezo, D. (2017). Governance structures in smallholder pig value chains in Uganda: Constraints and opportunities for upgrading. *International Food and Agribusiness Management Review, 20*(3), 307–319.

Paraskevopoulou, C., Theodoridis, A., Johnson, M., Ragkos, A., Arguile, L., Smith, L., et al. (2020). Sustainability assessment of goat and sheep farms: A comparison between european countries. *Sustainability, 12*(8), 3099.

Pérez-Lombardini, F., Mancera, K. F., Suzán, G., Campo, J., Solorio, J., & Galindo, F. (2021). Assessing sustainability in cattle silvopastoral systems in the Mexican tropics using the SAFA framework. *Animals, 11*(1), 109.

Poponi, S., Arcese, G., Mosconi, E. M., Pacchera, F., Martucci, O., & Elmo, G. C. (2021). Multi-actor governance for a circular economy in the Agri-food sector: Bio-districts. *Sustainability, 13*(9), 4718.

Rockström, J., Steffen, W., Noone, K., et al. (2009). A safe operating space for humanity. *Nature, 461*, 472–475.

Roos Lindgreen, E., Opferkuch, K., Walker, A. M., Salomone, R., Reyes, T., Raggi, A., et al. (2022). Exploring assessment practices of companies actively engaged with circular economy. *Business Strategy and the Environment, 31*(4), 1414–1438.

Sani, D., Picone, S., Bianchini, A., Fava, F., Guarnieri, P., & Rossi, J. (2021). An overview of the transition to a circular economy in Emilia-Romagna region, Italy considering technological, legal–regulatory and financial points of view: A case study. *Sustainability, 13*(2), 596.

Schader, C., Grenz, J., Meier, M. S., & Stolze, M. (2014). Scope and precision of sustainability assessment approaches to food systems. *Ecology and Society, 19*(3).

Schneider, A., & Meins, E. (2012). Two dimensions of corporate sustainability assessment: Towards a comprehensive framework. *Business Strategy and the Environment, 21*(4), 211–222.

Singh, R. K., Murty, H. R., Gupta, S. K., & Dikshit, A. K. (2009). An overview of sustainability assessment methodologies. *Ecological Indicators, 9*(2), 189–212.

Skunca, D., Tomasevic, I., Nastasijevic, I., Tomovic, V., & Djekic, I. (2018). Life cycle assessment of the chicken meat chain. *Journal of Cleaner Production, 184*, 440–450.

Soldi, A., Aparicio Meza, M. J., Guareschi, M., Donati, M., & Insfrán Ortiz, A. (2019). Sustainability assessment of agricultural systems in Paraguay: A comparative study using FAO's SAFA framework. *Sustainability, 11*(13), 3745.

Spence, L. J., & Rinaldi, L. (2014). Governmentality in accounting and accountability: A case study of embedding sustainability in a supply chain. *Accounting, Organizations and Society, 39*(6), 433–452.

Ssebunya, B. R., Schmid, E., van Asten, P., Schader, C., Altenbuchner, C., & Stolze, M. (2017). Stakeholder engagement in prioritizing sustainability assessment themes for smallholder coffee production in Uganda. *Renewable Agriculture and Food Systems, 32*(5), 428–445.

Tait, P., Saunders, C., Guenther, M., & Rutherford, P. (2016). Emerging versus developed economy consumer willingness to pay for environmentally sustainable food production: A choice experiment approach comparing Indian, Chinese and United Kingdom lamb consumers. *Journal of Cleaner Production, 124*, 65–72.

Talukder, B., & Blay-Palmer, A. (2017). Comparison of methods to assess agricultural sustainability. In *Sustainable Agriculture Reviews* (pp. 149–168). Springer.

Theurl, M. C., Hörtenhuber, S. J., Lindenthal, T., & Palme, W. (2017). Unheated soil-grown winter vegetables in Austria: Greenhouse gas emissions and socio-economic factors of diffusion potential. *Journal of Cleaner Production, 151*, 134–144.

UN. (1966). International covenant on civil and political rights. United Nations General Assembly Resolution 2200A.

UNESCAP. (2009). *What is good governance? United Nations economic and social Commission for Asia and the Pacific*, 1-3.

UNGC/IFC. (2009). *Future proof?: embedding environmental, social and governance issues in investment markets : outcomes of the Who Cares Wins Initiative, 2004–2008.*

United Nations General Assembly. (1948). Universal declaration of human rights (UDHR), Paris.

United Nations High Commissioner for Refugees (UNHCR). (2011). Global Trends 2011.

Van der Merwe, M., Kirsten, J. F., & Trienekens, J. H. (2019). Enforcement mechanisms and governance structures to protect a region of origin lamb product. *Supply Chain Management: An International Journal, 24*(5), 561–573.

Vergé, X., Maxime, D., Desjardins, R. L., & Vanderzaag, A. C. (2016). Allocation factors and issues in agricultural carbon footprint: A case study of the Canadian pork industry. *Journal of Cleaner Production, 113*, 587–595.

Veser, P., Taylor, K., & Singer, S. (2015). Diet, authoritarianism, social dominance orientation, and predisposition to prejudice: Results of a German survey. *British Food Journal, 117*(7), 1949–1960.

WCED. (1987). *Report of the world commission on environment and development: Our common future*. Oxford University Press.

Weber, O., & Saunders-Hogberg, G. (2018). Water management and corporate social performance in the food and beverage industry. *Journal of Cleaner Production, 195*, 963–977.

Wiedemann, S. G., McGahan, E. J., & Murphy, C. M. (2017). Resource use and environmental impacts from Australian chicken meat production. *Journal of Cleaner Production, 140*, 675–684.

Zira, S., Rydhmer, L., Ivarsson, E., Hoffmann, R., & Röös, E. (2021). A life cycle sustainability assessment of organic and conventional pork supply chains in Sweden. *Sustainable Production and Consumption, 28*, 21–38.